1.03

COST   25.95
20% DISCOUNT   (5.19)
TAX   1.46
          _____
          22.22

- 2 - DAHLINE & PLOSER
   3   MARTINS
   9   CARDINALS
  13 ? MARTIN PARK
  72 ? ✓   ✓
  77   WESTERN MINN / SOUTHERN MINNY
  78   FAIRMONT STATE CHAMPS
  79   JONI WALT MENKE
       SPIKE GRAHAM
  80   WALT MENKE
       DON DAHLINE
  81   JAY PLOSER
       HANDS PARK
  83   RON CRAVEN
  88   RON CRAVEN
 100   HOWIE SCHULTZ
 101   TONY WOLVERTON
 117   1963 HIGH SCHOOL TOURNAMENT
 117   1964   ✓   ✓   ✓
       118/119 1965   ✓   ✓   ✓
 119   1971   ✓   ✓   ✓
 140   120/121 1975   ✓   ✓   ✓
 141   131/132 1993   ✓   ✓   ✓

Batter-Up!

Celebrating a Century of Minnesota Baseball

by
Ross Bernstein

Nodin Press

"Batter-Up: Celebrating a Century of Minnesota Baseball"
by Ross Bernstein

(WWW.BERNSTEINBOOKS.COM)

Cover Painting by Duluth Artist Tim Cortes. To order a limited edition print of this cover painting, please call: (218) 525-4953.

ISBN 0-931714-97-4

Edited by Joel Rippel

Published by Nodin Press
530 North Third Street
Minneapolis, MN 55401
(612) 333-6300

Printed in Minnesota by Printing Enterprises, New Brighton

Photo Credits:
Minnesota Twins: 6,7,27-61,72,98,143,157
University of Minnesota: 82-96,149,151
Minnesota State High School League: 113-138
Minnesota Historical Society: 5,10,12,14-15,20-27,139,144-147,152-155
Dick Jonckowski Archives: 13,16,17,18,19,65,73,94,110
Duluth Dukes: 63-66,69-70,72,147
St. Paul Saints: 68,71-73
Brian Larson: 74-77,146
Pioneer Press: 81
Tim Cortes: 4
Sandy Thompson: 50,58,150
George Rekela: 11
David Sherman: 148,160
University of Minnesota-Duluth: 108-111
St. Cloud State University: 103-107
Minnesota State University, Mankato: 103-104,106-107
Southwest State University: 108,110
Winona State University: 108
St. Scholastica: 108
St. John's University: 98-99
University of St. Thomas: 99-100,102
Hamline University: 100
Gustavus Adolphus College: 100-101

Acknowledgements:
I would really like to thank all of the people that were kind enough to help me in writing this book. In addition to the countless pro, college and university Sports Information Directors that I hounded throughout this project I would like to sincerely thank all of the men and women that allowed me to interview them. In addition, I would particularly like to thank my publisher, and friend, Norton Stillman.

Tim Cortes	Ardie Eckhart	Tim Kennedy	Andy Johnson	Mike Cristaldi	Bob Nygard	Brian Larson
Harmon Killebrew	Karen Zwach	Howard Voigt	Dick Mingo	Gene McGivern	Mike Hemmesch	Bob Schabert
Paul Molitor	Anne Abicht	Paul Allen	Dave Wright	Larry Scott	Brian Curtis	Ryan Kapaun
Dick Jonckowski	Tim Trainor	Nick Corndor	Ron Christian	Andy Bartlett	Mike Herzberg	Joe Block
Joel Rippel	Bob Snyder	Chris Owens	Jen Walter	Steph Reck	Eric Sieger	Julie Arthur Sherman
Ann Johnson	Dave St. Peter	John Baggs	Ron Christian	Kelly Loft	Jim Cella	Don Dahlke
Randy Johnson	Don Stoner	Kurt Daniels	Rocky Nelson	Mark Fohl	Dan McMahon	George Rekela
Robert Claveau	Greg Peterson	Brad Ruiter	John Griffin	Jim Cella	Jeff Hagen	Donald Floyd Bernstein
Sandy Thompson	Troy Andre	Eric Sieger	Dan McMahon	LeAnn Finger	Andy Bartlett	Toddler Rendahl
Denise Johnson	Tom Jones	Bob Nygaard	Matt Pederson	Don Nadeau	Bruce Abbots	*H.J. Pieser*

For Sara and Campbell, the two loves of my life...

Cover Painting by Artist Tim Cortes

I would especially like to express my gratitude to Minnesota sports artist, Tim Cortes, for allowing me the privilege of showcasing his newest masterpiece entitled: *"The Old Ballgame"* on the cover of my new book. I couldn't be more pleased with the final product and simply can't thank him enough for all of his hard work. He is not only an amazing artist, he is also a wonderful friend. *(Contact Tim directly if you would like to purchase a signed, numbered, limited edition print of the cover painting — he even has multiple framing and matting options and can ship anywhere in the world.)*

One of the nation's premier photo realism artists, Cortes uses colored pencils as his preferred medium. Hundreds of his collectible lithographs have been sold throughout North America and his clients are a venerable who's-who of American sports. From Shaquille O'Neal to Mark McGwire and from Wayne Gretzky to Troy Aikman, Cortes has been commissioned to create countless commemorative works of art over the past decade. *(Check out some more of his works on the back flap of this book cover!)*

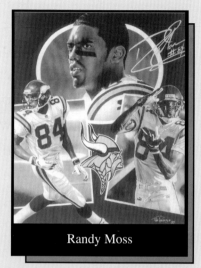

Randy Moss

His paintings have also been featured in numerous venues around the world, including: the US Hockey Hall of Fame, Franklin Mint, Kelly Russell Studios and Beckett's Magazine, as well as on trading cards, pro sports teams' game-day programs, and in various publications. Known for his impeccable detail, Cortes has dedicated his life to the pursuit of celebrating the life and times of many of the world's most famous athletes and the sporting events in which they play.

Cortes grew up in Duluth, where he later starred as a hockey goaltender at Duluth East High School. After a brief stint in the United States Hockey League, Cortes went on to play between the pipes for two seasons in the mid-1980s for the University of Minnesota's Golden Gophers. Cortes then decided to pursue his passion of art and sports full-time, and enrolled at the prestigious Minneapolis College of Art and Design. He has been painting ever since!

Today Tim lives in Duluth with his wife Kathy and their two children. He continues to play senior hockey and also gives back by coaching both youth football and hockey. In addition, in 2002 Tim was named as the goalie coach for the UM-Duluth Hockey Lady Bulldogs.

If you would like to purchase a signed, limited edition print of "The Old Ballgame" or any other of Tim's hundreds of works of art, please check out his web-site or contact his studio, where you, too, can own a piece of sports history.

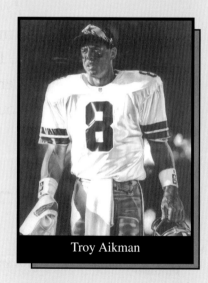

Troy Aikman

Squaw Valley Gold

1998 Olympic Gold

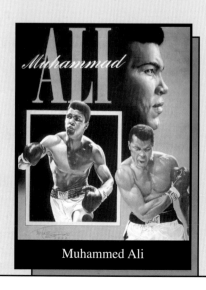

Muhammed Ali

TABLE OF CONTENTS

Harmon Killebrew is, in a word, a legend. Bigger than life itself, Harmon is also one of the most beloved sports figures of the 20th century. I had a chance to catch up with him recently in his native Idaho, where he reflected upon everything from the state-of-the-state of the game in the Land of 10,000 Lakes, to contraction, to strikes, to stadiums, to steroids. And, with everything bad about the game of baseball seemingly being whirled about these days, who better than to talk about the past, present and future of Minnesota baseball than a guy who simply represents everything good about the game — Mr. Baseball himself, Harmon Killebrew.

Harmon Clayton Killebrew Jr. grew up playing baseball in Payette, Idaho, and went on to become one of the most feared sluggers in Major League Baseball history. After turning down a football and baseball scholarship to the University of Oregon, Harmon went on to get his start with the Washington Senators. Then, in 1961, when the franchise was relocated to the Twin Cities, Harmon quickly became a fan-favorite in the Gopher State, assuming the role of being the Twins' on and off the field leader. His hustle and tenacity earned him the respect of his team-mates and, in turn, he became not only one of the game's fiercest competitors, but also a true gentleman as well.

When it was all said and done, Harmon had rewritten the record books. With 573 career round-trippers, Harmon was the second (only to Babe Ruth) in the history of the American League to hit more than 40 home runs, (eight times), 30-or-more home runs, (10 times), all while driving in 100-plus RBIs (nine times). Killebrew was the consummate team player, always more interested in his team's achievements rather than his own. "You know, it's fine to hit homers, but it's the RBIs that mean the most," he would often say. Over his career he tallied 1,584 RBIs, while garnering 2,086 hits and playing in 13 All-Star games. On May 4, 1975, his No. 3 was officially retired at Met Stadium, and on January 10, 1984, Killer became the first Twin ever to be inducted into the Baseball Hall of Fame.

From leading his club to the 1965 World Series to winning the Home Run Crown, Harmon could do it all. Quiet and unassuming, Harmon was always more interested in his team rather than personal accolades, and he is the first to deny his greatness. He is also quick to give thanks and appreciation to the game of baseball for everything it has done for him and his family. Today Harmon is retired and living in Arizona, spending as much time as possible with his kids and grandkids. In addition, he also stays involved with the Twins, where he does special events from time to time, sitting in on television and radio broadcasts, and helping with the organizations' charities as well.

A Minnesotan through and through, Harmon is torn these days. While he is elated to see his young Twins on the verge of greatness, at the same time he is saddened to see the game he loves so dearly struggle to find its identity in this new millennium. The money the players are making today is unconscionable in his eyes. Ah, if only he were playing today. Can you imagine what this guy would be worth? Funny you should ask... According to "Leveling the Field," a new book that calculates how much stars of the past would be worth if they played today, Harmon's 1967 season alone (*his stats of 57 homers, 145 RBIs and a .298 average were converted and adjusted to current standards*) would be worth $22.3 million in today's dollars! Anyway, with no further ado, here is the man who represents the little kid in all of us, Harmon Killebrew.

"When they originally told us that we were moving from the nation's capital to Minnesota, I was, frankly, a bit apprehensive about it. But when it finally happened it was just great. The people of Minnesota immediately embraced me and I grew to love it up there. The fans in Minnesota are as good, if not better, than any fans in baseball. They showed me so much love and respect, and I will never forget that.

"When I came to Minnesota I was already aware of the great baseball tradition that they had here. In fact, I had actually played against the Minneapolis Millers and St. Paul Saints in my earlier days. Old Nicollet and Lexington Parks had a lot of great ballplayers come through their gates through the years and that just added to Minnesota's great history. I have seen a lot of great players and great teams have come and go up there through the years, but there might be any better than this year's club.

"The 2002 Twins are just a wonderful story. This group of kids plays hard and plays solid, fundamental baseball — and that is really refreshing to see. I couldn't be prouder of these guys and hope they can keep it together for a long, long time. The organization has done a tremendous job of putting together this group of young players and it is really the story of the year in baseball. Certainly, Terry Ryan and Jim Rantz (the GM and Director of Minor League Operations) should be commended for the incredible job they have done in assembling this team from the bottom up. I also give them a lot of credit for all of their hard work in scouting and developing a solid minor league system, and it is great to see it finally pay off. And, what is truly amazing about all of that is the fact that they did it all with a heck of a lot less money than most of the other ball clubs. So, you just have to tip your hat to these guys for what they have done, it's great.

"On the other hand, however, it really makes you crazy to think about everything that is going on right now in baseball. I mean when I first heard that they were going to contract the Twins it made me physically ill. I mean to think that they would want to eliminate this franchise after all it has been through over the years was crazy. The Twins have such a great history, and not just in Minnesota, but all the way back to the beginning of the American League when they were the Washington Senators. I just feel so strongly about my old team and, of course, I don't want to see anything happen to it. Contraction would truly be a terrible, terrible thing for not only

Twins fans, but for all of baseball. This organization has such a proud heritage and to throw that away would be a tragedy.

"Now, as far as the strike being resolved, I couldn't be happier. I think it was just a terrible thing for both the players and the owners to even consider at the time. I mean with everything that has happened in the United States over this past year, it was just simply wrong and disrespectful to even talk about it. Call it what you want: a strike, a work-stoppage or a lock-out, it doesn't matter, it just didn't make sense. Gosh, with the economy the way it is right now, it is just in really poor taste. The fans would've lost, the players would've lost, the owners would've lost — everyone would've lost.

"They had to figure it out because the fans weren't going to tolerate much more of it. The salaries are outrageous and the fans can't even comprehend it. I am torn, because I am a former player, so I understand what the players are going through. A compromise had to be reached from both sides in order to preserve the game for the next generation, and I was glad to see them get this deal done.

"The 1994 strike was a different situation. The economy was different and the attitude towards the game was different. Plus, you had the Mark McGuire and Sammy Sosa home run race, as well as Cal Ripken's great streak to bring the fans back when it was over. Nowadays it is an entirely different situation. The fan base has already shrunk and baseball can't expect the fans to keep coming back and forgiving them.

"Frankly, it is a different situation for kids today as well. They have a lot of other choices for what to do in their spare time, and baseball isn't as high on their lists as it was a generation ago. If baseball isn't keeping them entertained, then they will certainly find something that will. Other sports have narrowed the gap and that is just a reality. I know that all of my grandkids just love to watch and play baseball, so anything that hurts the game, really hurts me, personally. I want my grandkids to have the same love of the game that I did and to be able to enjoy it way down the road with their kids as well.

"Another concern I have for the future of the game is steroids. I know it is being scrutinized in the media as of late with the big-leaguers, but there are plenty of kids in the lower levels of the game that are taking them too, and that has got to stop. We just need to keep the game as pure as we can. Baseball had always thought it was immune to that sort of thing and now we know it isn't. In fact, I really don't know how the issue has become an "issue." I mean it should be cut and dry. If they are not using them then let them be tested. What do they have to hide? For me it is not so much about them putting up big numbers with regards to home runs, it is more about the integrity of the game. Plus, it just isn't healthy for these guys to be taking that stuff. It is deadly and what is worse is that kids look up to them and see them doing it and think it is OK. That, more than anything, bothers me the most. So I am glad that this issue was addressed in the new labor agreement as well.

"Overall I would have to say that the game has really not changed that much since my days at old Met Stadium. Expansion has diluted the talent pool and it is especially difficult today for the hitters. I mean they get four or five pitchers thrown at them each and every game, from starters to middle relievers to set-up men to closers, and it is tough for them to get into any kind of rhythm. Others have said the ball is juiced and so are the bats. Heck, I always thought wood was just wood, but now that is a different story too. The ballparks are also smaller, there is more astroturf, the pitching is thinner and the players are just bigger and stronger today. But, a few things have remained the same. You still have to step up and hit the ball, you have to catch it, run, throw and do the fundamentals. That will always be the heart and soul of the game. All in all, I would have to say that the biggest change in the game today is the money — it is just way out of whack and hopefully the new labor contract will help to get this in order.

"I think overall baseball is at a crossroads right now. We are at a time when some changes need to be made and we need our leaders to step up to the plate to get some things done for the good of the game. We need to get the salaries back into a realistic situation so that the game can not only survive, but also thrive in the future. The bottom line is that there has to be some big changes made, and made soon, or we are just heading down the same road that we have been down before. It needs to be fixed and there is no better time than the present.

"It is tough for the people of Minnesota right now too. They have been struggling with all of the stadium issues that have been lingering for several years now, and that is unfortunate. On one hand they really want to keep professional baseball in Minnesota, but on the other hand they don't want to have to pay for it. I mean the cost to each individual is miniscule, really, when you think about it. I just don't know. I hope that in the end the powers-that-be will come together to figure this thing out so that we can get a new stadium and keep big-league baseball where it belongs. They just have to. I am positive and hopeful. I know that a lot of this is hinging on a new owner stepping up, but that it is a catch-22 as far as that new owner wanting a guarantee that the team will stay here and that they will get a new stadium. It is a very difficult situation and I hope it can be resolved because I really love the Twins and want them to stick around forever.

"But, overall, as far as the state-of-the-state of Minnesota baseball right now, I think that they are right at the top of the class with regards to having quality programs from the top to the bottom. There are so many individuals who have given so much of their time and energy to make sure that our kids can enjoy the game, and that is what it is all about. Sure, it is great to get our kids into colleges and even into the professional ranks, but it should mostly be about having fun. I will say, however, that it always amazed me as to just how good the quality of baseball was up there, considering it was a cold weather climate. Whether it was kids out playing for fun or college kids trying to get better, they were always out there, whatever the conditions were, and trying their hardest. That was just great to see.

"The one thing that I always took away from my time in Minnesota is that the people up there really cherish their free-time and know how to have fun — especially in the summertime, when they are not cooped up in the house. And, whether they are out in the yard or up at the lake, it always seemed like the fans made time to tune into the ballgame and support us. I never forgot that. Overall, I can't thank the fans of Minnesota enough for their amazing generosity and hospitality towards me over the years. It is a state with a wonderful baseball heritage and I was truly proud and honored to be a part of it."

Hey, did you know that Archibald Doc "Moonlight" Graham, from the movie "Field of Dreams" was really a real person from our very own Iron Range up in Chisholm? God, I love stuff like that! Yeah, I even looked it up. Archie played in one game, in 1905, with the New York Giants, but never got to bat. I mean when he got to come back to life in the movie and then wink, right before the pitcher threw him some chin music, I begged for more. And then, when he crossed the infield line to save Kevin Costner's little girl from choking on that hot dog, and knowing that he couldn't come back in to the game, I cried like a baby. Maybe that is why I am such a sucker for this game, I really do love it.

As a kid growing up in the cozy Southern Minnesota town of Fairmont I used to live for playing sports. Anything I could get my hands on I would play: football in the Fall, hockey in the Winter and, of course, baseball in the Spring and Summer. My first foray into the great Summer past-time, however, came with T-Ball. And, from there I graduated to Kiwanis, a youth baseball league that had games at the local Middle School. Now, for whatever the reason, as a pitcher I could throw a fastball that seemed to be about 100 mph at this point. But, consequently, I had pretty much zero accuracy. I can still remember opposing batters being absolutely horrified to face me. As a result, they would stand so far outside the batter's box that I would finally just toss an eephus pitch over the outside corner at about 25 mph for a strike. It wasn't pretty, but it worked. From there I played in VFW and then American Legion Ball. The camaraderie was the best, taking the bus from town to town, telling jokes and hanging out with your pals along the way.

In high school I was a third baseman and a pitcher: translation, I rode the pines quite a bit. I remember when I wasn't pitching I was either keeping the score book, or chomping through an entire giant bag of sunflower seeds. Sure, I even succumbed to peer pressure at one point and graduated from sunnies to chewing tobacco, but it was a short-lived experiment in being naughty. You see, one of my pals got some Skoal Bandits. You know, they were the kind that were nice and neat, in their own little pouch. So, I loaded up my cheeks with a couple of them and had at it. I made the small mistake of swallowing mine though, and after about an hour of violent heaving, decided that sunnies were probably a safer source of nutrition for me.

The highlight of my high school career at old Fairmont High would have to be our big road-trip to the Metrodome. It was there, for some district game or something, that I was able to give up a grand-slam, and get handed a 10-run loss. As a pitcher, it pretty much gets no better than to say you gave up a grand salami at the humpty-dump. After my heroics in the Dome, yours truly had a brief stint with the Minnetonka Millers during my freshman year of college. It was a college team and I was clearly way out of my league. After a couple of horrible outings on the mound as a middle-reliever, I called it a career after beaning a huge guy right in the ass. He wanted to kill me, so I decided right then and there that maybe I should hang up the ol' cleats for good.

I later played in my fraternity league, and then retired to softball. When I moved away to Chicago after college I was invited to play in a league with a couple of my hockey buddies. But when I showed up and got laughed at for bringing a glove, I decided that "kitten ball" just wasn't for me. Then, when I moved to New York City, another friend asked me to play. Just to be safe I asked him if I should bring my glove. He laughed and said of course. He also said to bring high-tops. I said great, it just so happened that I had high-top baseball spikes. At this point I was laughed at yet again as he said that they wouldn't work very well on black-top. Apparently the island of Manhattan was all out of dirt, so softball had migrated to asphalt. Needless to say, that was the end of my brief Big Apple softball experience.

I moved home a few years later and wound up getting a call from some of my old fraternity brothers who were playing in a league. They invited me back out to play and I reluctantly agreed. We got together and started to play catch. It was painful. I was dropping balls and popping out left and right. So, I figured it couldn't be me, it had to be my eyesight. With that, I went to see my eye doctor and got fitted for some glasses. I promptly went back out onto the field, where, full of confidence, I dropped a pop fly and flew out. After the season I called it a career.

I now officially live vicariously through golf and hockey, and watch the Twinkies on the tube. Like most Minnesotans I love the Twins, and can't believe what they have gone through in the last five years or so. These guys are like Rasputin, they just won't die. I mean from surviving the alleged move to North Carolina to being contracted, to strikes and stadium referendums — this organization has seen it all. As fans, this has obviously been extremely frustrating. I think we are all sick of hearing about luxury taxes, revenue sharing and salary caps — we just want to watch baseball!

I think my love affair with the game really kicked in to overdrive with these guys when I was in college. Sure, I had been to the old Met as a kid, but in 1987, when I was a freshman at the U of M, it was pure magic. When they won the pennant that Fall, I went nuts. My hand still hurts from all the gratuitous high-fiving that was going on around Dinkytown. I can still remember running through the streets of downtown Minneapolis with my buddies heaving roll after roll of toilet paper that we has just raided from our dormitory, Middlebrook Hall. It was amazing. Then, when they did it again four years later, I stayed in to watch it on TV. I just had to see the pandemonium from a more sober perspective. Once again, it was simply awesome!

Overall, I am a homer, and I love all forms of Minnesota baseball. Our history is an incredible journey that takes us way back to a time when we were just a territory, not even yet a state. In fact, baseball in Minnesota has had a long and amazing tradition, dating back to the pre-Civil War era of the 1850s. From the Millers and Saints to the Twins and Gophers, we have had the good, bad and the ugly. There have been so many obscure teams that have come and gone during that glorious century and a half. Some of them are hilarious. Come on, surely you can remember them all, right? Let's see!

OK, you know about the Twins and Saints, that's easy, and you might even remember the "old" St. Paul Saints and Minneapolis Millers, but do you remember the Minneapolis Brown Stockings or St. Paul Red Caps? The Twin Cities have certainly had their share of interesting ballclubs. What about the Minneapolis Minnies and St. Paul Apostles, or even the Minneapolis Unions or St. Paul North Stars, or the Minneapolis Keystones and St. Paul Gophers? Or how about the Minneapolis Roughriders or St. Paul Colts, or the Minneapolis White Shirts or just the plain ol' St. Paul Base Ball Club of the 1890s? Maybe the Minneapolis Bananas, Minneapolis Loons, St Paul Armours, St. Cloud Arctics or even the Minneapolis Millerettes will refresh your memory? OK, OK, lets try some easier ones. What about the old Stillwaters, or Winona Clippers, or St. Cloud Rivers Bats or even the St. Cloud Rox? No, maybe the Brainerd Muskies, Hastings Crescents, Red Wing Manufacturers or Crookston Crooks rings a bell. Surely you know of the Fargo-Moorhead Graingrowers and of the Virginia Ore Diggers, right?

If not, then obviously you followed the Warren Wanderers, Fairmont Martins, Alexandria Beetles and Mankato Mashers, yeah? Rochester had the Aces, Honkers, Roosters, Bears and Bugs, while Winona had the Silver Bells. Speaking of bells, maybe Duluth rings a bell. After all, the port city has had its share of teams over the past century or so, including the Whalebacks, Jayhawks, White Sox, Twi-Sox, Cubs,

Cardinals, Steelers, Dukes, and of course my personal favorite, the 1887 Northwestern League Duluth "Freezers." That tremendous name is followed by a close second place finish with the 1904 St. Cloud/Brainerd franchise, which was nicknamed the "St. Brains." (I can hear it now, "Here we go Brains... Here we go! Rah! - Rah!)

All in all though, I think the state-of-the-state of baseball in the Land of 10,000 Lakes looks great. And, we have done it without the luxury of being able to play outdoor baseball in the wintertime — a real disadvantage for our kids. The state of the state of our youth game in the Gopher State is as strong as ever too. That is a tremendous credit to our dedicated coaches and volunteers, who have seen to it that our kids have had every opportunity available to them to play and compete against the top levels of competition. Hey, don't just take my word for it, the proof is in the pudding:

Did you know that Minnesota has the second largest number of participants in the AAU program and also has the second largest number of teams participating in the American Legion baseball program as well? In addition, Minnesota Babe Ruth teams have gone on to compete in the Babe Ruth World Series in three of the last four years, with Lakeville coming in second place for the 16-year-old division in 2002. We have also had six teams in the last seven years go on to compete in the National American Legion World Series, including Tri-City (New Brighton), which won the national championship in 1999, and Excelsior which finished No. 2 in 2002. There are also a ton of kids playing in summer youth leagues, such as the Gopher State Baseball League, which has more than 3,500 kids suiting up each summer, and the 400-team Metro Baseball League, the largest independent traveling youth baseball league in the country.

And, many of our kids are moving on to play at the next level too. Our college and universities have been tapping into this reservoir of quality young ballplayers for years. Did you know that the Gophers, who have won over 40 games in each of the last three seasons and have emerged as one of the nation's elite programs, are more than 70% Minnesotan? So, who will the next Dave Winfield, Paul Molitor, Kent Hrbek, Jack Morris, Terry Steinbach or Jim Eisenreich be? Stay tuned, because there are a host of kids out there just waiting to bust loose and make Minnesota proud.

I would also like to say that the epiphany behind "Batter-Up!" was to celebrate the wonderful heritage of baseball that we, as Minnesotans, so dearly love and respect. Minnesota has an amazing baseball tradition, and I am honored and humbled to be able to bring so much of it to life for everyone to enjoy in my new book. When I first started writing this more than a year ago, I was immediately taken by just how much information there actually was about the sport of in our state. This led to an interesting dilemma on just how I was going to disseminate it all. I mean there are literally hundreds, if not thousands of players, coaches, administrators, media personalities and others, who are deserving of being in a book such as this, and as a result, it was extremely difficult to put it all together. Knowing this, I have to issue a caveat of sorts to explain my rationale for how I chose to tackle a subject that is so passionate and yet so controversial with so many Minnesotans — the game, and lifestyle of baseball.

I have chosen to focus primarily on the historical side of the game for this book, and tried to chronicle as best as possible the true history of the game over the past century and a half. It was an arduous task, but one that was inspiring to complete. All in all, there were some 400 sources that went into the project, not to mention an additional 50 or so interviews. Undoubtedly, and expectedly, whenever a book such as this is written, people usually get bent out of shape when they realize that so-and-so wasn't mentioned, or that he or she got more ink than him or her. I guess that is just the nature of the beast with stuff like this, and all I can say is that I tried to be arbitrary and objective in my research, and hopefully the vast majority of people that should be in here, are in here. For those who I have overlooked, or simply did not have the space to mention, I sincerely apologize. Believe me, it was a difficult process to have to eliminate so many wonderful biographies and funny stories because I simply did not have the real-estate to mention them. My main objective was to celebrate the positive aspects, such as the people, big games, history, and drama of baseball in the Gopher State, and hopefully I have succeeded in my mission. I would also like to add, however, that if any readers find any inaccuracies or mistakes in the book, to please e-mail me about it so I can correct it for the second printing. I am not to proud to say that with so much information covering such a long period of time, there are bound to be a few mistakes in here. Ultimately, I just want to get it right to preserve and chronicle our amazing history as best as possible.

With that, do you know what? I really can't wait to take my new daughter to her first ballgame. Let's just hope that all of this stadium mumbo-jumbo works itself out so that we can all enjoy playing hooky down the road to watch an afternoon ballgame under the clouds with our kids. That is what this great game is truly all about. So, sit back, relax, crack open a tall beverage, and get ready to read about some good ol' fashioned Minnesota baseball. Hopefully you will have half as much fun reading about and celebrating this amazing tradition as I did getting the opportunity to bring it all to life. Enjoy!

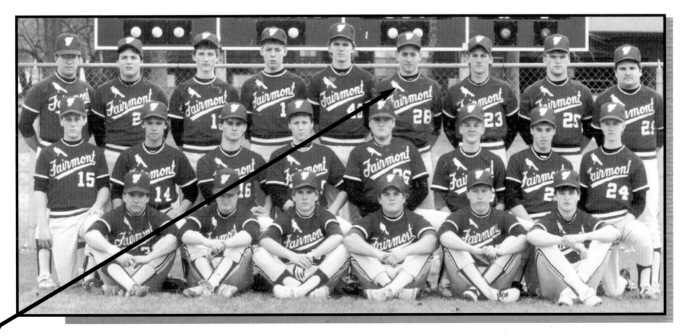

Yours truly, weighing in at a mean buck-sixty-five (*and batting about the same...*) for the mighty 1987 Fairmont Cardinals.

While the game of Baseball, or "Base Ball," as it was originally known, has emerged as America's national past-time, its origins are still a matter of controversy. A number of stick and ball games were played throughout the East Coast early in the 19th century, including "round ball," "one-old-cat" and "goal ball" among others. Since the dawn of time, however, it has been widely accepted that Major General Abner Doubleday invented the game in 1839 while he was a cadet stationed at West Point, New York. He supposedly dreamt up the game and its accompanying rules to provide a form of entertainment for his fellow cadets. As a result, the National Baseball Hall of Fame was later founded in Doubleday's home town of Cooperstown, New York, where it has remained ever since.

The first "official" baseball game, however, took place on June 16, 1846, in Hoboken, New Jersey, when the Knickerbockers squared off against the New Yorkers. A debate has been rekindled as of late though amongst many prominent baseball researchers and historians with regards to when and where the game actually began. You see, in 2001 some librarian discovered a little blurb in the obscure newspaper, "The National Advocate," that on April 23, 1823, a game of "base ball" was played at the corner of Broadway and 8th Street in lower Manhattan. The early reference to the game did not get specific, but certainly predates Doubleday's claim to fame by nearly 20 years.

Others have even speculated that the game crossed the pond from the United Kingdom, where the Brits played a game called "rounders," a popular schoolyard game which was similar to cricket. When those immigrants came to America, they hypothesized, the game evolved into an amalgam of what we now know as baseball. (In the game of Rounders, a player was "out" when an opposing player threw the ball at him. An adaptation of this was used in the "New York Rules," which saw a player "being out when touched by the ball while in the hand of the adversary.")

From those humble beginnings the game we know and love has grown into a mega-billion dollar industry — full of passion, controversy and a pure love of the game. And, while there is little controversy that the game first began out on the East Coast, it wasn't long after that it found its way over to the Land of 10,000 Lakes.

In fact, in 1853 Fort Ridgely, which had been established on the Minnesota River as a frontier post even prior to the Civil War, had become a center of military activity. Soldiers from the East Coast serving at the base undoubtedly introduced the game to the Gopher State, and the rest, they say, is history. According to several historians, many of the locals even remember the soldiers playing the new game of base ball there. Troops then moved back and forth to Fort Snelling in St. Paul and thus spread the game along the way.

Now, in as early as 1857, the now ghost-town of Nininger, Minn., fielded what is believed to be the first ever base ball team in the state. (To put this into perspective, it would be nearly two years later until the territory of Minnesota would become the 32nd state admitted to the Union!) Others quickly followed. St. Paul had a club called the "North Stars" and Minneapolis had the "Excelsiors." During this era the teams played with either "Town Ball" or "New York rules," no one is for sure.

By 1867 organized base ball had arrived in Minnesota with the formation of the Minnesota State Association of Base Ball Players. That year the organization sponsored a tournament in which the "North Star Club" of St. Paul claimed the first State Championship by beating the "Vermillion Baseball Club," 43-35. (This was later considered to be the first "town-team" championship.) That next year a handful of additional local teams from such far away exotic locales as: Stillwater, St. Cloud, Winona, Vermillion, Northfield, St. Paul and Minneapolis, competed in the tournament for

CHARLES BENDER

Minnesota's first Hall of Famer, Charles Bender, was a man of Ojibwa Native American descent. The "Chief" as he was affectionately known, was born one of 13 children near Brainerd on the White Earth Reservation in 1883. In 1900 Bender enrolled in the Indian School at Carlisle, Pennsylvania, where he would go on to star on the school's football, basketball, track and baseball teams. Baseball quickly emerged as his sport of choice though, as he became a dominant pitcher. He began playing semi--pro baseball, under an assumed name of course (so he didn't lose his Carlisle eligibility), and found that he could do quite well against the big boys. It was there, against the Chicago Cubs that the legendary Connie Mack saw the youngster play and immediately signed him to a pro contract.

The Chief would then go on to pitch for the Philadelphia Athletics, and later with Baltimore of the Federal League, and finally the Philadelphia Phillies, from 1903 to 1917 — compiling a career record of 212 wins and 128 losses, and also won three American League Pitching Winning Percentage Titles in 1910, 1911 and 1914. He was one of the most dominant pitchers of his day, leading his Athletics to five World Series appearances along the way. (He still remains the only pitcher ever to have nine complete games in the big dance.) He would pitch until he was 42, and was still tough as nails until the very end. After his playing days he went on to coach the Athletics from 1951 to 1953, and later served as either a coach or scout with the New York Yankees, Chicago White Sox, New York Giants and Philadelphia Athletics.

An avid hunter, fisherman and even a champion clay pigeon shooter and pro golfer in his latter years, the Chief was inducted into the Baseball Hall of Fame in Cooperstown in 1953.

The "Chief"

VINTAGE BASE BALL

George *"The Hit Man"* Rekela

Believe it or not, the Vintage Base Ball movement is alive and well in Minnesota. That's right, and leading the charge are the Quicksteps, a Twin Cities vintage base ball club, which plays other vintage teams from around the country using the game's original rules from 1858. Other teams in the area which compete in the annual Minnesota Vintage Base Ball Tournament include the Washington County Historical Society, Afton Historical Society Red Socks, Saint Croix Base Ball Club, Winona Lumber Barons and the Olmsted County Historical Society Roosters.

The teams even have historically correct uniforms, use mannerisms and speech typical of the day, and use the same equipment that was available during that era. Presently, there are over 100 established vintage base ball clubs throughout North America which play by rules ranging from the 1850s to the 1920s. For instance, the St. Croixs play by the 1860 "New York Rules," the same rules that were played by Civil War soldiers during times of leisure — ultimately helping to grow the game into what has become the national pastime.

the grand prize of a silver bell, which was given in lieu of a pennant. This was the infancy of amateur baseball in the state, and the fans were quickly learning the rules and beginning to take an interest. That year the Minneapolis "Unions" and Winona "Silver Stars" advanced to the Finals, where the Unions cruised to an easy victory. The Unions would prove to be the most powerful of all the clubs, hands down, winning the next five titles.

They were a bunch of men among boys in those days and were described by Minneapolis Journal writer, Joe McDermott, in his 1912 article: "The Unions did not wear uniforms as uniforms are known today. Their trousers were long and looped over their shoes and they ware shirts to match, on which their team name was printed. Most of the gladiators wore mustaches."

The game died down in popularity in the 1870s but then a renaissance occurred when Charles Smith, the head bookkeeper at the Hennepin County Savings Bank, put together a new team called the "White Shirts." The club played at various locales throughout Minneapolis and emerged as the team to beat of this era. Their main rivals were the "Lyndales," whom they often played for purses as large as $100 per outing.

The White Shirts changed their name to the Blue Stockings in 1876 and that same year a traveling team from Manchester came to town for an exhibition game. The team also brought something else with them as well, a curve ball, which had never been seen or even heard of locally. The visitors crushed the Blue Stockings, who were mesmerized by the curving balls, holding them hitless on the afternoon. It was even reported in the paper that next day that the crowd thought "Bohn (the opposing pitcher) was a magician."

Bohn was so good that the next year a new team, the "Brown Stockings," was formed with Bohn as its new pitcher. The team was backed by local businessman Frank Chase, who wanted to win at all costs. When he hired Bohn, so began the state's first semi-professional team. The Brown Stockings would play their games at a ball lot, complete with a fence and grand stand, on Nineteenth street in Minneapolis. The new team also played St. Paul's first semi-pro team, the "Saints," as well.

The popularity of the game remained steady during this era. One popular league was the Keystone Association, of which the Winona Clippers were a powerhouse in the late-1870s. Then, in 1883, the Minneapolis "Browns" were formed with Eddie Whitcomb serving as the team's owner, manager and shortstop. None of the players were paid but Whitcomb financed the operation with the understanding that he would donate a percentage of the gate receipts back to the boys from time to time. The fans loved it. It wasn't uncommon for as many as 3,000 spectators to show up for games, particularly to

watch the cross-town rivalry with the St. Paul "Red Caps" and a club from Stillwater. "Stillwater was the Browns most bitter foe," added McDermott, "and no matter how the game ended a free-for-all fist fight generally followed." The club also beat the traveling White Stockings from Chicago, avenging a previous loss from a few years back.

In 1884 professional baseball came to the Gopher State when the Northwestern League, a professional, minor league, was formed with teams from Minneapolis, St. Paul, Winona, Duluth and Stillwater, as well as six other teams from Illinois, Indiana, Wisconsin and Michigan. The Duluth Jayhawks won the Northwestern League title that year with a 46-33 record. (That next year the Jayhawks folded and were replaced by what this author feels might be the greatest nickname in Minnesota sports history: the Duluth "Freezers.")

It is also interesting to note that the "Stillwaters" were led by an African American pitcher by the name of Bud Fowler, who came to Minnesota to play baseball in the pre-Jim Crow era of racial relations in America. Fowler (whose real name was John Jackson) was already a well-traveled veteran second baseman, when he was recruited to come north for the summer. Just 10 years earlier, however, he became the first black to play in organized baseball.

This was also the beginning of the greatest rivalry in Minnesota baseball history: Minneapolis versus St. Paul. Minneapolis' team was known as the Millers that year, while their cross-river rivals were known as the St. Paul Base Ball Club. Their

Early Base Ball Rule Adaptations

1857 Nine innings was established as the length of a game
1858 Fly balls had to be caught on the fly
1859 The catcher now stood behind the batter
1866 The bunt was introduced, as was stealing bases by sliding
1867 The curve ball was introduced
1869 The glove was used for first time
1885 The catcher used a chest protector for the first time
1889 Four balls, instead of nine, constituted a walk
1890 Walks were no longer included as hits in batting averages
1891 The catcher first used a catcher's mitt
1893 The distance from the mound to home plate was pushed back from 50 to 60 feet
1895 The infield fly rule was adopted
1908 The catcher first used shin-guards
1909 A cork center ball was introduced

BOBBY MARSHALL

Bobby Marshall was the first great African American sports legend of Minnesota. The Minneapolis Central High School star went on to become the first man of color to play in the Big Nine (later the Big Ten) as an End for the Gophers. From 1904-06 he led the team to an amazing record of 27-2, while outscoring their opponents 1,238-63. In 1906 he even kicked a game-winning 60-yard field goal in the rain and mud to beat the University of Chicago, 4-2 (field goals counted 4 points back then). He received All-Western honors for all three of his years in Minnesota.

In addition to football, he earned all-conference honors as a first baseman on the baseball team and lettered in track as a sprinter. As a professional, he was a star in football, baseball, boxing and even hockey, where, in 1908, he became the first African American to play professionally, when he suited up for the semi-pro Minneapolis Wanderers. In baseball he played for the Colored Gophers and the Chicago Leland Giants professional Negro-League teams, and on the gridiron he played professionally with the Minneapolis Deans (which were undefeated with Marshall playing), Minneapolis Marines, Duluth Eskimos and Rock Island Independents.

He was such an incredible athlete, that after retiring from playing pro football at the age of 44, he even made a comeback at that age of 50 to play in an exhibition game at Nicollet Park. Marshall was such a durable athlete that he never sustained a major injury in nearly 30 years of football. He later became a grain inspector for the state of Minnesota and died on Aug. 27, 1968, at the age of 88. In 1971 he was inducted into the College Football Hall of Fame, and several years later was also named to the National Football Foundation's Hall of Fame. He will undoubtedly be remembered as one of Minnesota's greatest ever all-around athletes.

first meeting took place in St. Paul at the old West Seventh Street Grounds, where more than five thousand fans crammed into the park to see the historic match. A lot of side betting was on the line as well with tens of thousands of dollars being wagered. Carruthers was on the mound for Minneapolis and Elmer Foster for St. Paul as the Millers, who never even reached second base in this one, got spanked, 11-0. St. Paul had recruited many of the Millers top players to jump ship that year, adding even more drama to the young rivalry.

St. Paul was in contention to win the pennant that year until Foster snapped his arm in two during a game against Milwaukee late in the season. But when their season was over, something happened that made history. While the Minneapolis club folded after that season, St. Paul got a unique opportunity to join the Union Association, which was just finishing its season. Despite the fact that it was considered to be an "outlaw league," which meant that the team illegally lured players away from other leagues, the Union Association was the real deal back in the day — joining the National League and American Association as the three major leagues. The Union had teams from Pittsburgh, Philadelphia, Baltimore, Boston, Chicago, Cincinnati, St. Louis and Washington, but two dropped out late in the year, and as a result, St. Paul and Milwaukee, of the Northwestern League, were invited to fill in for what would prove to be just nine games.

With that, however, St. Paul, which renamed itself as the "White Caps," earned itself the distinction of being the state's first team ever to play major league baseball. One of the stars of that team was St. Paul native Joe Werrick, who, upon playing in the Union, became the second Minnesotan to play in the majors. (The first, however, was Minneapolis native Elmer Foster, who had played briefly with Philadelphia earlier in the year before signing on with St. Paul.)

(Interestingly, the fans didn't get a chance to see any of St. Paul's games, because all of the team's games were played on the road. Their barnstorming tour pro-

duced a modest 2-6-1 record, placing them ninth among the 12 teams. The St. Paul Base Ball Club disbanded at the end of that 1884 season and it would be another 77 years before Minnesotans would again have a major league baseball team to root for.)

In 1886 the Northwestern League was resurrected with six teams joining the fray: Minneapolis, St. Paul, Duluth, Eau Claire, Milwaukee and Oshkosh (Des Moines and La Crosse were added that next year). The Minneapolis and St. Paul clubs both had ballparks to play in, but had to go elsewhere on Sundays. That's because the city fathers prohibited baseball on the Sabbath. As a result, the teams and fans alike would hop on the Milwaukee Railways short line train and venture north to White Bear Lake, where they would resume the action out in the "burbs."

Two years later the Northwestern League folded due to financial problems, as well as from "raiding" by other leagues for its top talent. So, the Western Association was begun that year with franchises in Minneapolis, St. Paul, Des Moines, Sioux City, Milwaukee, Chicago, Kansas City and Omaha. But, due to late season flooding and thin fan support, the Minneapolis franchise, then called the "Minnies," was sold off to an outfit in Davenport, Iowa. The St. Paul franchise, known both as the "Saints" as well as the "Apostles," fared well in the circuit, playing there though the 1891 season — when they were relocated to Duluth, where they became the "Whalebacks."

The "Minnies" would return to the Western that next season, along with Denver, and stay there until 1893, when a new professional, minor league called the Western League was formed. Established in Indianapolis, the Western League was an eight-team circuit which featured clubs from across the Midwest. More importantly, however, was the fact that this was the first semi-pro league that pitted the rival Minneapolis Millers and St. Paul Saints against one another.

THE COLORED GOPHERS

MINNESOTA & THE NEGRO LEAGUES

African-Americans first began to play baseball during the Civil War era, but because of racism and "Jim Crow" laws, they would be forced to play in their own leagues — often barnstorming throughout the countryside playing anyone who would challenge them. The white professional leagues would sometimes hire young black men to play for them, but it was very inconsistent.

So, in 1920, an new league was formed with eight of the better black teams at the time to make up what would later be known as the Negro National League. Before long, rival leagues formed in eastern and southern states, allowing the game to thrive and flourish in the African American community. The leagues became sources of pride for their local towns and even became centerpieces for their economic development.

In 1945, a shortstop by the name of Jackie Robinson, who was playing for the Kansas City Monarchs, became the first African-American in the modern era to play on a white professional team when the Brooklyn Dodgers signed him. While the signing was an historic event in civil rights history — paving the way for other young black men who would later break through the color line, it also marked the decline of the Negro Leagues. Soon, the best black players signed contracts with the Major Leagues and before long the fans followed. The last Negro League teams closed up shop in the early 1960s.

Now, as far as the Negro Leagues in Minnesota, this is an interesting story that first takes us back to 1884, to the sleepy river town of Stillwater. It was there that the Northwestern League had started, complete with teams from Minneapolis, St. Paul, Winona, Duluth and Stillwater, as well as six other teams from Illinois, Indiana, Wisconsin and Michigan. What is significant about the "Stillwaters," however, is that they were led by an African American pitcher by the name of Bud Fowler. Fowler (whose real name was John Jackson) was already a well-traveled veteran second baseman by the time he was recruited to come north for the summer though. Just 10 years earlier he became the first African American to play in organized baseball.

With regards to actual Negro League teams in Minnesota, however, no official teams were ever represented here, but the state did have some all-black teams in the early part of the century. The most notable of those teams were the St. Paul Colored Gophers and Minneapolis Keystones. The Gophers were led by Minneapolis' Bobby Marshall, who would later be regarded as one of the best athletes in state history. In 1909 Marshall even led his Gophers past the infamous Chicago Leland Giants for the Negro Baseball Championship. (Rube Foster, the great pitcher who later founded the organized Negro Leagues, played for the Leland Giants and would also later pitch as a hired "ringer" for the Gophers in the years to come.)

Another interesting sidebar to black baseball history came in 1908, when a man by the name of Richard Brookins played for the Fargo-Moorhead Browns in the Northern League. The significance of this is that Brookins was the first documented African-American [outside of the Negro Leagues] to play organized baseball [as a career — not as a ringer playing for a couple months with a random team], in the 20th century.

Later, in the 1953, another Minnesotan, St. Paul native Toni Stone, played in the Negro Leagues when she signed a contract with the Indianapolis Clowns — becoming the first woman ever to play professional baseball for a men's team. Stone even got a hit off of future Hall of Fame Pitcher Satchel Paige that season! That next year she would play with the Kansas City Monarchs, a traveling all-star team which had won several pennants in the "Colored World Series."

A great story about the Gopher State and Negro League history comes from Southern Minnesota, where, in 1949, Hall of Fame Pitcher Hilton Smith spent his summer vacation playing baseball in tiny Fulda. As the story goes, the town desperately needed lights for its ballpark — so it could keep up with the Jones' in the local townball league. So, a man by the name of Richard Reusse (as in the father of celebrated Star Tribune columnist Patrick Reusse), who was an undertaker by day and the townball team manager by night, thought of a way to get it done. He and a few of his pals headed to Kansas City, where they proceeded to convince the great Hilton Smith, a star pitcher of the Kansas City Monarchs Negro League team, to come up to Murray County and become the mother of all "ringers" for the Fulda Giants.

Smith, now 42 and well past his prime, couldn't turn down the offer to spend five months in balmy Minnesota for a cool grand a month. Reusse then scrounged up enough money from the local businessmen to pay the man, and the rest they say, is history. Fulda had a great year, Smith had a nice summer vacation, and after the season, the town's voters approved a $12,000 bonding measure for lights at the ballpark. It was a win-win-win. And, appropriately enough, in 2001 Smith would go on to be inducted into the Baseball Hall of Fame alongside fellow Minnesotans Kirby Puckett and Dave Winfield — two players who openly acknowledged at the induction ceremony in Cooperstown that if it weren't for the efforts of pioneers such as Smith, they would never have had the chance to make it in the big leagues.

(It is interesting to note that while Smith's arrival in Fulda for an entire summer was an anomaly, other Negro League players had frequented Minnesota in years prior. They would come in either as individual "ringers-for-hire" or else come as members of traveling teams which did the circuit of townball and exhibition games on a nightly basis. Fairmont, for instance, had the great Satchell Paige play at local Martin Park as a ringer, while other teams such as the Colored Brooklyn Dodgers and even the Harlem Globetrotters Colored Team played there in the '30s as well. The teams, which were given a percentage of the gate receipts, usually let the locals get an early lead, to get the fans into it, and then come back to win. They were usually careful, however, not to win by too much — after all, they wanted to get invited back the next year!)

Other milestones in black baseball history in Minnesota include 1948 when Catcher Roy Campanella, who, after starring for the Baltimore Elite Giants, joined the St. Paul Saints to became the first black player ever to play in the American Association before going on to a Hall of Fame career with the Dodgers. Then, in 1949, the cross-town Millers followed suit, by signing another future Hall of Famer, Ray Dandridge, who, from 1933-49 had previously played with the Detroit Stars, Nashville Elite Giants, Newark Dodgers, Newark Eagles and New York Cubans.

Thanks to the pioneering efforts of the players who played in the Negro Leagues, African American stars of today such as Barry Bonds, Ken Griffey Jr. and Torii Hunter, can achieve their dreams on an equal playing field. And that is what is all about.

The history of baseball in the Mill City proudly starts with the Minneapolis Millers, who were a fixture in the Gopher State's sports scene for nearly eight decades. It was during this era that baseball fans from across the Upper Midwest flocked here to watch the best baseball around.

Back in the day, minor league baseball was a way of life, which oftentimes provided its players the opportunity to earn a comfortable living. As a result, many minor leaguers spent their entire

The 1905 Minneapolis Millers

careers at that level. It wasn't just a stepping stone to the major leagues, rather, it was a lifestyle which saw the fans and players establish a bond with one another unlike anything we can comprehend in today's world of big-time sports. It was a wonderful blend of young stars on their way up, and grizzled old veterans who were on their way down — both living and playing in harmony. And, because the teams of this era usually had no affiliation with a major-league club, which routinely shuffled its players up and down throughout its stable of farm teams, the players usually stuck around and let the fans get to know em'.

The roots of minor league baseball in the Land of 10,000 Lakes take us all the way back to the post-Civil War era of the late 1860s. It was then, in 1867, that Minneapolis' first recorded team hit the field as the Minneapolis "Unions." Men, who had learned the game out East during the Civil War, were now returning from Gettysburg and Bull Run to introduce the game back home.

Minneapolis has a long history of baseball, and has been involved with the game's development from the very beginning. Some of the early teams included the "White Shirts," which was the team to beat of the 1870s. The White Shirts changed their name to the "Blue Stockings" in 1876 and dominated the local scene until another club was created in 1883, called the "Minneapolis Browns," the state's first semi-professional team. Fans came out in droves to watch the Browns do battle with the St. Paul "Red Caps" and the

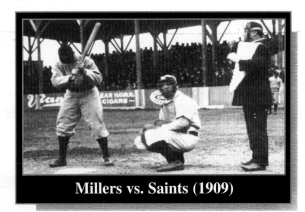

Millers vs. Saints (1909)

"Stillwaters."

The nickname "Millers" didn't come about until 1884, when the eight-team Northwestern League (the state's first professional circuit) opened up for business. (They were named, obviously, for the thriving flour milling industry which had sprung up along the Mississippi River.) Minneapolis, St. Paul, Stillwater, and (later) Winona had teams in the league, a minor league which also had clubs in neighboring Wisconsin, Illinois, Michigan, and Indiana. (Incidentally, the first meeting between Minneapolis and St. Paul teams occurred on June 2nd, at the West Seventh Street field in St. Paul. There, before 4,000 fans, Minneapolis was blanked, 4-0.) The league only lasted for one season, however, due to a lack of financing. Then, in 1888, the Minneapolis franchise transferred to Davenport, Iowa, where they finished the year with a 31-74 record.

Over the next decade or so Minneapolis would bounce around in and out of various leagues. One of the highlights of the 1890 season was when Millers Pitcher Red Killen hurled a 3-0 no-hitter against Sioux City. The club then advanced to the playoffs, where they faced off against rival Kansas City in one of the oddest series of all time. The series opened in KC with Millers' Pitcher Martin Duke taking the mound. It turned out that Duke's real name was "Duck," but he hated the name and had it changed. Well, some of the KC fans

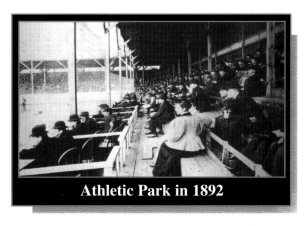

Athletic Park in 1892

found out about it and got an idea. That night, they smuggled a bunch of ducks into the stadium and, during the game, they would toss the squawking ducks out onto the field to taunt Duke while he was on the mound. He cracked and Kansas City won the flag.

In 1894 the Millers joined the upstart Western League. Originally established to rival the then established National League, a major league, the Western featured big-time players. At the time the Millers played in a small, intimate downtown ballpark located behind the West Hotel at Sixth Street and First Avenue North called simply the "Downtown Ballpark," or also "Athletic Park." (Prior to that the Millers played at Hiawatha Park near downtown Minneapolis.)

According to famed writer, David Wood, who wrote the article "Minneapolis' First Downtown Baseball Park," the ballpark's grandstand seated just 3,000 and the "bleaching boards," 1,600. It was described as "state of the art" at the time, complete with a "sturdy wooden fence 12 feet high surmounted by a 12-foot wire screen." In addition, the base-lines were "marked by a bed of clay two feet deep which makes a springy track and gives a chance for fast base running." The field was "as level as a board floor and almost as hard," and the dressing rooms located under the grandstands were described as "much more commodious than those generally provided for ball players — complete with lockers, bathrooms, and other necessary appliances." The area behind right field was also where the horses and carriages were parked.

Wood added that during this era most of the ballplayers stayed at the old Franklin Hotel and would then take the train to the park to get dressed. With them, the players used to carry their own bats which they "carefully packed in a custom leather case." Now, if a local youngster could convince one of those players to let him carry his bat case into the stadium for him, the boy, in return, would then be let into the game for free. This was a much better deal than having to pay the whopping 25¢ to sit out in the bleachers!

Minneapolis' first game there resulted in a 9-5 win over the hated Milwaukee Brewers. Some 3,000 fans, or "cranks" as they were then known, showed up on the cold and windy day to root on the

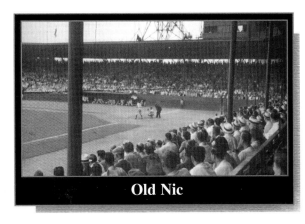
Old Nic

Millers to victory. It was at Athletic Park that the team's first star emerged, Perry "Moose" Werden, who knocked out 45 homers in 1895 — a single-season record which stood firmly until the great Bambino himself came along a few decades later and swatted 54 in 1926.

Midway through the 1896 season the Millers were evicted from the cozy confines of Athletic Park and were forced to find a new home. (The land was sold for development which later became the Butler Brothers Mail Order Company — a nine story building built in 1906 which would ultimately serve as the namesake of today's "Butler Square," next to the Target Center.) So, they moved into the newly constructed Nicollet Park. Located at Nicollet Avenue and 31st Street, by Lake Street in south Minneapolis, the ballpark had a seating capacity of about 4,000. More importantly, it was only 279 feet to clear the right field wall — making it a real hitter's delight. On June 19, 1896, the team christened its new digs by beating Milwaukee, 13-6, on Charley Frank's two-run homer, to win their inaugural game. The Millers just kept on rolling from there, claiming the Western League championship that year as well.

In 1900, in an effort to challenge the mighty National League, baseball tycoon Ban Johnson formed a new renegade league called the "American League." The AL then absorbed the eight Western League teams (Minneapolis, Milwaukee, Chicago, Cleveland, Detroit, Indianapolis, Kansas City and Buffalo) into its new circuit of big-time baseball. Shortly thereafter a war broke out between the two rival circuits with the American League raiding players left and right from the NL in an effort to even things out. The AL wanted to get into bigger cities though, so they quickly abandoned the smaller markets — including the Twin Cities. The Millers would go on to play one season in the big-time American League, finishing in last place. The Saints, however, were moved to Chicago by owner Charles Comiskey, and renamed as the White Sox — where they have remained ever since.

The next year the Millers left the American League and jumped ship yet again, this time becoming charter members of a new top-flight minor league called the "American Association" (along with teams from St. Paul, Milwaukee, Louisville, Columbus, Toledo, Kansas City and Indianapolis). The American Association, along with the International League and Pacific Coast League, comprised

the three major AAA minor leagues in the nation.

In 1904 Clarence Saulpaugh sold the Millers to W. H. Watkins, who also owned the Indianapolis team in the same league. Watkins lasted just a year though, as he wound up selling the club to St. Paul Saints Manager, Mike Kelley, who decided to cross the river and take over as president and manager of the Millers. Everything was going smooth for Kelley until one night in July of 1906 at Nicollet Park, when all hell broke loose during a game between the Millers and rival Columbus. Some 9,000 fans went ballistic in this one when a rookie umpire, who gave several close calls to Columbus — ultimately giving them a victory, nearly caused a riot to ensue. The ump was rescued by the police that night, but the next night the fans came prepared by smuggling in plenty of eggs and tomatoes. As the ump was about ready to say "Play-Ball," the fans let him have it and started pelting him.

As a result, the umpire immediately forfeited the game to Columbus. This, of course, led to pandemonium, in which a mob emerged with every intent of carrying out a lynching. Just then, a huge figure emerged from the crowd to restore the peace, It was none other than former Yale Football All-American, Pudge Heffelfinger. Now, according to former columnist George Barton, Pudge, who was long considered to be the greatest lineman of all-time, then promptly shouted: "Friends, you are about to do something that will forever disgrace the good name of Minneapolis — an act you will always regret. I am going to escort this man off the field and to his hotel. I warn all of you that anyone who harms him must answer to me!"

A few years later the attendance at Nicollet Park was dwindling, and as a result, the Millers were sold to Gus Koch of Milwaukee. In 1909 the Millers, managed by future Hall of Famer Eddie Collins, were led by a pretty good left-handed pitcher named "young" Cy Young. (He was of no relation to the "other" Hall of fame pitcher bearing the same name.) But the team struggled and Koch was tired of paying out big salaries, so he went ahead and sold the club to Mike and Joe Cantillon, who were the owners and managers of the Western League's Des Moines affiliate. The Cantillons knew what they were doing, and before long had turned the club around. They recruited a bunch a former major-leaguer's and had at it.

The 1910 squad posted a 107-61 record and won its first of three straight pennants. Pitcher Tom Hughes won a record 31 games

Nicollet Park

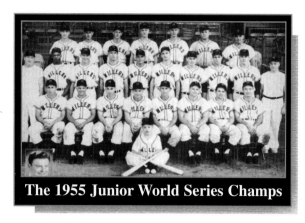

The 1955 Junior World Series Champs

that year, while Roy Patterson and future Hall of Famer Rube Waddell added 24 and 20 wins, respectively, in 1911. (Gavvy Cravath also hit 29 home runs for the Millers that year to set a new American Association record.) Righty Fred Olmstead won 28 games of his own in 1912, and with that, a dynasty was born.

One of the most exciting things about this era of baseball was the rivalry that evolved between the Millers and cross-town St. Paul Saints, who played just seven miles away at Lexington Park. These teams had it out for each other and the fans loved it. Highlighting these battles were the holiday double-headers which took place on Memorial Day, the Fourth of July and Labor Day, where the teams played a morning-afternoon double-header at the two different parks. The fans would hop on the street-cars to root for their teams and make a day of it — it was all the rage.

Another funny occurrence of this era produced what is still believed to be the shortest home run of all-time. It came one night at Nicollet Park when Miller Shortstop Andy Oyler stepped up to the plate during a game when the rain was coming down in sheets. Oyler then swung and chopped the ball straight down into the muddy infield just five feet in front of the catcher. The opposing players rushed the ball, but couldn't find it. The pitcher and catcher frantically searched as well, and by the time the second baseman finally found the muddy ball, it was too late — Oyler had slid across home plate for an inside-the-park-homer.

In 1915 the Millers won their fourth pennant under the Cantillons and had emerged as the team to beat in the entire league. The railroads were also chugging along, linking all the ballparks from city to city, creating a boom not only for the fans, but for the sport in general. But troubling times were ahead though, as World War I loomed just over the horizon. Sure, baseball rolled on, but many of the country's young men were being called into action. In the Spring of 1917 then-President Wilson signed a state-of-war resolution. As a result, many teams would participate in military drills before games under the instruction of a non-commissioned officer.

The war years were tough on baseball and the Millers were no exception. The nation was at war and people had more important things to do than worry about a game. More and more young men were being sent overseas and for the ones that stayed home, they were busy working long hours in war-related industries. Then, with attendance way down, something happened to boost morale. On May 24, 1918, some 1,200 fans came out to Nicollet Park to watch the

Joe Hauser

American Association's first ever night game. No, their were no lights, but with the new Daylight Savings Time act now in effect, the 7:00 p.m. game, which saw the Millers beat Toledo, 11-3, just got in before the sun set on a new day. Just a few months later, however, the season was cancelled after the Secretary of War ruled that baseball was a "non-essential industry."

The war ended in 1919 and with that the boys of summer returned to the ballparks across the land. That next year Mike Cantillon sold the Millers to a group of 29 local businessmen, headed by George Belden, president of the Minneapolis Athletic Club. Joe Cantillon, however, would stay behind the Miller bench for another five years to lead the club. Then, on October 7, 1923, after a 7-1 win over Indianapolis, the team was sold again. This time the buyer was someone pretty well known in Miller circles, and his name was Mike Kelley. Kelley was brilliant when it came to rebuilding ballclubs and wasted little time in re-tooling the Millers. He went out and bought a whole pile of aging major-leaguers and then re-sold them back to the major league's after they had padded their averages and hit plenty of homers in little Nicollet Park. In fact, most of the guys who had resurrected their careers in Minneapolis never went on to do a thing back in the majors. His plan was pure genius.

(One of the highlights of this era came on October, 14th, 1924, when Babe Ruth and Bob Meusel of the New York Yankees played in an exhibition game at Nicollet Park. The Great Bambino played for the "Odd Fellows," who were the Minneapolis amateur champions, while Meusel played for "Al Dretchko's All-Stars." Ruth played first base and went four-for-five with a pair of homers and six RBIs in the Odd Fellows' 8-5 victory.)

In 1928 the Millers were led by Duluth-native Spencer Harris, a .300 hitting speedy center fielder who played for 28 seasons before finally retiring at the tender young age of 48 as the minor-league career leader in runs, hits, and doubles. That same year future Hall of Famer Zack Wheat finished his career in Minneapolis after spending 18 seasons with the Brooklyn Dodgers.

The highlight of the 1929 season was a now infamous brawl that took place between the Millers and Saints in the morning game of the Fourth of July double-header at Nicollet Park. According to author Stew Thornley, the melee was described as "the most vicious affair ever witnessed at Nicollet," which "required fully a dozen policemen to quell the disturbance." As was described in Thornley's book, "On to Nicollet," the brouhaha began when Hughie McMullen spiked Millers Pitcher Huck Betts, who was covering first base on a routine ground ball. Betts then took the ball out of his glove and whipped it at McMullen's melon in retaliation. As the story goes, at that point all hell broke loose. Just then, reserve infielder Sammy Bohne who was coaching first at the moment, jumped in and gave Betts the business. That next morning legendary Minneapolis Journal columnist Halsey Hall's headline describing the story read: "Sammy Bohne Doesn't Play, But Gets More Hits Than Those Who Do..."

That next year Nick Cullop became the first American Association player ever to hit 50 homers, when he knocked out 54. The team, however, didn't fare as well as he did. Then, fully 17 years removed from their last pennant, the Millers got back into the action in 1932, winning their fifth American Association title. It was the height of the Great Depression and fans were finding enjoyment in one of life's inexpensive pleasures: baseball.

One of the big reasons for the team's turn-arounds that year was due to the acquisition of first-baseman Joe "Unser Choe" Hauser from the Baltimore Orioles of the International League. "Unser Choe" (a German expression for "Our Joe") lit it up that year for 49 dingers, as the Millers went on to set a single-season record for runs scored — nearly seven per game. In addition, Joe Mowry set an all-time league record by scoring 175 runs, while Art Ruble led the Association with a .gaudy 376 average.

When it was all said and done, the 100-68 Millers had claimed the title with nearly 10 games to spare. With that, the team made its first ever appearance in the Junior World Series, a post-season competition between the winners of the American Association and the rival International League. There, they battled the Newark Bears, a New York Yankees farm club full of fire-power. The series opened on the road, where the Millers took two of three, only to see the Bears even the series at 2-2 back in Minnie.

Game Five was a wild one that would go down in history for its infamous "Play of Six Decisions." With two outs in the ninth and the game knotted up at 8-8, Newark was rallying with runners at the corners. That's when Johnny Neun ripped a drive into short left-center that appeared to be caught on a beautiful back-handed dive by Center fielder Harry Rice. Now, the second and third base umpires both ruled the batter out, but the Bears protested. The two sides then spent 40 minutes arguing as to whether or not he caught the ball or not. Fully six decisions were made back and forth, and when it was all said and done, the umps finally overturned their original ruling that Rice had caught the ball. A formal protest of the game was then filed by skipper Donie Bush, but the representatives from both leagues could not get past their partisan bickering and the Bears 12-9 victory was allowed to stand.

Now, down three games to two, the Millers jumped out to an early lead in Game Six, but saw their title hopes disappear on a three-run, ninth-inning rally which gave the game to Newark, 8-7. The series, and perhaps one of the most bizarre protests in baseball history, were over.

The 1933 season was all about first-baseman Joe Hauser, who became the first ever pro player to hit 69 home runs in a single season. (By no surprise, 50 of the 69 dingers came at cozy Nicollet Park!) And, he could've hit 70, but rain canceled the last game. The record number was also complimented with 182 RBI's and 153 runs in 153 games as well. (The pro record stood until 2001, when outfielder Barry Bonds hit 73 for the San Francisco Giants.)

Incidentally, another landmark occurred that year at Nicollet Park when Minneapolis' very own General Mills unveiled a "Breakfast of Champions" advertising slogan for its "Wheaties" cereal on a billboard along the outfield fence. It would be the beginning of a wonderful relationship between the company and with sports. General Mills soon started to sponsor WCCO Radio broadcasts as well, and went on to endorse Babe Ruth years later. In fact, Wheaties even sponsored the first ever televised sports broadcast in 1939. Today, for an athlete to make the cover of the Wheaties box is as good as it gets!

(Wheaties, which were introduced back in 1924, were actually invented by accident when a health conscious Minneapolis man spilled bran gruel on a hot stove. The result was a crispy flake that not only tasted great but was nutritious to boot. The man contacted the Washburn Milling Co., the forerunner of General Mills, and the rest, they say, is history. His creation was turned into "Gold Medal Wheat Flakes," and later changed to "Wheaties.")

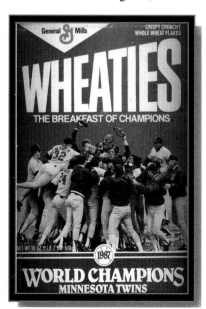

The Millers went ahead and won two more titles in 1934 and 1935 as well. One of the highlights of that 1935 season occurred when the legendary Yankees First Baseman Babe Ruth made an appearance at Nicollet Park in a game between the Minneapolis and St. Paul Policemen. Ruth played half a game with each team, but was held to just a double in five at-bats.

Billy Rigney

It is also interesting to note that in 1935 the Millers exercised a loop-hole in a little-known city ordinance which stated that games had to be stopped promptly at 6:00 p.m. (With no lights, teams were not allowed to start innings after 5:45 p.m.) So, in 1935, during a game with Toledo, the Millers saw a 3-0 lead disappear as the Mud Hens scored five runs in the top of the ninth. However, with the clock reading 5:55 p.m., the Millers pulled out the old stall tactic before the final out could be made. As a result, the score reverted back to the last full inning — thus giving the Millers a 3-0 win. (Years later, apparently someone looked it up and no such ordinance was found!) It is also interesting to note that Minneapolis and St. Paul were the last hold-outs when it came to night baseball in the American Association. In fact, by this time these two clubs were the only ones playing exclusively day games at home. So, shortly thereafter, the two clubs both installed lights at their respective stadiums.

In 1936 the American Association adopted a new playoff system called the "Governor's Cup," which saw the top four teams in the regular season duke it out for a spot in the Junior World Series. The Millers kicked it into overdrive that year, even becoming the first team to top 200 home runs in a season, but fell flat on bad pitching and wound up in fifth place.

Something exciting then happened in 1938. That was the year when a 19-year-old rookie from San Diego by the name of Ted Williams made his Minneapolis debut en route to a Hall of Fame career with the Boston Red Sox. Williams would stay just one season in Minnie before being signed by the Bo-Sox, but it was a wonderful one for baseball fans nonetheless. The chiseled right fielder lit up the league that year, becoming the first player to win the American Association's Triple Crown, hitting .366 with 43 home runs and 142 RBI's. Before long "Teddy Ballgame" had earned himself a reputation for being a hot-head. As legend has it, Williams' bad attitude even reached the point where Manager Donie Bush exclaimed to team owner Mike Kelley: "Either that kid goes or I go!" Kelley then calmly replied: "We're going to miss you, Donie…" (Williams, of course, would go on to survive two wars, hit 521 homers with the Red Sox, win a pair of Triple Crowns, become the last player to hit .400 in a season, and compile a career batting average of .344. Not bad!)

The 1940 season was all about Millers' superstar Ab Wright, who won the American Association Triple Crown that season with 39 home runs, 159 RBI's and a .369 average. The highlight of his spectacular season came on the Fourth of July, when he belted four home runs and a triple against the Saints for 19 total bases — a league record never matched.

Eddie Stanky

Gene Mauch

That next year the nation braced itself for World War II. Many of the Miller players were called to duty overseas, including Zeke Bonura, who was hitting .366 at the time. Baseball was allowed to continue operating during the war years, but the pool of available players was greatly reduced. Teams had to make do with what they had, and usually that meant playing guys who were either too old, too young, or deemed physically unfit to fight in the war. As a result, the war years were pretty thin as far as baseball was concerned. It was, however, relieving for the fans to have an outlet of fun during those trying times in American history.

In 1946 Mike Kelley, who had always prided himself on operating independently, finally got fed up with system and sold his beloved Millers to Horace Stoneham's New York Giants. After 52 years as a player, manager or executive, Mike had finally had enough. It had simply become too tough to compete for talent with the major league teams and their vast network of minor league affiliates. It became a classic case of "if you can't beat em', join em'." With that, the Millers officially became a farm team of the Giants.

A couple of native Minnesotans led the charge in 1947, beginning with Milaca's Carl DeRose, who was an ace pitcher with rival Kansas City. DeRose was suffering from an extremely sore arm and could barely pick up a ball by the time he faced the Millers on June 26th that season. Somehow though, DeRose fought through the pain to pitch what would prove to be the first perfect game in the history of the American Association. Apparently, DeRose was so sore that in the locker room after the game, he was unable to even lift his arm up to shake the hands of his elated teammates. The other Minnesotan who had a great season in 1947 was Catcher Wes Westrum, from Clearbrook, who hit .294 with 22 home runs and 87 RBIs for the Millers. (Westrum would later go on to become manager of both the Mets and Giants.)

In 1948 the managerial carousel went wild as manager Frank Shellenback resigned early in the season when he became ill. Center fielder Chick Genovese then took over until Billy Herman was hired to serve as the team's player/manager in mid-June. Herman, a perennial National League All-Star, was later inducted into the Hall of Fame in 1975.

That season also marked the end of the color line for Twin Cities baseball. On May 22nd of that year Catcher Roy Campanella appeared for the St. Paul Saints, who were by this time were a farm team of the Brooklyn Dodgers. The Millers would follow suit that next season when GM Rosy Ryan signed Ray Dandridge, who had previously played for the New York Cubans of the Negro American League.

Lu Clinton

Dandridge, who had played for 16 years in both the Negro and Mexican Leagues, was regarded by many as the greatest third baseman in the history of the Negro Leagues. Dandridge, who hit .362 that season, was actually 36 years-old. But, he said that he was just 30 — a common tactic by many older Negro Leaguers at the time who were hoping to make it in the big leagues. Incredibly, Dandridge, who was never given that chance to play in the majors, was elected to the Hall of Fame in 1987.

After that season, Giants owner Horace Stoneham announced that his Giants had purchased 20 acres of land in St. Louis Park with the intention of building a new stadium for their minor league affiliate, the Millers. The deal, however, never got done.

In 1950 Dandridge lit it up, hitting .311 while scoring 106 runs and driving in 80 more. For his efforts, Dandy was honored with the Silver Ball Award as the league's Most Valuable Player. In addition, the Millers, under Manager Tommy Heath, claimed their eighth Association pennant that year to boot. In addition to Dandridge's efforts, the team got great pitching from Dixie Howell, who tossed a no-hitter, and also from future Hall of Fame knuckleballer Hoyt Wilhelm.

In 1951 the Minneapolis baseball world was blessed with the arrival of a young rookie center fielder by the name of Willie Mays. His stay at Nicollet Park would be just 35 games, but he showed the fans of Minnesota that he was indeed the real deal. Mays opened the season for the Millers by going 2-for-6 in a 14-7 win over Columbus, and then hit safely in 12 straight games — a stretch which saw him hit a whopping .607. During his tenure as a Miller, Mays hit .477, hit eight home runs, knocked in 30 RBI's and scored 38 runs. So good was this kid that he practically single-handedly carried the Millers on his back during that first month of the season as the Millers won 21 of those outings.

With numbers like that it was no surprise when Giants Manager Leo Durocher called him up that May to come to New York. Willie responded by getting a homer for his first big-league hit. Worried that the fans of Minnesota would be upset, Giants owner Horace Stoneham bought ads in the local newspapers apologizing for his quick exit and explaining that Mays was necessary to the clubs' title hopes. (Of course, the "Say-Hey" kid would tear up the major leagues that year, earning Rookie of the Year honors en route to leading the Giants to the 1951 pennant — on Bobby Thomson's dramatic home run against the Dodgers. He would go on to play until 1973, hitting 660 home runs along the way. He finally landed in the Hall of Fame in 1979.)

That same year knuckleballer Hoyt Wilhelm won 15 games for the Millers. (Wilhelm would go on to play for 21 years in the Major Leagues before being inducted into the Hall of Fame in 1985.) The next couple of years would be up and down for this club. In July of 1954 the National League leading New York Giants came to town to play an exhibition game before 8,880 at Nicollet Park. The Millers beat the Giants 6-5, roughing up former Gopher and Winona native Paul Giel, who was pitching for the Giants, in the process. Willie Mays, who got the loudest applause, went 3-for-4 in the loss.

Later that season a real barn-burner took place when the Millers took on Indianapolis one afternoon. According to author Dave Mona, it was one of baseball's largest enforced exoduses. Here's what went down: Early in the game, Indianapolis Pitcher Herb Score beaned a Miller batter with a fast ball. A few innings later, Miller Pitcher Jim Constable nailed Score with a slow curve. Then, the umpire, Stan Landes, tossed Constable out of the game for what he believed was a deliberate beaning. Millers Manager Billy Rigney then charged onto the field to plead his case to Landes that if Constable were really trying to nail Score, he certainly wouldn't have done it with a slow curve. All hell broke loose at that point and before you knew it, Landes tossed Rigney. The dugout nearly emptied, and with that, Landes sent the entire Miller team to the showers. Everyone, that was, except for Chico Ibanez, a Spanish-speaking utility infielder who "was taking a siesta" out in the right field bullpen!

By 1955 a stadium debate had erupted in the Twin Cities. Just the year before the National League approved the transfer of the Boston Braves to Milwaukee, and there were also rumors flying around that the Giants and Dodgers would be moving as well. At the same time, the Millers and Saints both wanted bigger ballparks. Add to that the fact that many of the local big-wigs from both sides of the river had been trying for years to land a major league franchise for the area.

With that, a commission backed by the cities of Minneapolis, Bloomington and Richfield was appointed to select a new site for a new stadium. They came back shortly thereafter with the recommendation of a 164-acre parcel of land in Bloomington for $478,899. (Incidentally, a few years earlier the Minneapolis Baseball Association acquired a 33-acre plot of land for a stadium on Wayzata Boulevard, a quarter-mile west of the Belt Line, but when the Korean War erupted, a government ban was put on construction of new sports arenas.) The Bloomington site was then deemed "neutral" enough by both of the rival Minneapolis and St. Paul groups, which liked the fact that it was equidistant from both downtowns. Shortly thereafter, it was realized that St. Paul's bond money had to be spent within the city limits. So, they dropped out and went ahead with the construction of Midway Stadium — which would be built in St. Paul in 1956 for around $2 million.

With still no assurance of obtaining a new major league franchise, plans nevertheless got underway to determine just how much money was going to be needed to pay for a new state-of-the-art baseball stadium. So, a bond drive was set up by the Bloomington Chamber which then created an organization called the "Minute Men." The Minute Men's objective was to raise the necessary funds (roughly $5 million in private capital) to finance the construction of a new stadium. A year later the Minute Men had raised $2.2 million, but were still short. Then, a local investment bank cut the remaining $2.3 million bond offering to just $1 million. From there some 50 Minneapolis businessmen pooled together and ponied up the cash. (Incredibly, during this same time, the Minneapolis committee had to turn down an opportunity to purchase the Philadelphia Athletics because it was in the midst of its fund drive to build a stadium for a team that didn't even exist.)

Ground was then set to be broken on June 20, 1955. But before one single shovel load of dirt could hit the ground, another matter had to be addressed. You see, a farmer by the name of Paul Gerhardt hadn't been paid the $122,000 he was owed by the committee for his 50-acre parcel on which he grew radishes, onions, melons and sweet corn. So, he lined up his tractors as a barricade along what would become the first-base line and wasn't going to budge until he got some cash. The oversight was quickly remedied, however, and with that, the ground was officially broken on what would become Metropolitan Stadium.

Now, back to the 1955 season, where the Millers, under second-year skipper Billy Rigney, had their best season ever. Led by Pitcher Al Worthington, who led the Association with 19 wins, the Millers played sound, fundamental baseball that year. One of the early highlights came in June, when the New York Giants came to Nicollet Park for an exhibition game. There, despite a homer by Willie Mays, the Millers won the game, 9-5. After the game, however, the Giants took Second Baseman Wayne Terwilliger with them and left behind Outfielder Monte Irvin in Minneapolis. The club was in first place by mid-July and as a result, they were allowed to host what turned out to be their fourth ever All-Star Game. When it was all said and done, the Millers, led by Shortstop Rance Pless, who was named as the Association's MVP, won their ninth pennant in a yawner — by nine full games. The club set a new Association record with 241 homers, as Lennon and Wilson each knocked out 31 apiece.

Minneapolis then took on the Denver Bears, a Yankee farm club, in the first round of the playoffs. A total of eight homers were

knocked out of the park in Games One and Two as the Millers cruised to a 2-0 lead in the series. They took Game Three, 9-7, and then completed the sweep on Rance Pless' dramatic 13th inning homer in Game Four.

Next up were the Omaha Cardinals. The series opened up at Nicollet and once again the Millers took the first two games. They just kept on rolling from there, taking Games Three and Four to sweep the series. It was now back to the Junior World Series, an event they have not been a part of since 1932, when they lost to Newark.

The Series got underway with Minneapolis winning the opener versus the International League champion Rochester Red Wings. But Rochester rallied back to take a three-games-to-two lead. Then, in Game Six, with the Millers down 3-2 in the bottom of the eighth inning, George Wilson homered to tie it and then homered again in the tenth, giving the Millers a thrilling 4-3 win to even the series. Pitcher Al Worthington came in to close out the final three innings of this one, earning his third win of the series along the way.

Now in Game Seven, in what would prove to be the last-ever ballgame played at Nicollet Park, the Millers came out and gave the sell-out crowd of more than 10,000 fans their money's worth. Rigney went with closer Bud Byerly in this one, and he got in trouble early — giving up a lead-off home run followed by another. He didn't even last an inning as Floyd Melliere came in to mop-up midway through the first. Then, in the fourth, the Millers got a pair of home runs from Lennon and Sawatski, while future Hall of Famer Monte Irvin made it 5-2 with a solo shot of his own in the sixth. Then, when Rochester added a pair of their own in the seventh, Worthington came back out to try and save the day. He got some insurance that next inning when the Millers scored four more runs. He hung on from there as Minneapolis finally won their

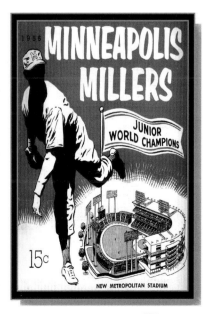

Willie Mays

first Junior World Series championship, 9-4. It was a story-book ending for one of Minnesota's grandest shrines, old Nicollet Park.

In 1956 the Millers moved into their brand spanking new ballpark, called Metropolitan Stadium. At the time, it was an engineering marvel, complete with a very unique cantilever design, which had no posts, poles or pillars holding anything up or obstructing any views. The stadium opened on time, despite a fiery explosion in February under the grandstand along the third-base line. With that, on April 24th, the first ever baseball game was played at new Met Stadium — in an American Association season opener nonetheless. The big opening day hoopla was dubbed "The Miracle of 78th Street," as Halsey Hall emceed the pre-game festivities.

"I didn't think this stadium would ever be built," said Giants Owner Horace Stoneham, in Joe Soucheray's article entitled, "Yesterday." "But you not only built a stadium, but one of the finest in the country. You ask if this compares with major league stadiums. It's as good as any and better than most of them." (Later that season Stoneham would state publicly for the first time that he was considering moving his Giants to Minneapolis. Stoneham had even engaged in negotiations with the Minneapolis major-league task force, but was bluffing of course, as he wound up moving his club to San Francisco that next year instead.)

The Wichita Braves pooped the party that opening day afternoon though, beating the Millers, 5-3, before nearly 19,000 fans. Millers Manager Eddie Stanky was even ejected in the fifth inning for arguing a call, giving the fans a reason to cheer. Stanky had replaced Bill Rigney, who was earlier promoted to become the manager of the New York Giants. One of the stars of this team was a kid by the name of Felipe Alou, a Latin American outfielder who would go on to become one of the longest tenured managers in the major league's.

(Finally, one of the highlights that year came during a pre-game exhibition when Millers' outfielder Don Grate threw a baseball 445 feet-one inch, the distance equivalent from beyond the centerfield fence to home plate, to set a new world distance throwing record.

Back in the day, throwing contests were all the rage and the kids absolutely loved to watch them.)

In 1957, when the Giants moved to San Francisco, the Millers were moved to Phoenix, Arizona, where they became the "Phoenix Giants." To fill the vacancy, however, the San Francisco Seals (a Boston Red Sox farm team) were moved to Minneapolis to fill the void. The "new" Millers then hit the field with a feisty player/manager by the name of Gene Mauch and a first base coach by the name of Jimmie Foxx — a future Hall

Ted Williams

of Famer. In addition, the Millers were blessed with a 19-year-old rookie by the name of Orlando Cepada that year, who would go on to become a Hall of Famer as well.

The Millers finished third in the American Association in 1958 with a record of 82-71. Even so, things looked promising for the young club as they headed into the playoffs, where they would face a tired Wichita club.

The Millers knocked off Wichita and then proceeded to upset Denver in the next round, to find themselves back in the Junior World Series. Their opponent would the mighty Montreal Royals, who were led by a young pitcher named Tommy Lasorda. The Millers took Games One and Two, 6-2 and 7-2, followed by Game Three, 3-2. Then, in Game Four, the Millers completed the sweep by downing the Royals in their own backyard, 7-1, to claim their second Junior Series Championship in just three years. It was a truly amazing season for the new ballclub.

"I remember sweeping Montreal four in a row and winning it all in 1958," said Mauch years later. "I was still playing and managing at that point, and it was a pretty special championship for me. That year was great, and I even still have the giant pennant from when we won that series."

The 1959 Millers were an amazing story. That year the Millers finished second in their division with an impressive 95-57 record. They opened the playoffs against Omaha, and the series went back and forth until the teams had won two games each. Then, back home at the Met for the fifth game of the series, the Millers new second baseman, who had just been activated before game-time, scored the game-winning run in the bottom of the tenth. His name was Carl Yastrzemski. (Like Ted Williams had done 22 years earlier, "Yaz" spent a season in Minneapolis playing Triple-A ball, before heading to Boston, where, ironically, he would succeed the great Teddy Ballgame in the outfield.)

The game was officially protested by Omaha, who challenged Yaz's series eligibility. The Omaha officials were proved to be right, and the league president ordered the game replayed. So, even without the services of Yaz, the Millers went out and still won the next game, to take the series. Led by their feisty manager, Gene Mauch, they then went on to beat the Fort Worth Cats for the league championship, earning a trip to the Junior World Series against the Havana Sugar Kings. (Incidentally, Fort Worth was led by a couple of Minnesotans — former Gopher Jerry Kindall and former Mankato State player Bob Will.)

This Junior World Series proved to be one of the most amazing spectacles in sports history. The first two games were played at Metropolitan Stadium, but because of cold weather and small crowds, Game Three was moved to sunny Havana. During the first two games of the series, the Sugar Kings, not quite used to Minnesota's balmy climate, could be seen in their dugout guzzling hot coffee and huddling around a fire they had lit in a wastebasket to stay warm. A series highlight was a two-run-homer hit by Mauch's brother-in-law, Roy Smalley, Sr., in a 6-5 Game Two victory. (Smalley's son, Roy Jr., would subsequently go on to play a key role in Minnesota Twins' history.)

Now, Cuba in 1959 was no longer a tropical paradise. The Cuban Missile Crisis and Bay of Pigs were just around the corner, and this area of the world was practically a military state. With that, the five games played in the Cuban capital drew more than 100,000 fans, not counting the thousands of Fidel Castro's gun-toting soldiers, who had stationed themselves throughout the stadium. Down three games to one, the Millers rallied in the series and won Games Five and Six.

With the series tied at three games apiece, the stage was now set for the much anticipated Game Seven. (Stew Thornley captured the scene best in his book "On to Nicollet) As Fidel, a former pitcher himself, made his entrance to the game, he walked by the Millers' bullpen with his hand on his revolver and said to the Minneapolis pitchers, "Tonight we win." It was looking great for the Millers as they built a two-run lead going into the eighth, but Havana came back. They evened it up in the eighth, and then in the bottom of the ninth, Havana's Don Morejon ripped a liner into center field. Raul Sanchez, who was on second, then rounded third and slid home ahead of

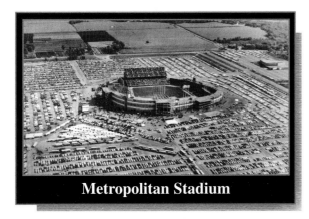

Metropolitan Stadium

Umphlett's throw to score what proved to be the winning run. The crowd erupted as the Sugar Kings had won the Junior World Series crown. The Millers came home dejected, but happy to be in one piece!

"I imagine it was about as gripping a time as I had ever experienced," said Mauch, who first met Castro when the two played together in the Cuban winter league in 1951 and knows him personally to this day. "It was standing room only every night," he added. "Fifteen minutes before game time, Castro would come walking in through center field with his entourage. Every fan rose and waved a white handkerchief and yelled 'Fidel,' 'Fidel!' Then he would come sit down behind home-plate. No baseball player in history was ever greeted the way he was greeted down there. About half of my players were afraid to win the championship game because there were Cuban soldiers on the bench with loaded rifles and bayonets. In fact you couldn't get from the batters box to the dugout without wading through 50 to 100 soldiers. A lot of my players were fearful, and wanted to get the hell out of there, I know that. The whole thing was quite an experience."

Interestingly, in 1959 a new circuit called the Continental League was formed. The renegade league was making a bid to become the "third" major league, and even announced that it had eight teams ready to play ball in 1961. Minneapolis-St. Paul was one of those teams, and the fans were getting excited. But, on October 27th, 1960, at 2:15 p.m., it was announced that Calvin Griffith was moving his Washington Senators to Minnesota. Major league baseball was finally coming to the Land of 10,000 Lakes, but that also meant it would be the end of the Millers and Saints. Oh, and by the way, the Continental League folded before it ever got off the ground.

In 1960 the Millers played their farewell tour under the tutelage of new manager, Eddie Popowski, as Mauch was called up take over the Philadelphia Phillies. The Millers finished fifth that season, missing the playoffs and post-season hoopla altogether. Left Fielder Carl Yastrzemski led the way though, producing a 30-game hitting streak along the way. (Yaz would go on to play for 23 seasons with the Red Sox, winning the Triple Crown in 1967, and retiring with more than 400 home runs and over 3,000 hits. He was inducted into the Hall of Fame in 1989.) The Millers played their final game ever on September 11th, beating Houston, 5-2, and finishing the season with an 82-72 record.

After nearly eight decades of play and nearly 60 years in the American Association, the Millers, champions of nine pennants, and owners of 37 first-division finishes, were done. They had won 4,800 games and lost 4,366 for a .524 winning percentage — best by a long-shot of all the teams which had ever played in the Association.

What had originally started as a weekend diversion back

in the 1860s, emerged as a wonderful slice of Americana. Minneapolis and St. Paul, bitter rivals until the end, finally had their common ground in the Twins. Peace could now resonate throughout the Twin Cities base-paths! The team's logo even depicted a Saint and a Miller shaking hands across the Mississippi River in a gesture of friendship and unity. This was taken even further as the "TC" logo, representing the Twin Cities, would be the focal point of the new uniforms.)

Old Nicollet was later torn down and replaced by a Norwest Bank Office. So many memories were created at that glorious old park, and now it was all gone. The old wooden bleachers, the rented cushions, the streetcars, real grass and even a lesser known tid-bit of old Nicollet's lore — that of Mike Kelley's big Dalmations, who used to wander onto the field from time to time and growl at opposing right fielders, it was all there. Old Nicollet was truly an intimate Minnesota treasure, alive now only in the memories of those lucky few who lived in this great era of baseball — but damn good memories nonetheless.

THE 7TH INNING STRETCH

Take me out to the ballgame

Take me out with the crowd

Buy me some peanuts and crackerjacks

I don't care if I never come back

Let me root, root, root for the hometeam

If they don't win it's a shame

Cause it's one, two, three strikes you're out

At the old ballgame!

For more than a 128 years the Saints have been synonymous with the Pig's Eye city of St. Paul. Also called the "Apostles" in their early years, the team's popularity grew in the post-Civil War baseball boom, and even gave people a renewed sense of hope and pride. The teams' history stretches back into a time when baseball was just a game and the players were bigger than life itself.

The first records of the game being played in St. Paul take us back to 1867 and the formation of the Minnesota State Association of Base Ball Players. That year the organization sponsored a tournament in which the "North Star Club" of St. Paul claimed the first State Championship by beating the "Vermillion Baseball Club," 43-35. (This was later considered to be the first "town-team" championship.)

By 1876 the Saints had established what would prove to be one of the best rivalries in baseball history with cross-town

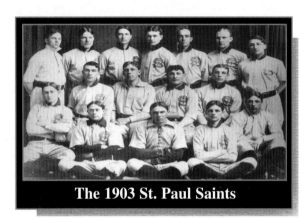

The 1903 St. Paul Saints

Minneapolis. The Saints were playing against Minneapolis' finest at that time, the "Brown Stockings." Then, by the early 1880s, another team, the St. Paul "Red Caps had established a solid rivalry with the Minneapolis "Browns," both of whom were considered to be semi-pro in status.

In 1884, the Saints fielded a team in the Union Association. The team played its games at the old West 7th Street Grounds and was owned by a gentleman named Charles Comiskey. That same year the Saints jumped to the Northwestern League, where they played through 1887. They were joined by several local teams from the area as well — the Minneapolis Millers, Stillwater and Winona, and played in a Midwest semi-pro that included clubs from as far away as Wisconsin, Michigan, Indiana and Illinois.

In this new league began one of the greatest rivalries in the history of modern sports — the Millers vs. Saints, which first took place on June 2nd in St. Paul before some 4,000 fans. The Saints won that one, 4-0, but rest assured, these two teams would have plenty of time to duke it out over the next 75 years or so.

Another interesting aspect of the league was the fact that the Stillwater "Stillwater's" had an African American pitcher on its squad by the name of Bud Fowler. Fowler, who was an outstanding athlete, had to endure a lot of prejudices just to play the game he loved. This was an incredible thing at the time, considering Fowler was among just a handful of colored players who had made it into professional baseball prior to the era of the "Jim Crow" segregation laws.

That year was a tough one for the Northwestern though, as financial problems and raiding by rival major leagues for the top players took its toll on all of the teams. (Those leagues included the National League, the American Association, the Eastern League and the Union Association.) As a result, the league folded that September. The Saints, however, also known as the "White Caps" at this point,

were then asked to finish the season in the rival Union Association. With that, the Saints thus became Minnesota's first ever major-league baseball team. It was a big mystery for the fans though, because the team played all of its games on the road, ultimately finishing with a 2-6-1 record during its brief flirtation in the "show." In the process the club earned the distinction of being the only major league club not to play a single home game.

(It is interesting to note that while St. Paul was the state's first major league baseball team, the first ever major league game played in Minnesota took place in 1891, when Columbus and Milwaukee, of the American Association, played their final series of the season at Athletic Park in Minneapolis — the Brewers beat Columbus that day, 5-0.)

That league also bit the dust after the year, and the Saints played an independent schedule over the next couple of seasons. In 1888 the Saints, along with the Minneapolis "Minnies," joined the Western Association. They would play there until 1891, when they then joined another pro circuit called the Western League. That affiliation would last just 18 games, however, as late that May the St. Paul franchise moved to Ft. Wayne, Indiana, where it played until the league folded later that year. (The professional, minor league Western League would reappear in 1894 with eight teams, including the Minneapolis Millers.)

After the season, Comiskey bought the 1894 Western League champion Sioux City Cornhuskers franchise, and moved it to St. Paul — where he renamed them as the "Saints." (They would still also be referred to as the "Apostles" during this era as well.) The Western League Saints played solid baseball from that point on, posting a winning record in four of the next five years, from 1895-99.

During this era the Saints played at an intimate little ballpark on the west side of Dale street, between Aurora and Fuller. The new park featured a grandstand which seated 1,500 fans, and two open bleachers which could handle another 750 people each. The park even had a big blackboard put up to be used as a scoreboard. A design flaw was soon discovered at Comiskey's new stadium, however, in that crowds of 1,000 or more fans were able to hike up a nearby hill along St. Albans and watch the game as plain as day. Comiskey was none to pleased about that, so he had some new stands and a fence erected along that side of the field to block their free view. The kids then rebelled by drilling hundreds of holes into the fence so that they could continue to watch the games without paying. Comiskey finally got the last laugh though when he had a second fence built just a foot inside the first one.

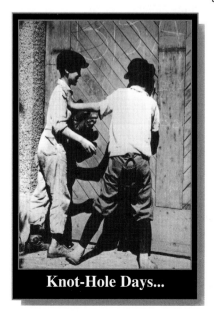

Knot-Hole Days...

Back in the day, the fans, known as "cranks," would huddle shoulder-to-shoulder around the baselines to watch their Saints. Tickets were just 50¢ for grandstand seats and merely a quarter to sit in the bleachers. It must have been quite a sight to see so many cigar-toting gentlemen with their dark overcoats and derbies, and all the ladies in their floor-length skirts and shawls arriving by horse-drawn carriage.

(Incidentally, Comiskey

was forced to move his Sunday games to the State Street Ballpark, which was located near the Mississippi River flats on the corner of State and Eaton Streets, because the local Fathers did not want baseball to interfere with the Sabbath. The State Street Ballpark, or "pillbox" as it was sometimes known — for its cozyness, was actually designed by renowned architect and St. Paul native, Cass Gilbert (1859-1934), who went on to become one of the leading lights of American architecture. Among his best known works were the Minnesota State Capitol, the Woolworth Building in New York City and the U.S. Supreme Court building in Washington, D.C. The Sunday rule for games, by the way, was lifted in 1910.

In April of 1897 the Saints moved into the newly constructed Lexington Park, which was located just a mile east between Lexington and Dunlap, just off of University Avenue. It was innovative in its day, complete with backs on the bleacher seats and imported English grass for the outfield. On April 30th the Saints christened their new digs with a 10-3 victory over Connie Mack's Milwaukee club. The intimate ballpark would serve as the team's home for the next six decades.

St. Paul went on a hiatus in 1900, but returned that next year to play in the American Association. That same year, Western League president Ban Johnson decided to challenge the established National League (which came to be back in 1876), by upgrading his Western League and turning it into a major league. He would call the new circuit the American League, where it still remains today.

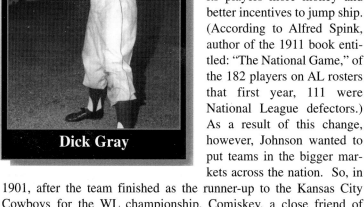
Dick Gray

The American League then raided the National League's talent pool, offering its players more money and better incentives to jump ship. (According to Alfred Spink, author of the 1911 book entitled: "The National Game," of the 182 players on AL rosters that first year, 111 were National League defectors.) As a result of this change, however, Johnson wanted to put teams in the bigger markets across the nation. So, in 1901, after the team finished as the runner-up to the Kansas City Cowboys for the WL championship, Comiskey, a close friend of Johnson's, packed up his Saints and moved them to the Windy City, where they have remained ever since as the Chicago White Sox. (He would name them the Sox in commemoration of the old Chicago White Stockings.) Other teams in the AL at that time included: Milwaukee, Detroit, Indianapolis, Buffalo, Kansas City and Minneapolis — which would finish in last place and fold after just one season.

Comiskey's move was not without its share of difficulty though. In fact, in order for him to go to Chicago, he had to jump through a couple of hoops set forth by Chicago Cubs Owner James Hart. Among them, he had to abide by the National Agreement (which stated that the players were tied to their current club contracts via options), and he also had to pay the outstanding debt on the now-defunct National League team from Cleveland. In return, Hart allowed Comiskey to build a new ballpark on the south side of town, far enough away that it wouldn't compete with his Cubbies, who played on the North Side at Wrigley Field. Hart figured that the stench alone from the nearby stockyards would eventually drive the Sox out of business. But, as usual, Comiskey got the last laugh, erecting a state-of-the-art stadium bearing his name and then winning the AL title that very next year. His White Sox have played there ever since.

(It is interesting to note that while Comiskey's White Stockings would go on to win a couple of American League Championships over the next several years, the one in 1919 would go down in history as one of the biggest sports betting scandals of the 20th century. These were the infamous "Chicago Black Sox," who allegedly fixed the World Series that year against the Cincinnati Red Sox. And, believe it or not, one of the alleged eight instigators was St. Paul native Charles "Chick" Gandil, a first baseman who had previously starred for Washington and Cleveland. The eight accused Black Sox, which included "Shoeless" Joe Jackson, were later mysteriously acquitted of the charges, but were nonetheless banned for life from baseball. Hey, at least they got to come back from the dead and

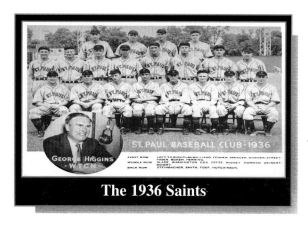
The 1936 Saints

play in that Iowa cornfield in "Field of Dreams" though!)

So, with their team headed east, St. Paul then landed a new franchise in the upstart American Association, which was equivalent to minor league status. (Many of the Western League cast-off's joined the new circuit, including Milwaukee, Kansas City, Toledo, Louisville, Columbus and Indianapolis.) Over the next several decades the Saints would play as an "independent" ballclub which meant that it could sell its up-and-coming prospects to any number of various major league teams. (The American Association would evolve into one of the strongest and most stable minor leagues in baseball, ultimately serving as the home of the Saints for the next half century.)

The Saints were managed by Mike Kelley, who also played first base alongside future Hall-of-Fame Manager Miller Huggins, who was at second. (Huggins would go on to achieve fame as the manager of the New York Yankees from 1918-1929, a stint which included guiding the infamous 1927 "Murderer's Row.")

The Saints got off to a quick start, winning pennants in two of their first three years in the Association. The 1903 club was led by pitchers George Ferguson and Charles Chech, who won 19 and 24 games, respectively, league batting champion Phil Geier, second-baseman Miller Huggins, and outfielders Spike Shannon and Jim Jackson.

In 1904 St. Paul won the American Association regular season title by eight games with a 92-52 record and advanced to the inaugural "Little World Series" (in 1932 it was renamed the "Junior World Series"), where they ultimately lost to the Eastern League champs from Buffalo, two games to one. That next season Kelley had a falling

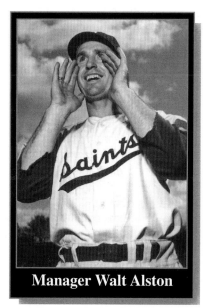
Manager Walt Alston

Don Demeter

out with Saints Owner George Lennon, so he put together some investors and jumped ship to the other side of the Mississippi River, where he became president and manager the rival Millers. He would be back a few years later though, in what would turn out to be one of the strangest cross-town love affairs in baseball history.

Throughout this period Kelley sold-off his top players to keep his team in the black. That's how it was in those days when you were a minor league team — you had to make money by developing young talent and then sell them off for the cash. Kelley was pretty aggressive though, and it caught up to him in 1907 and 1908, when he produced a pair of last-place squads.

(Over the years some of those transactions proved to be quite lucrative, including Bubbles Hargrave, who he bought for $500 and then sold to the Reds for $25,000; or Chuck Dressen and Tom Sheehan, whom Kelley acquired for $2,500 and then dished off to those same Reds for $40,000; while another was Clint Hartung, who he bought for a grand and then peddled to the Giants for a cool $25,000. Kelley, who never prided himself on being a great judge of talent, used to get his information from the umpires. He knew they made the best judges of talent and were a lot cheaper to consult with than scouts, so he would become friends with them and then milk them for everything they knew!)

Over the next decade or so, the team enjoyed moderate success. The highlights of every season, however, were the games versus the cross-town rival Millers. Twenty-two times per season these two got together to battle it out for bragging rights. And, on holiday weekends, there were double-headers at both Lexington and Nicollet Parks. The fans would ride the streetcars seven miles across town to watch their teams duke it out, making it bliss for the baseball aficionados.

In 1913 Mike Kelley sold the club to some local investors and got back with the Millers. As a result, the Saints finished in last place that next season. (There were two highlights of significance that year, however. The first was the outstanding play of Left Fielder Joe Riggert, who would go on to play for St. Paul for 12 seasons before hanging em' up for good in 1924. Riggert led the Association in triples with a career high of 23 that year, and would ultimately retire as the minor league career leader in three-baggers with 228. The other was the simple fact that Shortstop Bill McKechnie played on the team that year. McKechnie would go on to win nearly 1,900 games as a manager with the Pirates, Cards, Braves and Reds.) In 1915 a gentleman by the name of John Norton bought the Saints outright and brought Mike Kelley back to be his manager.

Phil Haugstad & Pat McGloth

(Kelley would manag the Saints for nine more years, winning titles in 1919, 1920 and 1922. After the 1923 season he purchased controlling interest in the Millers, managing them from 1924-31. When it was all said and done, he had won 2,390 games — the third highest among all managers in minor league history.)

With Kelley back at the helm, the team went from last to second place — a 41.5 game improvement from the year before! That year was also special in the sense that it would prove to be the only year in history that the two teams would battle for the league championship. The Saints came out just a game and half back though, as the boys from the Mill City edged them out in the last week of play.

In 1916 Lexington Park was rebuilt with an addition called the Coliseum Pavilion — a dance hall that shared the left-field wall with the ballpark. In order to make room for the new addition, the park's home plate had to be moved from the Lexington to the Dunlap side of the field.

The 1918 season was cancelled due to the onset of World War I. Young men were being called into action overseas, and baseball, like so many other things at that time, would have to take a backseat to what really mattered. Play resumed that next season, however, and the Saints responded by taking the American Association regular season title with a 94-60 record. From there they went off to face the Pacific Coast League champion Vernon Tigers in the Little World Series. The series was a best-of-nine games affair, the same length as the major league World Series of the day. The series was played out

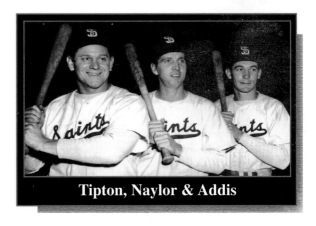

Tipton, Naylor & Addis

on the West Coast as well, because the weather was warmer during the late Fall. Vernon ultimately edged out the Saints, five games to four, in a tight series that wasn't decided until their were two outs in the bottom of the ninth inning of Game Nine. Twenty game winner Dan Griner was the pitching star for St. Paul, winning three of the Saints' games while giving up just two runs in 27 innings. Lefty Dick Niehaus won the other one on a six-hit shutout. Vernon was a rough bunch, often getting into fights with its opposing players, and using intimidation to win. So unsportsmanlike was this group, that the Saints refused to play them again. In his book "Barbary Baseball," author Scott Mackey reported, "In that series, not only did Vernon players taunt and bait umpires and opponents, they started several fist fights as well. At the close of the series, a riot erupted and American Association umpire Jim Murray was beaten by Vernon fans. Eastern writers labeled the Tigers and their fans 'thugs' and 'hoodlums' who damaged the good name of baseball."

As the team hit the roaring twenties, really good things started to happen. The team was gelling and the players were simply playing outstanding baseball. In 1920 the Saints jumped out to an 18-3 record and never looked back, winning the division by nearly 30 games with an amazing 115-49 record. (They scored 961 runs that year, more than 200 more than runner-up Toledo!) As a result, they are considered by many historians to be the greatest team in the nearly 100-year history of the American Association. Led by the pitching of 27-game winner Charley "Sea Lion" Hall, St. Paul led the league in most offensive categories, even batting a whopping .301 as a team.

Standouts including Goldie Rapp, Bubbles Hargrave, Howard Merritt, Steamboat Williams, Bruno Haas and Joe Riggert, helped the Saints produce that gaudy .701 winning percentage. In addition, First Baseman and lead-off batter Chuck Dressen was first in runs with 131 and stolen bases with 50, while center fielder and cleanup hitter Elmer Miller, a former Yankee, hit .333 and drove in 100 runs to boot. Also leading the way were Second Baseman Marty Berghammer and Shortstop Danny Boone, considered by many to be the best middle infield combination of the era.

From there it was a clash of the titans as the American Association champion Saints went on to face the International League Champion Baltimore Orioles in the Little World Series. The O's, who were one of the best in the business at that point, upset St. Paul, five games to one, to claim the best-of-nine series crown. The series was a dog-fight, which was best captured by legendary St. Paul Dispatch writer Don Riley, who wrote about it in a 1953 article: "The final game, at Lexington Park, nearly brought on a riot when the fans thought the umpires were costing the Saints the game. Danny Boone was almost bounced for throwing his glove into the stands to protest one decision. Headlines the next day called the work of the officials 'umpiracy.'"

After a dip in the standings in 1921, the Saints rebounded to finish strong in 1922, easily claiming the American Association pennant. It was a season that was, perhaps, even better than the 1920 club. St. Paul crushed its competition that year, finishing 15 games ahead of second place Minneapolis with a 107-60 record. The club utilized its roster of major league veterans to post one of the highest win totals in Association history. Led by the pitching trio of Sheehan, Benton and "Sea Lion" Hall, who each posted 20-win seasons that year, the club advanced to the Little World Series, where they again lost to the International League champion Baltimore Orioles, five games to two.

In the series, St. Paul's only victories came from veteran lefty Rube Benton, while Left Fielder Bruno Haas, arguably the most popular player who ever wear a Saints uniform, posted big numbers from the plate as well — finishing the season with a .323 average. Incidentally, the series was marred by a near-riot at the end of Game Seven in St. Paul, which the Orioles won 4-3. The fans were so upset about a blown call the umpire made late in the game, that he had to be

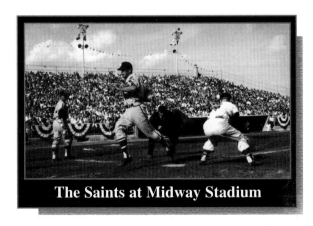

The Saints at Midway Stadium

escorted off the field by the cops after the final out when the crowd stormed the diamond.

The 1923 Saints posted a gaudy 111-57 record, but could manage just a second place finish that year. In fact, in the nearly 100-year history of the American Association, just two teams have posted better records than St. Paul's 111 victories in 1923. Unfortunately, the Kansas City Blues were one of them, ending the season with a remarkable 112-54 record. A big part of the Saints success that year, however, was due to its solid pitching staff. The club had four 20-game winners in "Sea Lion" Hall, Tom Sheehan, Cliff Markle and Howard Merritt. One of the stars on the team was Third Baseman Charley Dressen, who hit .304 and drove in 99 runs that year. One of

the biggest characters on this roster was a 22-year-old kid named Walter "Cuckoo Christy" Christensen, who hit .296 and led the league in walks with 102. Christensen was a real wild-man and liked to amuse himself by doing somersaults in the outfield — sometimes

Danny Ozark

even while waiting for a lazy pop-up to fall back to earth.

It is interesting to note that 1923 was also Mike Kelley's 18th and final season as St. Paul's manager. Five American Association championships and 12 first division finishes later, Kelley went on to purchase a controlling interest in the Minneapolis Millers, where he ultimately went on to serve as the team's president and manager.

In 1924, the Saints made it back to the top by winning their fourth American Association regular season title in just six years. They edged out Minneapolis by three games to post a 95-70 record behind the pitching of Cliff Markle and Howard Merritt, who each posted 19 wins apiece that year. From there the Saints went on to beat the International League champs from Baltimore, five games to four (with one tie), in the Little World Series. The Orioles held a four games to two lead in the series before the Saints rallied to win the final three games and capture what would prove to be their only Little World Series crown.

The Saints dipped in the standings over the next few years, but remained competitive nonetheless. In 1927 a shortstop by the name of Leo "the Lip" Durocher played for the Saints. (Leo, who would manage well into the 1970s, would go on to be inducted into the Hall of Fame in 1994.) Another highlight of this era came in 1928, when the "Sultan of Swat," Babe Ruth himself, came to Lexington Park to play an exhibition game. At that point, the Saints were a farm club affiliate of the New York Yankees, so the Bambino was out on a promotional tour.

For the fans, however, it was just great to be outside watching baseball. The holiday double-headers between the Saints and Millers were the highlight of any kids summer. A morning game at Lexington Park followed by a streetcar ride across the river for an afternoon double-header at Nicollet Park made for quite a day. While the fans loved these games, make no mistake, for the players it was a bitter rivalry. In one 4th of July twin-bill in 1929 at Nicollet Park a brawl erupted between the two teams that required more than a dozen policemen to break up. In the middle of the melee Millers reserve infielder Sammy Bohne, who was serving as the first base coach at the time, jumped into the mix and landed a couple big round-houses. That next day the headline over Halsey Hall's column in the Minneapolis Journal read: "Sammy Bohne Doesn't Play, But Gets More Hits Than Those Who Do…"

In 1930 future Hall of Fame Pitcher Lefty Grove won eight games for the Saints before going on to the New York Yankees, where he became a four-time 20-game winner. That next season the Saints won the American Association regular season title with a 104-63 record, but wound up losing the Little World Series to the International League champs from Rochester, five games to three. Leading the charge that year were pitchers Huck Betts and Slim Harris, who each tallied 20 wins, while Outfielders Harold Anderson,

George Davis, Ben Paschal and Cedric Durst batted .314, .343, .336 and .300, respectively. In addition, infielders Joe Morrissey, Jack Saltzgaver and Oscar Roettger hit .331, .340 and .457, respectively, as well.

The era from 1915-1931 was one of the most successful in Saints history as the club posted 17 winning seasons and won five American Association pennants along the way. In 1936 the Saints began serving as the primary farm-club affiliate of the Chicago White Sox. (Then, in 1942, the team switch its affiliation to the Brooklyn Dodgers, with whom they stayed tied to until 1960. Interestingly, the Millers were the top farm club of the New York Giants at this time as well, giving the Twin Cities a unique perspective into "Big Apple" baseball.)

In 1936 a new post-season policy was implemented by the American Association called the "Shaughnessy System," which saw the first and third place teams along with the second and fourth place teams face-off with the winners meeting in a final series. The Saints, who finished second that year, lost their initial playoff series to Indianapolis, four games to one.

The club fared well during the decade of the 1930s, but didn't capture its next flag until the 1938 season under Manager Foster "Babe" Ganzel. The Saints, behind the strong play of Second Baseman Ollie Bejma and Left Fielder Bit McCulloch, who each hit over .300 that season, won the American Association regular season title with a 90-61 record. From there the club went on to beat Milwaukee, four games to two, in the first round of the Association playoffs, but then lost to Kansas City, four games to three, in the Finals.

By now old Lexington had lights installed, making for some interesting double-headers with their rival Millers. The club went through a couple of crummy seasons in the early 1940s before finally making their next playoff appearance in 1944. The post-war boom was on now, and baseball was enjoying a surge in popularity like never before. On opening day 1946, some 21,449 fans crammed into Lexington Park to set an all-time attendance record.

In 1947 the Dodgers, the team's parent club, bought the Saints outright. Future Hall of Fame Center Fielder Duke Snider hit .316 with 12 home runs and 46 RBIs in just 66 games for the Saints that year as well.

In 1948 St. Paul finished third in the American Association with a 86-68 record. One of the big reasons for the team's success that year was due to the outstanding play of Catcher Roy Campanella, a future Hall of Famer who would become the first black player ever to play in the American Association that year. The famed Negro League star hit .325 with 13 homers and 39 RBIs in just 35 games that year before going in to win National League MVP honors three times for the Brooklyn Dodgers in the 1950s. From there the club went on to beat Indianapolis, four games to three, in the first round of the playoffs, followed by an identical margin over Columbus in the Finals. With that, the Saints were off to the Little World Series, where they ultimately lost to the International League champs from Montreal, four games to one.

The 1949 Saints, under Manager Walter Alston, won the American Association regular season title by just a half-game with a 93-60 record. (Alston would go on to man-

Roy Campanella

age the Dodgers from 1954-67, winning seven pennants along the way.) From there the team got upset in the first round of the playoffs by Milwaukee, four games to three. (The game was growing in popularity by this time and in 1949, the peak of the post-war boom, there

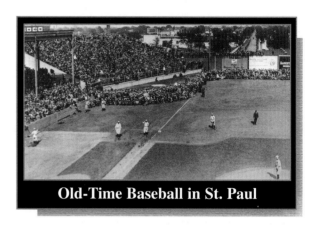

Old-Time Baseball in St. Paul

were 59 minor leagues with 448 teams playing throughout America — with an annual attendance of nearly 40 million fans.)

As the decade of the 1950s approached, several players were the keys to the clubs future success. While Snider and Campanella had brief stints with the Saints, others stepped up in their absence. Among them were pitchers Clem Labine and Phil Haugstad, as well as First Baseman Lou Limmer, Shortstop James Pendleton, Second Baseman Jack Cassini and Left Fielder Eric Tipton.

In 1951 the Saints finished second in the American Association pennant race with a 85-66 record. From there the club went on to beat Louisville, four games to one, in the first-round of the playoffs, but lost in the championship series to Milwaukee, four games to two. (Incidentally, that same year Lexington Park's right field wall was completely destroyed in a wind storm. This ultimately proved to be a blessing though for the team's left-handed hitters, who could now easily reach the newly rebuilt wall which was brought in some 35 feet closer to a more manageable 330 feet.)

The team fared just OK over the next several years, bud did sport a couple of big names on their roster in the early 1950s, including future NBA All-Star Bill Sharman, who played outfield here in 1952 and 1955, as well as Wayne "Twig" Terwilliger, who hit .312 while playing second base for the Saints in 1952.

They then got into the fray in 1955. This wasn't on the field though, but rather off of it, and in the court of public opinion. You see, at about this time there were many local sports aficionados who were trying very hard to lure a major league ballclub to the Twin Cities. Among the rumored candidates were the Giants and Dodgers, who both would eventually wind up in California. Anyway, in the early part of that year it was decided that a new stadium should be built to lure a potential big league team. Both Minneapolis and St. Paul public officials haggled and haggled over who, what, why, when and where it should be built. When the smoke had finally cleared, a bond drive was set up by local business interests known as the Minneapolis Minutemen to raise the necessary capital to finance the construction of a new stadium to be built in "Switzerland." This "neutral" site was located in the "demilitarized zone" of Bloomington, in a cornfield just south of the middle of nowhere. Equidistant from both downtowns, the spot seemed to be fair and equal for the two bickering sisters.

But shortly thereafter, St. Paul Mayor Joseph Dillon said "no thanks" to the new stadium and instead put into motion a new plan to start construction on a different stadium in the Midway area of St. Paul. So, with Brooklyn Dodgers President Walter O'Malley on hand, St. Paul held a ground-breaking ceremony of its own for the $2 million Midway Stadium just two weeks prior to the one in Bloomington. If the Millers were going to play in the posh new Metropolitan Stadium, then the Saints were going to get a new stadium of their own. Hmphhh!

On September 5, 1956, the final baseball game ever was played in Lexington park. There, a 19-year-old rookie pitcher by the name of Stan Williams beat, who else, the Minneapolis Millers, by final score of 4-0.

The 9,000 seat Midway Stadium opened on April 25, 1957, with a day-night double-header between the Saints and Wichita Braves. The Saints lost em' both, 7-2, and 9-1 before a combined total of about 16,000 fans. The season was up and down that year, but the club ultimately finished in the playoffs. There, they beat Wichita, four games to one, in the opening round, before losing, four games to two, to Denver in the Association Finals.

With their new ballpark the Saints were feeling pretty good. And, like the Millers, who had just moved into Metropolitan Stadium with the hopes of landing a big-league club, the Saints, too, felt that their ballpark would be suitable to lure a major league team of their own — to St. Paul.

The 1958 and 1959 seasons saw a couple of dismal fifth and seventh place finishes. Then, in 1960, it was announced that Calvin Griffith's Washington Senators would be moving to Minnesota that next year, where, renamed as the Twins, they would play their home games in Metropolitan Stadium. The news was expected, but a slap in the face nonetheless for St. Paulites. (It is interesting to note that the American Association received $600,000 for giving up its territorial rights for the Twin Cities.)

So, in that final season of action, the Saints, under future San Francisco Giants skipper Danny Ozark, managed a fourth place finish with a 83-71 record. The last game ever at Midway came on September 25, 1960, when the Saints beat the Louisville Colonels, 3-2, in Game Three of the American Association's playoffs. Three days later Louisville would take the series and put the final nail in the coffin. Pitcher Jim Golden tallied 20 wins that year, while infielders Johnny Goryl and Gail Harris each posted .300 averages at the plate. From there they went on to lose their playoff opener to Louisville, four games to two, thus putting an end to professional baseball in St. Paul for what would prove to be another three decades.

The Saints and their cross-town rivals from Minneapolis would high tail it out of Dodge in the Twins' wake, leaving behind just memories of a simpler day. In actuality, the Saints moved to Omaha that next year.

(For those wondering what ever happened to Midway Stadium after it's unsuccessful bid to lure the Twins to St. Paul, the 3,100 seat Municipal Stadium was torn down in 1981 to make way for the Energy Park business complex. Over the years the "White Elephant" was used for high school, college, and amateur baseball, as well as for high school football games. It certainly never lived up to its potential though, as its biggest tenants wound up being the Vikings, who used it as their Spring Training practice facility for years before moving into their posh Winter Park facilities in Eden Prairie. Oh sure, there were the two professional slow-pitch softball franchises who came and went, the Minnesota Norsemen and the Goofy's, but neither could hold a candle to what it would've been like if the Twins had chosen that site over the Met.)

All in all, those were some great years at old Lexington Park. Two fires, one in 1908 and another in 1916, nearly cost the old lady her life, but she hung on until

Wayne Terwilliger

the very end when a wrecking ball tore her down in 1957. Full of character and charm, they just don't build em' like old Lex any more. Now, as far as the players went, it was a regular who's-who of stars that came through St. Paul — either on their way up, or on their way down. Five players and one manager who wore the Saints uniform are now enshrined in the Hall of Fame in Cooperstown: Second Baseman Miller Huggins, Lefty Gomez, Walter Alston, Duke Snider, and Catcher Roy Campanella. And, as far as the official records go, St. Paul played in the American Association for 59 seasons, finishing

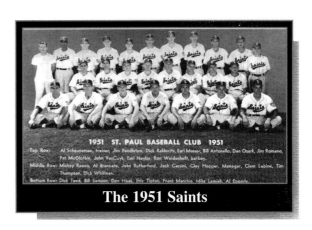
The 1951 Saints

with nine pennants and the second-best record of all-time.

Old time baseball was now out and the snazzy new Twins were in. Gone were the "Knot Hole Gangs," streetcar tokens for Saturday double-headers and "Coliseum Homers." It was a bygone era when the visiting teams always wore grey uniforms and the team managers were not in the dug-outs, but rather out in the open, coaching third base. It was, in a word, baseball. Pure and simple. The way it outta be.

(In 1993 the Saints would have a reincarnation of sorts, re-emerging after a 33 hiatus as the "new" St. Paul Saints, of the "Independent" Northern League. To learn more about the historic Northern League, and about the "New" Saints, please check out that chapter in the book.)

Old Lex

Perhaps no team in Minnesota sports history is as beloved as our Twins. From Harmon to Herbie and from Kaat to Kirby, this institution has seen it all. Two World Series titles and a whole lot of memories later, here is the story of how our very own Twinkies came to be.

Professional baseball in Minnesota has roots that go back for more than a century. Sure, we've had the Saints and Millers, who were farm-clubs of the New York Giants and Boston Red Sox, respectively, along with a slew of other minor league affiliates through the years — but big-time pro ball didn't get here until the mid-1950s. That's when the bickering sisters of Minneapolis and St. Paul both decided to build new stadiums in an attempt to lure major league baseball teams to their respective cities. The results were the $13.5 million Metropolitan Stadium, which was completed in 1956 in a 164-acre cornfield in Bloomington, and the $2 million Midway Stadium,

Bobby Allison

which was built that next year just off of Snelling Avenue in the heart of St. Paul's Midway District.

The purpose of those new venues was simple. While they would house the Millers and Saints, they would also allow the powers-that-be to be able to lure a major league team to the heartland and put Minnesota on the map. Earlier, in 1953, the National League's Boston Braves got permission to move to Milwaukee — a development which gave hope to the local powers-that-be that some other unhappy team might also be willing to move to the great northern tundra.

Among the teams that would be wooed over the next five years were none other than the Brooklyn Dodgers, Cleveland Indians, Philadelphia Athletics, Chicago White Sox, Washington Senators, New York Giants and Bill Veek's St. Louis Browns. While several of those teams used the Twin Cities as political pawns in attempts to get better stadium deals for themselves, others were serious about relocation, including the New York Giants, whose owner, Horace Stoneham (who also owned the Minneapolis Millers), stated publicly in May of 1956 that he was considering moving his club to the Twin Cities. But, the New York Giants eventually announced that they were moving to San Francisco for the 1958 season, and were joined by the Brooklyn Dodgers, who moved to LA that year as well. (This move to the west coast was significant because it meant that pro sports could be sustained logistically with the east coast. Jets could now allow for coast-to-coast travel, whereas in the past, the trains simply made it impossible. This boded well for Minnesota's chances in landing a team, considering the

fact that most people felt that our state was just on the outer reaches of the western frontier.)

During this time, several exhibition contests were played in Minnie, including the first-ever pro baseball game between two major league teams, which was played at the Met on August 5, 1957, with the Detroit Tigers beating the Cincinnati Reds, 6-5, before some 22,000 fans. (In an attempt to attract more fans, Gopher star George Thomas was signed by Detroit before the game.) Then, on July 21, 1958, the Washington Senators came to town, where they defeated the Philadelphia Phillies, 8-6, in an exhibition game before 16,000 at the Met. (Team owner Calvin Griffith was being courted big-time during this "propaganda trip," which lasted for more than a week, all in an attempt to show him how good life could be if he only moved his club here for good. For Griffith, who was tired of

Camilo Pascual

being pounded by the Washington media, the wooing was therapeutic.) That same month the LA Dodgers came to Midway, where they beat the Saints 3-0 in front of some 11,000 fans. (Visiting clubs were guaranteed $10,000 to play exhibition games here and the money generated for the Minnesota teams helped ease the financial load of the bond payments for the stadiums.)

Then, as the prospects dimmed, a new scenario emerged from the fog. In July of 1959, New York Attorney William Shea announced the formation of the newly created "Continental League," which was slated to emerge as the "third" major league, behind the American and National Leagues. So, under the leadership of Commissioner Branch Rickey, five franchises, including: Minneapolis-St. Paul, New York, Denver, Toronto and Houston, were then announced. But, by that next summer, the league was broke and folded before it ever saw the light of day. Major League Baseball, which viewed the rival circuit as a legitimate threat, then decided to eliminate any other would-be competitors by allowing the then eight-team National League to expand by adding the New York Mets and Houston Astros.

Down but not out, Minnesota still remained hopeful. Behind the scenes, local businessmen and sports aficionados including: Charles Johnson, Jerry Moore, Wheelock Whitney, Bill Boyer, Gordon Ritz, Chet Roan, Lyman Wakefield, Jr., Joyce Swan, Ken Dayton, Norm McGrew, Hugh Barber,

Jack Kralick

Don Knutson, Neil Messick Sr. and Sid Hartman, among others, had been keeping the wheels turning by doing everything from attending league meetings to raising money — but nothing was happening. By now their best bet was with the Washington franchise, who, under the ownership of Calvin Griffith, was eager to make a move out of the nation's capital and into the heartland. Calvin, Clark Griffith's adopted son, had assumed the club presidency when his father died just a few years prior, and was determined to move his club to get it back into the black. (Since assuming the role of owner, he was being wined and dined quite regularly by delegations from San Francisco, LA,

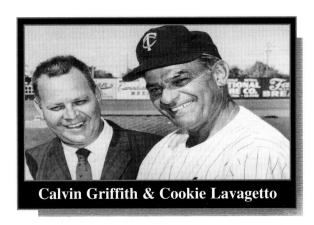

Calvin Griffith & Cookie Lavagetto

Dallas and Minnesota — all of whom wanted his franchise. The American League hadn't expanded in more than 50 years and cities knew that if they were going to get a team that they would have to get creative.)

Then, on October 26, 1960, Minnesota's prayers were answered when American League owners voted narrowly to allow Griffith to move his team to Minnesota. Helping the proceedings, no doubt, was the fact that the American League President, Joe Cronin, was a former Griffith family employee who just happened to be married to Calvin's sister. The evening prior to the big vote, Calvin had asked the Minnesota delegation for $250,000 in moving expenses, financial help from the local banks, plus a guarantee of a 40,000-seat stadium complete with 750,000 paid fans for each of the first three years. He had been playing this whole transaction extremely close to his vest through it all, and wanted to make sure it was a done-deal before the news hit the airwaves. It was a lot to swallow, but after a lengthy meeting, they agreed — and the rest, they say, is history.

The move, however, was not without its share of controversy. Sure, the Sen's had been pretty lousy through the years and were not making much money, but they were also one of baseball's oldest clubs, and the folks in D.C. were not thrilled about letting them go. When the news finally broke that Calvin was going to move them, there were threats from Congress and even a plea from then-President Dwight Eisenhower for the club to stay put. When it was all said and done though, the League had come up with a compromise of sorts. They would let Griffith move to Minnesota, and in return, grant Washington a new expansion team under local ownership. The "new" Senators would also be joined by the expansion Los Angeles Angels as well, who edged out Dallas in the voting. (Believe it or not, Calvin's wife, as well as his brother and sisters found out about the move to the Twin Cities through the media — that's how secret and last-minute the deal actually was!)

"If you had told me when I got up that morning that by the end of the day we'd have a baseball team in Minnesota, I'd have told you flat out you were nuts," said Griffith in Dave Mona's article: "Calvin Griffith: Not Even My Family Knew We Were Moving to Minnesota."

That next morning, Minnesotan's arose to a front-page headline reading: "Washington Senators to Move to Twin Cities in '61." After seven long years of frustration, Major League Baseball was coming to the Land of 10,000 Lakes. But their was big work to be done. The Met would need to be remodeled and expanded, tickets would have to be sold, and a front-office would need to be assembled. Oh, and they would also have to figure out a way to make a perennial cellar-dwelling team into a winner so that the fans would want to root for them.

Cesar Tovar

Yup, this was an exciting time for Minnesota sports fans. The Gopher Football team was fresh off of their national championship, as was the Gopher Baseball team as well. In addition, the National Football League was about to set up shop across town with the newly created Minnesota Vikings as well. Sure, the state lost the Minneapolis Lakers to Los Angeles that year, but optimism was running high with the addition of big-time baseball and football to the Gopher State.

As the team made preparations to move, excitement was building. Minnesota baseball fans had been loyal followers of the Millers and the Saints through the years and were treated to the likes of several future Hall of Famers, including: Willie Mays, Ted Williams, Carl Yastrzemski, Roy Campanella and Duke Snider. Their new team, which was renamed the "Minnesota Twins" (after the two Upper Midwest cities), did have a nucleus of young players that showed some promise. Among them were Harmon Killebrew, Camilo Pascual, Jim Lemon and Bob Allison — the American League's Rookie of the Year in 1959.

The team, under the tutelage of Manager Cookie Lavagetto, came together that Spring. Then, after a pretty solid exhibition season, seemed ready for the real thing. With that, they hit the road for the Big Apple, where they opened their inaugural 1961 season against Maris, Mantle and the eventual World Series champion New York Yankees. There, Pitcher Pedro Ramos out-dueled Whitey Ford to take the opener, 6-0, and get the season started out on the right foot. From there the team won four of its next five games before returning home, where, on April 21, they played their first home game, losing 5-3 to the new "expansion" Washington Senators before 24,606 fans at the Met.

The Twins hit the skids after that though. Finally, after going 29-45, a stretch which included a 13-game losing streak, Griffith fired Lavagetto and replaced him with Coach Sam Mele. In addition, to shore up his error-prone infield, he traded pitcher and hometown legend Paul Giel and Reno Bertola to Kansas City for Bill Tuttle, who was slated as the team's new third baseman. (Incidentally, Giel went on to play just one game with KC and then promptly retired at the age of 28. Royals Owner Charley Finley then demanded $50,000 from the Twins as compensation. Sorry Charley!) If that weren't enough, Calvin then brought in an aging Billy Martin from the Milwaukee Braves in

Ron Perranoski

Paul Giel

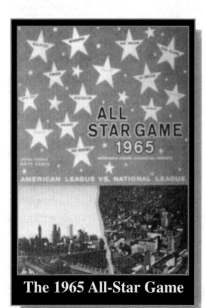

The 1965 All-Star Game

Al Worthington

Dean Chance

exchange for Billy Consolo. All in all the team struggled. The pitchers set records for allowing the most walks, hits and hit batsmen in the franchise's history, allowing more than a dozen base-runners per game. When the bleeding had stopped the Twins stood at 70-90, fully 38 games out of first place.

But, despite the weak showing on the field, some 1,256,722 fans came out to see major league baseball in Bloomington. And, there were a few bright spots, including Catcher Earl Battey, who led the team in batting with a .302 average. There was also rookie Shortstop Zoilo Versalles, who hit .280 while scoring 53 runs. Outfielder Bob Allison hit .245 with 29 homers and 104 RBI's, while Center Fielder Lenny Green went on a 24-game hitting streak as well. In addition, Pitchers Jack Kralick and Jim Kaat also won 13 and nine games, respectively. Perhaps the brightest star on this team was none other than Harmon Killebrew. Killer hit .288 with 46 home runs and 122 RBIs. Those numbers were impressive, but with Roger Maris hitting a record 61 homers against pitching staffs thinned by expansion drafts, Killebrew was forced to take a back-seat with the national media.

That off-season Griffith strengthened his porous infield by shipping Pedro Ramos to Cleveland for infielder Vic Power and Pitcher Dick Stigman — a native Minnesotan, and also shipped outfielder Dan Dobbek to Cincinnati for Catcher Jerry Zimmerman. Second and third base were also shored up by adding Bernie Allen and Rich Rollins too. With that, the team came out and played some inspired ball during that sophomore campaign, jumping from a seventh-place finish in 1961, to a strong, 91-71, second-place finish in 1962 — just five games behind the Yankees. In fact, they were in the pennant race all the way until late September. They even led the American League in attendance, drawing 1,433,116 fans to a stadium which only had a seating capacity of just 39,525. The pitching staff was the big key to the puzzle though as Camilo Pascual became the team's first 20-game winner; Jim Kaat wasn't far behind with 18 of his own; and Dick Stigman, Shorty Pleis and Ray Moore each contributed as well.

Perhaps the biggest story of the year, however, came on August 26th, when Jack Kralick pitched a historic no-hitter in a 1-0 win against Kansas City. (Only George Alusik's ninth-inning full-count walk kept him from a perfect game.)

Despite the team's offensive progress, a lack of defense was it's achilles heal. Zoilo and Rollins committed way too many errors and the outfield of Killebrew, Green and Allison were anything but fleet-a-foot when it came to chasing down hard liners. Offensively though, every Twin starter finished in dou-

ble figures in home runs, and Killer led the league with 48 home runs and 126 RBIs. And, as far as Rollins' porous defensive showing, he more than made up for it by knocking out 16 homers, driving in 96 runs and batting a cool .298. He was then joined by teammates Earl Battey, Jim Kaat and Camilo Pascual to play in the All-Star Game as well. Oh yeah, and one other thing — at the end of the season a young outfielder by the name of Tony Oliva got called up for a cup of coffee, where he hit .444 in 9 games.

In 1963, Minnesota, despite finishing with an identical 91 wins, dropped back a notch to third. But a nucleus was in place that proved could contend for the pennant. The team called up Jimmie Hall, who belted 33 home runs in his rookie season, and then traded lefty Jack Kralick to Cleveland for Pitcher Jim Perry — both solid moves. Perry shored up an already decent pitching staff which included the likes of Pascual, who again led the league in strikeouts (202) and finished with an impressive 21-9 record. In addition, Stigman won 15, Stange added 12 and Kaat pitched in with 10 of his own. But perhaps the biggest fan-favorite member of the rotation was none other than reliever Bill Dailey, who was greeted out of the bullpen by the team organist's own version of "Bill Dailey Won't You Please Come Home." He had 21 saves en route to striking out 72 in 108 innings. On the other side of the plate the Twinks hit a team-record 225 home runs. Killebrew led the American League with 45, while Allison and rookie Jimmie Hall added 35 and 33, respectively. Rollins hit .307, finishing third to Boston's batting champ Carl Yastrzemski, while Earl Battey slugged 26 homers and knocked in 84 RBIs. Once again, the team posted poor defense though, and lack of speed on the base-paths — two big strikes in their post-season quest. Still, they finished 21 games over .500 and proved to be very entertaining.

The story of the 1964 season was the phenomenal rise of right fielder Tony Oliva, who was named as Rookie of the Year that season. In fact, he was so impressive that he went on to win the league batting title with a .323 mark that included 32 home runs and 94 RBIs. Equally impressive that year was Killer, who led the American League with 49 homers — his fourth straight season of 45-or-more dingers. Major League Baseball's sultan of swat won the home run crown for the third straight year, putting him in a very select class. Only seven players had ever led their leagues in home runs for three or more consecutive years up to that point. The Pittsburgh Pirates' Ralph Kiner holds the all-time record of seven straight years, and Babe Ruth had two streaks — four in a row from 1918-21, and six in a row from 1926-31. Killebrew finished the 1964 season with some other very

HARMON KILLEBREW

Harmon Killebrew grew up playing baseball on the vacant lots of Payette, Idaho. The neighbor kids would emulate the late Hall of Famer Walter Johnson, who had played semi-pro ball just 15 miles away. What set Killebrew apart from other kids was his intense dedication to the game and his desire to improve himself. While many boys were content simply to play the game, Harmon would practice for hours in the backyard of his home, swinging his bat at imaginary pitches. He would become an Idaho high school football, basketball, and baseball sensation — even earning All-American honors as a quarterback. Upon earning 12 high school letters, he decided to accept a scholarship from the University of Oregon to play both football and baseball. He had a lot of other offers from competing schools, but his brother had gone to Oregon and he really liked it there.

But, after being heavily recruited by both colleges as well as major league baseball scouts, Harmon suddenly was presented with another interesting option. At the time, Idaho Senator Herman Welker was a close friend of Washington Senators owner Clark Griffith, and one of Welker's favorite subjects was talking about a certain local star playing baseball back in his home-state of Idaho. Welker persuaded the Old Fox to check out the kid, Killebrew, and Griffith immediately dispatched scout Ossie Bluege to Idaho. As the story goes, the first time Bluege saw him play, the 17-year-old Killebrew hit a 435-foot shot out of the park and into a sweet-potato field, prompting Bluege to call Griffith and proclaim, "Sign him up!".

Harmon truly wanted to go to college that fall, but when Griffith flashed a $30,000 signing bonus in front of him, he just couldn't refuse. So, Harm became the Senators first bonus baby. (The bonus-baby rule meant that players were forced to spend at least two seasons in the big leagues before being sent down to the minors. The rule was notorious for damaging young ballplayers by depriving them of necessary minor-league teaching and experience, and it would nearly ruin Killebrew's career.)

Harmon spent the required two seasons riding the pines in Washington, D.C., before spending two more years in the Senators' farm system. He received a "last look" in 1959 when he was placed on the team's major league roster. Three major league managers had expressed doubt that he would ever make it as a big league ballplayer. They saw his potential as a power hitter, but needed to be sold on Harmon the fielder, runner, and thrower as well. (Little did they know that early in his career, Harmon was actually the second fastest player on the team, his knees just got worse as he got older.)

That's when Calvin Griffith, who had succeeded his uncle as president of the Senators, decided to see what the family money had bought and insisted that Harmon be given an extended shot with the Senators. The new Washington third baseman surprised everybody in 1959 by becoming one of the most feared sluggers in the American League. Harmon led the usually dormant Senators that season, finishing with a surprising 42 homers and driving in 105 runs.

When the Senators moved to the Twin Cities in 1961, Killebrew continued his torrid home run hitting pace, winning three successive home run titles from 1962-64. He rose to Hall of Fame stardom in the early 60s in Minnesota, becoming the primary attraction at the old Met. On the field, Harmon assumed the position of Twins' team leader. His hustle and tenacity made him the complete player that had eluded him earlier on in his career. He became known as a fierce competitor, a solid fielder, and a true gentleman off the diamond.

"I was really apprehensive about moving to Minnesota to tell you the truth," recalled Harmon. "I liked playing in Washington, I thought it was a great place to play, and I really enjoyed the excitement of seeing and meeting all the presidents, congressmen, senators, and other famous people who would attend our games. Although I didn't like playing in the cold Minnesota weather, the warm hearts of the people made it warm up in a hurry. They were great. I really enjoyed the years I spent playing there, the fans were just wonderful to me."

Harmon went on to win the American League MVP in 1969, when he hit 49 dingers with 140 RBIs and 145 walks, all team records that still stand. In 1974, sensing that the end was near for his aging veteran, Calvin encouraged Harmon to retire and manage in the Twins farm system at AAA Takomah. Griffith was grooming Killebrew to be an eventual Twins manager, but the he wanted to play just one more season. So he declined Calvin's suggestion and signed on as a designated hitter with the Kansas City Royals.

On May 4, 1975, Harmon returned to Met Stadium, this time as a member of the opposition. His No. 3 was officially retired in a pre-game ceremony, and to top it all off, he smacked a homer to left field in his first at-bat. Minnesota fans went crazy as he rounded the bases in what some have said was the loudest ovation Twins fans have ever have given an opposing player.

"I think that being a Twin meant that I had an opportunity to play on a lot of great ballclubs, and play with some great players over the years," said Killebrew. "Just putting on that uniform and walking on that Met Stadium field to represent the Twins was about as big a thrill as anything for me."

Harmon Clayton Killebrew, Jr., will be remembered as one of the greatest home run hitters in history with 573 career round-trippers. He was the second (only to Babe Ruth) in the history of the American League to hit more than 40 home runs, (eight times), 30-or-more home runs, (10 times), all while driving in 100-plus RBIs (nine times). Killebrew was the consummate team player, always more interested in the team's achievements rather than his own, "You know, it's fine to hit homers, but it's RBIs that mean the most," he would say. Over his career he tallied 1,584 RBIs, while garnering 2,435 hits and playing in 13 All-Star games.

Because of his tremendous contributions to the game of baseball, on January 10, 1984, Killebrew became the first Twin ever to be elected to the Baseball Hall of Fame. At the induction ceremony, he went on to tell the gathering that he attributed much of his success to his father, who once explained to his mom regarding the families' sports-worn front lawn, that he was "raising children, not grass."

Harmon was more than just a slugger. He overcame his early fielding problems and emerged as a solid all-around baseball player. Twins manager Sam Mele recognized him as a genuine team leader whose presence in the lineup inspired the other players to do their best. Quiet and unassuming, Harmon was always more interested in his team rather than personal accolades, and he is the first to deny his greatness. He is quick to give thanks and appreciation to the game of baseball for everything it has done for him and his family.

In his hometown of Payette, there is a ballpark called "Killebrew Field." There also is a street named for him there as well, and his No. 12 football jersey still hangs prominently in the halls of his high school for all the kids to see. His hometown didn't forget him — nor will baseball. Killebrew ranks as one of the greatest right-handed sluggers of all time. "One of the quietest team leaders of all time," remarked a sportswriter, "but a leader nevertheless."

"He was a steadying influence on our teams," said his former teammate Rod Carew. "The greatest thing that I learned from Harmon was here was a man who would hit two or three home runs in a ball game one day, and then maybe strike out four times the next night. But, I never once saw him get upset or gesture to the fans even when people booed him. His whole career was one of dignity. I watched him day in and day out and saw that here was a future Hall of Famer who could handle harassment from the people in the stands and not let if affect him as a player. I knew that if he could do that, then I could, as well. Harmon was a great hitter and a great ballplayer."

"Harmon was just what you would expect," added Jim Kaat. "He was the perfect poster-boy for the Minnesota Twins. He was this big, hulking power hitter, very soft-spoken, a gentleman in every sense of the word, and he was the perfect person to be identified and associated with the Twins. I respect what he did on and off the field, and it was a great pleasure playing with him. Just the way he carried himself during good times and bad times was a great influence on all of us."

"You couldn't have played with a better person than Harmon," said Tony Oliva. "I think he was almost too nice to be a major league ballplayer. He is just a wonderful person, and I considered it to be an honor to be able to play baseball with Harmon."

impressive stats. He hit a modest .270 in 1964, but scored 95 runs and accumulated 111 RBIs to boot. With the addition of teammate Bob Allison's 32 homers, the two combined for 81, the most prolific homer-twosome ever for the Twins. At a sports banquet in Baltimore, Killebrew was presented with a crown of jewels, symbolic of the major league home run championship. He would join a select fraternity of prior winners, which included Mickey Mantle, Ted Williams, Ernie Banks, Eddie Mathews, Hank Aaron, Willie Mays and Roger Maris.

"Over my career I led the league six times in home runs", said Killebrew, "but that year was special because it was the first time I hit 49. That was probably one of my best years ever as an individual, but unfortunately we didn't win anything as a team."

The 1965 Twins were historic. They came out of nowhere and shocked the baseball world, while taking the fans of Minnesota on a ride they would never forget. They opened up the season on April 12th with a 5-4 win over the Yankees, it was perhaps an omen of good things to come for this promising bunch of kids. The season got off to a great start and by mid-season the team was poised to make a run for its first-ever trip to the post-season. Meanwhile, on July 13th, the baseball Gods shined down on Minnesota by letting Metropolitan Stadium host the state's first-ever All-Star game. And, while the National League won the 36th mid-summer classic, 6-5, local slugger Harmon Killebrew thrilled the 47,000 fans in attendance by smacking a tater for the AL. The AL had rallied back from a 5-0 deficit

The 1965 A.L. Champion Twins

TOP ROW: Jerry Zimmerman c - Frank Quilici if - Camilo Pascual p - Bill Pleis p - Rich Rollins if - Earl Battey c - Zoilo Versalles if - Joe Nossek of - Jimmie Hall of - Harmon Killebrew if - Tony Oliva of.
MIDDLE ROW: Jerry Kindall if - Dave Boswell p - Jim Merritt p - Andy Kosco of - Jim Kaat p - Don Mincher if - Dick Stigman p - Jim Perry p - Jim Grant p - Al Worthington p.
BOTTOM ROW: Ray Crump equipt manager - Sandy Valdespino of - Bob Allison of - Mel Nelson p - John Sain Coach - Hal Naragan coach - Sam Mele manager - Jim Lemon coach - Billy Martin coach - John Klippstein p - John Sevcik c - George Lentz trainer.
FRONT ROW: Batboys - John Natwick, Mark Stodghill, Dennis King.

Despite the efforts of those two players, however, the team finished with a disappointing 6th-place finish at 79-83. Pitching and defense were again where most of the finger-pointing turned to, as the team finished tied for worst in the league in overall defensive performance. So desperate were the Twins at second base that after trying five different second basemen, they went out and traded Lenny Green and Vic Power for former Gopher star Jerry Kindall. He was decent, but did not solve the answer to their riddle. They did acquire a few new pitchers that year though in Jim "Mudcat" Grant, Al Worthington, and Johnny Klippstein — all of whom would make contributions. Kaat was the ace with 17 wins, while Pascual and Grant added 15 and 11 respectively. Another key pickup was made that off-season when Griffith traded Pitcher Gerry Arrigo to Cincinnati for a minor-league second baseman by the name of Cesar Tovar. Tovar, who was beat out by a young infielder named Pete Rose, would go on to anchor Minnesota's infield for years to come.

to tie the contest before Ron Santo's RBI single in the seventh proved to be the eventual game-winner.

From there the Twinks rolled. They had a five game lead and were playing smart baseball. By season's end the team was hitting on all cylinders. Shortstop Zoilo Versalles led the league in at-bats, runs scored, doubles, and triples. Outfielder Tony Oliva batted .321 and won his second straight batting title. Mudcat Grant won 21 games to lead the league and Jim Kaat won 18 games as well. To top it off, the Twins had four 20-plus home run hitters: Jimmie Hall, Bob Allison, Don Mincher, and Harmon Killebrew. (Mincher came off the bench to hit 22 home runs and 65 RBIs during the pennant drive while filling in for Killebrew, who was hurt following a collision with Baltimore's Russ Snyder.) There was also the bullpen of Al Worthington, Johnny Klippstein, Jim Perry, and Bill Pleis who were, at times, untouchable. The Twins won with smart pitching, a solid defense, and clutch hitting.

HALSEY HALL

Halsey Hall was a Minnesota sports institution. With his now trademark line, "Holy Cow!", Halsey became synonymous with the sport of baseball. Hall wasn't just a beloved sports broadcaster though, he was also an accomplished journalist whose first newspaper byline appeared in the Minneapolis Tribune way back in 1919.

And, when Halsey wasn't calling games or writing about them, he was out on the speaking circuit doing sports banquets, where he became a world-class storyteller. Always a sucker for a good cigar and an "occasional" glass of scotch, Halsey was as colorful a character as there was. From his fear of flying to his love of soap operas, he was a classic.

Hall's storied career on the diamond first got going in 1933, when he broadcasted his first Minneapolis Millers game at Nicollet Park on WCCO Radio. He would also do play-by-play announcing for Gopher Football games during this era, where he coined the nickname of "Golden Gophers." In 1961 Hall became a member of the original Minnesota Twins broadcast team, along with Herb Carneal and Ray Scott. He would stay there until 1972, until retiring to focus on public speaking and promotional work. He still was able to do the pre-game ceremonies at Met Stadium though, as he attended nearly every game he could.

Sadly, Halsey died of a heart attack at his home in St. Louis Park on December 30, 1977, at the age of 79. Perhaps Halsey's close friend and colleague, Dick Cullum, said it best at his funeral: "Halsey Hall laughed his way through life, and he kept the rest of us laughing, too."

ZOILO VERSALLES

Brought into this world on December 15, 1940, in a one-room straw hut in Marianao, Cuba, Zoilo Versalles was born to baseball and poverty. Although he was still small, at the age of 12, he was fast enough to play sandlot baseball. Not being able to afford a glove of his own, he shared a glove from an opposing player when the teams switched sides.

The young shortstop's favorite player was Willie Miranda, then a great star in the Cuban National League who would later play for the Yankees and Orioles. At 14, he had all the tools that made up a great shortstop: an arm, the hands, the eyes, and speed. As he grew older, Versalles taught himself to read by slowly sounding out the players names on the rosters and in the sports pages of the local paper. Baseball had become his life, and would eventually be his ticket out of poverty.

He was discovered by "Papa Joe" Cambria, the Washington Senators scout who found him in Cuba. He helped him come to America where he would become a hero to his native Cubans. Cambria's advice to the young Zoilo: "Eat, sleep, and think baseball." Cookie Lavagetto, manager of the Washington Senators, had a simple formula for his team's success: "Tight pitching and a healthy Zoilo Versalles at short."

Zoilo Versalles was one of the greatest players ever to play for the Twins. From 1961-1967, his Twins career batting average was .252, while he had 1,046 hits, scored 564 runs, belted 86 homers, knocked in 401 RBI's, and stole 84 bases in a total of 1,065 games. His greatest season, of course, was that of 1965, when he led the Twins to the World Series and was named as the American League MVP.

On November 28, 1967, Zoilo was traded to the Dodgers for Pitcher Ron Perranoski and Catcher John Roseboro. He would bounce around for a few more seasons before finally retiring in 1971. Sadly, Zoilo, who made his home in the Twin Cites area, passed away in 1995.

Here is what a few of his teammates had to say about him:

"Zoilo was the best Twins shortstop ever," said Tony Oliva. "And, there was nobody better in the league than Zoilo in 1965. He could hit and could catch everything. He covered a lot of ground at shortstop, so nothing got by him. He was a great friend and was like my brother. It was comforting for me to have someone to talk Spanish to, because I spoke very little English."

"Zoilo had a real fine year in 1965," said Harmon Killebrew. "He played a great shortstop, and he hit real well too. He was kind of erratic at times as a young player, but he certainly learned to play the game. He was a big reason we won the pennant that year."

"We had played together in the minors as well, and he was a great talent," said Jim Kaat. "He had as good a year as any ballplayer could have in 1965. I don't know how he did it all, because mentally there was so much additional pressure on him because he was taking care of his family responsibilities on top of everything else. Coming out of Cuba from a situation that we all would consider poverty, and then all of a sudden becoming a star in the major leagues, it was very difficult for him to handle and his career fizzled out a lot quicker than it should have."

"He was a hero of mine as a kid, so I really looked up to him," said Dave Winfield. "He had a unique style and flare and was just a great ballplayer. I once got a chance to meet him, and it was a genuine thrill for me."

On September 26, after battling Chicago and Baltimore for the right to represent the American League in the World Series, the Twins, behind Kitty Kaat, clinched the honor when they beat the Washington Senators on their home field, 2-1. Champagne corks popped following the win as the team knew it was now playing the role of Cinderella. (That Sunday, back at Metropolitan Stadium, the Twins' score was displayed on the scoreboard during the Vikings game against the Lions. When the fans saw it, they rose en masse to cheer them on.) Minnesota finished in first place during that magical year, seven games ahead of the pack with a club-record 102 wins. They would then go on to face the mighty Dodgers of Los Angeles in that fabled October get-together, the World Series. L.A., which had to win 14 of its final 15 games to edge out the San Francisco Giants, were also playing red-hot baseball. It would prove to be a study in contrasts as the power of the Twins would challenge the speed, defense and pitching of the Dodgers.

The Twins now were presented with the monumental challenge of facing the heavily-favored Los Angeles Dodgers and their ace pitchers Sandy Koufax and Don Drysdale, who had won 26 and 23 games, respectively. "The Twins are game, but they are not in the same class as the Dodgers, they'll be lucky if the Series goes to five games," one national sportswriter noted.

Finally, on October 6, the game got underway at the old Met with Vice President Hubert Humphrey tossing out the first ball. From there Mudcat Grant threw the first pitch of the first World Series ever to take place in Minnesota. He would be driven by the familiar chatter of his shortstop Versalles, as he chanted, "Hubba-Hubba-Hubba—Cat!" Then, in a shocker, Dodger ace Sandy Koufax decided to sit out the opener to attend Yom Kippur — the holiest of Jewish holidays. His place was taken by the almost equally feared Don Drysdale, a six-foot-six right-hander. The Dodgers struck first with a Ron Fairly home run in the second, but Minnesota answered with a homer of their own, this one from Mincher. Minnesota scored six unanswered runs in the third, highlighted by a Versalles three-run tater. The 47,797 fans cheered as their Twins took Game One, 8-2.

Game Two featured a pitcher's duel between two of the greatest baseball has ever seen, Koufax and Kaat. Scoreless through five, left-fielder Bobby Allison then made an historic diving, sliding circus catch off Jim Lefebvre's sinking liner to end a fourth-inning scoring

Celebrating the A.L. Crown

Frank Quilici

threat. The game was still scoreless until the sixth, when Oliva doubled to score Zoilo, with Killebrew coming in on the next play. In the bottom of the seventh Versalles tripled and scampered home on a Perranoski wild pitch. To add some salt to the wound, Twins pitcher Jimmy Kaat knocked in Allison and Mincher with an eighth-inning liner. Minnesota was shocking the baseball world, winning, 5-1, and threatening to sweep Los Angeles.

Back at the Chavez Ravine for Game Three, reality bit as Dodger lefty Claude Osteen faced off against Camilo Pascual. The stars were out in force for this one as well, with Frank Sinatra, Gregory Peck, Doris Day and Milton Berle among the spectators in attendance. The Twins threatened early with Killebrew and Zoilo on the corners, but that would be as close as the Twins would get that day, as they were both thrown out in run-downs. The Dodgers' John Roseboro then singled in the fourth, knocking in Fairly and Jim Lefebvre. L.A. added two more runs late, as the Minnesota bats remained quiet. They went on to take the game by the final count of 4-0.

In a replay of game one, Grant and Drysdale were rematched for Game Four. Errors and miscues were the story of the day for the Twins though, as the Dodgers got two easy runs early. Killebrew and Oliva smacked solo taters to make it 3-2, but errors by Hall, Oliva, and Frank Quilici in the sixth, accompanied by a Lou Johnson solo homer in the eighth, opened the flood gates. Los Angeles went on to win the game, 7-2, tying the series at two games apiece.

Game Five then featured a rematch of the titans, Kaat and Koufax. This time, Sandy would have the last laugh though as he did something that only one other pitcher had been able to do all season — shut out the Twins at Met Stadium. Koufax went on to take the game, 7-0, striking out 10 for the huge shut-out victory. Maury Wills led the Dodgers with a four-hit performance that equaled the entire Twins' hitting attack as the Dodgers went ahead three games to two with the series headed back to Bloomington.

The Twins were now 0-for-Osteen in their last seven tries under Mele. But the Mudcat, despite not feeling well, had the performance of his life in the sixth game of this epic battle. With Earl Battey aboard, Allison started off the festivities in the fourth by slamming an Osteen offering over the Met's left field wall. In the fifth, Grant masterfully pitched his way out of a bases-loaded, no-outs jam. Then, Mudcat amazed the Metropolitan Stadium crowd by going deep for a home run with Allison and Quilici on board to make it 5-1 in the sixth. Fairly homered for the Dodgers in the seventh, but it was too little too late for Los Angeles. The Mudcat had

Billy Martin & Earl Battey

pitched a six-hit, complete-game gem to tie the series at three games apiece. It would now all come down to the pivotal Game Seven.

In what turned out to be their third World Series go-around, it was Koufax vs. Kaat one last time. No one could believe that Koufax was going to pitch on only two days rest, but he did. In the third, Zoilo singled off Sandy, and then stole second as the hometown fans cheered, only to have the home plate umpire wave him back to first. Dodger announcer Vin Scully, explained the call to the millions of radio and TV listeners across the nation: "Umpire Ed Hurley has just ruled that batter Joe Nossek interfered with catcher Roseboro's

**A trio of broadcasting legends:
Herb Carneal, Halsey Hall & Ray Scott**

throw. Versalles is going back to first, and manager Sam Mele is coming out of the dugout." Mele protested, but the call stood. The next batter, Oliva, struck out, ending the potential rally.

In the top of the fourth, Kaat served up a dinger to Johnson, then was abused for a double followed by a single, good enough for another run. That would be all for "Kitty," as relief pitcher Al Worthington was sent in with the Twins down by the score of 2-0. In the fifth, Twins second baseman Frank Quilici doubled off the left field wall. Then Rich Rollins, batting for Worthington, walked, setting the table for Versalles. Zoilo ripped the Koufax offering down the line, only to have L.A.'s Jim Gilliam make the catch of his life, robbing Versalles and the Twins of the World Series crown. Koufax then retired 12 Twin batters in a row before Killebrew could manage a single off him in the ninth. With the tying runner at the plate, Koufax stuck out Battey on three straight. Allison was now the last hope. With the count 2-2, the Twins left fielder whiffed. The game ended 2-0, and the Dodgers were World Series champions for the second time in three years. The Twins, who had captured the attention and respect of all baseball, had played their hearts out.

Just how good was Koufax? He had pitched his second

The old Met

shutout of the 1965 World Series while striking out 10 batters. And, for the Series, he finished with an astonishing ERA of 0.38 in 24 innings pitched — holding the Twins to a measly team batting average of just .195. Minnesota was simply no match for possibly the greatest pitcher of all time.

"It was an unusual year for me, missing much of the season

TONY OLIVA

Pedro "Tony" Oliva grew up in the western province of Cuba, on his father's farm in Pinar del Rio, about 100 miles from Havana. He went to school through the 8th grade in a two-room wooden schoolhouse. He grew up as one of 10 kids; five boys and five girls. (He told his father he was a lucky man because he had hit .500!) Baseball consumed his life, and it would be his ticket out.

"When I was a boy, we would help my father with the work on the farm after school, then play baseball," said Oliva. "We grew tobacco, oranges, mangos, potatoes, corn, and raised cows, pigs, chickens, and horses. My father loved the game and always found time for my brothers and me to play it. He helped all the kids play and enjoy the game by going to Havana and buying gloves, bats, and balls for us. Once he came back to the farm with nine gloves. We kept them in our house, and when the kids came to our farm to play baseball, they used them."

He got his big break when he was spotted by Cuban scout, "Papa" Joe Cambria, and came to the states for a tryout. His teammates on his Cuban team even chipped in to buy him some clothes for his trip. "Since I didn't have a passport, I had to use my brother Antonio's. So, everyone started calling me Tony," said Oliva. "I found I liked the name. In fact, I liked it better than Pedro, so I didn't ever tell anyone my real name."

The newly-christened Tony was invited to a rookie camp with the Twins, and in 1961, he led the league with a .410 average. After one-year stints in Class A and AAA, he made it to the majors in 1964. As a rookie with the Twins, Oliva led the American League with a .323 batting average, becoming the only rookie ever to win the batting title. He was named Rookie of the Year, earning every penny of his lavish $7,500 salary.

That same year, Tony got a new teammate from his native Cuba, Zoilo Versalles. Twins manager Sam Mele said simply, "Now I've got two kids from Cuba!" The two became instant friends. "Best roommate I ever had," said Versalles of Oliva. "He doesn't smoke, doesn't drink, and doesn't snore. All he does is eat, sleep, and breathe baseball."

Oliva would go on to become one of the greatest players in Twins history. One of the highlights of his career was when he led his team to the World Series in his sophomore year, winning another batting crown en route to being named American League Player of the Year by the Sporting News. "It was a great series and something I will never forget," said Oliva. "I look at it this way, there were two champs -- one from the American League and one from the National League. But, only one team can win when you play seven games. Anything could've happened that last game, and we got beat by the Dodgers."

Tony won a Gold Glove in 1966 and captured a third batting crown in 1971. In 15 seasons, six of which were affected by a knee injury, Oliva would finish with 1,917 hits, 220 home runs, 947 RBI's and had a career average of .304. His prowess as a hitter was demonstrated in the fact that he led the league in hits five times, and his 220 career home runs rank third all-time among Twins. An eight-time All-Star, his number six was officially retired on July 14, 1991.

From 1962-1976 Tony was simply awesome. He could hit for power and average as well as run, field, and throw. His versatility made him one of the most feared hitters of his day. If not for knee problems which cut short his career, Oliva would have been a certain choice for the Hall of Fame. He became a part time coach in 1976 and upon his retirement from the game that same year, Oliva began coaching for the Twins, where he has been ever since. Tony-O will forever be remembered as one of the Minnesota Twins all-time greats.

"I would like to be remembered as a ballplayer that gave 100 percent and also a person that was able to get along with everybody," said Tony. "I think the fans here in Minnesota are great, and it was a pleasure to play here for them. I have lived here for over half of my life and my family, and I am grateful to the good people of Minnesota."

As far as the Hall of Fame goes, Tony has his own views: "Everybody thinks I should be in the Hall of Fame except for the people that vote. I feel a little bit disappointed. I think I should be in the Hall because I achieved so much. It was too bad that I got hurt, but there were people that did less in the same amount of time than I did that got in. A lot of pitchers now in the Hall of Fame, who pitched against me, have told me over the years that when they were asked by baseball writers who they felt should be in the Hall that isn't, they said me. I had a lot of great accomplishments in my career, and I hope I can still make it in through the back door."

Here is what a few of his teammates had to say about him:
"He was like a brother to me," said Rod Carew. "He was the one who took me under his wing when I was a rookie. He even taught me how to tie my first necktie. He allowed me to be his roommate for nine years, and he taught me how to handle myself and how to handle people. He always had that great smile about him. He was never upset at people for anything, and that was one of the reasons that even today the people have a great love affair with this guy. He is a tremendous person aside from being a tremendous baseball player. We knew where we came from. We came from nothing -- countries where we wouldn't have been able to make the type of living that we were to make by playing professional baseball."

"He didn't have any legs left when I got there," said Gene Mauch. "But I remember in 1976, it was Tony's birthday, and he beat Mark Fidrych all by himself that day, going four-for-four He was one of the all-time greatest hitters. He's not recognized nearly as much as he should be."

"Here's a guy that deserves to be in the Hall of Fame," said Harmon Killebrew. "He was a Rod Carew - type hitter, with power. He was one of the finest hitters that I have ever seen. He could hit the ball all over the park and he was the best off-speed hitter that I ever saw. You could throw him 99 fast-balls and one change-up and he'd hit it out. He was such a great hitter."

"Tony is special to me," said Jim Kaat. "Tony has been short-changed with regards to the Hall of Fame. He was one of the greatest hitters and all-around players in all of baseball. If you were to ask catchers from the 1960s who they feared the most with the winning run on base: Killebrew, Carew, or Oliva, and they would say Tony was the guy pitchers feared most. Jim Palmer and I have talked about that at length and that's how he felt. Tony was a combination of average, power, speed, and he could drive the ball to produce runs. He was as good a pure hitter as there was."

"Tony is just a really nice guy and a great human being," said Tom Kelly. "He was such a gifted player. When he used to hit, he could take a low and inside pitch down the right field line, and the next time he'd take the same pitch down the left field line. He could hit the ball anywhere he wanted. I was in awe watching that man play baseball."

"He was my guru as far as hitting goes," said Kirby Puckett. "He and I were just so much alike, we were just apples-to-apples. We were the same kind of hitters - wild swingers who were able to do what we wanted to do with the bat. He was one of the greatest and without a doubt, he should be in the Hall of Fame."

JIM KAAT

Born in Zeeland, Mich., Jim Kaat was the model of baseball consistency. From 1959 to 1983, the red-headed southpaw become the first pitcher in major league history to ply his trade for 25 years. Winning 20 games several times throughout his career, he was more than just a good pitcher; he ranks up there with the likes of Bob Gibson and Bob Lemon as among the best at all aspects of the game. Though he only had a lifetime .185 batting average, Kaat was nevertheless highly respected as a hitter, considering he belted out 16 home runs over his career. What might be most amazing, however, was the fact that Jim was awarded 16 consecutive gold gloves for his spectacular fielding, a record unlikely to ever be matched by another pitcher.

After a remarkable 25 seasons in the majors, Kaat had appeared in 898 games, placing him fifth in history in the category, and he won 283 of them. With a lifetime ERA of 3.45, Kaat fanned 2,461 batters, had 31 career shutouts, 180 complete games, and 18 career saves.

As a member of the Minnesota Twins from 1961-1973, Kaat won 189 games, posted a 3.30 ERA, struck out 1,824 batters, and was selected for an appearance in the All-Star game in 1962 and 1966. The 1961 season was the first time that Jim pitched more than 200 innings for the Twins. For 10 out of 11 succeeding Twins seasons, he appeared in more than 200 innings for the club. In 1966, he pitched in 304 and two-thirds innings. During his stint with the Twins, he pitched 23 shutouts. He led the team in pitching in 1964 with a 17-11 record and an ERA of 3.22. Two years later, his 25 wins against only 13 losses led the major leagues. He was the Twins opening-day pitcher in 1965 and 1967. Kaat was also the recipient of the Twins Joseph W. Haynes Pitcher of the Year Award in 1966 and 1972.

On August 15, 1973, Kaat was unceremoniously sent packing for the Windy City to join his new team, the White Sox.

"I would have liked to have played my entire career in Minnesota," he said. "I was heartbroken when I heard Calvin Griffith had put me on waivers. Yet, in the back of my mind, I knew what was going on because the Twins had gradually phased me out of being a regular starter and made me into a long reliever. In 1973, I was coming back from a wrist injury that had happened the year before while I was sliding into second base. It took me a while that year to get my stuff back together, and I knew that I was getting stronger and healthier, but could sense the end was near.

"I remember getting a phone call from Calvin while I was golfing at the Minnetonka Country Club, and he told me that the White Sox had picked me up on waivers. That night I went in to clean out my locker and to personally thank Calvin for the years I had in Minnesota. Calvin said 'You know, I really would have liked to have kept you, but my manager told me that he didn't think you could pitch in the big leagues anymore.'

"Then, when I went down to the locker room to pack my bags, I saw Frank Quilici, the manager, and said to him, 'Thanks a lot, good luck, and I appreciated the opportunity.' Frank's words were, 'You know, I would have liked to have kept you, but Calvin didn't think you could pitch in the big leagues anymore.'

"I remember driving to Chicago that day, and it was a very difficult trip for me, reminiscing on my days in the Twin Cities. I really enjoyed it in Minnesota and would have loved to have finished my career there. Looking back, in retrospect, it was a great break for me. Going to Chicago was a stepping stone for me to play another 10 years in the majors, and I got to experience a World Series win with St. Louis in 1982."

After his days as an active player ended, Kaat returned to the Twin Cities as a broadcaster. He teamed with Ted Robinson to do Twins KMSP-TV broadcasts in 1988. The following year, he and Robinson joined WCCO-TV and Midwest Sports Channel on Twins games. He served as a Twins broadcaster until 1993, when he moved to the Big Apple to broadcast Yankees games. One of the all-time greats, Kitty will be undoubtedly be remembered as one of the best pitchers ever to throw for the Twins.

"I think after 25 seasons in baseball, I can look back and honestly say that I never gave less than a maximum effort," reflected Kitty. "Throughout my career, I never had to turn the ball down and was ready to play every day. I take pride in the fact that I never missed a start because of a sore arm, and I felt that I gave the Twins their best days work for their money. I'll never go down as one of the all-time greats, but in my mind I feel good about the fact that I got the most out of my abilities. It meant a lot to me that my teammates had confidence in me, and that I was the guy that they wanted on the mound when we had a big game to win."

Here is what a few of Jim's teammates had to say about him:

"Jim was a great pitcher and was always a great competitor," said Harmon Killebrew. "He was one of the finest fielding pitchers that I have ever seen. I mean, he won 16 gold gloves as a pitcher — that's just incredible. He should be in the Hall of Fame."

"Jim was great to be around," said Rod Carew. "He was one of the best hitting pitchers in baseball and one of the top left-handers in the game. Being around Jim and watching him perform day in and day out was an inspiration to me as a young player coming up. He is a very classy person."

"He is a very nice guy and was a good teammate," said Tony Oliva. "He was a pitcher that was great to play behind because if you ever made an error, he would never say anything bad to you about it. He would just say 'come on, let's go!' He was a pleasure to play with, and I really like him."

"I really like Kitty," said Jack Morris. "He was a great pitcher. He does a super job broadcasting the games on TV and is just a super guy."

"He is a great guy and a great announcer," added Kent Hrbek. "I saw Kitty play at the old Met many times. He had a very unorthodox pitching style, and he would just come right at you with whatever he had. He would tell you to your face that his pitches probably couldn't even break a pane of glass, but, nonetheless, he knew how to pitch and was just a great pitcher. He is a super great guy who can play golf from both sides."

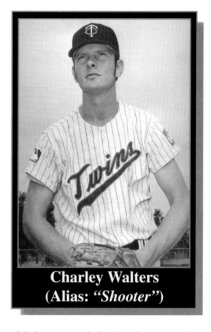

**Charley Walters
(Alias: *"Shooter"*)**

due to a dislocated elbow, but a great year nonetheless," said Killebrew of the 1965 Series. "After winning the first two, we thought we had a chance to sweep the series. Sandy Koufax had such a great game on only two days rest, throwing mostly fastballs to us. I'll always remember getting the last hit of the Series off of Koufax and that we still had a chance to win it right up to the final out."

"We had such a good team that year," added Jim Kaat. "When you're in your mid-twenties, it was so exciting just being there, and I don't think you ever realized how difficult it was just to get there. My feeling at the time was that we were good and going to the Series was going to happen to us more than once. So, maybe I didn't think there was enough sense of urgency. We were enjoying all the festivities, and that may have taken a little of the focus off our winning as well. From an individual standpoint, I can remember sitting on the bench next to pitching coach Johnny Sain in Game Two. I had never seen Sandy Koufax in person, and I had heard a lot about him. After seeing him pitch for a few innings, I remember telling Johnny that if we gave up just one run, this game would be over. What stands out in my mind is just thinking that there was no way we could win against him, because he looked completely unbeatable."

After the season Zoilo Versalles was named as the American League MVP. There had been some question as to whether or not he would win it, after all, his competition was a regular who's who of baseball: Yankee Pitcher Mel Stottlemyre; Tiger Shortstop Dick McAuliffe; Oriole Third Baseman Brooks Robinson; and Red Sox Right Fielder Carl Yastrzemski. At the annual team dinner, Twins owner Calvin Griffith gave Zoilo the good news.

"My next announcement should wipe away any last doubts as to why the Minnesota Twins won the pennant this year. I've just received word from the commissioner's office of the choice for the Most Valuable Player in the American League for 1965. The choice is Zoilo Versalles of the Minnesota Twins!"

"That year," said Minneapolis Star sportswriter Max Nichols, "Zoilo became the senior shortstop in the American League. He carried the Twins on his strong, if not broad, shoulders when Harmon Killebrew was

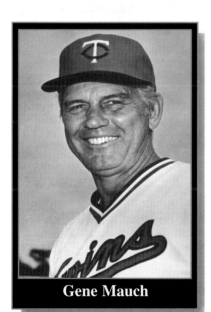

Gene Mauch

injured. This was the year that the Minnesota Twins have a champion among many champions."

Upon receiving the honor, Zoilo was asked to say a few words. He stood silent for a moment, as a hush fell over the audience. Perhaps he was thinking, just then, of growing up on the dusty streets of Marianao, Cuba, and all he had gone through in his life to get to where he was at that moment. As he stood next to the trophy, he said: "I am just lucky. Lucky to get a base hit, lucky to get a home run, lucky to steal a base, and lucky to be here."

At that point, manager Mele responded: "And we are the luckiest of all, because we have a player like Zoilo Versalles!" Yet, Zoilo would insist that the honor should be given to his best friend Oliva. "Tony's hitting brought us the pennant," he added. "He was the most valuable to our team."

Minnesota started off slowly in 1966, but wound up coming on strong in the second half to win 89 games that season. They eventually finished a close second to the eventual champs from Baltimore. One of the reasons the Twins couldn't repeat their performance of a year ago was due to all of the injuries the team sustained. When quality players such as Bobby Allison and Camilo Pascual were out of the lineup, it forced Mele to juggle the roster. Another bright spot, however, was the play of Harmon Killebrew, who had 39 home runs and 110 RBI, and Tony Oliva, who hit .307 with 25 homers and 87 RBI. Overall, it was a down year, highlighted by one game in particular, when overweight catcher, Earl Battey, who after an apparent single, was thrown out at first base from right field by Boston's Lu Clinton. Battey's performance prompted the wry sports writer Halsey Hall to recall some years later that watching him round second base "looked like he was pushing a safe." The lone bright spot that year was the performance of Pitcher Jimmy "Kitty" Kaat, who posted a phenomenal 25-13 record, with an impressive 2.74 ERA and 205 K's.

"For a pitcher, and all pitchers realize this, sometimes it's not always how you pitch, but when you pitch," said Kaat. "Sometimes you have those years when you pitch mediocre, your team scores a lot of runs, and then when you pitch well, you win 2-1. That's the kind of year I had in 1966. I won a lot of games by blowouts, but I also won the close ones. It all just came together for me and I just happened to pitch on the right day a lot that year."

The 1967 Twins were all about two newcomers, Pitcher Dean Chance, acquired in a trade with the California Angels, and a rookie from Panama by the name of Rod Carew. Chance recorded the fifth ever 20-victory season by a Minnesota hurler, and became the ace of the staff. So good was Chance, that on Aug. 6, he threw a 5-inning no-hitter

Jerry Koosman

Jim Eisenreich

against Boston, winning 2-0. And, just for good measure, he decided to throw another one just three weeks later in a 2-1 victory over Cleveland. Carew, meanwhile, made the All-Star team and established himself as one of the game's best pure hitters. For his efforts he was awarded the Rookie of the Year Award. (Griffith also unloaded veterans Pascual and Bernie Allen to Washington for reliever Ron Kline.)

Overall it was a solid season for the Twins, who wound up going down to the wire with Boston and Detroit for the title. Midway through the season, with a 25-25 record, Manager Sam Mele was canned in favor of Cal Ermer, who then led the team to one of the best pennant races in the modern era — going 66-46 down the stretch. Entering the last week of the season, Boston, Chicago, Minnesota and Detroit were separated by just one game. So, the season came down to a two-game stint with the Red Sox, in Boston, where Minnesota needed just one victory to clinch the pennant. They lost the first game, despite a decent performance on the mound from both Kaat and Perry, 6-4. Killer even launched his 44th homer of the season, but Carl Yastrzemski's three-run shot of his own sealed this one for Boston. Then, in the other game, the Twins took an early 2-0 lead as Oliva doubled home Killebrew, who later drove in Tovar with a single. The BoSox rallied and pulled ahead late. Minnesota put together a two-out rally in the eighth though, as Oliva and Killebrew singled and Allison crunched a shot off the left field wall which brought Oliva home. But Yastrzemski then threw out Allison, who was trying to stretch a single into a double. With the 5-3 loss, the season was over. For the record, Oliva hit .289 with 17 homers and 83 RBI's while Killebrew hit .269 with 44 dingers and 113 RBI's.

Prior to the 1968 season, Griffith decided to scuttle veterans Zoilo Versalles and Mudcat Grant, trading them to the Dodgers for Catcher John Roseboro and relievers Ron Perranoski and Bob Miller. In addition, longtime Catcher Earl Battey retired. This season was a disappointing one for the Twins, who sank to a dismal seventh place in the AL with a 79-83 record, 24 games behind the Detroit Tigers. One of the big reasons for the slide was due to the fact that Killer suffered an All-Star game hamstring injury, which sidelined him for nearly the entire second half of the season. A few changes affected the Twins this year as well, including the fact that the AL pitching mounds were lowered and the strike zones were also narrowed in an effort to give hitters a better chance. A few bright spots, however, did include Tony Oliva's .289 batting average, good for third in the league, followed by Ted Uhlaender's .283, which was fifth. One other highlight occurred on September 22nd, in a 2-1 win over the Oakland A's, when Venezuelan utility-

Mickey Hatcher

man extraordinaire Cesar Tovar became just the second player in history to play all nine positions in a game. He even struck out Reggie Jackson!

That next season Cal Ermer was canned, and the infamous Billy Martin was hired to take over. In addition, the American League was divided into two, six-team divisions — of which the Twins were designated to the Western Division. Martin wasted little time in making a name for himself this season, leading the Twins all the way to the AL Western Division Finals, where they ultimately

Butch Wynegar

lost the Championship Series in three games to Baltimore. The star of the year was Harmon Killebrew, who came off his injury to be named as the league's MVP. Killer hit 49 home runs and drove in 140 runs that season, while Rod Carew captured his first silver bat with a .332 average. Carew even tied a major league record that year by stealing home an incredible seven times. Other big contributors included: Cesar Tovar, who stole a career-high 45 bases and hit .288, while Tony-O led the league with 197 hits. In addition, Pitchers Jim Perry, Bob Miller and Ron Perranoski each made big contributions in the teams' pennant chase, as did Catcher John Roseboro, Shortstop Leo Cardenas (acquired in a trade with the Reds) and First Baseman Rich Reese.

Martin's explosive personality inspired this group of over-achievers, who wound up edging past the Oakland A's to wrap up the inaugural American League West Division title with a 97-65 record. (So aggressive was Martin that even Harmon Killebrew stole eight bases!) Then, in the American League Championship Series, the Twinks met up with the Baltimore Orioles, in B-Town's Memorial Stadium. On paper the series looked solid: Minnesota led the league in batting and Baltimore in pitching. The O's were led by a venerable all-star cast including: Second Baseman Dave Johnson, Outfielders Paul Blair and Frank Robinson, Third Baseman Brooks Robinson, First Baseman Boog Powell and Pitcher Dave McNally, who won 15 straight games that season.

Game One opened in Baltimore with Perry facing Mike Cuellar. Tied 3-3 tie in the ninth on Boog Powell's homer, this one went into overtime. There, the Birds' Mark Belanger scored on a Paul Blair squeeze play in the 12th to give Baltimore a dramatic 4-3 win. Game Two was another pitchers duel, with Minnesota's Dave Boswell scattering seven Baltimore hits over 10 scoreless innings before giving the reins to Ron Perranoski in the 11th. Orioles Pitcher Dave McNally gave up only three hits in this one, and it all came to an end when pinch hitter Curt Motton lined a single off of Perranoski to score Powell in the 11th to seal the deal. Game Three of the ALCS was

John Castino

held back at the Met. Baltimore's Jim Palmer pitched a decent game, but the O's pounded Minnesota's pitchers for 18 hits. As a result the Twins fell flat on their faces, losing 11-2, in front of just 32,735 fans to finish out an otherwise tremendous year.

Manager Earl Weaver's strategy of walking Killebrew early and often, frustrated the slugger and wreaked havoc on the team's chemistry that post-season. (Incidentally, Appleton, Minn., native Jerry Koosman went on to win the deciding game of the World Series that year as the Mets beat Baltimore in five games.)

Led by All-Star Right Fielder Tony Oliva, the Minnesota Twins won the AL Western Division for the second year in a row in 1970. This was indeed a wild year for Minnesota baseball, and it all started out with a pre-season managerial change. The popular Billy Martin, who had led the Twins to an impressive 97-65 record and the American League West title only the year before, was fired by owner Calvin Griffith and replaced with former Minneapolis Miller player-manager Bill "Captain Hook" Rigney. (Rigney earned his nickname "Captain Hook" because he used to pull his pitchers early and often when they got into hot water on the mound.)

There was endless speculation as to why the fiery Martin was fired. Maybe it was because he punched the Twins traveling secretary, or maybe it was his fight he got into outside a Detroit bar, or possibly it was because he publicly aired his grievances about the Twins front office management to the press. Regardless of the reason, the fact remained that Calvin canned him. The whole mess didn't bode well with the fans. "Bring Billy Back" bumper stickers were everywhere, and there was even a country-western song that uttered, "Are you leavin' Billy Martin? It's a shame, it's a shame."

But Rigney, the Twins new skipper, ignored the distractions and went on to guide his team to a 98-64 record and their second straight Western Division title. The season started off well for the Twins. But, midway through the season, pitcher Luis Tiant broke his shoulder, so the Twins brought up a 19-year-old rookie to replace him by the name of Bert Blyleven. Bert went on to have a pretty good year, winning 10 games for the Twins. One of the highlights that season came on May 20 against the Kansas City Royals, when Rod Carew became the first Twin ever to hit for the cycle. (Carew had his knee torn up by a runner at second base early that year though, and sat out for much of the season as Frank Quilici and rookie Danny Thompson filled in for him.)

The Twins pitching staff was led by Jim Perry (the brother of future Hall of Famer Gaylord), who, with 24 wins, a modest 3.03 ERA and 168 strike-out's, became the first Twin ever to win the Cy Young Award. And, whenever Perry needed help, closer Ron Perranoski came in to mop up. Ron's American League leading 34 saves, combined with Stan Williams' 15, made up the best bullpen in the league. Throw in Jim Kaat and Tom Hall, and statistically the Twins had the second best pitching staff in the league that year.

The Twins bats were also hot in 1970, Killebrew hit 41 dingers with 113 RBI's, and Carew, Tovar, and Oliva all hit .300 or better. As a team, the Twins would go on to lead the American League in batting. Tony-O had another of his fabulous seasons in 1970, cranking out the most hits in the American League for the fifth consecutive year, with 204, and once again leading his club to the post-season. He led the team in batting with a .325 average, while driving in 107 RBI's, scoring 96 runs, and hitting 23 homers. And don't forget his league-leading 36 doubles as well.

The Twins were champions of the American League West, and the 1970 playoffs were a rematch of the year before, with, unfortunately, the same results. Being swept by the Orioles the season prior, observers might have thought that some sort of revenge factor would've been motivating the Twins. They were wrong

On October 3, the Twins opened the American League Championship Series at the Met. Minnesota jumped out to an early one run lead in Game One, but Perry got rocked as the O's went on to beat the Twins, 10-6. Baltimore pitcher Mike Cuellar hit a grand slam

TWINS ALL-TIME CAREER PITCHING STATS

CAREER WINS

189	Jim Kaat	1961-73
149	Bert Blyleven	1970-76, 85-88
128	Jim Perry	1963-72
112	Frank Viola	1982-89
96	Dave Goltz	1972-79
93	Brad Radke	1995-2001
88	Camilo Pascual	1961-66
75	Kevin Tapani	1989-99
67	Dave Boswell	1964-70
61	Scott Erickson	1990-95

EARNED RUN AVERAGE

2.67	Dean Chance	1967-69
3.03	Jim Merritt	1969-68
3.19	Jim Perry	1963-72
3.28	Bert Blyleven	1970-76, 85-88
3.29	Jim Kaat	1961-73
3.31	Camilo Pascual	1961-66
3.35	Dick Woodson	1969-70, 72-74
3.36	Mudcat Grant	1964-67
3.48	Dave Goltz	1972-79
3.49	Dave Boswell	1964-70

SAVES

254	Rick Aguilera	1909-98
108	Ron Davis	1982-86
104	Jeff Reardon	1907-09
88	Al Worthington	1964-69
76	Ron Perranoski	1968-71
54	Mike Marshall	1978-00
51	Bill Campbell	1973-76
43	Doug Corbett	1908-82
42	LaTroy Hawkins	1995-2001
34	Mike Trombley	1992-99

TOTAL GAMES

505	Eddie Guardado	1993-2001
490	Rick Aguilera	1989-99
460	Jim Kaat	1961-73
376	Jim Perry	1963-72
360	Mike Trombley	1992-99
348	Bert Blyleven	1970-76, 85-88
327	Al Worthington	1964-69
286	Ron Davis	1982-86
260	Frank Viola	1982-89
247	Dave Goltz	1972-79

COMPLETE GAMES

141	Bert Blyleven	1970-76, 85-88
133	Jim Kaat	1961-73
80	Dave Goltz	1972-79
72	Camilo Pascual	1961-66
61	Jim Perry	1963-72
50	Frank Viola	1982-89
37	Dave Boswell	1964-78
36	Geoff Zahn	1977-08
34	Dean Chance	1967-69

The 1985 All-Star Game

and was later relieved by Dick Hall, the 40-year-old "junk-baller," who came in to mop up by allowing just one hit in the final five innings. Killebrew pounded out a two-run homer in the fifth, but the Orioles hung on to take it.

In Game Two it got a lot worse. Baltimore topped their first game power surge by crushing the Twins 11-3, despite homers by Oliva and Killebrew. Baltimore held a close 4-3 lead after eight and then exploded in the 9th, peppering Perranoski and Luis Tiant for seven runs, including Johnson's three-run homer.

Back in Baltimore for Game Three, Rigney sent Kaat up against Jim Palmer. It wasn't even close, and Earl Weaver's Orioles went on to complete the sweep. Palmer struck out 12 and allowed just six Minnesota hits in this one as Kaat was replaced in the third by Blyleven. Baltimore scored five runs in the first three innings, and another in the eighth to ice it. In the first two years of the ALCS, the Twins were 0-6, all six losses coming at the hands of mighty Baltimore. The O's went on to the World Series again and this time shut down Cincinnati's Big Red Machine in five games.

"Losing two years in a row to the Orioles was tough," said Oliva, who batted .500 in the ALCS. "After the first game, I thought that we had a chance to beat Baltimore, but we lost a very tough play-off series to a really good team. That year was a lot of fun and winning the West for the second time was a real thrill. We had a great ball club back then, and it was too bad we just couldn't make it past that next round to make it to the World Series like we did in 1965. There were a lot of great players on that 1970 team, and we were like a family."

Regrettably, for the Twins, this would be the end of the line for a while as the team would struggle over the next several years. For the previous six seasons the team had played outstanding fundamental baseball, but would go downhill quickly from there. After the season Bob Allison retired. Killebrew, although one of the game's best ever, never again hit more than 28 home runs, and Tony-O would go on to suffer a series of knee injuries which hobbled him for years to come. Perry, Kaat and Blyleven were a solid 1-2-3, but the team could never get anything going after that. They had holes in their infield and could find an effective stopper either. As Minnesota was aging, the Oakland A's were coming of age — it was soon to be their turn.

In 1971 Minnesota drew just 945,000 fans, marking the first time in their 11 seasons that they failed to draw one million. Sure, Killebrew had 28 homers, including his 500th, and a league-leading 119 RBIs. In addition, Tovar hit .311 and Carew followed with .307 as well. Heck, Perry even won 17 ball games. And, despite his knee

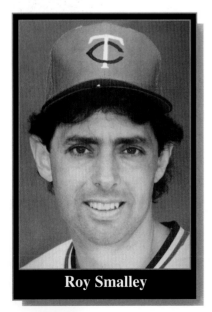

Roy Smalley

injury, Tony-O, now an eight-year veteran, wound up winning his third American League batting title with a .337 average. But the decline was on and it wasn't pretty. It was officially a "rebuilding" period in Minnie.

A players' strike that April set the early tone for the 1972 season as the Twins drew an all-time low 797,901 fans to the Met that year. Rigney was replaced on the bench that next season by former player and coach Frank Quilici. Quilici, a big fan favorite, known for his enthusiasm and character, managed to get the club into contention by mid-August. They faltered down the stretch though, and wound up with a 77-77 (.500) record good for third in the AL. A couple of bright spots that season included: the stellar play of Rod Carew, who won his second batting title with a .318 average (with no homers!), and also the acquisition of a 29-year-old rookie outfielder by the name of Bobby Darwin, who, after spending a decade lost in the Dodgers' minor league system, emerged to hit 22 homers and knock in 80 RBI's. Tony O was injured that year, as was Jimmy Kaat, who broke his wrist while sliding into second base after posting a tremendous 10-2 record through July.

Calvin did some house cleaning that off-season, unloading the likes of Jim Perry, the team's all-time winningest right-hander, and Cesar Tovar, the league leader in hits just one season earlier. He also dealt reliever Wayne Granger to St. Louis in exchange for pitcher John Cumberland and outfielder Larry Hisle. Hisle was the real prize here as he would soon develop into one of the League's big hitters. The 1973 Twins rebounded that season to hit an impressive .270 — the highest team average in the Major Leagues. Leading the charge was 20-game winner Bert Blyleven, who was simply awesome on the mound. The team slumped late though, and couldn't recover. No one on the squad hit 20 homers and the offense was timid at best.

One bright spot, however, was that the league voted to add the designated hitter — a blessing for the now hobbled Tony O, who hit .291, on 16 homers and 92

Jeff Reardon

RBI's. In fact, Oliva holds the distinction of hitting the first ever dinger by a DH, when he did so off Jim Hunter on April 6th that year in the Twins 8-3 season-opening victory over the A's. The other highlight was the play of Rod Carew, who won his fourth batting title with a huge .350 average while leading the league in hits and triples. After staying in the race through July, it turned out to be another .500 season for Minnie, as they went 81-81 — 13 games behind first-place Oakland. Another big loss for the team was that of Jim Kaat, who was released that August and then signed by the White Sox.

Another interesting story was that of Pitcher Eddie Bane, who, after compiling an incredible collegiate record of 41-4 at Arizona State, was given the biggest ever signing bonus to date by the Twins. More than 45,000 fans showed up to see the highly touted rookie in his debut against the Kansas City Royals, which he lost by the score of 5-4. How would he do that year? He finished the season with an 0-5 record and was promptly sent down to Tacoma.

The 1974 Twins posted an 82-80 mark, only good enough for third place in the West — eight games behind the A's. The season was dotted with several outstanding individual efforts though, including Carew's league-leading .364 average and Darwin's 25 homers and 94 RBI's. Most importantly, however, was the fact that 1974 would

ROD CAREW

The son of a Canal tugboat worker, Rod Carew came into the world in a unique way. On October 1, 1945, in Gatun, Panama, Olga Carew went into labor on a speeding train. As luck would have it, a physician, Dr. Rodney Cline, just happened to be on that same train along with nurse Margaret Allen. They delivered Olga's baby right there on the train. The baby was a boy. A grateful Olga named her son Rodney Cline Carew, after that doctor, and nurse Allen became Rod's godmother.

As a boy Rod played baseball, listened to major league games on his radio and dreamt of going to the United States and becoming a big leaguer. One day, his godmother Margaret Allen wrote a letter to his mother from New York City. She encouraged them to pack-up and move to New York to pursue a better life. So, in 1962, at the age of 16, Rod, his mother, brother, and sisters, moved to Harlem where his mother supported the family by working in a factory.

Speaking little English, young Rod had trouble fitting in at school. He was wary of the many drug dealers and thugs operating in his neighborhood. Rod spent his afternoons working in a grocery store to help support his family and, in doing so, dearly missed his passion, baseball. Then his luck changed when he tried out for a weekend sandlot baseball team, which played in the shadows of Yankee Stadium in the Bronx.

He played shortstop and second base for the Cavaliers where he hit consistently and with power. During the course of one season, he batted .600. Word of Carew's skill soon reached Herb Stein, a New York City transit detective, who also scouted young talent for the Minnesota Twins. Stein watched Rod play in several games and was impressed. "He was spraying hits all over the place," said Stein. "He had a pair of wrists that just exploded." Stein told Hal Keller, head of the Twins' farm system, to come see Carew play. That day, Rod went 6-for-7 with two singles, three doubles, and a grand-slam home run. He had officially been discovered.

When Minnesota came to town to play the Yankees, team officials invited Carew inside for a pre-game tryout. After easily putting two balls into the Yankee Stadium seats, Twins manager Sam Mele looked around nervously to see if any of the hometown team had seen Rod in action. Then the cautious Mele ordered, "Get that kid out of here before somebody else sees him!"

A month later, in June of 1964, Rod signed his first big-league contract with the Twins. Minnesota agreed to pay him an immediate bonus of $5,000, a minor league salary of $500 a month, and a future bonus of $7,500 when (and if) he made the major league roster. Although other big league teams had started to show some interest in him, Rod was anxious to sign with the Twins. He took the $5,000, gave some money to his mother, bought some new clothes, and put the rest in the bank.

He spent two years in the Twins farm system before Calvin Griffith called-up the 21-year-old for the start of the 1967 season. By the end of that season, he would be named Rookie of the Year and be selected to the All-Star Team. From there he just kept on going, leading the Twins in nearly every offensive category for years to come. Without question though, his best season was in 1977, when he was the biggest story in sports.

After switching over from second base to play first base, Rod had the greatest season of his incredible 19-year big league career. He nearly became the first hitter since Ted Williams to break baseball's magic .400 mark. Carew appeared on the cover of Sports Illustrated with the Splendid Splinter himself during that season. Rod's face also appeared on the cover of Time magazine with the headline, "Baseball's Best Hitter." He batted over .400 for the first half of the season, and his final .388 average was good enough to earn him his sixth batting title, while rapping out 239 hits, the most in the majors since Bill Terry hit 254 nearly 50 years earlier. He also scored 128 runs, hit 14 homers, and stole 23 bases. He struck out only 55 times in 616 at-bats. He had 38 doubles, 16 triples, and drove in 100 runs. At season's end the Twins' No. 29 had won the MVP award and for the 11th straight year was selected for the All-Star team, this time with the biggest number of fan votes ever recorded.

Afraid that he was going to lose Carew to free agency, Calvin Griffith traded him to the California Angels on February 3, 1979, for outfielder Ken Landreaux and some prospects. And so it went that Carew would finish his career in California some eight years later.

No true Twins fan will ever forget the graceful power of Rod's smooth hitting style. Carew was a career .328 hitter in 19 big league seasons and won seven AL batting titles (second only to Ty Cobb and Honus Wagner). He hit .300 or better for 15 consecutive seasons and finished with 3,053 hits, scored 1,434 runs, belted 92 homers, knocked in 1,015 RBIs, and stole 353 bases. He was named to 18 consecutive All-Star teams. He was elected to the Baseball Hall of Fame on the first ballot on January 8, 1991. His No. 29 was retired by the Twins on July 19, 1987. Carew was the greatest pure hitter of his era, a true wizard with the bat.

"I enjoyed the Twin Cities, and I really enjoyed the people," said Rod. "I came there as a young kid, still learning a lot about playing the game. In the years that I was there I really matured as a person and as a baseball player. I appreciated the Twins organization, Mr. Griffith, and the way the fans there treated me and responded to me."

(There were some oddities to Carew's brilliant baseball career. For example, he treated his bats with extreme tender love and care, putting them in a hot closet next to the clubhouse sauna to "bake out the bad wood." He also washed his bats in alcohol to clean off the sticky pine tar, because he "loved to use a clean bat." Like a lot of ballplayers, Rod chewed tobacco during games. He said that a big plug of chew would stretch his facial muscles so he could squint more, and as a result, see the ball better. He used to drink Coca-Cola almost non-stop, sometimes gulping down more than a dozen glassfuls per game. Sometimes, he would ride his bicycle from his home to the ball park, a distance of some 15 miles. He loved to chase balls for the pitchers during batting practice, and once, during a game, he even fined himself when he quit running after giving up on a foul ball that blew fair. An amazing bunter, he used to impress his teammates by putting a handkerchief at various spots throughout the infield and dropping bunts onto it.)

Here is what a few of his teammates had to say about him:

"We were roommates for 10 years," said Tony Oliva. "Between the two of us I would tell people that our room was hitting over .700, even though his average was always higher than mine. Rod was a remarkable ballplayer, a great person, and a good friend."

"He was one of the finest hitters I ever saw and the best bunter ever," said Harmon Killebrew. "He used to come out early to the park and practice his bunting. He could drop that ball down the third base line and, with the speed he had, nobody could throw him out. He was just outstanding and just a great, great hitter."

"I followed Rod Carew's career when I was growing up, and I thought he had the best pair of wrists of anybody I ever saw," said Paul Molitor. "The way he could wait and put the ball out to left field was incredible. He was a very gifted hitter who studied the game, knew how to take advantage of pitchers and their weaknesses, and had a remarkable, outstanding major league baseball career."

"In California, we had as close a relationship as any player and manager ever had," said Gene Mauch. "He knew how much I respected him and I felt like he felt the same way about me. It was a great privilege for me to manage Rod Carew. Watching him almost bat .400 was a season of the greatest hitting that I ever saw, and I played with Ted Williams. Watching him operate with the bat that year was incredible."

"He was such a talented hitter, and I really enjoyed watching him do what he could do," said Jim Kaat. "He was a real magician with the bat. I have a warm relationship with him to this day."

"I remember when I got my first hit, it was against the Angels, and Rod was playing first base," added Kirby Puckett. "I stood on base and said to him: 'How ya doin' Mr. Carew? I just want to tell you that I've been a big fan of yours, and it's my pleasure to meet you, man, because you're awesome, and I'm a rookie so I'm gonna shut up now and be quiet!' 'Please call me Rod,' he said to me. 'I know you're a rookie, and I just want to tell you to just keep playing, keep enjoying yourself, and keep playing the game the way you know how. And, the most important thing you should know, is to learn how to play when you're hurt, and you'll be just fine.' I will always remember that. Rod Carew is the very best there is."

Gary Gaetti

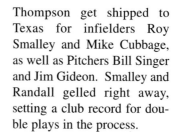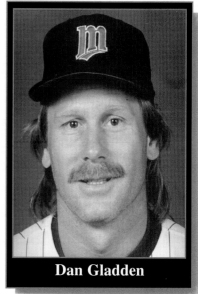

Dan Gladden

be the last year Harmon Killebrew would wear a Twins jersey. "Mr. Baseball," who would finish his illustrious career with 573 home runs, went on to play one final season with Kansas City that next year before finally hanging it up for good. Of course, his No. 3 jersey was later retired and he was also inducted into the Baseball Hall of Fame in 1984 as well.

As far as that season went, there were winning streaks and losing streaks, but nothing to write home about. Oliva and Killebrew each tallied 13 homers and shared the designated hitter role, while Carew added to his collection of silver bats by very quietly winning his third straight batting crown with an outstanding .364 average.

That next season was a wash for the Twinks as they finished with a dismal 76-83 record, good for just fourth, several miles south of the first place Oakland A's. Lost salary arbitration, injuries and bad luck all contributed to the team's demise that year as Hisle, Blyleven, Bostock, Decker, Braun, Brye and Soderholm all went down at one point or another during the season. Overall, it was an unhappy and unhealthy ball club. OK, there were a few bright spots. Carew, who was moved to first base, won another batting title (Rodney upped his homer total in 1972 from 0 to 14 that year), and several rookies made names for themselves as well, including outfielders Danny Ford and Lyman Bostock, as well as Jim Hughes, who led the club in victories with 16. In addition, Dave Goltz, a Rothsay, Minn., native posted 14 wins too. On an inspirational note, after being treated for leukemia at the Mayo Clinic that year, Shortstop Danny Thompson put his disease into remission and returned to the starting line-up. On the last day of the season Calvin canned Quilici and hired former Minneapolis Miller player/manager, Gene Mauch. Mauch was a 16-year veteran of National League managing and was considered by most to be a great tactician. But, with less than 750,000 fans showing up that season, he was going to have his hands full.

Prior to the 1976 season getting underway, a groundswell of support started to emerge for the team to construct a new stadium. In fact, Calvin Griffith had publicly stated that he wanted to start the dialogue for not just a stadium, but for a domed-stadium to be built. As the movement grew, Hubert H. Humphrey said in a speech to the state's legislators that "Without professional sports, the Twin Cities would be just a cold Omaha."

With that, the disciplinarian Mauch got busy and wound up leading his club to an 85-77 record and a third-place finish — the team's best since 1970. There was some good drama that year too, as a couple of trades played a big part of the team's success. The first sent Danny Walton to the Dodgers in return for Second Baseman Bobby Randall, while the other saw Bert Blyleven and Danny

Frank Viola

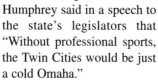

Thompson get shipped to Texas for infielders Roy Smalley and Mike Cubbage, as well as Pitchers Bill Singer and Jim Gideon. Smalley and Randall gelled right away, setting a club record for double plays in the process.

Another good addition was that of rookie catcher Butch Wynegar, who wasted little time in making a name for himself by being named to the All-Star team. The pitching was much better this year, thanks to the efforts of Bill "Soupy" Campbell, who led the club with 17 wins, and also that of Dave Goltz, who pitched in with 14 of his own. The team got hot late and won 12 of 14, surprising everyone by moving into second place in early August. They folded down the stretch though and came back to earth shortly thereafter. On the sad side, after several seasons of playing with bad knees, the remarkable Tony-O, who hit just .211 that year, decided to finally call it quits. Oliva spent his entire playing career in the Twins organization, winning three American League batting titles in his 11 seasons with Minnie. (His No. 6 was later retired in 1991.)

In 1977 state legislators approved a bill to build a replacement for Met Stadium. So, some $55 million in bonds were sold with the intent to be repaid with revenue from the new stadium, as well as from some public money which included various hotel and liquor taxes.

Now, on the field, Mauch seemed bound and determined to shake things up. So, he brought a ton of candidates into training camp that year and came out with 10 new Twins on the roster. Complete with youth, speed and hitting, the team had a bunch of young prospects poised to do some damage in the future. The big story of the year though, was that of Rod Carew, who flirted with .400 and became a bonefide superstar before the eyes of the nation. More than a million fans passed through the Met's turnstiles, that year, mostly to see Carew win the American League's MVP award. He led the league in average (.388), hits (239), runs (128) and triples (16), and also knocked in 100 RBI's to boot. For his efforts, the six-time batting champ received a lot of national attention, appearing on the covers of several national magazines including, Sports Illustrated and Time, where the headline read: "Baseball's Best Hitter." Carew also hit 14 homers, stole 23 bases and struck out just 55 times in 616 at-bats. At season's end the Twins' No. 29 had won the MVP award and for the 11th straight year was selected for the All-Star team, this time with the biggest number of fan votes ever recorded. He also received the treasured Roberto Clemente Award for distinguished service by a ballplayer to his community.

Carew carried the Twins on his back that year, willing them into a tough pennant race with Kansas City,

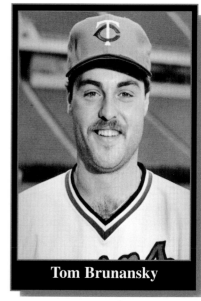

Tom Brunansky

Chicago and Texas, who were all battling for first place until after Labor Day, when the Royals ran away with it. Carew's hitting was infectious too, as Glenn Adams, Lyman Bostock and Larry Hisle (this group of hitters was affectionately known as the "Lumber Company"), also played great, posting .338, .336 and .302 averages, respectively. Hisle also led the AL with 119 RBI's as well. In addition, Goltz won 20 games, while Tom Johnson added 16 of his own. As a team, the Twins posted a .282 batting average, the best in the bigs, while tallying 867 runs — nearly 5.5 per outing. But,

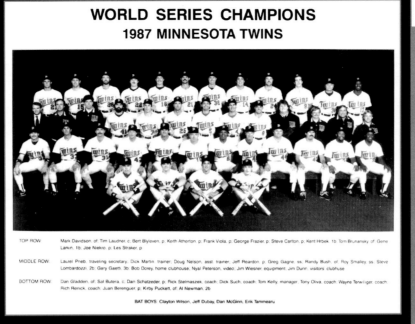

WORLD SERIES CHAMPIONS
1987 MINNESOTA TWINS

TOP ROW: Mark Davidson, of; Tim Laudner, c; Bert Blyleven, p; Keith Atherton, p; Frank Viola, p; George Frazier, p; Steve Carlton, p; Kent Hrbek, 1b; Tom Brunansky, of; Gene Larkin, 1b; Joe Niekro, p; Les Straker, p

MIDDLE ROW: Laurel Prieb, traveling secretary; Dick Martin, trainer; Doug Nelson, asst. trainer; Jeff Reardon, p; Greg Gagne, ss; Randy Bush, of; Roy Smalley, ss; Steve Lombardozzi, 2b; Gary Gaetti, 3b; Bob Dorey, home clubhouse; Nyal Peterson, video; Jim Wiesner, equipment; Jim Dunn, visitors clubhse

BOTTOM ROW: Dan Gladden, of; Sal Butera, c; Dan Schatzeder, p; Rick Stelmaszek, coach; Dick Such, coach; Tom Kelly, manager; Tony Oliva, coach; Wayne Terwilliger, coach; Rich Renick, coach; Juan Berenguer, p; Kirby Puckett, of; Al Newman, 2b

BAT BOYS: Clayton Wilson, Jeff Dubay, Dan McGinn, Erik Tammearu

group of overachievers. This rebuilt club very quietly emerged as legitimate contenders in the AL West, making a lot of believers along the way. Leading the charge out of the gates was Shortstop Roy Smalley, whose .340 batting average was good enough to earn himself a starting roster spot on the American League All-Star team. By mid-May the team had jumped out to first place and wound up hovering around with the big boys for most of the season. In fact, they even got into a pennant race with Kansas City, California and Chicago that lasted until the final week of the season, when they hit the wall and wound

in the end, the team's solid hitting couldn't make up for pitching depth, and they faltered down the stretch to finish at 84-77, fully 17 games behind first-place Kansas City. Perhaps the highlight of the season, however, came on June 26th, when 46,463 fans, the largest regular season crowd ever to cram into the Met, showed up to watch the Twins, led by Glenn Adams' record eight RBI's, destroy the White Sox, 19-2, to jump into first place in the West. And, in the process, Carew raised his batting average to .403 that day, teasing Ted Williams' record in the process.

After the season Calvin opened the free agency flood gates though, and let Hisle, the second best hitter in the AL, and Bostock, the league's top RBI man, go to Boston and California, respectively. In addition, Angels' outfielder "Disco" Dan Ford was traded for catcher Danny Goodwin and First Baseman Ron Jackson. And, veteran New York Mets lefty Jerry Koosman, an Appleton, Minn., native, was acquired in exchange for a pair of young pitchers. As a result, the club was forced to add several players to its lineup, including veterans "Iron Mike" Marshall and Jose Morales, as well as rookies Hosken Powell, "Bombo" Rivera, Darrell Jackson, Willie Norwood and Roger Erickson. Goltz led the way with 15 wins from the mound, while rookie Roger Erickson added 14, but in the end the club slid back to a 73-89 record. They did manage to make a mini-run at the All-Star break, but fell to fourth-place to finish 19 games behind the Royals.

The lowlight of the season came in September, when a controversy rocked the team. As a result, Rod Carew, who would win his seventh batting title that year, wound up being traded to the California Angels, in exchange for Dave Engle, Paul Hartzell, Brad Havens and Ken Landreaux. Here's how it went down. On September 28th of that year, Twins owner Calvin Griffith allegedly made some off-handed racist comments in a speech to the Waseca Lions Club. Little did he know, but there was a newspaper reporter in the audience who reported the story several days later in the Minneapolis Tribune. After reading the remarks, Carew was infuriated and vowed never play for the Twins again. Calvin was apologetic and insisted that his words were misunderstood and taken out of context, but the damage had been done. With that, Calvin, knowing that he would have to pay a fortune to keep Carew in his free agent year anyway, agreed to trade him. So, that off-season, Carew accepted a $4 million contract with the Halos. It was an illustrious 12-year career in Minnesota for Rodney, who wound up compiling a .334 lifetime batting average with the Twins. (He would, of course, be elected into the Baseball Hall of Fame in 1991.)

Now, as far as the team went, it was a surprising year for this

up finishing fourth, with a respectable 82-80 mark. Kenny Landreaux was particularly impressive, batting .305 with 15 homers and 83 RBI. And, while Jackson couldn't come close to filling Carew's shoes, he did manage to hit 14 homers and 68 RBI's — just two fewer than his predecessor the season before. The highlight of the year though came at the award ceremony, when rookie Third Baseman John Castino, who hit .285 and played solid "D," was named as the co-winner of the AL Rookie of the Year Award along with Toronto Shortstop Alfredo Griffin. In addition, Jerry "Kooz" Koosman, who went just 3-15 with the Mets in 1978, won the AL Comeback Player of the Year award with a 20-12 record, while Reliever Mike Marshall led the league with 32 saves as well. More than one million fans showed up that year to watch this bunch of rookies and veterans make a run for the post-season.

By now the Metropolitan Sports Facilities Commission had picked the site in downtown Minneapolis where a domed stadium was to be built for use by the Twins, Vikings and Gophers. Then, on December 20th of that year, the ground was broken on the Hubert H. Humphrey Metrodome. Taking 2.5 years and approximately $68 million to build, it would be Major League Baseball's third domed stadium along with Houston and Seattle, but the first "air-supported" structure of its kind.

Meanwhile, out on the diamond, the Twins digressed in 1980 by posting a marginal 77-84 mark, good for third in the AL West. One of the big reasons for the teams' downfall was the lack of decent pitching. Things got real bad on June 6th, when the ace of the staff, Mike Marshall was released. While the spin on the move was the he was off to a bad start, insiders thought that it was due to his involvement in a possible players' strike earlier in the year. It wasn't just pitching though, as the teams' defense was porous at best.

Then, on August

Greg Gagne

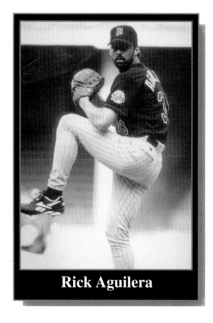

Rick Aguilera

Scott Erickson

24th, after a 3-2 loss to Detroit, Gene Mauch upped and quit as manager. At 54-71 he had had enough and could stomach no more. So, he was replaced by Coach Johnny Goryl. Under Goryl the team rebounded and even posted a 12-game winning streak en route to a 18-7 September record. As a result, Goryl was re-signed to manage the club in 1981. A few bright spots included a club record 31-game hitting streak by Landreaux, as well as Second Baseman Rob Wilfong's fielding record that year. In addition, John Castino continued to develop, hitting .302, with 13 homers and 64 RBI's, while rookie Pitcher Doug Corbett won eight games while adding 23 saves to boot. From the mound, the Kooz won 16 games after signing a three-year contract extension with the club, and Zahn added 14 of his own. After the season Goltz signed with the Dodgers as a free agent.

The 1981 Twins got off to a dismal 11-25 start, and with that the Johnny Goryl era was over. That's right, after just 72 games behind the bench, Gorly was canned in favor of the Twins original 1961 second baseman, Billy Gardner. And, although it was his first stint in the bigs, he had a tremendous track record down in the minors, where he posted six championships in 13 seasons. Overall, 1981 was a disappointment though, as the Major League Players Strike placed a black cloud over the entire season. On June 12 the players walked off the job and didn't come back for more than two months. The Twins, after stinking up the first half, did manage to finish with a 41-68 overall mark and were even in contention for the Western Division crown for much of the "second half" of the season. Injuries did this club in at the end as Smalley, Castino, Wynegar, Jackson, Erickson, Goodwin and Mickey Hatcher (who was acquired in an off-season trade for Landreaux), all were among the walking wounded. Plus, not one Twin reached double figures in homers. Ouch! There were some promising young rookies coming up through the system though, including Third Baseman Gary Gaetti and Catcher Tim Laudner. The most promising, however, was a first baseman from Bloomington by the name of Kent Hrbek, who beat the Yankees in his major league debut with a towering 10th inning game-winning home run.

When it was all said and done, the fans said good bye to the old Met. Sure, just 469,090 fans made the pilgrimage that season, but it was an important part of Minnesota's baseball history — and that shouldn't be forgotten. So, on a cold, rainy day on September 30th, after the Twins lost a 5-2 ballgame to Kansas City, she was put to rest. Not the prettiest thing to look at, the Met had character and old-school charm. The bleachers didn't match, the scoreboard was old and run-down, and the grass was beat up quite a bit from the Kicks soccer team. But the diehards

Chuck Knoblauch

didn't care, because they loved to be outside watching baseball. That was what it was all about. Oh, and by the way, the real reason why the team got out of Dodge and headed up 35W to Minneapolis was because the Vikings had threatened to move to another city unless the Met was either expanded or a new stadium was built. The Metropolitan Sports Facilities Commission wisely chose the latter. (No one wanted to see what happened to the old Minneapolis Lakers happen to their beloved purple.) So, after more than a decade of political wranglings amid the Twin Cities political landscape, not to mention the countless proposals as to where this albatross should be located, the state caved and the dream (or nightmare, depending on how you saw it...) of the Dome finally became a reality. (Did you know their was even talk of doming the U of M's Memorial Stadium? Other locales included the State Fair, Midway Stadium, and even the proposed "Lakeville Earth Stadium," which died like all the rest.)

Minnesota's brand new multi-purpose domed stadium opened for business in downtown Minneapolis on April 3rd, 1982, with an exhibition between the Twins and the Phillies. Fittingly, Pete Rose got the Dome's first hit. Then, on April 6th, some 52,279 fans crammed into the HHH Metrodome to watch the Twins play their inaugural game — which turned out to be an 11-7 loss to the Seattle Mariners. That season was a wild one, as the teams quickly realized that the balls flew out in a hurry in that big bubble. In fact, it wasn't long before it was being referred to as the "Homerdome." (To put it into perspective, there were 115 home runs hit at the Met in 1981, while 191 dingers were launched in the Dome in 1982.)

So, just how did the Twinkies do in 1982 under their new circus big-top? How about a franchise-worst record of 60-102. That's right, they stunk! But, it was all part of a grandiose plan, or so they would have us think, to get this promising group of youngsters to take the places of all those grizzled old veterans. So began the exodus. First, Roy Smalley was shipped to the Yankees for All-Star reliever Ron Davis and a minor league shortstop by the name of Greg Gagne. Also going to the Big Apple were Wynegar and Erickson, who were traded for John Pacella, Pete Filson and Larry Milbourne. Lastly, Rob Wilfong and Doug Corbett were sent packing to California for a promising right fielder by the name of Tom Brunansky.

This bunch of kids struggled at first, but showed great promise as the season went on. Leading the charge that year were First Baseman Kent Hrbek, Third Baseman Gary Gaetti, Left Fielder Gary Ward and Right Fielder Tom Brunansky, who each slugged 23, 25, 28 and 20 homers, respectively. (Hrbek would go on to finish second in the balloting for AL Rookie

Kevin Tapani

KENT HRBEK

Kent Hrbek was born on May 21, 1960, and grew up just a stone's throw from Metropolitan Stadium in Bloomington following the Twins and playing baseball. As a child growing up, literally, in the shadows of Bloomington's Metropolitan Stadium, Kent Hrbek often fell asleep to the sounds of cheering Twins and Vikings fans. It's no wonder then, that he grew up as a die-hard Minnesota sports fan. From his days of rounding the bases on the T-ball field to "touching em' all" in the Dome, Kent went on to become one of Minnesota's greatest home-grown baseball players.

"Tony Oliva was my hero, and I always idolized him," said Kent. "My mom even sewed a big #6 on the back of my T-Ball jersey, so I could wear his number."

Herbie went on to star at Bloomington Kennedy High School where he batted .480 his senior year, while playing great defense.

"He was an excellent fielder," Buster Radebach, his high school coach would say. "He was a student of the game and he studied it." It was in American Legion ball where Hrbek started to get noticed. His coach, Red Haddox, recalled that fans were simply in awe of his massive home runs. "He could handle the glove and could run for a big man," said former Twins owner Calvin Griffith who went to see one of Kent's Legion games. "I could see that his stroke alone was sufficient to gamble on him." So, in the 17th round of the 1978 draft, Herbie became a Twin, accepting a $30,000 offer.

After a brief stint in Visalia, where he was voted the MVP of the California League, Herbie got the call to come up to the show. He didn't waste any time in making a name for himself either, belting out a game-winning homer in the 12th inning at Yankee Stadium to give the Twins a thrilling win on August 24, 1981. He finished second to Cal Ripken in the Rookie of the Year voting, and was the lone rookie on the All-Star team in 1982.

"My sister probably sent in 10,000 votes on her own!" Kent said jokingly in regards to the All-Star balloting. He also made the cover of Sports Illustrated that year with the title: "Best of the Worst," and even appeared on the ABC-TV's Good Morning America show. Herbie had officially arrived.

While Kent's best season might have been in 1984, when he finished second in the MVP race after hitting .311, he will probably be best remembered for his Game Six grand slam in the 1987 World Series against Atlanta. A .282 lifetime hitter over his 14-year career in Minnesota, Hrbek is among the leaders in nearly every offensive category with 293 home-runs, 1,086 RBI's, 1,749 hits, 903 runs and 2,976 total bases. He retired in 1994 and his No. 14 was formally retired on August 13, 1995. While Kent Hrbek was probably appreciated most by his teammates and the fans for his upper-deck power and agility, he will also be remembered as one of the best fielders ever to play first base. Being a Twin meant everything to this gentle giant.

"I thought being a Twin was just about the greatest thing in the world," he said. "Being from Minnesota, and being just a huge sports fan, I have always rooted for our teams, whether it was the Twins, Vikings, North Stars, Timberwolves, or Gophers - I just wanted our teams to win. I don't think there is anybody that wanted to win a ball game more than Kent Hrbek, and there probably never will be!"

"I had a great time playing," added Kent, on how he would like to be remembered. "I liked to put on a show and have a good time and make people think that I wasn't so much different than they were, because I was a major league baseball player. People always thought that I had too much fun on the field, but having a good time was the only way I played well. I'd like to think that I was a fun-loving guy who felt like 'Hey, don't look at me badly because I could drink a beer and I was a major league baseball player.' There are too many guys now that thought they were so much better than others because they were major league baseball players, and I could never stand that! Let me tell you, you're not better than me because you can hit a 90 mph fastball, and because you make $6 million a year! Don't think that your sh-- doesn't stink, because it does!"

Here is what a few of his teammates had to say about him:

"He was awesome," said Kirby Puckett. "He was the best first baseman that I ever played with. He was one of the best teammates that I ever had. He was a great person, fun to be around and he made every day special coming to the ball park. I always felt that he should have won several gold gloves and been on more all star teams. He's like me, just care free and just wanted to play. He loved what he did and he played hard every day. He got hurt a lot at the end, I think he separated that shoulder like three or four times, but they were all tough injuries during the call of duty. You knew that whenever you had Herbie and me in the same clubhouse, it was going to be loud and something would always be going on. Herbie always made me laugh, and he didn't even have to try."

"Kent is a fun-loving guy and he always played and conducted himself that way whether he was on or off the field," said Tom Kelly. "He was such a talented hitter and player, and he enjoyed playing the game. He probably wanted to win more than any other player I have managed. He had such a desire and will to win. He was a home grown athlete who was just a great player."

"He was a guy that I truly don't think I got to know very well," said Jack Morris. "He was a lot more of a fun-loving guy than I thought he was as an opposing player. I can only describe him as a good guy and a good person. He never really had anything bad to say about people, he was a positive, funny guy. He was a great competitor."

"He grew up with me," said Tony Oliva. "I coached him all the way through the minor leagues and into the big leagues, he was a wonderful player and a great person."

"I said for about five years that Hrbek was the best fielding first baseman that I have ever seen, and I played with Keith Hernandez, and I saw Don Mattingly up close for several years as well," said Jim Kaat. "I think that when he was healthy, he was as good as anyone in the game. He was a throw back to my era. All he wanted to do was play baseball and go home and hunt and fish and have fun. He really enjoyed the game and he played it well."

of the Year and even appear on the cover of Sports Illustrated with the caption "Best of the Worst...") In addition, Bobby Castillo, who was acquired that off-season from the Dodgers, won 13 games. He was the only shining light on this pitching staff though, as the team struggled here immensely. Take Terry Felton for instance. In 1982 he finished the season at 0-13! There was another rookie who showed some promise, however, a tall, lanky left-hander from New York by the name of Frank Viola, and the fans could sense that he was going to be a good one.

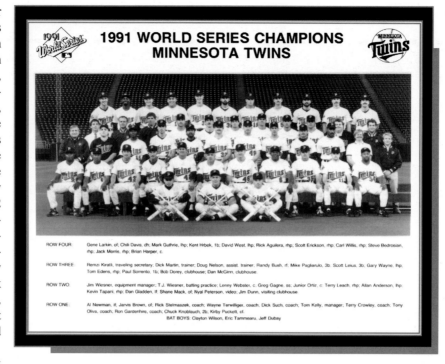

1991 World Series

1991 WORLD SERIES CHAMPIONS MINNESOTA TWINS

Minnesota Twins

ROW FOUR: Gene Larkin, of; Chili Davis, dh; Mark Guthrie, lhp; Kent Hrbek, 1b; David West, lhp; Rick Aguilera, rhp; Scott Erickson, rhp; Carl Willis, rhp; Steve Bedrosian, rhp; Jack Morris, rhp; Brian Harper, c.

ROW THREE: Remzi Kiratli, traveling secretary; Dick Martin, trainer; Doug Nelson, assist. trainer; Randy Bush, rf; Mike Pagliarulo, 3b; Scott Leius, 3b; Gary Wayne, lhp; Tom Edens, rhp; Paul Sorrento, 1b; Bob Dorey, clubhouse; Dan McGinn, clubhouse.

ROW TWO: Jim Wiesner, equipment manager; T. J. Wiesner, batting practice; Lenny Webster, c; Greg Gagne, ss; Junior Ortiz, c; Terry Leach, rhp; Allan Anderson, lhp; Kevin Tapani, rhp; Dan Gladden, lf; Shane Mack, of; Nyal Peterson, video; Jim Dunn, visiting clubhouse.

ROW ONE: Al Newman, if; Jarvis Brown, of; Rick Stelmaszek, coach; Wayne Terwilliger, coach; Dick Such, coach; Tom Kelly, manager; Terry Crowley, coach; Tony Oliva, coach; Ron Gardenhire, coach; Chuck Knoblauch, 2b; Kirby Puckett, cf.
BAT BOYS: Clayton Wilson; Eric Tammearu; Jeff Dubay.

Gabriel Murphy for the sole intent of purchasing the Twins and moving them to Florida.

When the 1984 Twins headed for Orlando to open Spring training, there was a renewed sense of optimism. There was also a whole bunch of major goings-on's, going on. Among them was the fact that Calvin Griffith was threatening to exercise an obscure option in his 20-year lease contract and move the Twins to Tampa. In that clause it stated that: "the club had to draw an average of 1.4 million fans in any three year period or he could break the lease and move the team." So, in an effort to stop Calvin, a group of local investors got together to buy up as many tickets as possible in order to keep the Twins in Minnie. Ticket buy-out plans were organized and "Save the Twins" task forces were even assembled. This went on into June, until a local multi-millionaire banker and businessman by the name Carl Pohlad stepped in and bought the team for $36 million from Griffith and his sister Thelma Griffith Haynes, thus keeping the Twins safe at home. The final buyout took place on September 7th, and with that, after 72 years, the Griffith era in baseball was over.

The fans were happy to finally have some security in their team not leaving, and they responded by playing respectable .500 baseball that season by going 81-81. Pitchers Mike Smithson and John Butcher, who were acquired in an off-season trade with Texas in exchange for Ward, gave the club a pair of decent starters to go along with Frankie Viola, who went 18-12 that year. The "Bruise Brothers" (Bruno and Herbie) were once again leading the charge as Hrbek finished second in the AL MVP balloting with a season that included a .311 average, 27 taters and 107 RBI's. Bruno, meanwhile, knocked out 32 homers and 85 RBI's as well. In addition, Kirby Puckett was called back up from Toledo in June to replace Jim Eisenreich and wasted little time in making a name for himself, hitting .296 in the lead-off spot while making nightly circus catches out in center field to boot. (He even got four hits in his first Major League game against California.) Other players who really stepped up that year were Mickey Hatcher, Ward's replacement in left field, who hit .302 with 69 RBI's, and Tim Teufel, who hit 14 homers and knocked in 61 runs while filling in for the injured John Castino at second. And, while Davis led the club with 29 saves out of the bullpen, the team also re-acquired Smalley at shortstop.

When it was all said and done, this bunch of kids had emerged as contenders in the AL West, going all the way into the last week of the season before being eliminated. They wound up finishing the year at 81-81, in a tie with California for second place.

In fact, by Sept. 16th, with just two weeks to go in the regular season, Minnesota was sitting at 75-72 and was a full game in first place. It was an exciting, blue-collar, bunch of kids who were making it happen out on the field that year, and the fans were loving every minute of it. The Metrodome fans, who were so starved for good baseball, showed their appreciation at the Twins' last home game of the season when they called them back onto the field and gave them a very moving, spontaneous 10-minute standing ovation. The honeymoon ended, however, when Minnesota set out on a seven-game road trip to both Chicago and Cleveland, where they came up just short. It

One of the biggest surprises of that season, however, was the stellar play of Center Fielder Jim Eisenreich, who beat out Mitchell for the starting role. Eisenreich, a St. Cloud, Minn., native, had made the leap to the bigs all the way from Class A and had all the tools to be a star. He jumped out of the gates by hitting over .300 and was playing stellar defense out in the pasture as well. But Jim had a nervous disorder known as Tourette's Syndrome, and didn't deal well with the pressure of playing in front of large crowds. As a result, Eisenreich left the team in 1984 and returned to St. Cloud, where he played amateur ball. He would try again two years later, and he succeeded with the Royals, Phillies and Marlins. He was an inspiration to millions.

The 1983 Twins finished just 10 games better than the previous years' version at 70-92, but did show a lot of promise. This core of youngsters had real potential and were starting to gel together as a unit. Leading the charge was "Bruno," who tallied 28 homers, while "Herbie" drove in 84 runs for good measure. A couple of other nice surprises included Outfielder Mickey Hatcher, who hit a career-high .317, and Catcher Dave Engle, who hit an impressive .305. In addition, free agent pick-up Ken Schrom posted a 15-8 record on the mound to pace Minnesota to a fifth place finish in the AL West. One of the highlights, er… lowlights, of the year came on April 14th, when the Metrodome roof deflated due to a tear caused by heavy snow. The team's scheduled game with California was, of course, postponed.

It is also interesting to note that that attendance dipped to 858,939 that year, showing that the novelty of the new Dome was wearing off. The fans were saying loud and clear that they weren't going to come to the ballpark just for the eye candy, they wanted to see a good product on the field. In addition, there were rumors floating around that because of poor attendance and fan support, the team was considering moving. In fact, it was even announced that a group from Tampa Bay had purchased the minority stock of long time board member

Ron Coomer

KIRBY PUCKETT

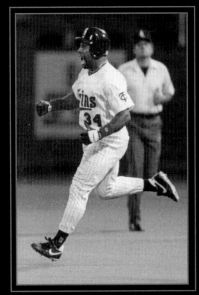

Kirby Puckett was born March 14, 1961, in Chicago. He grew up in the Robert Taylor Homes, a public housing project on Chicago's tough South Side, just down the road from the White Sox's Comiskey Park. Kirby's dad, William, was a postal worker, and his mom, Catherine, stayed at home in their 14th floor apartment to take care of Puckett's nine brothers and sisters. Kirby usually came home from school, did his homework, then went out to play ball.

"It was a long haul, coming from where I came from," said Kirby. "I can remember as a kid I broke up so many lamps and windows up in my room hitting the ball around — even with a wadded up sock ball. I was just playing baseball, just doing what I loved to do."

In 1973, his family moved out of the projects and into a better neighborhood outside of the city. Kirby would begin school at Calumet High School where he would emerge as a star third baseman. Kirby found it hard to get noticed by any major league scouts or college recruiters.

"Not too many scouts came to the ghetto to see me play." said the Puck. "We didn't even have a field, so we just played in a forest preserve that didn't have any fences or anything."

Kirby persevered through it all and graduated in the top 20 percent of his class. From there his luck would change though. At a Kansas City Royals free agent try-out camp, among several hundred hopeful kids, Bradley University coach, Dewey Kalmer, offered him a scholarship. Puckett did well at Bradley, even making the all-conference team.

Then, one year later, in 1982, tragedy struck when his father died of a heart attack. Kirby wanted to be closer to home and his family, so he left Bradley and enrolled at Triton Community College in River Grove, Ill. Puckett came into his own there, finally getting the attention of some scouts. But most of them just weren't impressed. They thought he was too short to play to be a big league prospect. Then his luck changed again. Jim Rantz, the Twins' director of minor leagues, took a chance on the fireplug-shaped ballplayer.

Once he was in organized baseball, Kirby tore up the minor leagues. There was Elizabethton, Visalia and finally Toledo. Virtually everywhere he went, he won the league's Player of the Year award. Then, while playing for Toledo in Old Orchard Beach, Me., he got the call to come up to the "show." Cal Ermer, the Mud Hens manager, called him in to tell him the good news and that he had to get on a plane to Los Angeles right away. Kirby didn't disappoint either. On May 8, 1984, Puck became the sixth player in AL history to get four hits in his major league debut. He had arrived.

Puckett's career was a storied one. There were two World Series and two ticker-tape parades down the streets of Minneapolis. There was game six in the 1987 "Cinderella-Series," against the Cardinals, when he got four hits and scored four runs to carry the Twins. And there was the "Worst-to-First Series" of 1991, when, in that game six, Kirby had one of the greatest games of his life. In that contest, Puck robbed Braves outfielder Ron Gant of a home run on a Ringling Brothers-like grab off the plexiglass, and then, to top it all off, in the 11th inning, with the game tied at three, Kirby hit a shot off Atlanta's Charlie Liebrandt that was the greatest homer in Twins history.

His bat didn't always make for heroics though. There was the Tony Oliva-inspired home-run epiphany during spring training in 1986, when, during batting practice in Orlando, Puck hit 10 consecutive balls over the fence, and after each hit, heard a strange sound. "Little did I know that they had some kind of auto show going on next door," said Puckett. "A motorcycle cop drove out onto the field where he told Kirby, "Swing at one more pitch, and I'll put you in jail!" Kirby's monster fly-balls had been breaking car windshields.

He was incredible. Only Willie Keeler had more hits in his first 10 years in the big leagues (2,065) than Puckett (2,040). In 12 seasons and 7,244 at bats with Minnesota, Kirby finished with a career batting average of .318, which included 2,304 hits, 1,071 runs, 1,085 RBIs, and 207 homers. He won a league MVP, played in 10 All-Star games, was named an All-Star game MVP, finished with a .989 percent fielding percentage, and earned six Gold Gloves. He was also awarded the treasured 1996 Roberto Clemente Man of the Year Award by Major League Baseball for his outstanding community service.

Tragically, in 1996, Kirby's career was ended due to irreversible retina damage in his right eye. Amazingly, his last trip to the disabled list was also his first. "I knew that baseball wasn't going to last forever," said Kirby. "It was great living in a fairy tale for 12 years, and I enjoyed every minute of it. I just thank God that I got the chance to live out the dream I had since I was five years old. Isn't that the way life's supposed to be?"

Puckett went on to add that he finds it remarkable that anyone could feel sorry for a man who, in 1997, despite not being able to play, is in the final year of a $6-million contract. He grants himself but one regret, he would have liked to have reached 3,000 hits. His trademark smile, goatee, and bald head, are only some of the reasons why Kirby is the most popular athlete in Minnesota history. His boyish enthusiasm for baseball is his greatest trait and his positive attitude not only inspired his teammates but the fans as well. From his patented after-the-hit "bat-flip," to his in-depth explanations on his hitting style, which included: "I'm just trying to get my hacks man..." and "I'm just seeing the ball good man..."

Then, in August of 2001, Kirby, who went on to serve as the Twins' Executive Vice President of Baseball, was inducted into the Baseball Hall of Fame in Cooperstown, N.Y., alongside his teammate and friend, Dave Winfield. Kirby will always be remembered in Minnesota as simply the best ever.

"My first love was always baseball, and it still is baseball," said Kirby. "I've lived a dream, man, and being a Twin means everything to me." "I was a gamer, and I came to play every day," he added. "I never took the game for granted. Not for one day. I had a smile on my face, but when I stepped between the white lines, I tried to hurt you because that was my job, man. I took my job very seriously because I knew that people paid their hard earned money to come see me play, and I wanted to give them the best possible show that I could every time I steeped onto a baseball field. I always did the little things that could give my team the edge, and that's why my teammates loved me. No matter what, with the game on the line, I wanted to be the man. I thrived on that, and that's what made me the player that I was. I never thought of myself as a superstar or anything like that, I'm just Kirby. My mom used to always tell me what goes up has to always come down, and sooner or later, all those people that you treated badly on the way up, you see again on the way down. I've remembered those words."

JACK MORRIS

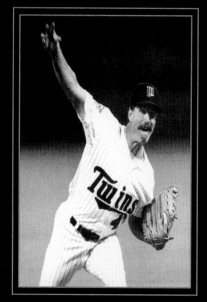

From the ballparks of St. Paul, Jack Morris went on to play high school ball at Highland Park and then in college at Utah's Brigham Young University. From there he was drafted by the Detroit Tigers, and went on to become one of baseball's all-time greatest pitchers.

Growing up in Minnesota Jack Morris was clearly a home-town kind of a guy who loved his hometown team.

"Like a lot of kids growing up in the Cities, I followed the Twins," he said. "My heroes were guys like Harmon Killebrew, Tony Oliva, and Bob Allison."

As a pro, Jack was the only pitcher to have won 14 or more games in each year in the 1980s and three times he won 20 or more games in a season. Although some were critical of his perennially high ERA, Jack would shrug and say that he was paid to win games, and that his contract did not stipulate that the margin of victory be by a shutout or by a score of 6-5.

The winningest pitcher of the 1980s, Jack Morris was a workhorse, notching double-digit wins in 14 of his 16 full seasons in the majors while finishing in the top 10 in Cy Young Award voting seven times. He won a trio of World Series titles as well, winning his first in 1984 with Detroit, his second in 1991 with his hometown Twins, and his third in 1992 with the Toronto Bluejays. He was also very durable, being relegated to the disabled list just twice in his 18-year career. He had a solid fastball, a hard slider, and excellent split-finger to make his pitching arsenal one of the best ever. Morris even hurled a no-hitter against the Chicago White Sox on April 7, 1984, matching the earliest date in a season a no-no was thrown. Among the most reliable pitchers in history, he holds the AL record with 515 straight starts, once going more than 10 seasons missing only one scheduled start. An excellent all-around athlete who was often used as a pinch runner, he also holds the major league career record for put-outs by a pitcher, with 387.

Perhaps Jack's finest moment came in the seventh and deciding game of the 1991 World Series, when he tossed a thrilling 10-inning complete game thriller for his hometown Twins over Atlanta. For his efforts, the aging righty was awarded the World Series MVP Trophy.

"Every ballplayer whether they signed out of high school or college probably has some kind of dream of playing with their hometown team," said Jack of his return home to Minnie. "And I was no different. After being drafted by Detroit and playing there through the years, I thought I might finish my career there. But as the political football of baseball goes, you gotta do what you gotta do, and when the opportunity arose to come play for Minnesota, it was like a dream come true. The 1991 season was a fairy tale."

Jack had spent 14 seasons with the Tigers before coming back to Minnesota — where he would wind up staying for just one season before getting out of Dodge.

"As players, we don't always recognize what points of light come across our paths until after they're gone," said Jack. "I never had any intention of leaving Minnesota when I was here, I never wanted to, but I understand what happened. Mr. Pohlad had to save his money for a guy named Kirby Puckett. He lost several great players and really the nucleus of a ball-club, because of the fan appeal of one player. I'm not blaming anybody, Kirby did what he had to do, and he was justified in doing it. Carl Pohlad did what he had to do, and all of us players who left the Twins did what we had to do as well. It was just unfortunate that we couldn't have kept it together - because I wanted nothing more than to win it all again with that same group of guys."

After his heroics with the Twins, Jack signed with Toronto, followed by stints in Cleveland and Cincinnati before finally hanging up his spikes at the tender age of 40. In 1994 Jack opted to come home and become the ace of the Northern League's St. Paul Saints, where he ended up leading the league with a 2.61 ERA. When it was all said and done Jack finished his illustrious career with 254 victories and 175 complete games. He retired during that season though, to spend more time working his ranch in Montana.

A die-hard Minnesota fan, Jack will always be remembered as one of the best. "I think people need to know that I loved the game of baseball," said Jack. "I really appreciate and respect the game and had fun playing it. I realize that I am rough around the edges. I've never really been well versed enough to be smooth and sensitive to everybody, because I was so driven in one direction - and that was to win. I blocked out a lot of distractions. It was the price of winning. In the process I turned off a few people. I just want people to know that I gave it all I had, and winning was most important to me. I think that when you are a perfectionist like myself, the only way you're justified in your effort is to win. It creates a huge burden on you - and you become your own worst enemy as well as your own worst critic."

Here is what a few of his former teammates had to say about him:

"Jack was a very competitive player," said Tom Kelly. "He was very intense about his job and was very workman-like as a pitcher. He knew how to win games and took the ball every four or five games. He was a great pitcher."

"His game seven performance was the most jacked up I have ever seen a pitcher pitch in a ballgame, and I don't think there will ever be another game pitched like it," said Kent Hrbek. "To me that was the single most gutsy performance by a pitcher that I have ever seen."

"Tiger Jack was probably one of the most intense people that I have ever been around," said Kirby Puckett. "He was a warrior and gave you everything he had. Whatever he had going, he would use to get it done, and that's the mark of a great pitcher. He protected us as well. I mean if another pitcher threw at us, he would throw at their players - and that is the way the game is supposed to be played. He took the ball no matter what and wouldn't miss a start, and I respected him greatly for that."

"He was a hard-nosed ball player and I respected the way he went about his work," said Dave Winfield. "He was a tough, mean competitor, like a Bob Gibson. I remember when you got a hit off of him, he would talk to you on the bases, telling you it was luck, and to wait for the next one!"

"Jack and I grew up competing against each other in St. Paul," said Paul Molitor. "To finally become teammates together in Toronto was special. Jack was always known as the best athlete in St. Paul when I was a kid. He had the best arm of all the city pitchers, and was a tremendous basketball player as well. He instilled fear in many hitters at the high school and American Legion levels. Jack was a fierce competitor and was the guy that you wanted to give the ball to in the big games. In 1991 he was amazing."

all came down to the now infamous "Jamie Quirk Game" in Cleveland, where Quirk, who was just signed that day from the White Sox, hit a two-out ninth inning homer to beat the Twins and all but kill their pennant dreams. They had one last chance that next night, and with Frankie Viola on the mound, seemed to be poised to keep themselves on life-support. There, they jumped out to a 10-0 lead by the fifth, but, as luck would have it, they squandered it away, losing 11-10. Later that night the Royals clinched the pennant. It was a devastating loss for the Twins, but they were determined to come back and redeem themselves that next year.

(In the interesting and weird department, on May 4th of that season, Seattle's Dave Kingman hit a pop-up straight up into a drainage hole in the Metrodome's roof, where, to the amazement of the bewildered John Castino who was waiting patiently below for it to fall back to earth, it stayed forever. As a result, he was awarded a ground-rule double, and his legacy, known as the "Kingman Rule" still lives on.)

That next year, 1985, the team was poised to take off, but fell short of expectations. Early in the season Manager Billy Gardner was let go and he was replaced with Ray Miller, the highly regarded pitching coach of the Orioles. The young players were responding well to Miller, however, who was much more of a disciplinarian than the laid-back Gardner, and they respected his ideology to the game. Miller guided them to a respectable 50-50 record for the remainder of the season, where they ended up with a less than spectacular 77-85 record — 14 games behind the eventual World Series champion Royals in fourth place. On the plus side, 1,651,814 fans came out to see the Twins, setting a single-season attendance record in the process. When it was all said and done, Kirby led the team with a .288 batting average; Bruno led the club with 27 homers; and Herbie, who battled through a sore shoulder for much of the season, led the club with 93 RBI's. On the mound, Frankie Viola once again had an 18-win season, while Smithson added 15 of his own. Perhaps the best news the pitching staff got came on August 1st, when Bert Blyleven returned to Minnesota in a trade with Cleveland for pitchers Rich Yett and Curt Wardle, and minor leaguers Jay Bell and Jim Weaver. The savvy veteran helped to develop this young staff and even pitched in with eight wins of his own down the stretch.

Another highlight that year came on July 16th, when Minnesota played host to the 56th annual All-Star Game. Nearly 55,000 fans packed into the Dome to watch the National League beat the AL, 6-1, in a yawner. Minnesota's sole representative, Tom Brunansky, went hitless in his only at-bat, but did manage to win the Home Run Derby the day before.

The expectations were high going into the 1986 campaign. This group of youngsters had showed a lot of promise up to this point and the fans were ready for some big dividends to start paying off. It came as a big let-down then, when the team plummeted to a 71-91 record, which could officially be considered a "rebuilding year." In fact, the management, led by the new executive vice-president/General Manager, Andy MacPhail, even went as far as firing Miller on September 12th. He was, in turn, replaced by Tom Kelly, himself a former Twin. Early in the season the Twins sent Pitcher John Butcher to Cleveland for lefty Neal Heaton, and also unloaded reliever Ron Davis to the Cubs for relievers George Frazier and Ray Fontenot. They even acquired Keith Atherton from the A's, but these guys were far from the answer to this staff's woes. Leading the way offensively was the "G-Man," Gary Gaetti, who hit 34 homers and drove in 108 runs. Herbie and Bruno added 29 and 23 homers, respectively, while Kirby added 31 of his own to go along with his gaudy .328 average.

The 1987 Minnesota Twins were, in a word, awesome. Their story is perhaps one of the greatest in sports. It all began during that off-season when GM Andy MacPhail set the early tone by acquiring ace reliever Jeff Reardon. Was he the missing piece of the puzzle? Heck, most baseball pundits predicted another season of mediocrity for these Twins,

probably no better than fourth in the AL West. Boy were they wrong!

The Twins took baseball by storm in 1987, featuring a lineup that was comprised of Minnesota's own "Fab-Four," the quartet of Herbie, Kirby, Bruno and the G-Man. They even added a new kid by the name of Dan Gladden, a hard-nosed left fielder who was full of grit and determination. The team played up and down that season but overall, played solid fundamental baseball under Manager Tom Kelly.

One of the highlights this season came on August 3rd, when Pitcher Joe Niekro was ejected from the Twins 11-3 win in Anaheim. Niekro, a crafty old vet, got caught with his hand in the cookie jar in this one as he coughed up a five inch emery board out his pocket after being accused of doctoring knuckle-balls. Busted!

The Twins finished the regular season with a modest 85-77 record, but it was good enough to win the West. Frank Viola began to show great consistency as a starter along with veteran Bert Blyleven, who, believe it or not, was with the Twins the last time they were in the American League Championship Series back in 1970. Leading the charge was Kent Hrbek. After being stiffed for the All-Star Game, Herbie took out his anger on opposing teams, finishing with a career-high 34 home runs and adding 90 RBI's to boot.

So, in the first round of the post-season, the Twins prepared to do battle with the Detroit Tigers. Detroit, with the best overall won-loss record in the bigs, was predicted to crush the Twins, whose record was just the ninth best in baseball. The Twins thought differently though and took the first two in Minnesota and then went on to win two of the final three in Detroit. Tim Laudner's double off Tigers ace Jack Morris was the difference in Game Two, and in Game Four they took the lead for good on Greg Gagne's fourth-inning home run. Leading the way in the series was Gary Gaetti, who was named as the ALCS MVP.

Now it was on to the World Series, where the Twins would face the St. Louis Cardinals. The first two games weren't even close. In game one, the first World Series game ever played indoors, the Twins blasted St. Louis, 10-1, thanks to Dan Gladden's grand slam. The second game was another cakewalk, an 8-4 victory, highlighted by homers from both Gary Gaetti and Tim Laudner. Just when it looked like a series sweep for Minnesota, the Cards came back and took the next three games in St. Louis. The Twins hung in there Game Five on Gaetti's eighth-inning, two-run triple, but the Cards held on for a 4-2 win. One victory for the Cardinals at the Metrodome, and St. Louis would be world champions.

Game Six was a wild one. Down in the fifth, the Twins retaliated behind Don Baylor's three-run homer, and then slammed the door on the Cards thanks to Kent Hrbek's childhood dream-come-true. With the Twins up 6-5 in the sixth, Herbie would make history that night. The big first baseman then proceeded to hit a 439-foot grand salami over the center field wall, and into a sea of white homer hankies. (The Star Tribune sold more than a million hankies during the playoffs!) The series was now even at three games apiece. As the Bloomington native circled the bases with his fists pumping and his mouth wide open, he remembered playing out that very play a million times before in his own back yard – just a stone's throw from the old Met. The Twins, behind Puckett's four hits and

Marty Cordova

CYCLE PERFORMANCES

Player	Date	Team	At-Bats	Score
Rod Carew	5-20-70	at KC	5	10-5
Cesar Tovar	9-19-7	Tex	5	5-3
Larry Hisle	7-4-76	at Bal	5	8-6
Lyman Bostock	7-24-76	at Chi	4	17-2
Mike Cubbage	7-27-78	Tor	4	6-3
Gary Ward	9-18-80	at Mil	4	8-9
Kirby Puckett	8- 1-86	Oak	5	10-1

score four runs, went on to take Game Six, 11-5 to even it up at three games apiece.

Said teammate Roy Smalley after Game Six: "Before Kent went up to bat I looked at Frank Viola and said, 'You watch... This is too set up. This is too much like a storybook. It's too perfect.' "

"It is something I will never feel again," said Herbie after the big game. "People talk about thrills in baseball. Just making the big leagues was a thrill. Hitting a home run at Yankee Stadium in my first game in the big leagues was a thrill. Hitting a grand slam in the World Series in your home state — that is indescribable."

Game Seven had all the drama you could ask for. The Cardinals scored first in this one with a pair of runs in the second, but the Twins rallied with runs in the second and fifth, and then took the lead on three walks and an infield single in the sixth. Frankie V. then held St. Louis scoreless on just two hits after the second, and ace reliever Jeff Reardon came in to retire the Cards in order in the ninth to bring Minnesota its first world championship. It was truly a wild one. Three Twins were thrown out at home plate. Greg Gagne drove in the winning run on an infield hit. Frankie "Sweet Music" Viola pitched eight beautiful innings, giving up only two early on. And, fittingly Jeff Reardon came in for the ninth, getting the final out on McGee's ground ball to Gary Gaetti. When the G-Man threw the ball across the diamond to Herbie at first, the Twins had won the game, 4-2, earning the title of baseball's World Champions. As Carl Spackler (alias: Bill Murray from the classic movie Caddyshack...) said so prophetically, it was truly a "Cinderella-Story."

In the series finale, the Minnesota fans had actually grown quite fond of the parachute-topped edifice better known as the "Homerdome," a true testament to its' inexplicable magic it had provided the Twins. Frank Viola would earn Series MVP honors, and for Herbie, there would be ticker-tape parades, presidential meetings, and even Late Night with David Letterman.

"I just step back and think of the guys that I played with back then," Hrbek would later recall. "Great guys, like Viola, Gaetti, Brunansky, Laudner, and Bush. We grew up in the big leagues together, we lost in the big leagues together, and then, in 1987, we were the best in the world together. I can still remember sitting on the clubhouse floor after the game. Everybody thought we all were drunk as pigs, but we weren't, we were all just mentally and physically spent. It was something that we had all worked so hard for, and had so much fun doing, that when it was over we just soaked it all in and enjoyed it."

"That team was the closest-knit group of guys I've ever been around," added Kirby Puckett. "It was unbelievable. I mean win or lose, every night you could find at least a dozen of us eating together at a restaurant. We hung together, and we won together. I still remember, after we won Game Seven, a bunch of us were just sitting there on the floor in the clubhouse, drinking champagne, and staring at each other like, 'What did we just do?' I've had a lot of people ask me since then, 'How did it feel?' And you know what? I can't tell them. It's something you have to experience for yourself to get it. It was something only the people in that room could understand."

"Being it was my first full year as a manager, it was a very special thing," said Manager Tom Kelly. "It was a new experience for me getting into the playoffs and into the World Series. Typically, we are somewhat afraid and apprehensive about new experiences because we don't know what to expect. There was a lot of cautious optimism surrounding the whole experience. The playoffs were a little

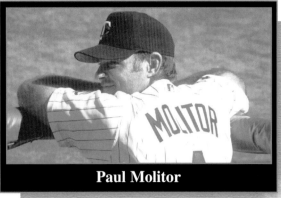

Paul Molitor

more nerve-racking than the Big Dance, but, all in all, it was an incredible experience."

By 1988, all of Minnesota was still dizzy and hungover from the World Series hoopla that had swept through the state during that magical season a year earlier. So, that next season, people were more interested than ever to see if the club could repeat as world champs. Fans turned out at the Metrodome in droves. In fact, the Twins became the first American League team ever to draw three million fans, as 3,030,672 people passed through the Metrodome turnstiles to watch the reigning champs defend their title. The faithful wanted to see up-close a part of the history, that for many of them, had unfolded before their eyes only on the television.

On the field, the 1988 Twins finished with a quite respectable 91-71 record en route to a second place finish in the AL West. In fact, it was the Twins' first 90-win season since 1970. Minnesota battled Tony LaRussa's Oakland A's for the better part of the season, but in the end the Athletics were too tough and won the AL crown with an amazing 104 wins.

As a group, the Twins placed second in the major leagues with a collective .274 batting average. Kirby Puckett had another monster year, batting .356 (the highest by a right-handed hitter in the A.L. since Joe DiMaggio's .357 back in 1941), while leading the league in hits with 234. The "G-Man," hit .301, Hrbek hit .312, and previously-unheralded pitcher Allan Anderson, who was called up from Portland (AAA), won 16 games while producing the league's lowest ERA at 2.45. In addition, closer Jeff Reardon notched a club-record 42 saves, good for second in the Majors.

As for their skipper, the remarkable Tom Kelly, he reaped the benefits of leading his ballclub to the 1987 World Series and was honored by managing the 1988 All-Star game. He was joined at the All-Star festivities in Cincinnati by Kirby Puckett, Tim Laudner, Gary Gaetti, Jeff Reardon, and Frank Viola — who also just happened to be the starting and winning pitcher for the AL, as they beat the NL, 2-1. Viola's heroics weren't confined to the 1988 All-Star Game though. He picked up right where he left off in 1987, when he won the World Series MVP, this time winning the coveted Cy Young award as the league's best pitcher. The 1988 season was a dream for Viola as he led the league with 24 wins, posted a 2.64 ERA, and struck-out 193 batters. He also set the Twins record for the all-time best winning percentage that season at .774.

The man ultimately responsible for the success of the team was manager Kelly. The Twins skipper never made a lot of noise in the dugout, yet was able to lead his team all the way to the promised land occupied by baseball's world champions. Kelly's soft-spoken, 'lead-by-example' attitude filtered throughout the club-house and became infectious with all of his players. He was a stickler for the fundamentals, and it was no coincidence that his team committed a Major League record for the fewest errors (84) while posting a .986 fielding percentage. T.K. carried with him the reputation of being a fan favorite, a media darling, and all-around good guy. Perhaps the biggest compliment paid to him is that he was referred to as a "players' manager."

In 1989 the Twins got off to a so-so start. They weren't going to make it to the post-season, so management decided to shake things up at mid-season by trading away their best pitcher, Frank Viola, to the New York Mets, in exchange for five young pitchers. They felt that they could get good value for the lefty, so they pulled the trigger on a block-buster deal that brought to the Twins several

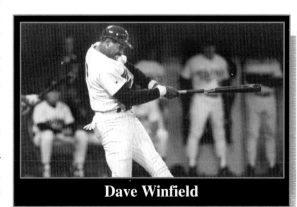

Dave Winfield

top rookies, including a pair of starters in southpaw David West (considered to be the Mets' top prospect) and Kevin Tapani, as well as relievers Tim Drummond and Jack Savage. In addition, Minnesota also acquired a proven, 28-year-old veteran in Rick Aguilera. As far as the team went, they finished in 5th place with an 80-82 record. Allan Anderson led the pitching staff with yet another 17 wins, while the Puck won his first batting title with a .339 average — it was his fourth straight 200+ hit season. Following the season, veteran reliever Jeff Reardon opted to sign a fat three-year contract with the Red Sox. Boston also made a play for Hrbek, but in the end Herbie stayed home, signing a 5-year, $14-million contract of his own.

The 1990 Twins were horrible. They finished in last place with a paltry 74-88 record. There were a few shining stars emerging though, including Catcher Brian Harper, who emerged as one of the game's best hitting catchers with a .294 average. He also had the Majors' longest hitting streak of the season at 25 games. Another emerging star was Left Fielder Shane Mack, who, after being called up, surprised everyone by hitting .326 and stealing 13 bases. As far as the pitching went, it was pretty ugly. However, Aguilera, who was converted from a starter to a stopper in the bullpen, wound up notching 32 saves. And, rookie right-hander Scott Erickson finished the season with eight wins and a solid 3.27 ERA. Minnesota also made history that year, when, on July 17th, in Boston, the team turned a pair of triple plays in the same game. The first one came in the fourth with the bases juiced and former Twin Tom Brunansky hitting a liner to Third Baseman Gary Gaetti. Gaetti then stepped on the bag for the first out, then tossed it to Al Newman at second for the second out, only to see Newmie chuck the relay to Herbie at first to nail the lumbering Bruno for No. three. Then, in the eighth inning, with runners on first and second, Jody Reed topped a grounder to Gaetti, who once again executed the 5-4-3 triple play to Newman and Herbie.

Well, the good thing about finishing in last place, is that the only place to go from there is up. And that is exactly what the 1991 "worst to first" Twins did. These Twins were a full-circle success story that will forever be remembered for Jack Morris' World Series heroics.

After the teams' best pre-season ever at their new spring training facility, the Lee County Sports Complex in Ft. Myers, Fla., (they moved after playing 55 years in Orlando), the squad slithered to a pathetic 2-9 start, courtesy of a pair of ugly West Coast swings. They rebounded though, and stayed strong under the guidance of T.K. Early on in the season, many Twins fans had a good feeling about this new bunch of players. Some even went as far as predicting an inkling of destiny when the Twins tore through the American League that summer, reeling off 15 wins in a row en route to winning the West. One of the reasons the club was playing so well was due to the unbelievable pitching of Scott Erickson, who, at one point, won a club-record 12 consecutive games en route to closing the gap on first-place Texas.

They then went on to easily win the ALCS, beating the Toronto Blue Jays four games to one, to earn a trip back to the World Series. One of the highlights of the ALCS came in Game Three, when pinch hitter Mike Pagliarulo won it for the Twins on a home run to right in the 10th inning. Kirby then homered in Games Four and Five to seal the deal for Minnie.

Now, in the World Series, the Twins would face another cellar-dwelling team from 1990, the resurrected Atlanta Braves, who had beaten the Pittsburgh Pirates, 4-3, in the NLCS. The World Series got off to a great start for Minnesota. The Twins won Games One and Two in front of the Metrodome faithful, 5-2, and 3-2, respectively. Game Two was not only highlighted by Kent Hrbek's now famous all-star wrestling tag of Atlanta's Ron Gant on first base. In addition, Chili Davis hit a two-run homer in the first inning, while Scott Leius added one of his own in the eighth.

The series then shifted south, to "Hot-Lanta" where the Braves won all three of the next games, highlighted by a 14-run shellacking of the Twins in Game Five. Up three games to two, the Braves then returned to the Dome to try and wrap it up. Kirby Puckett thought differently though and played the game of his life in Game Six. First, Puck robbed Braves outfielder Ron Gant of a home run in the third on a Ringling Brothers-like grab off the Plexiglas. Then, after a Terry Pendleton homer to tie it up, Puckett regained the lead for his twins on a sacrifice fly. Atlanta knotted the score again in the

seventh to send it into extra innings, only to see Kirby take over in the 11th. There, with the game tied at three, Kirby stepped up and hit a towering shot off Atlanta's Charlie Liebrandt that was without question the greatest home run in Twins history, giving Minnesota a thrilling 4-3 win and evening the series at three games apiece. "We'll see you tomorrow night!", said legendary broadcaster Jack Buck following the big hit.

Eddie Guardado

The locker room was surprisingly calm before the world championship Game Seven. In fact, the clubhouse television sets were all tuned to football games when the players arrived — so the players could set their fantasy football line-up's! Manager Tom Kelly had named Jack Morris as his starter in the most important baseball game of 1991, while Atlanta Manager Bobby Cox countered with John Smoltz, a Detroit native who grew up worshipping that very same Jack Morris.

The game was a back and forth pitching duel that went scoreless into the top of the eighth. That inning would prove to be one of the most tense of the series. With Lonnie Smith on first, Terry Pendleton hit a liner to the gap. Then, Smith, who was running on the pitch, mysteriously eased up and slowed down as he was rounding second. Replays showed that Twins Second Baseman Chuck Knoblauch put on a fabulous deke, faking that he was going to catch the ball coming in from the outfield. Little did Smith know however, that the ball was, in reality, still rolling around in the outfield at the time. By this time he realized what was going on he could only advance to third. Gant then hit a squibber to Hrbek for an easy out, followed by Sid Bream who hit into a 3-2-3 double play to end the inning. Morris leaped into the air pumping his fist up to the sky as the Twins had dodged a huge bullet.

Through the tenth, the Twins and Braves matched donuts on the scoreboard. It had now become only the second Game Seven in World Series history to reach extra innings. Kelly would later say: "There was no thought of changing pitchers. Morris could rest in November; the outcome of October was his to decide."

Dan Gladden then led off the last of the 10th with a broken-bat single that he somehow managed to stretch into a double. Knoblauch, who would be named Rookie of the Year that season, had just one sacrifice bunt all year. He got his second on that night though by moving Gladden to third. The Twins were now 90 feet from their second title ever. After intentionally walking Kirby and Herbie to load the bases, Gene Larkin now stood at home plate for the at-bat of his life. Larkin jumped on the first pitch and then hit a fly ball to left-center. Atlanta Left Fielder Brian Hunter, who was playing in, could only look on helplessly as the ball flew over his head and landed on the turf. The rest, they say, is history.

"The Twins are gonna win the World Series!", shouted legendary announcer Jack Buck after the huge hit. "The Twins have won it!"

Fittingly, Morris was the first to grab Gladden as he touched the plate. Two mobs of players, one at home and

Brad Radke

TOM KELLY

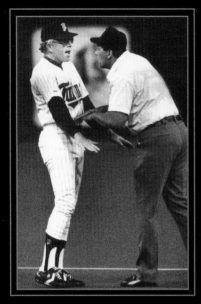

Tom Kelly's soft-spoken, 'lead-by-example' attitude filtered throughout the clubhouse and became infectious with all of his players. Tom has carried with him the reputation of being a fan favorite, a media darling, and all-around good guy. Perhaps the biggest compliment paid to him is that he is referred to as a players' manager. His career has been a long and winding one, with its roots in Minnesota.

Jay Thomas Kelly was born on August 15, 1950, in Graceville, Minn. His family ultimately moved east, and Tom grew up in New Jersey. Baseball had always played a role in his life because his father, Joe, was a Northern League pitcher during the 1940s and later played in the New York Giants system. Tom went on to become an outstanding ballplayer at St. Mary's High School in South Amboy, N.J. He went on to attend Mesa Community College in Mesa, Ariz., and also Monmouth College in West Long Branch, N.J.

T.K. fulfilled a boyhood dream in 1968 when the expansion Seattle Pilots selected him in the fifth round of the Major League Baseball free agent draft. So, he reported to Newark to play in the minor leagues. In his first year he hit an impressive .317, led the league in stolen bases and became a league all-star. From there it was off to Clinton and Jacksonville, until 1971, when he was signed as a free agent by the Twins. After spending a year in Charlotte, he began a four-year stint in Tacoma, the Twins triple-A club.

Then, in 1975, Kelly got the call he had been waiting for his entire career - he was going to the show. On May 19, he got his first major league hit when he singled off Detroit's Joe Coleman. It wasn't a very long stint in the bigs, 127 at bats in 49 games to be exact. But it was something he had dreamed of during his entire career as an active ballplayer. So, for a career minor leaguer, those 1975 Twins games were pretty special to him. He ended up with 23 hits, while driving in 11 batters, scoring another 11 runs and batting a buck-eighty-one. Kelly's lone dinger of his career came off Tigers pitcher Vern Ruhle.

"It's something you always dreamed about, to play at the major league level," said Kelly. "As a minor leaguer, you were always working towards that goal. I got the opportunity, but I wasn't good enough to stick around. At least, I did have a chance which was great for me, and it is something I will always remember."

After a season at triple-A Rochester, Kelly caught another break. This time he found his calling as he would spend the next three years in Tacoma and Toledo as player and as a manager. In 1979 and 1980, he managed a Twins' farm team in Visalia, where he led the club to two consecutive divisional titles. He was also named the California League Manager of the Year for two years in a row. He then was promoted by the Twins to Orlando where he was named manager of the year after guiding his team to the league championship.

In 1983, he got another call to the majors, this time as the new Twins' third base coach, becoming the first Minnesotan to ever become a member of the Twins' managerial staff. In 1986, T.K. took over the Twins' managerial duties from a faltering Ray Miller.

In 1987, Kelly became only the fifth manager in baseball history to win a pennant as a rookie when the Twins beat the Cardinals in the World Series. For his efforts the 37-year-old was named American League Manager of the Year. It was a tremendous victory for all of Minnesota and T.K. was given much of the credit. And deservedly so, for it was he who supplied the glue to hold the players together.

Kelly's heroes won their second World Series over the Atlanta Braves four years later. Tom thus became first Twins manager ever to lead his club to two divisional titles (and subsequent world championships) and the third manager ever in baseball history to have won two World Series and never lost one. In 1991, Kelly again was named American League Manager of the Year, and was also named WCCO Radio's 1991 Distinguished Good Neighbor, an award given annually to someone who brings honor to the state of Minnesota. In 1992, managed the American League All-Star team in San Diego. (It was the AL over the NL in a 13-6 rout.) Fittingly, Kirby Puckett was the All-Star Game MVP.

In 2001 T.K. stepped down as Twins manager and handed the reigns to long-time coach, Ron Gardenhire. When the dust had finally settled, Kelly's career resume was simply amazing. Very quietly he became entrenched as baseball's longest-tenured manager, managing 2,385 games in his nearly 20 years behind the bench in Minnie. In addition, he also became the all-time winningest manager in Minnesota history, having won 1,140 games.

TK also won a pair of World Series' in a span of five years. This may not sound impressive until one realizes that the Chicago Cubs have not won a single World Series since 1908, or the Red Sox since 1918. Kelly will no doubt go down in history as the greatest Twins manager.

"In 1975, I was just so happy to be in the big leagues that it didn't mean much to me right away," said Kelly. "But after being in the organization for 20-some years, I think it's very special, and I put more credence to it now than I did then. The Minnesota Twins have been good to me and my family. I feel like a part of the organization, maybe not an intricate part, but a piece. I feel like it's more of an honor now. We try to convey that point to the players, that it is an honor to wear the Twins' uniform. We think it's important that they represent the uniform as well as they represent themselves and their families."

On his longevity as Twins manager, T.K. was humble: "It just shows that I have had a lot of good players here over the years, and good players make managers look good. You have to remember that any manager is only as good as his players, and I've been very fortunate. I think it's the result of a good Twins minor league system, good scouting, and good coaching. It's not just one person, and there are a lot of people involved. The game itself can beat you up. All the time I spent playing and managing in the minor leagues with the bus rides, the traveling, and the wear and tear was tough. I am 46 years old, but I am starting to feel the 'longevity' of the game maybe a little more than the average 46-year old -- it's catching up to me. But I am grateful to be where I am, and I do think it is an honor to be the manager of the Minnesota Twins."

Here is what a few of his players had to say about him:

"T.K. will always be my favorite manager," said Kent Hrbek. "He's such a great guy. He was like my mother at the ballpark. He knew how I was feeling when I walked in the door just by looking at me. I just think he is an awesome manager, and I just love the guy."

"I consider Tom to be the most fair manager that I ever played for," said Jack Morris. "He let everybody know that there were no superstars on our team, and I think that the players respected that."

"We go way back," said Kirby Puckett. "I played for T.K. back when I was in the instructional leagues, and we always got along well. All he ever asked of me was that I gave a 100 percent, and I've always listened to whatever he has to say."

"Even before I came here I had the greatest respect for Tom Kelly," said Paul Molitor. "The way that his teams would perform in last-place seasons, or in championship seasons was remarkably consistent, and that definitely relates to the manager's control and leadership. It says a lot about how he can handle teams in this era of players, who maybe don't have the respect that the major league baseball deserves. Coming to the Twins, he surpassed my expectations as a manager in the manner of how he handles teams, rosters, and the ups and downs of a typical season."

the other at first, eventually merged in the center of the diamond in a sea of chaos. The hated Atlanta Braves had been tomahawk-chopped by the Minnesota Twins in one of the greatest World Series' ever.

"By 1991, we knew what to expect, so I think I enjoyed that one a little bit more because I knew what was going on," said Tom Kelly. "I wasn't as nervous this go around as I was in 1987. I frequently use the phrase 'storybook-like' to describe the games that series, because each game was like turning a page in a book to find out what was going to happen. Having the games come down to the ninth inning and the last at-bat was incredible. We were very fortunate to win, because either team could have easily won. What was really rewarding was the fact that we went from last place in 1990 to first place in 1991. It was also very special to me because we proved that smaller market teams could still win it all."

With five games decided by a single run, this series was, in a word, incredible. In front of 55,118 rabid fans at the teflon tent, Morris had pitched a seven-hit, 10-inning, 1-0 shut-out gem. Jack won two pivotal games for his Twins in the World Series, and they were the most important — the first and the last. His performance in Game Seven will go down in baseball lore as possibly the greatest ever. His two wins coupled with an amazing 1.17 ERA, easily earned him the Series MVP.

"Of course, Don Larsen's perfect game was incredible, but with regards to Morris' pitching performance in game seven of the 1991 World Series, I don't think there has ever been a better pitching performance under pressure, ever," said former Twins pitching great Jim Kaat.

"I wasn't really aware of what was going on historically when I was in that game, because my focus was strictly on getting out the Atlanta Braves and making sure that the fans at the stadium and everyone else watching would not go away disappointed," said Morris. "I've only watched the replay of Game Seven a few times because I get kind of choked up. I've recognized and realized that as soon as the game was over that it was probably my best day ever. Nothing else would compare in my career, and I recognize that I could never do any better than that, so I should just take it and appreciate it."

Amazingly, when Jack was asked just what was going through his mind when he took the mound in that 10th inning, it was something all Minnesota sports fans could relate to. Here's what he had to say: "I don't mean this in any derogatory way, but Fran Tarkenton had a big influence in that game. I remember growing up in Minnesota and watching the Vikings lose their third Super Bowl. I know that it is unfair for me to say that Fran was the reason they lost, because obviously it's a team sport. But you know, I think there were so many people that were disappointed in the Vikings, and particularly in Tarkenton, because he was the leader. The quarterback and the pitcher are considered to be the team leaders, and they are the people with the most influence on the outcome of a game. As I sat there, and the game progressed, I just couldn't help but think of the Vikings and those Super Bowl losses. During that seventh game, I looked up in the Metrodome crowd and saw all these people, just exhausted from screaming and cheering, but going absolutely berserk, wanting a winner so bad, and a sort of calmness came over me. It was like something was driving me from that point on, and I just refused to let the fans of Minnesota go home disappointed. I knew that we were going to win, if it took all night long. We weren't going to be losers, we weren't going to be the Vikings."

After the season ended and all the tickertape was cleaned up from the parades, the honeymoon ended abruptly when Morris made an announcement — he was going to sign with Toronto. Although the Jays offered him a lot more money than the Twins did, the fans were upset nevertheless. They were simply crushed to see their hometown hero leave so soon.

In 1992 the Twins made big news even before the season started when Kirby Puckett signed a new, fat contract during a live, made-for-TV extravaganza. There had been Kirby sightings in Boston, New York, and even one in Des Moines. Would he stick around and finish his illustrious career with Minnesota? The suspense was ended on December 4th, when, in a circus-like atmosphere, he inked a five-year, $30-million deal that made him the highest paid player in baseball. (Incidentally, that dubious honor ended just for a

few hours later when Barry Bonds signed his deal with the San Francisco Giants.)

A.J. Pierzynski

That season was, by all accounts, a success. The Twins went 90-72 to finish in second place, but couldn't catch the Oakland A's. They did, however, achieve several record-setting individual and team accomplishments. Among them was Tom Kelly winning his 523rd game, the most of any Twins manager in team history. There was also Kirby Puckett's fabulous year which included reaching 200 hits for the fifth time; knocking in 100+ runs and 100+ RBI's and hitting over .300 for the seventh time in nine seasons. In addition, he also belted out three grand slams en route to twice being named the American League Player of the Month. Other Twins to notch the 100-run plateau included Shane Mack and Chuck Knoblauch, who each had good years as well. Finally, reliever Rick Aguilera got his 109th save to become the Twins' all-time saves leader.

In 1993 Minnesota saw the return of one of its greatest native sons, Dave Winfield. The greatest all-around athlete to ever hail from the Gopher State, "Winnie" came home that year to get the 3,000th hit of his illustrious career. Fresh off his World Series run north of the border in Toronto, Winnie was the lone bright-spot on an otherwise mediocre Twins season. The big day came on September 16th, when the Dave hit No. 3,000 off Oakland's ace closer, Dennis Eckersley, becoming only the 19th player in major league history to achieve that mark.

"It was great," said Winfield. "I was so glad to come home and to have been able to accomplish such a major milestone in front of my home crowd in the Metrodome. That was definitely a special event for me in my career, and it's something that I will always remember."

Winnie's achievement wasn't the only highlight, however, as Kent Hrbek reached 1,000 RBI's, and Brian Harper became just fourth catcher in more than four decades to hit .300 in three consecutive seasons. To top it off, on July 13th, in Baltimore, Kirby Puckett earned All-Star Game MVP honors by hitting a homer and an RBI double in the mid-summer classic. Aggie also pitched well in the bullpen, but Scott Erickson led the Majors in losses, with 19. Overall, Minnesota finished with a 71-91 record, which left them tied for fifth place with the Angels.

The 1994 season was an interesting one to say the least. Several highlights were overshadowed by a big lowlight at the end of the year, when a labor dispute ignited a season-ending strike in mid-August. Among the goodies that year were Scott Erickson's no-hitter in a 6-0 win over the Milwaukee Brewers on April 27th. Kirby Puckett also garnered his 2,000th career hit that year on April 8th vs. Oakland, and then, on June 26th vs. Kansas City, he homered off Mike Magnante to become the team's all-time hits leader with 2,086. In addition, Chuck Knoblauch had an 85-game errorless streak and led the bigs in dou-

Doug Mientkiewicz

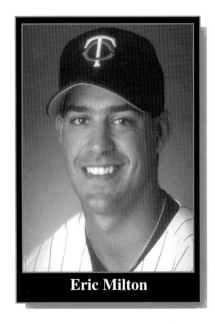

Eric Milton

bles, while Terry Ryan replaced Andy MacPhail as the team's new GM. Now, on the not so good stuff side of things, on August 4th, long-time First Baseman Kent Hrbek announced his retirement after 13 years of outstanding play for the Twins. When it was all said and done, the Twins finished with a 53-60 record, good for just fourth in the new American League Central Division.

Because of the pending strike, the 1995 season did not begin until April 26th. As a result, a modified 144-game schedule was played that year. The new schedule didn't matter much for the Twins, who stunk it up by going 56-88 to finish in dead last, fully 44 games out of first place. It was an overall crappy year. Sure, Right Fielder Marty Cordova, who hit 24 homers, drove in 84 RBI's and stole 20 bases, won the Rookie of the Year award, but other than that there wasn't much to write home about. The front office started to make rumblings about the economic feasibility of the Metrodome, and with that the exodus began. First to go was the teams' all-time saves leader, Rick Aguilera, who was sent to Boston; followed by Scott Erickson, Kevin Tapani and Mark Guthrie, who all followed. Finally, Kirby Puckett, who scored his 1,000th career run, his 1,000th career RBI and his 200th career home run that year, was tragically hit in the face by Cleveland's Dennis Martinez, ultimately ending his season. That next Spring he would later be diagnosed with glaucoma, an incurable eye condition, which would ultimately cause him to retire from the game he so dearly loved. It was the end of an era for Minnesota sports fans as one of the most beloved athletes of all-time had his career cut tragically short. (Puck, who was quickly named as the team's vice president of baseball, would, of course, go on to be inducted into the Baseball Hall of Fame in the Summer of 2001.)

In 1996, while the fans were mourning the retirement of Kirby Puckett, another home-town hero came home — Paul Molitor. A former Cretin High School and Golden Gopher star, Molitor had established himself as one of the game's greatest all-time hitters. Molly led the Twins that year with an outstanding .341 average and also led the league in hits with 225. Then, on September 16th, in a road game against the Kansas City Royals, with Jose Rosado on the mound, Paul made history. With the entire state of Minnesota waiting in anxious anticipation, Molly became the 21st player in major league history to get 3,000 hits. He did it in style too, becoming the first player ever to get it with a triple. In an otherwise ho-hum Twins season, Paul Molitor had made baseball fun again.

"I definitely tried to put it on the very back burner," Said Molitor on the 3,000th hit. "You don't go about assuming that you're going to get 211 hits in a year when you're going to turn 40 years old. When that ball got into the gap and I got to third, it finally sunk in. I found out afterwards that no one had ever hit a triple on their 3,000th hit, and that made it kind of special too, because it adds to the uniqueness of joining what is already a pretty small group of people. It's my most memorable game in

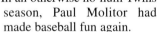

Torii Hunter

baseball and just having it happen to me as a member of the Minnesota Twins was amazing."

The Twins, who hopelessly chased a wild card spot that year, finished with a 78-85 record — good for fourth place in the Central. Leading the charge behind Molly was Second Baseman Chuck Knoblauch, who got an All-Star nod by batting .341 with 13 homers and 72 RBI's. The club also added a few veterans that year to bolster their roster. Among them were Rick Aguilera, who was brought back as a free agent. In addition, Third Baseman Dave Hollins, Center Fielder Roberto Kelly and Catcher Greg Myers all suited up in the Red, White and Blue as well.

That off-season the Twins added another Minnesota native, this time signing New Ulm's Terry Steinbach, who had very quietly become an all-star catcher for the Oakland A's. In addition, they also inked free agent Pitcher Bob Tewksbury. But the real story that off-season was the start of the stadium debate. The Twins presented the public with artist renditions of a new stadium, as well as a model and video showing how a retractable roof would work. Then, team owner Carl Pohlad announced that he would contribute $82.5 million in cash as a contribution to the new outdoor stadium and donate 99% of the team's stock to the state of Minnesota. The "catch" however, was that in reality, Pohlad's "contribution" was really just a loan. The public was now skeptical and as a result, the legislature shot it down. Later that year Major league baseball team owners even voted to allow the Twins to explore moving to another state.

That Fall Pohlad signed a letter of intent to sell the team to North Carolina businessman Don Beaver for $140 million if the legislature didn't approve a stadium. Shortly thereafter a special session of the Minnesota House voted against a proposal that would have financed a ballpark exclusively with taxes and fees on players, fans and broadcast stations. From there Pohlad offered to raise $111 million of a $411 million stadium, meaning that the state would have to fund the rest of the cost. That too, didn't fly. Fans were devastated and convinced the team was leaving. But Beaver's deal in Charlotte fell through and the team was forced to stay put. Perspective buyers were few and far between, but one perspective local ownership group did emerge: Clark Griffith, son of Calvin Griffith, who offered to buy the team for $86 million. No dice Clark.

Now, as far as the 1997 season, here's how it went down: It was a long, frustrating year, complete with nagging injuries and underachieving performances. The result was an ugly 68-94 finish. The biggest highlight of the year was the outstanding performance of Pitcher Brad Radke, who notched 20 wins and finished third in the Cy Young voting. In addition, Radke also put together a remarkable 12-game winning streak in 12 consecutive starts, an accomplishment achieved just twice in the past half-century. Other highlights included the retirement of Kirby Puckett's No. 34 on May 25th, and also the reunion of the 1987 World Series championship team in mid-August.

That off-season the Twins were forced to honor Chuck Knoblauch's demand for a trade. So, on February 6th, they shipped the disgruntled second baseman to the New York Yankees in exchange for pitching prospect Eric Milton, Right Fielder Brian Buchanan and Shortstop Cristian Guzman. Those three would be joined by a host of other promising youngsters that year, including Left Fielder Matt Lawton, First Baseman Doug Mientkiewicz, Third Baseman Corey Koskie, and Center Fielder Torii Hunter. Pretty soon, this cast of kids would be turning heads in the bigs — just like the bunch from 1987 had done. But for now, they would have to take their lumps. And that is exactly what they did that year, posting a 70-92 record. It was the team's sixth consecutive losing season. The other big news of 1998 was the retirement of future Hall of Famer, Paul Molitor. The 21-year veteran played his last game on September 27th at the Metrodome, and fittingly, he singled to right field off Cleveland's Doug Jones in his last at-bat.

Incidentally, that August Carl Pohlad signed a two-year lease with the Metrodome, which included one-year options to stay for the 2001, 2002 and 2003 seasons. Much to the chagrin of the fans and players alike, the stadium debate would linger. In fact, that next year it gained momentum and became nightly news. Here are some of the highlights and lowlights of this unbelievable saga: On June 26th the Minneapolis City Council narrowly voted to approve a resolution in support of exploring plans to build a Twins stadium. Later that month St. Paul Mayor Norm Coleman announced a plan to build a ballpark in St. Paul. Then, in August Governor Ventura set up a "special fund" for citizens to donate their sales-tax rebate checks to in order to fund a new stadium. (About $86,000 was collected, but later returned.) That next month Timberwolves Owner Glen Taylor and Wild Owner Robert Naegele Jr. agree to buy the Twins from Pohlad for $100 million, as long as state officials and voters alike of St. Paul approved a plan to build the ballpark in downtown St. Paul. Less than 60 days later a referendum in St. Paul was shot down soundly by the voters that would have imposed a half-percent city sales tax to fund the city's one-third portion of a proposed $325 million ballpark. The saga would continue.

On the field that year, T.K. and crew decided to just have fun. So, they brought out no less than 17 rookies to see who could cut it with the big boys. The highlight of the year, however, came on September 11th, when Eric Milton tossed a 7-0 no-hitter vs. Anaheim. Milton, who was the big prize from the Knoblauch trade, was now starting to emerge as one of the AL's top young pitchers. In addition, Shortstop Cristian Guzman and First Baseman Doug Mientkiewicz and Third Baseman Corey Koskie were emerging as one of the league's top infields. Add outfielders Torii Hunter and Jacque Jones, and you had the nucleus of a solid ball-club. Sure, they went just 63-97 that season, but they showed that they had a lot of potential.

The 2000 Twins finished with a 69-93 record, good for their fourth straight 90-loss season. While the team was struggling on the field, the fans were struggling off of it by trying to alleviate the stadium issue. Two new groups emerged that off-season to try and mediate the situation. The first was "New Ballpark Inc.," which consisted of a group of business and government leaders who were lobbying for a scaled-back, mostly privately financed stadium in downtown Minneapolis. The other, "Minnesotans for Major League Baseball," which was comprised mostly of prominent business and civil leaders, came together as a panel to suggest ways to keep the Twins in Minnesota.

As far as the 2000 highlights went, Matt Lawton was the big hitter this year, batting .305 and making his first All-Star appearance. In addition, Corey Koskie hit .300, Jacque Jones batted .285, and Cristian Guzman led the Majors with 20 triples. As far as pitching went, Eric Milton and Brad Radke were emerging as a solid one-two punch, while veteran reliever LaTroy Hawkins had found his niche as a closer.

In 2001 the Twins started to put it all together. They finished at 85-77, their first winning season since 1992, and got the attention of all of Major League Baseball. The Twins also drew 1,782,926 fans in 2001, an increase of 732,927 over their 2000 attendance. Minnesota hung around for most of the season at or near the top of the Central Division. At the All-Star break it looked like they were going to runaway with it, but they slid down the stretch to finish in second place behind Cleveland. Leading the way that year were First Baseman Doug Mientkiewicz and Center Fielder Torii Hunter, who single-handedly rejuvenated the enthusiasm at the Dome. Mientkiewicz went on a 15-game hitting streak in April and wound up leading the club in batting, with a .337 average, even winning a Gold Glove award for his stellar play at first base.

Hunter, on the other hand, wound up becoming a regular on ESPN's Baseball Tonight Show, where he was routinely shown as part of their "Web Gems" segment, making diving, circus catches out in center field. Torii led the club in at-bats, home runs and outfield assists, and was second in RBI's, runs, and total bases. He was even rated Best Defensive Outfielder in the American League by Baseball America and went on to win his first Gold Glove Award as well. After the season Manager Tom Kelly, the winningest all-time skipper in Twins history, decided to retire. Fifteen years and 1,140 wins later, the Graceville, Minn., native had had enough. He was replaced with long-time Assistant Coach Ron Gardenhire. "Gardy," much like T.K., was a real players' manager, and had the respect of the players and fans alike.

As far as the off-the-field stadium woes were going, it was only getting worse. That January "Minnesotans for Major League Baseball" released their report recommending that the Twins put up

Jacque Jones

half of the cost for a new ballpark, about $150 million, and that the rest could be funded without new sales, property or income taxes. Then, in March, the Minneapolis City Council voted to accept the "New Ballpark Citizens Committee's" recommendation to support "New Ballpark Inc.'s" plans for a smaller, more intimate open-aired ballpark built primarily with private money. New Ballpark Inc. would later announce that it could raise about $50 million towards the cost of a new stadium but the rest would have to come from a preferred stock offering. Finally, a bill for a $300 million open-air ballpark, which called for Twins owner Carl Pohlad and private sources to contribute $150 million, made its way to the floor of the State legislature. There, however, different versions were thrown around like paper airplanes and the final proposal was bogged down in the final weeks because of the tax and budget impasse that forced a special session.

The grand-daddy of them all came on November 6, 2001, when Major League Baseball owners voted to eliminate two teams before the start of the 2002 season. The teams weren't mentioned by name, but were later revealed to be the Twins and Montreal Expos. The legal events involving efforts to force the Twins to play at the Metrodome for the 2002 season were fast and furious and here's how it went down: On November 16th, Hennepin County District Judge Harry Crump granted a temporary injunction, sought by the Metropolitan Sports Facilities Commission, requiring the Twins, contrary to their owners' objection, to play out their season. A few days later the Twins and Major League Baseball appealed the case and requested that the Minnesota Supreme Court hear of the case. They promptly said no thanks, and instead told the state's Court of Appeals to hear the case as soon as possible. About a month later a three-judge panel heard the arguments and decided to uphold Judge Crump's opinion. Baseball, of course, sought an accelerated appeal to try and get a ruling before opening day. But the Supreme Court declined to hear it and the Twins said "Play Ball!" in 2002.

As the soap opera continued, on June 6th of 2002, the Metropolitan Sports Facilities Commission (MSFC) settled its lawsuit against Major League Baseball and the Minnesota Twins to keep the ball club playing in the Metrodome through the 2003 season. In addition, MLB agreed not to contract or eliminate the team in 2002 or 2003 or relocate the team during that time. Most importantly though, MLB acknowledged that Minnesota has historically has been a strong baseball market and also agreed to work with local participants to build a new ballpark.

Following that announcement the Minnesota House of Representatives and the Minnesota Senate closed the 2002 legislative session with a vote in favor of a new ballpark bill. Governor Ventura then signed the bill into law. Now, what that meant, however, was that the new law would not impose a statewide tax. Instead, funding for the proposed $330 million open-air, roof-ready

Cristian Guzman

TWINS ALL-TIME CAREER BATTING STATS

BATTING AVERAGE

.334	Rod Carew	1967-78
.318	Kirby Puckett	1984-95
.309	Shane Mack	1990-94
.306	Brian Harper	1988-93
.304	Tony Oliva	1962-76
.304	Chuck Knoblauch	1991-97
.286	Larry Hisle	1973-77
.284	Steve Braun	1971-76
.284	Mickey Hatcher	1981-86
.282	Kent Hrbek	1981-94

RUNS

1,871	Kirby Puckett	1984-95
1,847	Harmon Killebrew	1961-74
950	Rod Carew	1967-78
903	Kent Hrbek	1981-94
878	Tony Oliva	1962-76
713	Chuck Knoblauch	1991-97
648	Bob Allison	1961-78
646	Gary Gaetti	1981-98
646	Cesar Tovar	1965-73
564	Zoilo Versalles	1961-67

HITS

2,384	Kirby Puckett	1984-95
2,085	Rod Carew	1967-78
1,917	Tony Oliva	1962-76
1,749	Kent Hrbek	1981-94
1,713	Harmon Killebrew	1961-74
1,276	Gary Gaetti	1981-98
1,197	Chuck Knoblauch	1991-97
1,164	Cesar Tovar	1965-73
1,046	Roy Smalley	1976-82, 85-87
1,046	Zoilo Versalles	1961-67

HOME RUNS

475	Harmon Killebrew	1961-74
293	Kent Hrbek	1981-94
220	Tony Oliva	1962-76
211	Bob Allison	1961-78
207	Kirby Puckett	1984-93
201	Gary Gaetti	1981-98
163	Tom Brunansky	1982-88
118	Roy Smalley	1976-82, 85-87
98	Jimmie Hall	1963-66
96	Randy Bush	1982-93

RBI'S

1,325	Harmon Killebrew	1961-74
1,086	Kent Hrbek	1981-94
1,085	Kirby Puckett	1984-95
947	Tony Oliva	1962-76
758	Gary Gaetti	1981-98
733	Rod Carew	1967-78
642	Bob Allison	1961-78
485	Roy Smalley	1976-82, 85-87
469	Tom Brunansky	1982-88
409	Larry Hisle	1973-77

stadium would have to come from other sources which might include: the Twins or other private sources paying $120 million in cash; having the state sell $330 million in revenue bonds and then lending the money back to the host city; or even having the state invest the $120 million from the Twins or other private sources into a gift fund which would in turn generate interest income (over 30 years) that would help repay the $330 million in bond principal. It was also declared that the ballpark's host city would be allowed to raise local food, liquor and hotel taxes up to 5%, subject to a voter referendum.

Translation: There was still a lot of work to be done before Minnesota was going to get a new stadium. The bottom line was that the Twins, Vikings and Gophers all needed a new facility. While the Metrodome, which was just 20 years old at the time, was still a modern facility, it lacked the necessary amenities and profit centers that would allow the clubs to remain competitive financially against their respective competition. The new stadium would need more luxury suites, more concessions, more parking, and more opportunities for corporate sponsorship. And, as far as the baseball fans were concerned, they just wanted to be outside in the Minnesota summers. There was a reason that the cross-town minor-league St. Paul Saints were selling out all of their games at Midway Stadium — they were outside!

Midway through the 2002 season, however, a big monkey wrench was thrown into the stadium saga when Hennepin County was shut out of the process from participating in helping to finance a new stadium. (The legislature stipulated that two communities couldn't combine their efforts.) It all came back to sibling rivalry. You see, the two bickering sisters of Minneapolis and St. Paul, who have fought over the Lakers, North Stars, Vikings, Twins, Timberwolves and Wild, were once again cannibalizing each others chances for getting this thing done. Proposals were flying everywhere and politicians were messing the whole process up but good. With Hennepin County out of the mix the City of Minneapolis was left to try and get the proposal done. They had a great site, behind the Target Center in downtown Minneapolis, but were limited by how much money they could donate and how much taxing could be done for the project.

St. Paul, meanwhile, had several sites of its own, and lobbied hard to get the deal done across the river. But when the Twins balked and decided not to give them an exclusive deal to try and raise the money via a voter referendum in July of that year, the Pig's Eye city said no thanks to the Twins.

The reality in all of this is that baseball's economic situation was way out of whack. And as a result, the "powers that be" in Minnesota were demanding that they make serious economic changes, including implementing a workable revenue sharing system, before they were going to sign off on a new ballpark. Plus, the politicians also wanted MLB to approve a 30-year guarantee that there would be a Major League franchise in Minnesota. The politicians were close to pulling the trigger on this deal, but wanted a few more assurances that they weren't going to be left holding the bag if MLB opted to contract more teams.

In sum, more than 50 new stadiums, arenas and ball-parks have been built over the past decade in America, giving those cities a pedigree "big-league" status. They also provide a great environment for big companies to come to those cities and also produce an unquantifiable sense of community pride which is a wonderfully healthy and positive quality of life benefit. The difference today, however, is that the political landscape and local business community has changed. Back when the Dome was being lobbied, key business leaders stepped up and got stuff done. That corporate culture is no longer in the Twin Cities though as many of the major employers who were locally owned and able to make local decisions back then, are now headquartered elsewhere and run by big, bureaucratic conglomerates.

The bottom, bottom line is this. The Dome is outdated and needs to be replaced. The Vikings and the Gophers will ideally wind up back on campus, under an open-air retractable roofed outdoor stadium — where football was meant to be played. Then, hopefully the Twins will get a small, intimate outdoor stadium of their own. Whether it's in St. Paul or Minneapolis, no one cares. They just want them to stay put and have them around for their kids' kids to see for generations to come. That is what it is all about. Hey, it's like Hubert

BERT BLYLEVEN

One of the most beloved Twins of all-time is Pitcher Bert Blyleven. Blyleven, who pitched in the major leagues for 23 seasons, including 11 with the Twins, retired in 1992. The right-hander from Holland first joined the Twins at just 19 years of age back in 1970 and went 10-9 with a 3.18 ERA that year, earning A.L. Rookie Pitcher of the Year honors along the way. He quickly became the rock of the Twins rotation, consistently leading the club in wins, strike-outs and innings pitched.

He would ultimately have two separate stints with the Twins, also playing with Texas, Pittsburgh, Cleveland and California as well. One of the highlights of his career came in 1977 when as a member of the Texas Rangers, Bert tossed a no-hitter by California, 6-0, at Anaheim Stadium.

On baseball's all-time list, Blyleven ranks fourth in strikeouts (3,701), eighth in games started (685), ninth in shutouts (60), 13th in innings (4,970), and 23rd in wins (287). He posted double figure wins in 17 different seasons and in 1989 was voted Al.. Comeback Player of the Year. He also pitched in two All-Sear Games, three Championship series and two World Series — with the Pirates and later the Twins, where he finally got his ring. With stats like that, the next stop for this guy has got to be Cooperstown, and the Hall of Fame.

Bert finally hung up his cleats at the age of 42 and later became the color commentator for Twins television broadcasts. There, the "Dutchmen" has become quite the "czar of the telestrator" alongside his partner in crime, play-by-play man extraordinaire, Dick Bremer. Now, fans from across the Midwest are coming to the Dome in droves, sporting homemade signs reading: "Circle Me Bert!", in hopes that he will "circle" them on the TV monitor for all to see.

H. Humphrey once said: "Without professional sports, the Twin Cities would be just a cold Omaha."

With all of that behind them, the Twins somehow put on their game-faces and played baseball in 2002. It wasn't easy, but nearly every fan of the game from coast-to-coast was rooting for them. If ever their was a David vs. Goliath case, this was it. And do you know what? The Twins responded big-time, by busting loose all over the American League.

Inspired, the team hit the field to do battle with the odds of the world against them. They hung in there though. Among the early highlights the 2002 season was a 6-5, 15 inning thriller on June 10th, which saw Minnesota face Atlanta for the first time some 11 years after one of the greatest World Series ever. So tough was this bunch of kids that by July 24th, the Twins had built up a 14-game lead in the Central. They had just won nine of ten series, including a series sweep of rival Cleveland, and were poised to go the distance. And, they were doing it all short-handed as well, as Radke and Mays were both injured through much of the first half. Pitchers Kyle Lohse and Johan Santana stepped it up big-time, as did middle reliever and J.C. Romero. The club also made a mid-season transaction, sending club-house favorite Brian Buchanon to San Diego, in order to make room for rookie Right Fielder Michael Cuddyer, who had been tearing it up in Class AAA. Minnesota even had three All-Stars that year as well, with Center Fielder Torii Hunter, Catcher A.J. Pierzynski and Closer Eddie Guardado, who led the league in saves through the break.

The season was shaping up nicely for the Twins. Midway through the month of August the team had a magic number of just 16 and Cristian Guzman was even sporting a 23-game hitting streak as well. But everything nearly came to a screeching halt shortly thereafter when the players threatened yet another strike. The contract between the owners and the players union was set to expire at the end of the regular season and the players figured the only leverage they would have was right then. So, they threatened to walk off the field by the end of August unless they were able to reach a compromise.

The timing couldn't have been worse. With the nation fighting the war against terrorism and the specter of September 11th just around the corner — not to mention the sad state of the nation's economy, it was a real mess. The Twins: survivors of a move to North Carolina, the threat of contraction, and now a self-inflicted work-stoppage. What could possibly be next, locusts?

With that, the two sides got together for several weeks of marathon negotiations. Nobody wanted a repeat of the last strike in 1994, a 232-day work stoppage that forced cancellation of the World Series. So, on the morning of the deadline, and with just hours to spare, baseball averted a strike when negotiators pulled off a miracle by agreeing to a tentative labor contract. Amazingly, it was the first time since 1970 that players and owners accepted a new collective

bargaining agreement without a work stoppage. While Commissioner Bud Selig called the deal "historic," Players Union Leader Donald Fehr said: "All streaks come to an end, and this was one that was overdue."

With the deal the players' association had lifted the minimum salary from $200,000 to $300,000, and the average salary of its members to $2.38 million per season. The union also received a guarantee that the owners wouldn't eliminate any teams through the 2006 season. And for the first time, players agreed to mandatory, random testing for steroids. The deal also penalized teams for big spending on player salaries and gave poorer teams a bigger share of the wealth.

As part of the agreement, all teams would have to share 34 percent of their locally generated money, up from 20 percent. That money would then be divided equally among the 30 franchises with the intent of leveling the playing field. Also, a luxury tax was levied on high-payroll teams to try to limit the escalating player salaries. (Teams will now pay a tax varying from 17.5 percent to 40 percent of total player salaries above $117 million in 2003, $120.5 million in 2004, $128 million in 2005 and $136.5 million in 2006.) The bottom line here was that small market teams like the Twins now finally had a chance, and the big market pigs like the Yankees, whose $242 million revenue in 2002 was $40 million higher than any other club, could no longer "buy" themselves a World Series.

With the strike averted, the Twins went back to business with a renewed sense of vigor. By September 6th their magic number was at just 8, with the White Sox slowly falling out of the picture. That night the vaunted Homer Hanky made its triumphant return to the Metrodome as the Oakland A's, winners of a record 20 straight games, came to town to do battle. Brad Radke was masterful in this one though, throwing a five-hit, 6-0 shut-out to snap the A's streak cold. It was Radke's 100th career win and it couldn't have come at a better time.

Then, on September 15, the Twins, targeted for contraction the previous November, clinched the AL Central with a 5-0 win over the defending champion Cleveland Indians.

"Bud Selig couldn't

Joe Mays

get rid of us," said Jacque Jones during the team's wild champagne celebration in the clubhouse. "The White Sox couldn't get rid of us. The Cleveland Indians couldn't get rid of us. Here we are, and we're staying."

With the post-season in the bag the team cruised during the last two weeks. A couple of highlights did occur in that stretch though, including the one on September 18th, when Closer Eddie Guardado made history by earning his 43rd save of the season — surpassing both Jeff Reardon and Rick Aguilera to become the team's all-time single-season saves leader.

As the regular season winded down, the team was playing inspired baseball. Each night a new hero would seemingly emerge to lift the team to victory. Take September 25th for instance. That was when David Ortiz slammed a 12th inning game-winning homer off Cleveland Pitcher David Maurer (an Apple Valley High School alumni) to win the game 7-5. Then, on September 30th Bobby Kielty came off the bench to hit a two-run homer in the eighth to get the game-winning hit against the White Sox. It was Kielty's second consecutive game-winning hit in as many nights.

With that, the Twins regular season was in the books at 94-67. Both Jacque Jones and A.J. Pierzynski led the team by hitting .300, while Jones also led the club in hits, with 173 and runs, with 96. Jones also hit 27 homers and added 85 RBIs as well. Torii Hunter, who finished the year with a .289 average, led the team in home runs (29), RBIs (94) and stolen bases (23). In addition, Cristian Guzman again led the club with triples, with five, while hitting .273 to boot. A trio of Twins had 37 doubles: Jones, Hunter and Corey Koskie, who also hit .267 for the year. Doug Mientkiewicz had 122 hits and finished with a .261 average, while David Ortiz added 20 homers, 75 RBIs and wound up with a gaudy .500 slugging percentage.

As far as pitching went, Rick Reed came on strong and led the team with a 15-7 record and a 3.78 ERA. Eric Milton and Kyle Lohse each had 13 wins, while Brad Radke and Joe Mays, who were injured for much of the year, finished with 9 and 4 wins, respectively. In addition, Tony Fiore, J.C. Romero and Johan Santana added 10, 9 and 8 wins, respectively, out of the bullpen. And, while LaTroy Hawkins rebounded to go 5-0 in relief, the big story of this pitching staff was that of "Everyday Eddie" Guardado, who set a team record with 45 saves.

The next stop was Oakland, and the mighty A's in the

American League Divisional Series. And for a brief moment, before all the of the post-season hoopla that was about to besiege them, the team reflected.

From Doug Mientkiewicz's lucky rally spot in the dugout (where he sits on the ground and magically wills his team to victory), to Torii Hunter's thrilling home-run robbing circus catch of Barry Bonds shot to center field at the All-Star game, this team had seen it all. Contraction, strikes, moves, new stadiums — this bunch was like Rasputin — they just wouldn't die.

Perhaps it was when Torii Hunter got intentionally beaned in the ribs late in the season in a game against Cleveland. Instead of charging the mound, Hunter picked up the ball and rifled it back at the pitcher — sending a collective message to teams everywhere that these Twins were not about to lay down and be intimidated by anyone. These guys were for real and wanted to let the fans know how much they meant to them during this wild roller-coaster ride of a season.

"We went through a lot this past winter," said Pitcher Brad Radke. "But it all worked itself out. I mean most of the guys didn't know if they were going to even play this year or not. So, to come through all of that is amazing. Now, to have gone through all of the contraction, strike and stadium issues, to be in the post-season is great. Everybody feels good about the situation that we are in now and that is just good for this organization. We feel that this core group of players has an unlimited potential and that this can just be the starting point for years to come. Now, as far as the fans go, they have been the biggest part of this whole thing and they have gone through a lot more than we ever did. The fans stuck with us, came out to the park and supported us. So, as players, we want to thank them and let them know how much we appreciate what they have done for us."

"We have gone through a lot throughout these last few seasons and this past year was an interesting one to say the least," said Pitcher Joe Mays. "We knew that if they (management) kept us together that we were going to doing some great things this year, and we did. It was just a matter of us going out there and playing the game like we have been taught and the way we know how. We had a lot of injuries this year, and it has been tough, but we still hung in there and made it to the post-season. These guys never give up and that is why I love playing with them. I mean it doesn't matter if we were down by five or up by five, these guys continued to play the game hard from the start to the finish. And that is what this game is all about. And, as far as the fans go, they have been awesome for us this year. They have come out through thick and thin to support us and that has been just tremendous. They bring a lot of enthusiasm and a lot of energy, which makes it a lot easier for us to play the game. I mean for me, pitching just once every five days, the other four days I am a fan just like them. So I can see how great it is to watch this team. It has been a great season and one I will remember for a long, long time."

"As a group we have waited seven or eight years for this," said First Baseman Doug Mientkiewicz, "so it is great to finally get to the playoffs. It is also very rewarding to see the fans of Minnesota get to enjoy this too. They have been there for us the entire way and deserve this as much as we do."

"This season has just been an incredible ride," said Catcher A.J. Pierzynski. "Not only did we have the whole contraction mess but then the strike too made it an unbelievable roller coaster ride for everybody. A lot of people never gave us a chance to do anything this year but we believed in ourselves. This group of 25 guys in this clubhouse is very tight though and we were there for each other throughout the entire season. We believed in ourselves and were rewarded with something very special. It is an amazing feeling. And you can't say enough about our fans. They have stuck with us through all of this and we can't thank them enough for their support. It was a long winter up here and it was an even longer process for this team to make it to where it is now but it was definitely worth the wait. Let's just

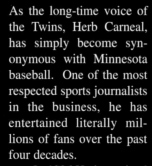

hope more good things can happen for this team, like a new stadium, and I am sure good things will just continue to grow from there."

"For me winning the division means a lot," said Second Baseman Luis Rivas. "I have been here for a while now and we have played hard for a lot of years to get to this point. So to have this finally happen is very special to all of us."

"We are really thankful to our fans who stuck around through contraction, through the strike talks and through all of this stadium stuff," said Center Fielder Torii Hunter. "It has been a lot to deal with but they have been there with us the whole way. I am very appreciative to them and I hope that they keep coming out to support us for a long time. If they keep coming we will try to keep winning and hopefully they will have some fun baseball to watch. This season has had it all. We have struggled to get to where we are right now and had to get there through contraction and a new labor agreement that almost cost us a first place finish. When we clinched the Central it was just a huge relief and it has been great to celebrate with my teammates on just what this season means to all of us. To make it to the playoffs after all that is very rewarding and I am just glad to be a part of this team. After all that bad stuff, something really good came out of it and that is pretty special to all of us."

"I would also really like to thank the fans for supporting us this season," said Third Baseman Corey Koskie. "I mean to play in front of 40,000 fans is so exciting and we just can't thank them enough for sticking with us this season."

"This has been such a special season for us," said Manager Ron Gardenhire. "Of course last year we came close, and this year we were able to get it done. It has been tough though. But winning our division title and getting into the playoffs was a very special thing. We felt like we did something pretty special for a lot of people and that means an awful lot to us. Our fans have been through so much but have hung in there for us and we appreciate it. These fans are very knowledgeable too. They have seen some great baseball years from the Harmon Killebrews to the Tony Olivas and from the Kent Hrbeks to the Kirby Pucketts. So for our fans to have gone through all that they have gone through over the past few seasons, we dedicate this Central Division title to them. It is a very special achievement for us and something that we will never forget."

"After being on the 1970 and 1987 post-season teams, and seeing what all they went through, it is amazing to see what this 2002 club has done," said former Twins Pitcher and current broadcaster Bert Blyleven. "I think to get the big picture you really have to go all the way back to 1995, when these kids started to come up through the organization and start to develop in to outstanding big-leaguers. I am just so happy for all these young kids and wish them nothing but the best, they really deserve it. It is just so refreshing to see how this club was put together. I mean most of them came up through the team's minor league system and that is so nice to see. And you could see that most of the country was rooting for these guys as they went into the post-season, considering everything they had gone through up until that point."

"It's a real compliment to these players for all of their hard work over the past few years to make it to the playoffs," said former Twins Left Fielder and current team broadcaster Dan Gladden. "It really says a lot about the dedication of these players and of the coaching staff."

"A lot of hard work has come to fruition in the sense that we had to redo everything under the guidance of GM Terry Ryan," said former Twin and current Third Base Coach Al Newman. "Terry took a lot of heat for a team that finished in last place for a lot of years. So it has been a long rebuilding process, but a rewarding one nonetheless. I am so happy for Terry Ryan now because he took more heat than anybody and a lot of people were calling for his hat. He stuck with it though and through his leadership we built from within. So this championship is one for the entire organization. We all did it and are very proud of each other from the top down."

"I just can't say enough about this group of guys, this has been an amazing story," added former Twin and current team Vice President Kirby Puckett. "They got a little taste of success last year and now they put it all together for this season. It is a great story. People were saying that they were a fluke in 2001 and stuff like that

so for them to come out and win the Central Division is a huge achievement. I am really proud of these guys. They started out in Spring Training working hard and now it has all paid off, I am just so happy for them. For the first time in 12 years there was playoff baseball in Minnesota and that is great. I am just so glad that they were able to avoid a strike and let this season be played out. It was destiny after that!"

It is also very important to note that much of the credit for the success of this ballclub was due to good drafting and development. With one of the smallest payrolls in the American League, the Twins showed the world that they were indeed for real. Their farm system, under the

Catcher Joe Mauer, from Cretin High School, was the Twin's No. 1 overall pick of the 2001 Draft. As the National Player of the Year in Football, Mauer even turned down a scholarship to play at Florida State University.

tutelage of Jim Rantz, the Twins' director of minor league operations, was paying big dividends. Fully 23 of the 30 players on the teams' active roster had played just for the Twins in their careers. Translation: this program was developing solid talent and keeping them at home.

Rising stars such as First Baseman Doug Mientkiewicz, Catcher A.J. Pierzynski, Third Baseman Corey Koskie, Second Baseman Luis Rivas, and outfielders Jacque Jones and Torii Hunter all came up from down on the farm. Add to that the draftees of Michael Cuddyer, Denny Hocking, and Matthew LeCroy, as well as pitchers Brad Radke, Eddie Guardado, LaTroy Hawkins and J.C. Romero, and one could see that the scouting reports were right on the money. In addition, they had brought in some inexpensive key free agents that year who were panning out big-time. Among them were Catcher Tom Prince and outfielders Bobby Kielty and Dustan Mohr, who all made big contributions in 2002. On top of all that, GM Terry Ryan had made some good trades over the past few years in acquiring Shortstop Cristian Guzman and DH David Ortiz as well as pitchers Eric Milton, Joe Mays, Kyle Lohse and Rick Reed. (Both David Ortiz and Joe Mays were discovered while playing A-Ball in Wisconsin, and then came to Minnesota via trades with Seattle — Ortiz for Dave Hollins and Mays for Roberto Kelly.)

With that, the Twins 2002 post-season got underway in Oakland as Game One of the ALDS pitted Brad Radke against Tim Hudson. The young Twins opened this one by making three errors and allowing four unearned runs in the first two innings. Ouch! Especially when you consider the fact that the Twins were the best defensive team in the majors that season, making just 74 errors. But Minnesota rallied back. Corey Koskie hit a two-run homer in the third, and Mientkiewicz added a solo homer of his own in the sixth. Jacque Jones' then smacked a game-tying RBI double, only to see Koskie's bases-loaded grounder drive in the go-ahead run. Pierzynski then added his fourth hit of the game, a run-scoring triple in the seventh against Cory Lidle, to seal the deal. Starting pitcher Brad Radke hung in there and Eddie Guardado came in to cap four innings of scoreless relief from Johan Santana and J.C. Romero to get the save.

Joe Mays got the nod in Game Two against Oakland's Mark Mulder — one of the best pitchers in the league. This one was a blow-out as Oakland jumped out to a 3-0 first-inning lead on a three-run dinger by Eric Chavez and stretched the margin to 8-0 by the end of the fourth inning. Cristian Guzman led off the

Corey Koskie

sixth with a homer, but it was too little too late. Oakland went on to take the game by the final of 9-1 as the series now shifted back to Minnesota. The Twins were feeling good about their chances after leaving the Bay Area with the series tied at one game apiece though.

After an 11 year absence Game Three saw the return of post-season baseball to the Dome. The record crowd of 55,932 Homer Hanky-waving fans were hushed early in this one though as the opening play of the game saw All-Star Center Fielder Torii Hunter dive and misjudge a Ray Durham liner that ultimately turned into an inside-the-park-home run. First Baseman Scott Hatteberg then followed with a homer to right off Starting Pitcher Rick Reed to make it 2-0, marking the first time in post-season history that a game started with back-to-back homers.

This was a wild one all right, that seemingly had it all. The Dome was being bashed by the media, which had now nicknamed her as the "bag-lady." Well, the "domefield" advantage was working early on as Scott Hatteberg overran a foul pop-up by 20 feet because he couldn't see it, and Second baseman Mark Ellis later butchered a pop-up for an error in the second. It didn't matter though. The Twins didn't have their bats working and they were swinging at poor pitches all night. Oakland's Terrence Long homered in the fourth to make it 3-0, only to see Minnesota rally.

A bloop single by A.J. Pierzynski in the fourth scored Torii Hunter to make it 3-1. Corey Koskie followed with a triple and an RBI single by Hunter in the fifth tied the game at 3-3 to bring the noisy crowd to their feet. But Oakland lefthander Barry Zito, who struck out eight Twins, hung in there and kept his team in it. Then, in the top of the sixth, Jermaine Dye hit what would prove to be the fourth homer off of Reed and put it out of reach. The A's went on to win it 6-3, and took a 2-1 lead in the best-of-five series.

Minnesota roughed up Oakland Pitcher Tim Hudson for seven runs in the fourth inning, and Eric Milton shut down the Athletics as the Twins forced a decisive fifth game in the ALDS with an impressive 11-2 victory in Game Four. MVP candidate Miguel Tejada gave Oakland an early lead with a two-run homer, but that was all the offense the A's could muster on this day.

Doug Mientkiewicz, who went 3-for-4 with a two-run homer for the Twins, started a fourth-inning rally with a single while A.J. Pierzynski reached on a one-out walk. Then the A's came completely unraveled as the record crowd of 55,960 went nuts. All in all there would be a pair of wild pitches, a hit batter, two errors, four hits and seven unearned runs in one of the wildest innings in playoff history. Tejada threw Luis Rivas' grounder over the third baseman's head, allowing Mientkiewicz to score and give the Twins a 3-2 lead. Pierzynski then slid home on a wild pitch by Hudson only to see Jacque Jones get beaned. A's First Baseman Scott Hatteberg later fielded Cristian Guzman's grounder and threw it wildly to Catcher Ramon Hernandez, which

Ron Gardenhire

allowed Rivas to score and make it 5-2. Corey Koskie got his fifth RBI of the series with a single that scored Jones, and then Guzman scored on a wild pitch by Ted Lilly. Torii Hunter then smacked a double to center and was later driven in by Mientkiewicz. Mientkiewicz also added a two-run homer in the seventh to make it 11-2 as the Twins cruised into Game Five back in Oakland.

Gave Five was historic as Brad Radke pitched seven outstanding innings to beat Oakland, 5-4, for the second time in the ALDS. This one was a real nail-biter right down to the final out. The Twins played aggressive baseball in this one, as evidenced by Cristian Guzman, who was thrown out at third base when he tried to stretch a double into a triple in the first inning. Minnesota got on the board in the second inning when Second Baseman Denny Hocking singled home Matthew LeCroy off of 19-game winner Mark Mulder. Jacque Jones then struck out with the bases loaded to kill the rally, but the Twins added another run in the third when Guzman doubled and then scored on LeCroy's single.

Oakland's Ray Durham hit a solo homer in the third to keep it close, but he was the only A's player to get to second base against Radke. Reliever J.C. Romero came in for the Twins in the seventh and got Terrence Long to ground out to end the inning. Gardy then put in LaTroy Hawkins in the eighth, and he answered by dramatically striking out Miguel Tejada to end the inning and preserve the team's one run lead.

The ninth was a wild one as All-Star Catcher A.J. Pierzynski hit a two-run homer against Billy Koch to finally give Minnesota some breathing room. David Ortiz then added an RBI double for insurance to make it 5-1. Now, just three outs away, "Everyday Eddie" Guardado came in to finish it up. With a four run cushion it was going to be easy, right? Wrong! Eddie got rocked big-time, as Mark Ellis' three-run homer with one out in the ninth inning brought the A's to within one run of tying. Then, Pinch Hitter Randy Velarde singled with two outs to bring the winning run to the plate — Ray Durham. So, with the collective hearts of nearly every Minnesotan hanging in the balance, Eddie came up huge and got Durham to pop up to second baseman Denny Hocking and end the game. It was Oakland's third straight Game Five ALDS loss in as many years. With that, the "Contraction Kids" were headed to the American League Championship Series. The Twins went nuts and piled on each other at the pitcher's mound. They would continue their party in the clubhouse, where they all took champaigne showers and celebrated.

Next up for the Twins were the wild card winning Anaheim Angels, who had beaten the mighty New York Yankees in the NLDS. In the process they had now given Minnesota the home-field advantage for the ALCS, which opened at the Dome.

Joe Mays was the difference in Game One of this improbable AL championship series as he picked apart the Angels bats for eight strong innings and hung on for a 2-1 win. The drama was everywhere in this one, especially due to the fact that the commissioner himself, Bud Selig, was there live and in-person. The very man who had tried with all of his might to eliminate this team was now back — giving the Twins even more reason to win it all.

Inspired, the Twins went ahead in the second in this one when Torii Hunter doubled, advanced on a wild pitch and then came home on A.J. Pierzynski's sacrifice fly. Anaheim tied it in the third on singles by Adam Kennedy and David Eckstein, followed by an error on Cristian Guzman, who booted a Darin Erstad grounder. After Luis Rivas walked and Guzman singled in the fifth, Koskie then drove in the go-ahead run with a hard double which landed just inside the right-field line. Guardado then came in for the ninth and got the big save as the 55,562 screaming, Homer Hanky-waving fans in the Metrodome went nuts.

Mays, who allowed just four hits, no walks and one unearned run, called it "the game of my career" and described the atmosphere as simply "overwhelming."

Rick Reed took the mound for the Twins in Game Two against Ramon Ortiz and this one got ugly early. Darin Erstad got the Angels on the board first with a first inning homer to quiet the Metrodome fans. Anaheim then added three more runs in the second, two of them unearned because of a costly error by A.J. Pierzynski — who couldn't hang on to a throw home after Reed had caught a runner off of first base. Then, in the sixth, Brad Fullmer homered off of Reed to make it 6-0 and seemingly out of reach. But the Twins rallied and knocked Pitcher Ramon Ortiz out in the sixth when Corey Koskie hit an RBI single followed by Doug Mientkiewicz's two-run single of his own to make it 6-3.

Now, in the eighth, a two-out walk to Torii Hunter and a single by Mientkiewicz put runners at the corners. That's when Angels Manager Mike Scioscia pulled his 20-year-old rookie Reliever Francisco Rodriguez and put in his horse, Troy Percival, a gunslinging fire-baller who had simply dominated the Twins through the years. Percival's first victim was Bobby Kielty, who represented the tying run at the plate. He got ahead 1-2 in the count and then Kielty took a called third strike over the inside corner to kill the rally. Percival then mopped up with a perfect ninth for the save. Game over.

Eric Milton, who no-hit the Angels in September of 1999, got the nod against Jarrod Washburn in Game Three back in Anaheim. There, the Angels won a heart-breaker, 2-1, despite some solid pitching from both sides. Milton pitched well but gave up a solo homer to Anaheim's Garret Anderson in the second inning to fall behind early. The Twins answered in the seventh, however, to tie it on to Jacque Jones' double which scored Dustan Mohr — who led off with a single. J.C. Romero then served one up to Troy Glaus, who knocked it out of the park in the eighth-inning to give the Angels a 2-1 lead. The Rally Monkeys were out in full force following the big hit and the Twins couldn't recover. Washburn, a Wisconsin native who grew up worshipping the Twins, was masterful and pitched outstanding baseball in this one. The Twins came out swinging in the ninth against Closer Troy Percival, but the 100 mph fire-baller needed all of four pitches to retire the side and earn the save. The Angels were now up two games to one and the momentum had clearly shifted.

Game Four was closer than the score revealed, but painful for Twins fans nonetheless. The two teams were deadlocked in a scoreless pitching duel through six innings when Radke got into some trouble. Radke retired the first nine hitters he faced and came into the seventh having given up just two hits. That's when Darin Erstad led off the inning with a single, stole second and reached third on A.J. Pierzynski's throwing error. After Tim Salmon walked, Troy Glaus drove a single to center which scored Erstad to make it 1-0. Radke then struck out Brad Fullmer, only to see Scott Spiezio bloop a double to score pinch runner Alex Ochoa and make it 2-0. The Angels would add five more runs in the seventh and eighth innings to ice it.

The Twins did have a few scoring chances in this one, particularly in the third when they got two hits, but failed to capitalize. Pitcher John Lackey, a 23-year-old rookie who joined the team midway through the year, wound up striking out seven and pitching a gem. Minnie did manage a meaningless run in the ninth but it was too little too late as they wound up on the wrong end of a 7-1 ballgame.

Game One winner Joe Mays now faced Kevin Appier in Game Five with nothing to lose. With their backs against the wall, the Twins came out swinging in this one and went up 1-0 in the first when David Ortiz smacked a two-out double off the wall to score Corey Koskie (who had walked) from second. The Twins added another in the second when Right Fielder Dustan Mohr doubled and then scored on A.J. Pierzynski's single. The Angels cut the lead in half in the third when Adam Kennedy hit a solo homer to lead off the inning and make it 2-1. The bottom of the fifth was a disaster for Mays though as Scott Spiezio led off the inning with a solo homer and was immediately followed by Adam Kennedy, who hit his second long-ball of the afternoon to give his halos a 3-2 lead.

The 2002 Central Division Champs!

Jacque Jones then led off the sixth with an infield single and reached third on a fielders choice, followed by a past ball. But by now the Angels had taken out Appier and put in the bespectacled wonder, Brendan Donnelly, who threw nothing but heat. So, with two outs and a full count, Ortiz went down swinging — leaving Jones stranded at third.

By the seventh the Twins were getting desperate, but they hung in there and made a little magic. It all started on Doug Mientkiewicz's lead-off single, followed by a single from Dustan Mohr, followed by yet another one-bagger from A.J. Pierzynski, which loaded the bases. Bobby Kielty then came in to pinch-hit for Luis Rivas, and Bobby was able to draw a walk off of Reliever Francisco Rodriguez. The young fire-baller then served up a wild pitch to Jacque Jones which scored Mohr. Jones then hit a sacrifice fly to center which scored Pierzynski to give the Twins a 5-3 lead. As A.J. slid hard into the catcher he gave the safe sign for all to see. The Twins were back in business.

The lead didn't last long though, as Twins Reliever Johan Santana came in and started what would turn out to be one of the most painful innings in franchise history. He first served up a single to Bengie Molina and yet another to Spiezio, followed by Adam Kennedy's amazing third homer of the game to give the Angels a 6-5 lead. (This guy hit just seven homers all year!) The rally monkeys and inflatable thunder bats at Edison Field exploded and the Twins were sent back to earth in a hurry. But wait, it gets worse. After a single by Erstad, Reliever LaTroy Hawkins then came in with no outs and gave up singles to both David Eckstein and Tim Salmon to load the bases. Enter the third Minnesota reliever of the inning: J. C. Romero. Well, Romero picked up where the others left off by walking Garret Anderson to make it 7-5. After striking out Troy Glaus to get the first out, Romero then gave up yet another single to Ochoa to bring in another run and make the tally 8-5. Tack on a wild pitch and it was now 9-5. Then, believe it or not, Shawn Wooten drilled a single to center to drive in two more runs and make it 11-5. It was painful to even watch at that point. Gardy then came out and yanked Romero and put in the fourth reliever of the inning, Bob Wells. Wells responded by giving up a first pitch single to Chone Figgins, followed by an Adam Kennedy single. (Hey, at least it wasn't another Kennedy home run...) Wells then plunked Eckstein to bring in another run and make it 12-5. The fans of Minnesota were now witnessing a meltdown of monumental proportions. Erstad then hit a fielders-choice to bring in one more to make it 13-5. Alex Ochoa then struck out to finally end the bleeding. It was a 10-hit, 10-run disaster that would ultimately cost this team a chance to get back to the World Series.

Torii Hunter's double play ended the eighth inning while Kyle Lohse came in to mop up. Fittingly, Angels Closer Troy Percival came in to put the final nail in the coffin in the ninth. Percival, who had a lifetime ERA of 0.00 against the Twins, wasted little time in taking care of business so his boys could get back to the clubhouse to start popping the bubbly. It was an ugly end to an otherwise brilliant season for our beloved Minnesota Twins.

Well, there you have it. Our 2002 Twins sure made us proud. From contractions to stadiums to strikes, these guys somehow aspired to truly become America's Team. As fans we have seen it all over the past four decades and are poised for greatness in the upcoming years as well. That is, of course, if the organization chooses to keep this core group of kids together. Let's hope so. Let's also hope that the next 40 years of Twins baseball can be as entertaining and exciting as the last. (Oh yeah, let's root-root-root for a new stadium too!)

A Cinderella Story...

MINNESOTANS IN THE MAJORS

HOME-TOWN	NAME	MAJOR LEAGUE DEBUT	HOME-TOWN	NAME	MAJOR LEAGUE DEBUT
Albert Lea	Mike Dimmel	1977	New Ulm	Brad Gulden	1978
Appleton	Jerry Koosman	1967	New Ulm	Doc Hammann	1922
Austin	Bill Burdick	1888	New Ulm	Brian Raabe	1995
Beaulieu	Charlie Roy	1901	New Ulm	Terry Steinbach	1986
Bemidji	Bryan Hickerson	1990	Nimrod	Dick Stigman	1960
Brainerd	Bullet Joe Bush	1912	North Branch	Lee Quillen	1906
Brainerd	Todd Revenig	1992	Olivia	Blix Donnelly	1944
Browerville	Lew Drill	1902	Pelican Rapids	Dave Goltz	1972
Brown Co	Burt Hart	1901	Pine City	Rube Walberg	1923
Clearbrook	Wes Westrum	1947	Prosper	Bryan Houck	1912
Cloquet	Chief Chouneau	1910	Rochester	Michael Restovich	2002
Cottage Grove	Kerry Ligtenberg	1997	Roseau	Kerry Taylor	1993
Duluth	Steve Foucault	1973	Royalton	Carmen Hill	1915
Duluth	Spence Harris	1925	St. Cloud	Jim Eisenreich	1982
Duluth	Bill Phyle	1898	St. Cloud	Joe Jaeger	1920
Duluth	Jerry Ujdur	1980	St. Cloud	Fred Spencer	1912
Duluth	Rip Wade	1923	St. Cloud	Henry Thielman	1902
Edina	Paul Siebert	1974	St. Cloud	Jake Thielman	1905
Faribault	Jimmy Pofahl	1943	St. James	Mike Kingery	1986
Faribault	Mike Mason	1982	St. James	Gary Mielke	1978
Fertile	Arlo Brunsberg	1966	St. Louis Park	Tom Niedenfuer	1981
Graceville	Bill Davis	1965	St. Paul	John Anderson	1958
Graceville	Tom Kelly	1975	St. Paul	Fred Baczewski	1953
Halstad	Tony Brottem	1916	St. Paul	Tom Burgmeier	1968
Heron Lake	Garland Buckeye	1918	St. Paul	Bill Carney	1904
Hibbing	Roger Maris	1957	St. Paul	Paul Castner	1923
Jordan	Ollie Fuhrman	1922	St. Paul	John Crooks	1889
Lake Crystal	Moxie Meixell	1912	St. Paul	Gene DeMontreville	1884
Lake Elmo	Pete Lohman	1891	St. Paul	Lee DeMontreville	1903
Lamberton	Bob Gebhard	1971	St. Paul	Lou Galvin	1884
LeRoy	Bob Mahoney	1951	St. Paul	Chick Gandil	1910
LeSueur	Roger Denzer	1997	St. Paul	Henry Gehring	1907
Libby	Frank Jude	1906	St. Paul	Angelo Giuliani	1946
Little Falls	Mike Poepping	1975	St. Paul	Tom Johnson	1974
Mankato	Lou Polchow	1907	St. Paul	Jerry Kindall	1956
Marshall	Bill Gullickson	1979	St. Paul	Mike Lynch	1902
Marshall	Greg Olson	1989	St. Paul	Carmen Mauro	1948
Minneapolis	John Blanchard	1955	St. Paul	Paul Molitor	1978
Minneapolis	Bert Brenner	1912	St. Paul	Jack Morris	1977
Minneapolis	Ralph Capron	1912	St. Paul	Hap Morse	1911
Minneapolis	Steve Comer	1978	St. Paul	Walt Moryn	1954
Minneapolis	Brian Denman	1982	St. Paul	Andy Nelson	1902
Minneapolis	George Dumont	1915	St. Paul	Mickey Rocco	1943
Minneapolis	Joe Fautsch	1916	St. Paul	Larry Rosenthal	1936
Minneapolis	Elmer Foster	1884	St. Paul	Howie Schultz	1943
Minneapolis	Jack Graham	1946	St. Paul	Rob Quinlan	2002
Minneapolis	Gary Hargis	1979	St. Paul	Tom Quinlan	1990
Minneapolis	John Hickey	1904	St. Paul	Joe Werrick	1884
Minneapolis	Kent Hrbek	1981	St. Paul	Dave Winfield	1973
Minneapolis	Ellis Johnson	1912	St. Paul	Dan Smith	1992
Minneapolis	Dave Maurer	2000	Sauk Rapids	Rip Repulski	1953
Minneapolis	Alex Remneas	1912	Slayton	Mike Johnson	1974
Minneapolis	Dave Robinson	1970	Sleepy Eye	Dana Kiecker	1990
Minneapolis	Mike Sadek	1973	Springfield	Bob Hegman	1985
Minneapolis	Pat Scanlon	1974	Springfield	Les Rock	1936
Minneapolis	Frank Stewart	1927	Staples	Loren Bain	1945
Minneapolis	Guy Sularz	1980	Stillwater	Jim Rutherford	1973
Minneapolis	Dave Thies	1963	Sturgeon Lake	George Cunningham	1916
Minneapolis	Carl Thomas	1960	Thief River Falls	Wayne Nordhagen	1977
Minneapolis	George Thomas	1957	Tyler	Milt Nielsen	1951
Minneapolis	Pete Turgeon	1923	Waseca	Jerry Terrell	1973
Minneapolis	Joe Visner	1885	White Bear Lake	Rip Conway	1918
Minneapolis	Charley Walters	1969	White Earth Reservation	Chief Bender	1903
Minneapolis	Don Wheeler	1949	Willow River	Ernie Nevers	1926
Minneapolis	Cy Wright	1916	Winnebago	Harry Chozen	1937
Minneapolis	Jack Zalusky	1903	Winona	Gene Corbett	1936
Minnetonka	Jim Brower	1999	Winona	Paul Giel	1954
Minnetonka	Tim McIntosh	1990	Winona	Julie Wera	1927
New Ulm	Fred Bruckbauer	1961			

(Source: Glenn Gostick & Total Baseball, 2001)

THE NORTHERN LEAGUE

The Northern League is one of the oldest professional minor league organizations in Upper Midwest baseball history, and its roots take us back to 1902, when it was first started as an independent league. That next year it became a Class D league, after joining the newly created National Association of Professional Baseball Leagues, the governing body of minor league baseball. At the time, the NAPBL classified the minor leagues throughout America into either Class A, B, C, or D status — thus assuring more equal competition for each team according to city populations, financial resources, ballparks, roster sizes and player salaries.

The Northern League, meanwhile, had set its mid-season player limit to 14, and set the maximum player salary to $1,200 per season. (The league had a "salary limit" at this point, in order to prevent the larger cities, which generated more revenue than the smaller ones, from hoarding the best players.) The league was also a training ground, if you will, for American Association teams such as the St. Paul Saints and Minneapolis Millers, who sent young players there to get a little more seasoning. In addition, the league's short schedule allowed for many of the area's top collegiate ballplayers to come out and get a summer tune-up before school started.

With that, the league set out to do business, setting up ballparks and holding try-outs. It was a real wild ride, but that first season came out without a hitch. And, while teams came and went during the first few years of the league's tumultuous existence, some of the original clubs included the: Duluth "Cardinals," & later the "White Sox," Crookston "Crooks," Fargo "Browns," Grand Forks "Forkers," Superior "Longshoremen" and the Winnipeg "Maroons."

In the early going of the league, Duluth emerged as the first major threat. Pitcher Henry Gehring, who tossed a no-hitter in a 5-0 victory over visiting Superior, led the league with 13 victories that season en route to leading his White Sox to the 1904 league championship. That next season the Longshoremen disbanded and were replaced by the St. Cloud/Brainerd "St. Brains." Duluth would go on to make it two in a row, however, as they took the pennant with a 64-34 record.

In 1906, in an effort to grow and prosper, the six-team Northern League combined with the four-team Copper Country Soo League (a resort league from the Upper Peninsula of Michigan which featured four teams: the Hancock Infants, Houghton Giants, Calumet Aristocrats and Lake Linden Sandy Cities) to form the Northern-Copper Country League. The Northern League teams would take trains to Duluth and then board steamer ships for the rest of the journey to the U.P. across Lake Superior. Once there, they would stay for two week stretches, playing each of the teams (which were all within a few miles) on different nights.

The league would disband following the 1908 season

though, with many of its members joining either the Minnesota-Wisconsin League or Western Canada League. The Northern League tried to regroup that year, but did not finish the season, ultimately resulting in what would turn into a five-year hiatus.

(It is very important to note, however, that during that 1908 shortened Northern League season, a man by the name of Richard Brookins played for Fargo. The significance of this is that Brookins was the first documented African-American [outside of the Negro Leagues] to play organized baseball [as a career — not as a ringer playing for a couple months with a random team], in the 20th century. Jackie Robinson's debut with the Montreal Royals wouldn't come until 1946.)

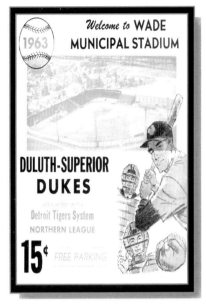

Most of the Northern League teams relocated to the Minnesota/Wisconsin League, including Duluth, which won the 1909 title, Winona, Rochester, Red Wing, Eau Claire, Wausau, La Crosse and Superior. (The Red Wing "Manufacturers" folded in 1911, however, after losing to the Winona "Clippers," 16-7, in a MWL game which saw just seven fans attend.) Shortly thereafter Winona took the 1912 MWL crown the then four team league folded.

That same year the Central International League, which featured several former Northern League teams including: the Duluth White Sox, Superior Red Sox and Virginia Ore Diggers, among others, became the second coming of the

Northern League.

That next year Virginia, Winona, Grand Forks, Fort William/Port Arthur and Winnipeg were added, as were the Minneapolis "Roughriders" and St. Paul "Colts." The Colts, however, lasted until July 23rd, when, with a 28-54 record, they relocated to La Crosse, WI. (Minneapolis and St. Paul's

affiliation with the league would last just one season, but it made for some good baseball at old Nicollet and Lexington Parks. The Millers and Saints, both of the American Association, gave the other local teams permission to play in the minor league that year, but the idea

got canned shortly thereafter.)

(It is also interesting to note that future Hall of Fame Pitcher, Rube Waddell, who had gone 12-6, with the Millers just the year before, played for both the Minneapolis "Roughriders" as well as the Virginia "Ore Diggers" that season before finally retiring.)

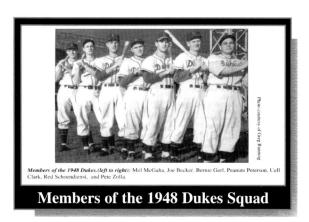

Members of the 1948 Dukes Squad

Members of the 1948 Dukes.(left to right): Mel McGaha, Joe Becker, Bernie Gerl, Peanuts Peterson, Uell Clark, Red Schoendienst, and Pete Zolla.

Duluth came back in 1914 to take the Northern League crown with an 82-43 record. That next year Grand Forks and Grand Rapids both dropped out, while the Fargo-Moorhead Graingrowers went on to win the title the following season with a 74-49 record. (Incidentally, Moorhead's last title had come back in 1897, while in the Red River Valley League.)

Virginia and Fort William/Port Arthur both followed suit in 1916, and in 1917, after Fargo-Moorhead took its second straight title, the then four-team Northern League disbanded. It was the onset of World War I, and young men from across America were being called to action. Baseball was about to come to a screeching halt.

Believe it or not, the Northern League would not be resuscitated until 1933, when it was brought back to life with seven teams: Crookston, Fargo-Moorhead, Brainerd, Winnipeg, Superior, East Grand Forks and Eau Claire. (Little Falls was in but dropped out just prior to opening day.) With that, the Northern League was back in business.

(It is important to note that at this particular junction of baseball history, something happened that was quite significant in ensuring the survival of the minor leagues. You see, back in this era of baseball, major league teams, in their never-ending quest for talent, used to take players (known as "raiding") from their minor league clubs and lure them away with little restraint — often without even compensating the minor league clubs in return. But, in 1920, the major leagues elected Judge Kenesaw Landis to serve as their commissioner. Landis saw the value in the minor leagues as feeder systems, and quickly sought to protect their rights. He also enforced provisions regarding the transfer of players between clubs and leagues, in order to preserve their survival.)

It is interesting to note that when the Northern League made its triumphant return, it was during the height of the Great Depression. A lot of other minor leagues from around the nation had gone belly-up around this time, and as a result, the Northern found itself packed with some of the top young talent in American baseball.

Red Schoendienst

That first year back, 1933, former Left Fielder Bruno Haas, who had played with St. Paul and the Philadelphia A's, was instrumental in getting the old Northern League back on its feet. He contacted local club owners, encouraged them to get back into the game and somehow coordinated a 126-game schedule.

(Former St. Paul Saints shortstop Lute Boone was also helpful in reviving the League. In addition to serving as the league's president, he also owned, managed and played for the Crookston team — whom he named after his native Pittsburgh Pirates.)

One of the most important things the league did in the early going was to contact a gentleman by the name of Hugo Goldsmith, a sporting goods manufacturer from Cincinnati, who, according to historian Herman D. White, "agreed to pay part of the out-of-pocket expenses of organizing the league as part of a contract by which his company was to furnish each club 10 dozen baseballs free for spring training in exchange for their buying their uniforms and equipment from his company."

White contended that without this contract, it was unlikely that the league would have gotten off the ground — because the league had a rule that stated at least one new ball had to be used in each game. Apparently cheaper balls were used for practices and all foul balls were promptly returned by the fans, although the kids were allowed to keep the homers.

Baseball during this era was not as glamorous as one might think. The Northern was so broke that it couldn't even afford to pay for an office staff. Because there was no office for the teams to report into, the player-managers of the teams would meet at various highway intersections to exchange information as they ventured on to their next games.

According to historian Herman D. White, try-outs were also a no-frills experience. When former Chicago White Sox Centerfielder Johnny Mostil was hired to manage the Eau Clare club, he often sent out training camp invitations that looked like this:

"Dear Frank: I would give you a trial with the Eau Claire club and the proposition is this: $40 per month and expenses on the road. You pay your own expenses at home and in training; also your own transportation to training camp. You furnish your own uniform, shoes and cap for training. We start training about April 20th and the season starts May 4th. Kindly let me know if this is satisfactory to you."

And, in addition to those select few who were sent "formal invitations," it wasn't uncommon for several hundred more boys (between the ages of 16 and 20) to hike or even hitchhike across the country to attend one of those try-out camps with the hopes of earning just one of those precious 14 roster spots. It was equally as tough for the manager, who had no coaches or assistants to help evaluate all of those players.

Then, when the team was assembled, it was an even bigger adventure trying to get to the games — which often took more than a day to get to. Usually, all 14 players, plus the manager (and sometimes a fat umpire too) had to cram into just two seven-passenger Studebakers, to make the journey from such far away locales as

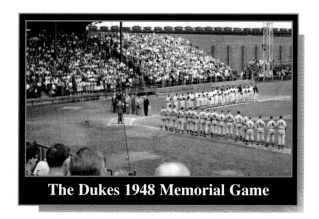

The Dukes 1948 Memorial Game

Duluth's Denny McLain

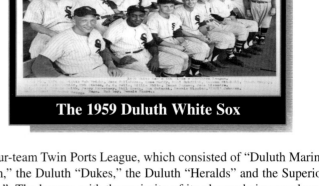

The 1959 Duluth White Sox

Crookston to Winnipeg. One of the cars would then pull a trailer which carried all the baseball equipment. Then, when they got there, they would often stay at a second-rate motel, usually for a dollar per night. (Some players would even stay at the homes of local families as well.)

Now, back to the 1933 season, where Superior took the first championship of the reborn Northern League. Superior's club was operated by Frank Wade and his son, Dick, who was a former major league outfielder with the Washington Senators. The Wades were from Duluth, however, so that next season they moved the team back across Lake Superior, where their Sox would play at Athletic Park — a combination baseball and bandstand with seating for about 2,000.

(A new ballpark called the Duluth-All Sports Stadium was built in 1941 on the southeast corner of what is now the "Wade Stadium" parking lot. [The ballpark was renamed in his honor in 1954.] Complete with nearly 400,000 bricks from old Grand Avenue, the "Wade," as it was affectionately known, became the "Wrigley Field of the Northern League.")

That next year the White Sox were led by a kid named Wally Swanson, who stole a record 60 bases — a record that was never broken by anyone, including future Hall of Famer Lou Brock, who would steal 38 for St. Cloud in 1961. In 1934, Fargo-Moorhead, now renamed the Twins, took the title thanks to Gus Koch's 36 homers.

In 1937 Duluth (now called the Dukes), under player-manager Dutch Dorman, won what would prove to be Wade's only pennant. They finished second to Superior the following season and in 1939, Duke's superstar Robert Schmidt led all of professional baseball with an astonishing .441 batting average. (Incidentally, the Dukes were named in honor of former Duluth Hornets hockey star, Herbie Lewis, a man of great character and class who was nicknamed as the "Duke of Duluth" before going on to a Hall of Fame career with the Detroit Red Wings.)

By this time the economy was turning around and baseball was growing in popularity. The Northern League was doing pretty good as well. One of the big additions that came during this era was when the American League began sending its umpires to the Northern League to do their training. Not only did the AL pitch in for their salaries, they also gave the league an entire new crop of outstanding umpires — which really changed the game for the better.

By the early 1940s the nation was at War and baseball was pushed to the back burner. As a result, the Northern League shut down from 1943-45. But, while many of the nation's young men went off to war, many others stayed back — and wanted to play ball. So, it wasn't uncommon for small, independent leagues to sprout up in order to fill the void. One of those leagues was

the four-team Twin Ports League, which consisted of "Duluth Marine & Iron," the Duluth "Dukes," the Duluth "Heralds" and the Superior "Bays." The league, with the majority of its players being employed in the local war plants and shipyards, would have the distinction of being the only pro league to ever play under the Class E label. The league, like many others of its kind, however, folded after just 19 games.

After our boys started returning home from overseas, a post war baseball boom hit with a fury. So, in 1946, after a three-year interruption, the Northern League resumed with the St. Cloud Rox, in just their first year, beating Duluth, 7-6, to claim the crown. Leading the charge for the Rox were Ed Gittens, who drove in 99 runs that season, and Tony Jaros, the former Gopher and future Minneapolis Laker basketball star, who belted out 14 homers as well.

Then, on the morning of July 24th, 1948, a tragedy occurred which forever changed the league. That night the Duluth Dukes were

ROGER MARIS

Roger Maris was born in Hibbing and grew up loving the game of baseball. As a kid his family moved to Fargo, where he went on to star in football, basketball and track at Shanley High School. Then, during the summers, he played baseball for the Fargo American Legion team.

From there Roger was all set to play football at the University of Oklahoma when a Cleveland Indians scout saw him play in a Legion game. So impressed with the kid was the scout, that he convinced him to stick with baseball. With that, he was assigned to the Indians Class C farm club — the Fargo-Moorhead Twins. There, Maris won the 1953 Rookie of the Year award en route to leading his hometown club to the Northern League Championship. Shortly thereafter, he was called up to the "Show."

In 1959 Maris earned the starting right fielder's job for the Kansas City A's. In 1960 he was traded to the Yankees, where he hit 39 home runs, won a Gold Glove and was named as the American League's MVP. Then, in 1961, he won his second MVP and made history when he broke Babe Ruth's epic record of 60 home runs in a season. He did it in high fashion too, hitting No. 61 during the last game of the season — a record that stood until 1998, when Mark McGuire finally topped it. But Maris would forever have to live with an asterisk next to his name in the record books, pointing out that he had set the mark in a season that was two games longer than the Bambino's.

Maris struggled with the New York media after that and could never get out from under the shadow of Ruth's record. He became an isolated star on a team of superstars, namely Mickey Mantle, who was one of his closest friends. Roger was later traded to the St. Louis Cardinals, where he helped lead them to a pair of World Series appearances in the late 1960s. He retired in 1968 with 2,134 career major league hits and a lifetime batting average of .281. Roger Maris tragically died of cancer on December 14, 1985 at the age of just 51. He was one of Minnesota's best ever.

CITIES THAT HAVE BEEN REPRESENTED IN THE NORTHERN LEAGUE

Aberdeen (South Dakota) Pheasants 1946-1971
Bismarck-Mandan (North Dakota) Pards 1962-1964, 1966
Brainerd (Minnesota) Muskies 1935
Brainerd-Little Falls (Minnesota) Muskies 1934
Brandon (Manitoba) Angels 1908; Greys 1933
Cavalier (North Dakota) (no nickname) 1902
Crookston (Minnesota) Crooks 1902-1905; Pirates 1933-1941
Devils Lake (North Dakota) (no nickname) 1902
Duluth (Minnesota) Cardinals 1903; White Sox 1904-1905, 1908, 1913-1916; Dukes 1934-1942, 1946-1955
Duluth-Superior (Minnesota-Wisconsin) Twi-Sox 1956-1958; Dukes 1959-1970, 1993-1997
East Grand Forks (Minnesota) Colts 1933
Eau Claire (Wisconsin) Cardinals/Bears 1933; Bears 1934-1942, 1946-1953; Braves 1954-1962
Fargo (North Dakota) (no nickname) 1902-1905; Browns 1908
Fargo-Moorhead (North Dakota-Minnesota) Graingrowers 1914-1917; Twins 1933-1942, 1946-1960; RedHawks 1996-97
Ft. William-Pt. Arthur (Ontario) Canucks 1914-1915; Canadians 1916
Grand Forks (North Dakota) Forkers 1902-1905; Flickertails 1913-1915; Chiefs 1934-1935, 1938-1942, 1946-1964
Huron (South Dakota) Phillies 1965-1968; Cubs 1969-1970
Jamestown (North Dakota) Jimmies 1936-1937
La Crosse (Wisconsin) Colts 1913
Madison (Wisconsin) Black Wolf 1996-1997
Mankato (Minnesota) Mets 1967-1968
Minneapolis (Minnesota) Millers 1913
Minot (North Dakota) Why-Nots 1917; Mallards 1958-1960, 1962
Rochester (Minnesota) Aces 1993
Sioux City (Iowa) Explorers 1993-1997
Sioux Falls (South Dakota) Canaries 1942, 1946-1953; Packers 1966-1971; Canaries 1993-1997
St. Boniface (Manitoba) Saints/Bonnies 1915
St. Cloud (Minnesota) Rox 1946-1971
St. Paul (Minnesota) Saints 1993-1997
Superior (Wisconsin) Longshoremen 1903-1905; Red Sox 1913-1916; Blues 1933-1942, 1946-1955
Thunder Bay (Ontario) Whiskey Jacks 1993-1997
Virginia (Minnesota) Ore Diggers 1913-1916
Warren (Minnesota) Wanderers 1917
Watertown (South Dakota) Expos 1970-1971
Wausau (Wisconsin) Lumberjacks 1936-1942, 1956-1957
Winnipeg (Manitoba) Maroons 1902-1905, 1908, 1913-1917, 1933-1942; Goldeyes 1954-1964, 1969, 1993-97
Winona (Minnesota) Pirates 1913-1914

traveling on their team bus from Eau Claire to St. Cloud, when, on Highway 36, near the Dale Street exit in St. Paul, a heavily loaded chemical truck crossed the center line and collided head-on with the bus. An explosion ensued and by the time the smoke had cleared Outfielder Gerald "Peanuts" Peterson of Proctor, Outfielder Gilbert Tribble of Duluth, and Pitcher Donald Schachman of St. Louis, as well as club manager George Treadwell, from Superior (who was driving the bus), along with the truck driver, James Grealish were all killed at the scene. Infielder Steve Lazar of Oliphant, Pa., would later be pronounced dead at the hospital.

Six other players in the crash were critically injured, while the remaining seven sustained minor injuries. (Luckily, one of the motorists who had stopped to help was a doctor. He and a local farmer, Frank Kurkowski, who was working in his nearby field at the time, both heroically helped to pull several of the men from the fiery wreck.) Of those 13 players, only four ever played professional baseball again.

The tragedy was tough on the entire league, but the other teams tried to pitch in by doing whatever they could to show their solidarity. They started by immediately replacing the players on Duluth's roster, so the team could resume play just a week later — after all of the funerals. (The Dukes also got some replacement players from both the St. Louis Cardinals— with whom the Dukes had a minor league affiliation with, as well as from the Duluth "Steelers," which played in the Arrowhead Amateur League.) In addition, ball clubs from around the nation put on benefit games to raise money which was later distributed equally among the injured players and the families of those who were killed. Even the truck driver's family was included.

Baseball's popularity continued to grow throughout the 1950s, and the Northern kept chugging along as well. (Another league in Minnesota during this era was the Class B "Three-I League," which featured teams from southern Minnesota, including Rochester and Winona.) More and more players were making pitstops in the league en route to the major leagues, providing plenty of good action for the fans.

St. Cloud's Lou Brock

THE NORTHERN LEAGUE'S MAJOR-LEAGUE AFFILIATIONS

Crookston: Chicago White Sox 1936; St. Louis Cardinals 1937; Boston Red Sox 1938

Duluth: (St. Louis Cardinals 1937-1942, 1946-1950; Cincinnati Redlegs 1954-1955

Duluth-Superior: Chicago White Sox 1956-1959; Detroit Tigers 1960-1964; Detroit Tigers & Chicago Cubs 1965; Chicago Cubs 1966; Chicago White Sox & Chicago Cubs 1967; Chicago White Sox 1968-1970

Fargo & Moorhead: (North Dakota-Minnesota) Cleveland Indians 1934-1940; Pittsburgh Pirates 1947-1948; Cleveland Indians 1953-1957; New York Yankees 1958-1960

Mankato: New York Mets 1967-1968

St. Cloud: New York Giants 1946, 1948-1957; San Francisco Giants 1958-1959; Chicago Cubs 1960-1964; Minnesota Twins 1965-1971

St. Cloud won another title in 1950 and in 1952 an 18 year-old rookie shortstop by the name of Henry Aaron suited up for the Eau Claire Bears. The Fargo-Moorhead Twins won the 1953 crown thanks to a kid from Hibbing by the name of Roger Maris, who, after being named as the N.L. Rookie of the Year, went on to stardom with the New York Yankees. The Twins took the 1954 title as well, as Frank Gravino belted out an amazing 108 home runs over that two year stretch.

One team in particular though, the St. Cloud Rox, seemed to be loaded with an abnormal number future major leaguers. Maybe it was the water? Among them were Andre Rodgers, Leon Wagner and Frank Funk, who led the Rox to the Northern League championship in 1955. That next year the Rox featured a kid by the name of Orlando Cepeda, who won the Northern League Triple Crown that season before going on to a Hall of Fame career with St. Louis and the Giants. (The "Baby Bull" was named as the National League's Most Valuable Player as a member of the Cardinals in 1967, and from there the All-Star first baseman went on to compile a .297 lifetime average in the majors (nine times hitting over .300) while hitting 397 home runs to boot.) In 1958 the Rox took the regular season title behind future Hall of Famer Matty Alou, and in 1961 St. Cloud featured future Hall of Famer Lou Brock, who would go on to become the all-time leading base-stealer in MLB history.

Another highlight of this era came on August 8th, 1956, when future Twins Pitcher Jack Kralick threw a no-hitter for Duluth in a 5-0 win over Fargo-Moorhead. (Incidentally, Fargo-Moorhead was led by future major league All-Star Pitcher Jim Perry, who would later play for the Twins.) Duluth, which was managed by former Minneapolis Miller home-run king Joe Hauser, went on to beat Eau Claire for the Northern crown that year. (Kralick, of course, would go on to throw the first Twins no-hitter in history as well, in a 1-0 win over Kansas City before nearly 24,000 fans at the Met on August 26th, 1962.)

In 1963 the Northern League once again changed its affiliation, this time from Class C to Class A — with rosters now being made up primarily of rookie minor leaguers. Fargo had dropped out by this time, but the Duluth-Superior Dukes, as they were now known (the Duluth franchise relocated to Wausau before the season), remained as one of the top teams in the league throughout this era, winning titles in 1957, 1961, 1963, 1969, and 1970. In fact, Bill Freehan, Willie Horton, Jim Northrup and Mickey Stanley all played for the Dukes in the 60's before going on to form the nucleus of the 1968 Detroit Tigers World Series title team.

In 1965, however, because of pressures from the cold weather (oftentimes major league farm directors were reluctant to send a young pitcher up north to play in the cold) and also from the major leagues, the Northern League went from 120 games a season to just 70. The Rox then went on a tirade, winning four straight titles from 1965-68. Among the stars of this era were Bob Brooks, Nate King, Lou Smith, Bob Gebhard, Ron Keller, Mike Colin, Louis Stephen, Bob Castiglione, Steve Brye, Gary Reierson, Steve Christopher, Alex Rowell, Bobby Jones, Jim Nettles, Tom Ferraro and future Minnesota Twins pitcher, Dave Goltz. The Dukes rounded out the tumultuous '60s by winning a pair in 1969 and 1970, thanks to the outstanding play of Jim Mueller, Steve Houck and Dan Rourke.

The Vietnam War was also starting to heat up and young men from across the nation were being drafted into service. Baseball, as in previous times of war, would have to take a back seat. All of those factors helped to contribute to the league's ultimate demise in 1971, when, with baseball interest at a low point in America, the "third"

WALLY GILBERT

Wally Gilbert is arguably one of Minnesota's greatest ever all-around athletes. A graduate of Duluth Denfeld High School, Gilbert went on to Valparaiso University in Indiana, where he served as captain of the football, basketball and baseball teams there. In football, he earned All-American honors starring as a halfback, punter and drop-kicker extraordinaire.

In the late 1920s and early 1930s he played third base for the Brooklyn Dodgers and Cincinnati Reds. When those same Dodgers moved to Los Angeles in 1957, the Sporting News named him as the starting third baseman on the all-time Dodger team. In addition to playing on several pro touring basketball teams, including with Two Harbors, the Duluth Tank Corps, the Denver Tigers and the Buffalo All-Americans, he was also a champion curler, back at the old Duluth Curling Club.

But perhaps his most memorable role in professional Minnesota sports came on the gridiron, where he starred alongside future Hall of Famer's Ernie Nevers and Johnny Blood, as a halfback and kicker with the NFL's Duluth Eskimos in the late 1920s. Wally's deadly drop-kicks beat several teams, including the likes of the Green Bay Packers, and Chicago Cardinals. He once booted a record 61-yarder!

Late in the 1930s, Wally married his long-time sweetheart, Mary McKay, and settled down. But he didn't slow down! He continued to play and manage in the Northern League with both Wausau and Winnipeg, and when World War II broke out, he and some buddies organized a semipro baseball team out of Duluth.

Gilbert worked and lived in Duluth for the remainder of his life, until he passed in 1958. The obituary, in the Duluth News Tribune on Sept. 7th of that year, led with a fitting headline: "Duluth's greatest all-around athlete is dead."

Northern League, was shut down for what would prove to be a 22 year hiatus. The Rox took the title that year, but it would all be for not as the great Northern League had its lights turned off. At the time, the Northern League, often referred to amicably as the "Polar Circuit," was the oldest league in the lower classifications of the minor leagues.

While many of the Northern League teams split up and found new leagues to play in (mainly townball leagues), others simply folded into the night. The Northern League would again be pulled off of life support in 1993, when the league opened just as it had done back in 1902, with an "Independent" status.

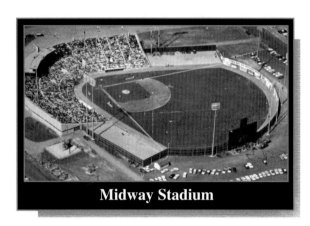
Midway Stadium

The "New" Northern League

In 1993 minor league baseball made a triumphant return to the Upper Midwest when the Northern League, after a 22-year absence, rose from the dead as a six-team "Independent" Class A league. Leading the charge to resuscitate the old NL was Baseball America publisher Miles Wolff, the former owner of the legendary Durham Bulls — an Atlanta Braves affiliate which was made famous in the movie starring Kevin Kostner entitled "Bull Durham." Wolff could see that the game was growing in popularity once again, and knew that the Upper Midwest was the only region in North America without an active professional minor league system at that time. He knew of the great baseball history and tradition in the area, and figured that a new league, with a short 72-game schedule, would be a home run.

Among the charter members of the upstart league that first year were a trio of Minnesota teams: the St. Paul Saints, Duluth-Superior Dukes and Rochester Aces, as well as clubs from Sioux Falls, Thunder Bay and Sioux City. The Saints, which played their home games at Midway Stadium, were managed by former major lea-

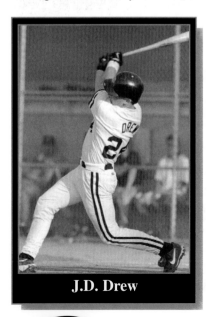
J.D. Drew

guer Tim Blackwell. Midway Stadium, which was renamed from Municipal Stadium in 1994, was also expanded that next year to seat more than 6,300 fans. The Saints were the big hit of the league. After all, they were owned by a group which included Mike Veeck, the son of Hall of Fame Owner Bill Veeck, and Bill Murray, the much celebrated actor and comedian.

The crowds came out in record numbers to see the Saints that inaugural season as the team had 25 home sell-outs and drew more than 168,000 fans. Among the

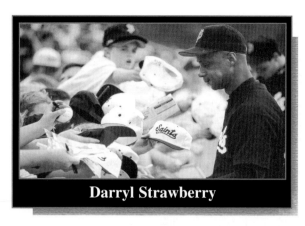
Darryl Strawberry

stars on this club were ex-Chicago Cub star Leon Durham, who made his presence felt right away when he hit a 10th inning game-winning grand slam in a 7-4 come-from-behind victory against the Dukes early in the season.

The team played solid baseball that first year and became the media darlings of the airwaves. Veeck, a marketing genius, made coming to the ballpark an adventure. He knew that Twins fans, as loyal as they were, wanted to see outdoor baseball — and that is exactly what he gave them. The team posted a 42-29 regular season record that season and then went on to beat the Rochester Aces, three games to one, to win the inaugural NL championship.

Two players from league would go on to sign pro contracts that next year as well: Saints Pitcher Mike Mimbs, who inked a deal with the Philadelphia Phillies, and Duluth-Superior DH Jeff Grotewald, who signed with Kansas City. (Other players from the NL that year which went on to sign pro deals included Cuban Shortstop Rey Ordonez, who would go on to star for the New York Mets, and Kevin Millar, who went on to excel with the Florida Marlins.)

That next year the Rochester Aces folded and relocated to Winnipeg, where they became the Goldeyes, and promptly won the Northern League crown. The Saints, meanwhile, finished in third that next season at 43-36, out of the playoffs. However, the team did have a few stars, including Matt Stark, who had a 23-game hitting streak, as well as Third Baseman Vince Castaldo, who was named as the league's Most Valuable Player. In addition, the Saints set a professional short season attendance record with 241,069 fans walking through Midway Stadiums turnstiles.

The 1995 Saints were led by new manager Marty Scott, the former farm director of the Texas Rangers. His Saints played inspired ball that year, claiming the first and second half league titles and even tying a league record with 53 wins to boot. From there the Saints cruised into the playoffs, where they defeated the Winnipeg Goldeyes, three games to one, to win the NL championship. Leading the way for the club that year were First Baseman Dan Peltier, an ex-Ranger who led the league in hits with 119; Reliever Bruce Walton, who set a league record with 29 saves; Left Fielder Doug O'Neill, who tallied 17 home runs; and ex-major league outfielder Darryl Motley, who was signed midway through the year.

That next season a divisional format was adopted after Fargo-Moorhead and Madison were added as expansion franchises. That was a wild year for the Northern League all right, and

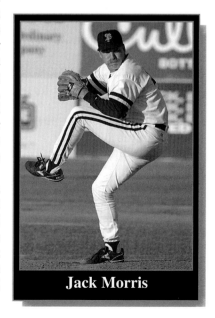
Jack Morris

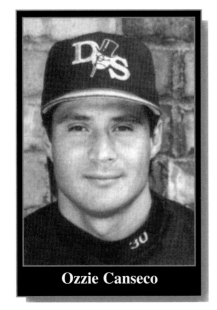

Ozzie Canseco

Anthony Lewis

especially for the Saints, who were signing major leaguers left and right. While J.T. Bruett became the first ex-Twin to play for the Saints, the big news that season was the signings of ex-major league stars Darryl Strawberry and Jack Morris. Strawberry, who was on a rehab assignment in St. Paul, was looking to get back to the bigs, while Morris was just looking to have some fun after an amazing 14-year career as a pitcher, where he won World Series rings with Detroit, Minnesota and Toronto.

Strawberry came out of the gates swinging, hitting his first homer against Duluth in just his second game as a Saint. He would go on to hit .435 in 29 games and set a club record with 18 home runs in just 108 at-bats. With the "Straw" playing like that, it was no surprise that the New York Yankees bought his contract early that July and promoted him straight to the majors within a couple of days. He would go on to help lead the Yanks to their first World Series title in 15 years. Jack, meanwhile, a St. Paul native, went 5-1 during in the first half of the year, but then got frustrated in the second half and retired midway through the season. Even in his 40s, Jack could still bring it, as he still finished up as the league's ERA champ with a 2.61 mark.

Later in the year the team brought in yet another former big-leaguer, First Baseman Glenn Davis, who knocked out three grand slams in the second half of the year. Another highlight of that season came when Saints Pitcher Joe Miller pitched the first no-hitter in club history against Thunder Bay. From there the Saints swept past Madison in the Eastern Division finals, and kept it going in the title series against Fargo-Moorhead.

St. Paul rallied from a six-run deficit to win Game One of the best of five series against the RedHawks. They then took Game Two and finally hung on to edge FM, 4-3, in the third game thanks to Joe Biernats triple in the top of the ninth to seal the deal. It was the Saints third Northern League crown in just four years.

Overall the Saints won both halves of Northern League's Eastern Division with a 45-40 record. In addition, the club sold out all of its home dates en route to drawing more than a quarter-million fans to Midway that year. The league as a whole drew more than one million as well.

In 1997 the Northern League was all about the Duluth-Superior Dukes, who defeated the Winnipeg Goldeyes, three games to two, to win the their first championship since 1956. The Dukes got to the Finals by downing the defending champs from St. Paul, three games to two, in the Eastern Division Championship Series.

Mike Meggers hit 32 homers and had 99 RBIs that season for the Dukes, while Pitcher Jeremy McGarity led the league in strike-outs with 142.

The highlight of that year, however, was the debut of Ila Borders, who became the first woman ever to pitch on a regular basis for a pro-fessional men's baseball team when she laced em' up for the Saints. Borders drew hordes of media around her every time she took the mound that year, but she handled it like a pro. She even struck out the first batter she ever faced, Duluth-Superior's Jeff Jensen, in a pre-season game. She would make amends with him soon enough though, because late that June she was traded to those very Dukes, where she would become a fixture in the team's rotation. The lefty from Whittier College appeared in seven games that season, finishing with an ERA of 7.50.

Another interesting event of the 1997 season came in early July, when the Saints signed future Major League All-Star Centerfielder, J.D. Drew. Drew, who was selected as the second over-all pick of the first round of that year's amateur draft, was unable to come to terms with the Philadelphia Phillies — so he wound up play-ing out the year with the Saints before going back into the draft again the following season. (He would play part of that next season in St. Paul, where he flirted with .400, before finally signing with the St. Louis Cardinals.)

This was the trend in St. Paul. Because it was an independ-

SOME NORTHERN LEAGUERS IN THE MAJORS

Player	Years	N.L. Team	Major League Team(s)
Jeff Grotewald	1993	Duluth-Superior	Houston
Mike Garcia	1993	Rochester	Pittsburgh
Ken Grundt	1994	Sioux Falls	Boston
Mike Cather	1995	Winnipeg	Atlanta
Joel Bennett	1996	Newburgh	Baltimore, Philadelphia
Joe Grahe	1997	Bangor	Philadelphia
Mike Porzio	1997	Sioux City	Colorado
Jeff Zimmerman	1997	Winnipeg	Texas
Chuck Smith	1998	Sioux Falls	Florida, Colorado
Jeff Sparks	1998	Winnipeg	Tampa Bay
Terry Pearson	1997,00	S.F. & Duluth	Detroit
Joey Eischen	1999-00	Adirondack	Montreal
Nate Field	2000	Sioux City	Kansas City
Mike Mimbs	1993	St. Paul	Philadelphia Phillies
Rey Ordonez	1993	St. Paul	New York Mets
Doug Dascenzo	1995	St. Paul	San Diego Padres
Dan Peltier	1995	St. Paul	San Francisco Giants
Darryl Strawberry	1996	St. Paul	New York Yankees
Kevin Millar	1993	St. Paul	Florida Marlins
J.D. Drew	1997-98	St. Paul	St. Louis Cardinals
Frank Charles	1993	St. Paul	Houston Astros
Eddie Oropesa	1993	St. Paul	Philadelphia, Arizona
Scott Stewart	1996	St. Paul	Montreal Expos
Luis Lopez	1995	St. Paul	Toronto Blue Jays
Roy Smith	1998-99	St. Paul	Cleveland Indians

ILA BORDERS

Considered by many to be one of the greatest female athletes of all-time, Ila Borders has gone out and made a name for herself in a very big way. A real trailblazer for women of all sports, her story is truly amazing.

As a high school senior at Whittier Christian (Calif.) back in 1993, Ila defied the odds be being named as the MVP of her baseball team. Later that year, Ila made history by becoming the first woman ever to earn a college baseball scholarship, when Southern California College took a chance on her. She played well, but struggled at times. Then, as a junior, she transferred to Whittier College, in hopes of getting more time on the mound.

On May 29, 1997, Ila made history again when she became the first woman to sign a contract with a men's professional baseball team, the St. Paul Saints. Then, on May 31, she became the first woman to pitch in a regular season game, when she took the mound against the Sioux Falls Canaries. Ila struggled, but hung in there. Many were skeptical of her, thinking that her signing was merely a publicity stunt to attract more media attention.

Just a few weeks later, after appearing in just seven games with the Saints, the lefthander was traded to the Duluth-Superior Dukes. There, Ila made history once again, this time by becoming the first woman to start a men's pro game, when she took to the hill against those same Sioux Falls Canaries. Ila did much better this time around and settled in as a regular starter in the team's rotation. Then, on July 24, 1998, Ila finally did it. She became the first woman to win a men's pro game when she got a 3-1 decision over those very Sioux Falls Canaries.

Borders started the 1999 season in Duluth before being traded to the Madison Black Wolves. She made 12 starts that year, going 1-0 and posting an impressive 1.67 ERA. Ila stayed with Madison before eventually retiring in 2000 at the age of 25. Presently, among other things, Ila is a teacher, does motivational speaking and continues to inspire little girls from around the world.

A real pioneer, Ila has proven that women, if given the chance, can do anything men can do — oftentimes even better. For her efforts, Ila's game-ball, glove and uniform are on display in the Baseball Hall of Fame in Cooperstown, N.Y., commemorating her remarkable achievements. In addition, in 2000 Ila was voted No. 98 in Sports Illustrated's "Top 100 Female Athletes of the Century."

"I don't see myself as a pioneer," said Borders, "I just see myself as someone who loves baseball."

Madison's Nate Vopata, who hit a game-winning two-run homer in the 7th.)

In 1998 the Fargo-Moorhead RedHawks swept the Saints in three straight to win their first title of the modern era. Leading the charge for the RedHawks were a quartet of All-Stars. Chad Akers had a record 30 doubles, scored 79 runs and 111 hits that season, while Torry Wells had 20 homers to boot. In addition, John Knott stole a record 30 bases, while Pitcher Jeff Bittiger had a record 12 wins to go along with his gaudy 1.94 ERA.

The Saints, who defeated Thunder Bay, three games to two, to win the Eastern Division Championship Series that season, were led by yet another former big-leaguer that year in former Detroit Tigers Catcher Matt Nokes. Nokes, who hit .351 with eight homers and 50 RBIs, was also the hero of the playoffs against Thunder Bay. There, in the deciding fifth game, with the score tied at 1-1 in the bottom of the ninth, Nokes stepped up and smacked the game-winning home run to end the series. (It should also be noted that in the 1997 & 1998 seasons, Saints slugger David Kennedy hit a record 38 homers.)

Following the 1998 season, the Northern League decided to merge with the eight-team Northeast League, thus creating a 16 team league now competing in 12 states and two Canadian provinces. In 1999 the two league merger produced a new Northern League format to determine a champion. Under the new system, a five-game league championship series now pitted the champs of the Northern League Central vs. the Northern League East. And, in that first year of action, Albany downed Winnipeg to take the inaugural crown.

After finishing last in 1999 with a 35-49 record, the 2000 Dukes, under rookie player/manager Benny Castillo, came out and took the Central Division title. Leading the charge for the Dukes that season were Anthony Lewis, Jim Rushford and Tony Mitchell, who simply terrorized Northern League pitchers. In one game during August, Mitchell caught fire, going 6-for-6

ent team with no major league affiliations, and because the team was located in a big metropolitan city, major leaguers either on their way up or on their way down were eager to come there. For big-shot athletes, being in the Twin Cities was much better than getting marooned in some tiny town in the middle of nowhere.

(That season also marked the league's first ever All-Star Game, which was played in August at Midway Stadium before a sell-out crowd of 6,329. The East defeated the West, 2-1, thanks to

including a trio of dingers for 9 RBI's in a 21-12 rout over the rival Saints. From there they cruised, taking the second-half crown along the way. They would finish with an outstanding 53-33 record, and then go on to beat Madison, 6-3, in a one-game showdown.

Next up were the Saints, who they then eliminated in the first round of playoffs, three games to one. Then, in the next round, the Dukes swept Fargo-Moorhead, who, themselves had just swept Winnipeg in the West Divisional Series. This series was close though, especially in the deciding Game Three, where the

Duluth's Historic Wade Stadium

The Duluth-Superior Dukes

MIKE VEECK & BILL MURRAY

While Marvin Goldklang is the Chairman of the Saints, the two guys who really run the show are Mike Veeck, the President, and Bill Murray, whose title reads: Owner & Director of Fun.

A baseball lifer, Veeck has been with the new Saints since the beginning. The Veeck family has became synonymous with baseball ever since their involvement which started back in the early 1900s, when Mike's grandfather ran the Chicago Cubs. Veeck's father, Bill, was a Hall of Fame owner with the St. Louis Browns, Cleveland Indians, Chicago White Sox and the then-minor league Milwaukee Brewers. A marketing wizard, Veeck will best be remembered for signing Larry Doby, the first African American to play in the American League, planting the ivy on the Wrigley Field outfield brick walls, and for once sending a midget, 3-foot-6 Eddie Gaedel, to the plate to bat for the St. Louis Browns. Mike has been the big reason for the Saints success, continually coming up with new marketing and promotional ideas. He is truly one of the most innovative minds in the game.

Bill Murray, meanwhile, is a comic genius. And, as a lifelong baseball fan, it was no surprise when he became an investor in the club at their inception back in 1993. As a part-part-time first and third base coach for the Saints, his biggest achievement came back on August 10th, 1997, when he played a major role in what would turn out to be the biggest comeback in franchise history. According the team's media guide, here is how the big game went down:

"The Saints fell behind the Sioux Falls Canaries, 9-2, after three innings. With the second half pennant race in full swing, Murray replaced manager Marty Scott as third base coach and instigated a remarkable rally. The Saints chipped away at the Canaries' lead, closing within 9-8 after seven innings. In the bottom of the eighth, and current base-running coach Lamarr Rogers on second base with two out, Murray took a daring chance sending the speedy Rogers home on a single to shallow left field. Rogers barely beat the throw, leading the Saints to a 10-9 win."

(And for what it is worth, this author's favorite Bill Murray movies are, in no particular order: "Caddyshack," "Stripes," "Meatballs," "Ghost Busters," "What About Bob," "Groundhog Day" and "Space Jam" — which Bill can be seen proudly wearing his Saints cap during a basketball scene with Michael Jordan.)

RedHawks rallied back from a six run deficit to send the game into extra innings. There, in the 10th inning, Center Fielder Bernard Caston's sacrifice fly put the Dukes ahead for good — giving them their first Northern League Central Division Championship.

From there the Dukes advanced on to the Northern League World Series where they ultimately were swept by East power Adirondack, three games to none. Manager Benny Castillo, who was named Central Manager of the Year, and his "Benny's Bombers" played outstanding ball that year. Anthony Lewis captured the Triple Crown with a .368 average, 33 homers and 89 RBIs while Tony Mitchell was right on his heels with a .352 average, 26 homers and 87 RBIs. In addition, Left Fielder Jim Rushford was named Central Division Rookie of the Year as well.

In the year 2001 the New Jersey Jackals defeated the Winnipeg Goldeyes to take what would prove to be the third combined-league titles. The Saints, meanwhile, fell to 37-53 under new manager Doug Sisson. One positive for that next season, however, was when former Saints pitcher Scott Stewart won the job of starting closer for the Montreal Expos. Stewart started out hot right out of the gates, earning 12 saves in 12 chances with a 1.69 ERA entering the second half of the season.

Winnipeg took the 2002 crown while Fargo-Moorhead came in a close second. The Saints and Dukes, meanwhile, finished in fourth and fifth places, respectively, and out of the playoff hunt. Sadly, at the end of the season, it was announced that the Duluth Dukes would be relocating to Kansas City, where they would play in a new $15 million stadium near a new racetrack and other attractions. Poor attendance and a ballpark "unable to operate in the 21st century" were reasons for the clubs departure. The franchise, with roots extending back for nearly a century, will certainly be missed. One can only hope that the team will be able to find a new ownership group in the years to come and be resurrected from the dead once again. The old Wade will be ready for them when they do.

Today, even with occasional franchise shifts, the Northern League is rock solid. It uses Major League Baseball rules, complete with wooden bats and designated hitters. In addition, team rosters are 22-men deep with a maximum of four veterans and a minimum of five rookies. This balance works well, considering the bread and butter of the league consists of minor league veterans and rookies just out of college.

Presently, there are 16 teams which play an 86-game schedule divided into two 43-game halves. Playoffs then consist of a five-game divisional series, followed by a best-of-five conference final,

The Dukes All-Time All-Star Team

First Base:	Don Mincher
Second Base:	Dick Newberry
Third Base:	Wally Gilbert
Shortstop:	Harold Reiser
Outfielders:	Joe Schmidt, Willie Horton & Morrie Arnovich
Catcher:	Bill Freehan
Pitchers:	Jack Kralick, Cloyd Boyer & Denny McLain
Manager:	Bob Swift

(Voted on by Twinports fans at 100th Anniversary)

WAYNE TERWILLIGER

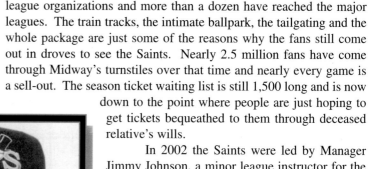

Wayne "Twig" Terwilliger is a Minnesota baseball legend. The year 2002 represented his 55th season in professional baseball and his eighth as a coach for the St. Paul Saints. As a second baseman, Twig made his Saints debut back in 1952 when the team was a Dodgers minor league affiliate. He hit .312 that season and then went on to a very productive nine-year Major League career.

From there he got into coaching and managing, until finally making it back to Minnesota to become the third base coach from 1987 to 1993 — enjoying a pair of World Series titles along the way. He then made his triumphant return to St. Paul in 1995 and has been at Midway ever since.

Terwilliger has played, coached or managed more than 5,000 professional ball games and is one of just five men known to have been in pro ball for at least 50 consecutive seasons. (Don Zimmer, Connie Mack, Bill Fischer and Jimmie Reese are the others). Following the 2002 season Twig finally hung up his cleats and retired to Texas. Nut before he could get out of Dodge, St. Paul Mayor Randy Kelly signed a proclamation designating a day in late August as Wayne Terwilliger Day in St. Paul.

which leads to a five-game league championship series pitting the champs of the Northern League Central vs. the Northern League East. The Central Division consists of St. Paul, Duluth-Superior (now Kansas City), Gary, Sioux Falls, Sioux City, Schaumburg, Joliet and Winnipeg, while the Eastern Division features Brockton, Berkshire, Allentown, Elmira, Adirondack, Quebec, New Jersey and Albany-Colonie.

The success of the league can be credited in large part to the early success of the St. Paul Saints. And the success of the Saints can be directly attributed to the marketing genius otherwise known as Mike Veeck. Like his father before him, Vecek gave the fans what they wanted — entertainment. From a pig who delivers the baseballs to the umpire before each inning, to offering haircuts and massages in the bleachers during games, to having whoopee cushion giveaway night, to taking a hot-tub in the outfield, it's all in good fun. And that is what is all about. (Incidentally, Veeck's father once even sent a midget into a major leauge baseball game to force the opposing pitcher to shrink his strike-zone!)

Veeck wasn't afraid to hire the first woman in professional baseball, and he also wasn't afraid to make a dream come true for Dave Stevens, who, in 1996, became the first player born with no legs to play pro ball. Baseball, by nature, is boring. So Veeck made it un-boring by giving the fans things to do during the down-time between innings — things like inflatable sumo suit wrestling and watching little kids race giant hot dog mascots around the base-paths on a hot summer night. It was pure genius.

And a decade after the Northern League opened its doors back up for business, the Saints have figured out the formula for success. Some 60 former Saints have had their contracts sold to major league organizations and more than a dozen have reached the major leagues. The train tracks, the intimate ballpark, the tailgating and the whole package are just some of the reasons why the fans still come out in droves to see the Saints. Nearly 2.5 million fans have come through Midway's turnstiles over that time and nearly every game is a sell-out. The season ticket waiting list is still 1,500 long and is now down to the point where people are just hoping to get tickets bequeathed to them through deceased relative's wills.

In 2002 the Saints were led by Manager Jimmy Johnson, a minor league instructor for the Houston Astros who had replaced former skipper Doug Sisson. He was the club's third manager in as many years and will definitely have his hands full in the future. There are no celebrities on his roster, but there are a handful of youngsters on the rise, including All-Star Pitcher Jake Whitney, as well as Outfielders Ryan Ruiz and Keith Williams, along with First Baseman Jason Hill, who all hit over .300 in 2001. In addition, Left Fielder Kevin Roberson, who played briefly with the Mets and Cubs in the mid-1990s joined the squad in 2002 and led the league with 27 homers. The Saints have won only a one playoff game in the past three seasons, however, and are looking to get back on top in what has become one of the toughest and most respected minor leagues in the nation.

Bob Zupcic

Through it all, the Northern League has been there. For more than 100 years now, this league has been providing ballplayers and fans alike the opportunity to enjoy the game as it was meant to be played. It is "old school" in that there are no big salaries, no team planes and no multi-million dollar TV contracts. It's just plain old baseball with a proud history...the way it oughtta be.

And, through the years, 14 Minnesota cities have been represented in the league, including: the Brainerd Muskies & Brainerd-Little Falls Muskies; Crookston Crooks & Pirates;

Fargo-Moorhead's Chris Coste

Dave Stevens

Duluth Cardinals, White Sox & Dukes; Duluth-Superior White Sox & Dukes; East Grand Forks Colts; Fargo-Moorhead Graingrowers, Twins & RedHawks; Mankato Mets; Minneapolis Roughriders; Rochester Aces; St. Cloud Rox; St. Paul Colts; Virginia Ore Diggers; Warren Wanderers; and Winona Pirates.

In addition, the Northern League has produced its share of future major league stars. From the original era there were a bunch, including: Hank Aaron, Roger Maris, Bob Feller, Don Larsen, Lou Brock, Willie Stargell, Joe Torre, Gaylord & Jim Perry, Jim Palmer, Orlando Cepeda, Denny McLain, Vada Pinson, Matty Alou, Jim "Mudcat" Grant, Larry Hisle, Greg Luzinski, Dave Goltz, Charlie Walters, Bo Belinsky and Leon Wagner, as well as future managers Earl Weaver, Cal Ripken, Sr. and Dallas Green. Oh yeah, there was one more guy worth mentioning… Bob (*I must be in the front row!*) Uecker.

Joe Miller

Now, in the modern era, Major Leaguers including Jack Morris, Darryl Strawberry, J.D. Drew, Matt Nokes, Rey Ordonez, Leon Durham, Mike Cather, Darryl Motley, J.T. Bruett, Scott Stewart and a host of others have made there way through the Northern League. All in all, over the past decade, several hundred players have been sold to major league organizations.

Considered to be the pre-eminent modern era independent league, the Northern League's success has paved the way for other independent leagues across North America. In addition, the league has proven that with some savvy grass-roots marketing and a decent outdoor ballpark, you can stay afloat and even thrive. Today's sports-entertainment dollar is spread pretty thin. The fans have more choices now than ever on just how they are going to be entertained, but the Northern has carved out a niche that is hopefully here to stay for a long, long time.

MINNESOTA AND THE MINORS

The Loons' Jeff Jonckowski

While the Millers and Saints provided Minnesota with years and years of minor league entertainment, they weren't the only show in town. The Northern League was also an outstanding minor league circuit, boasting dozens of major league affiliate programs along the way. Countless other leagues have come and gone through the years as well. There was the Keystone Association of the 1870s, the Red River Valley League of the late 1890s, the Northern-Copper Country League of 1906, the Minnesota-Wisconsin League of 1908, the Central International League of 1910, the Twin Ports League of 1943, the Three-I League of the 1950s, and the Western and Southern Minny Leagues of the 1950s and '60s.

The minor leagues have played a vital role in the development of the game of baseball. When the National Association of Professional Baseball Leagues (the original governing body for the minors) was created back in 1902, there were just 14 leagues with 96 clubs playing in America. It was created to preserve the rights of the teams, so that they wouldn't be raided from the major league teams. Since then, they have grown to be a formidable partner of Major League Baseball. Today Minor League Baseball is an entity all of its own with various classes and classifications that draws nearly 40 million fans to its games. It has certainly come a long way.

But minor league baseball isn't just about the "farm teams" of the bigs, it is also about the smaller, local leagues which provide countless opportunities for players either on their way up, or simply on their way down. For some it is a way to play in a league with tougher competition than town ball, while for others it is just for fun. For whatever the reasons, it is important to note that Minnesota has had several other minor and developmental leagues which have truly made a difference.

In June of 1994 the four-team Independent North Central League opened up shop with teams from Minneapolis, Brainerd, Chaska and Hibbing. Former Gopher and Atlanta Braves Catcher, Greg Olson, managed the Minneapolis Loons that season and played a pivotal role in starting the new circuit. That next season the league joined the upstart Prairie League, an eight-team circuit which now included teams from Regina, Saskatoon, Moose Jaw, Brandon, Minot, Bismarck and Aberdeen. (The Loons, which played their home games at the U of M's Siebert Field, also had future Atlanta Braves Pitcher Kerry Ligtenberg on their roster that season as well.)

Another league began play in 1994 as well, the Northwoods League, which began with franchises in Rochester, Kenosha, Wausau, Manitowoc and Dubuque. The League, which competed in a 56 game schedule between June and August, was made up of "All-Star" teams of college players. The Rochester Honkers claimed the first league title that year with a 31-15 overall record. Waterloo was added in 1995 and that next year the Dubuque Mud Puppies relocated to St. Cloud, where they were renamed the River Bats. In 1998 the Northwoods League joined forces with the Prairie League, adding three new teams to the circuit with Austin, Brainerd and Grand Forks. The Rivers Bats took the NWL crown that year when they swept the Honkers in the Finals.

The Mankato Mashers joined the fray in 1999, while the Honkers edged the River Bats in the Championship Series for the second year in a row. That same year the NWL saw its first alumni make it to the show when former Dubuque Mud Puppy pitcher Jeff Weaver made his first start for the Detroit Tigers on April 14th against the Minnesota Twins. St. Cloud took the title in 2000, while in 2001, teams from Alexandria and Madison were added to the mix. In 2001 the All-Stars of the NWL even beat Team USA, 1-0, becoming just the first team that year to shut them out.

The league, which has evolved into the premier summer collegiate circuit in the Midwest, has really gone on to become the real deal. League-wide attendance has reached nearly 300,000 fans per year, while several hundred NWL alumni have gone on to play some level of professional baseball. Among the players in the league are Twins Manager Ron Gardenhire's son Toby, an infielder who plays at Arkansas-Fort Smith Junior College, as well as Joe Gaetti, the son of ex-Twins Third Baseman Gary Gaetti, who plays centerfield at N.C. State.

TOWN TEAM BASEBALL

Amateur baseball (or Base Ball as it was known back in the day) has long roots in Minnesota that extend all the way back to the 1850s, when Minnesota was still two years away from being recognized as the 32nd state admitted to the Union. Town-team Baseball, or "Town ball" as it is known, represents all that is good about the sport of baseball. Its players are amateurs and play simply for the love of the game. As a result, it has grown in popularity to the point where today, it is not only one of the most popular games in town, it is simply a lifestyle for families from Ada to Zumbrota.

The first recorded amateur team to hit the diamond in Minnesota came back in 1857, when the citizens of Nininger, now a ghost town, decided to organize a baseball club. The game was brand new at the time, and would develop in the Gopher State after the early stages of the Civil War, when soldiers who learned about it out East returned home from battle to play at Fort Snelling. From there the game's popularity grew like wildfire. Some of the early teams of this era included the St. Paul "Olympics," St. Paul "North Stars," St. Paul "Saxons," Red Wing "Crescents," Stillwater "St. Croix," Hastings "Vermillions," St. Cloud "Arctics," "Minneapolis Unions" and Minneapolis "Excelsiors."

In 1867 the "Minnesota State Association of Base Ball Players" was formed and shortly thereafter the first ever state amateur baseball tournament in the state was held. According to historian Cecil Monroe, who wrote "The Rise of Baseball in Minnesota," the organization's purpose was to "improve, foster and perpetuate the game of baseball and to cultivate kindly feelings among the different members of the Base Ball Clubs." St. Paul's General Henry Sibley was named as the first president, and so began one of Minnesota's most treasured sporting events, the annual state town-team tourney.

The inaugural state tournament, which would feature two classes of competition and a $5 entrance fee, was held in St. Paul that September 24th, at the North Star grounds. The first game of the tourney was a blowout as the game between the St. Cloud Arctics and St. Paul North Stars was called off in the sixth inning, with the North Stars leading by 50 runs. Game Two was much closer as the North Stars edged out the Vermillions, 58-40, to claim the first title. (Incidentally, the Vermillions won their playoff game against St. Cloud by the score of 100-44!) After the game President Sibley awarded a silver ball, which would become emblematic to future state amateur champions, to the captain of the winning team. Then, in the second class, the Saxons and St. Croix each split their games. But, because the St. Croix club had to get home, they tossed a coin to determine a winner — which came up in favor of the Saxons.

There it was, the first ever state tournament, in the books. It wasn't without its share of controversy though. "Bickerings, accusations of unfairness, and some-times disputes so bitter as to interrupt a game now arose," according to Monroe. So from that point on, the teams had to agree on a set of rules that would be consistent throughout the tournament, and they would therefore have to abandon their local "house" rules that they were accustomed to. In addition, in order for a team to win the best-of-five game tourney, their players "must have been members of the club in good standing for 30 days prior to the match." This cleaned up a lot of improprieties in the game, but they still had a long way to go.

Eventually cash was substituted for trophies, and with that came "ringers" — or hired guns. They were most always pitchers, usually grizzled veterans who had been around the block and who could go on just a day or two of rest. They even had a fancy name for these guys, "competent baseballists."

The interest in the sport grew quickly. That year, a local newspaper editor remarked that: "The game of Base Ball has become so much the style that nearly every village and hamlet has its club, and to be a member of the first nine is now looked upon as being nearly as honorable a position as a seat in the Legislature."

By the 1870s some new clubs in the state emerged as contenders, including: the Northfield "Silver Stars," Hastings "Crescents," Winona "Clipper," "Unions" and "Blue Stockings" of Minneapolis, and the "North Stars" and "Red Caps" of St. Paul. And, although these clubs professes to be strictly amateur in status, they, like their predecessors, did not shy away from hiring a professional "ringer" or two, especially when the big bucks were on the line for a large tournament.

Town ball continued to grow in popularity right up through the turn of the century, despite the fact that numerous semi-pro and minor-professional leagues got thrown into the mix. There was still a place for the amateur game though, and the format flourished — particularly in smaller, rural areas throughout the state. In small-town America, being on a town team was like being royalty. It gave communities a sense of pride and helped them to form a sense of identity. Summers were planned around the teams' schedules, and their games were front-page news. There was also a lot of gambling associated with the games in the early years as well. In fact, some ballparks were even located within horse track infields, so that an entire day of betting could be had by all. And, with all of that money on the line, the need for "ringers" grew ever more prevalent.

Dassel Players — 1913

Howard Lake (1900)

★ WRIGHT-STAR LEAGUE ★
ALL STAR
BASEBALL GAME
Co-Leaders
BUFFALO
AND
ELK RIVER
VS.
ALL STARS

SATURDAY NIGHT, JULY 7 8:15 P.M.
BUFFALO MEMORIAL PARK
[In Case Of Rain, Game Will Be Played Monday Night, July 9]

ALL STAR ROSTER

Don't Miss This Big Attraction!
Admission: Adults 50¢, Children 25¢

July 7, 1956

Men from as far away as St. Louis and Chicago were now making the trip to Minnesota to play ball for the highest bidders.

For many of those smaller farming communities, however, the game was more difficult than in the bigger cities. Permanent baseball fields were few and far between, as were gloves and uniforms. But the games were no less important in the country than in the city. Early on, it brought new settlers together at a time when social gatherings were a rarity. The really rural areas played "pasture ball," which, in some instances, even brought livestock into play. In fact, it wasn't uncommon for a family farm to host several hundred neighbors to watch a good pasture ball game on a Sunday afternoon picnic out in a newly plowed field.

In 1924 the State Amateur Baseball tournament was begun thanks to the efforts of Roy Dunlap, the Editor of the St. Paul Pioneer Press and Dispatch. Dunlap encouraged the newspaper to sponsor the tournament, which eventually featured eight teams — each representing a regional district. The Association of Minnesota Amateur Baseball Leagues governed the event and established the ground rules from the get-go. The tournament was first held in St. Paul, making for quite a trek by train for the outstate teams. (It was particularly unfair to the rural teams because most of the players were farmers, and couldn't be away for any long period of time during the crucial harvesting season.) But they did it, and the tourney was, by all accounts, a big success. That year the St Paul Armours, behind the outstanding play of tourney MVP George (Lefty) Boche, beat Stillwater to claim the first ever Town Team State Tournament title.

This system was good but not great. Many of the out-state teams felt that their league champions should be entitled to go to the State Tournament, while others thought that only region champs should go. Finally, in 1934, a regional setup was approved by all the leagues, which saw eight regional champions plus 11 outstate league champions attend to the tournament. Two years later they canned the 11 outstate league champions though, and the rest, they say, is history.

The roaring '20s were the good ol' days for town ball. One of the highlights of this era came in October of 1924, when the great Bambino, Babe Ruth, came to Minnesota. The Babe had just led his Yankees to the World Series title and was in the midst of a 19-game western city barnstorming tour to promote the game of baseball, as well as himself. The Babe

Delano (1906)

Buffalo (1912)

Maple Lake (1931 Class B Champs)

Darwin (1936 Class A Runner-Ups)

Winsted (1948 Class A Champs)

was the biggest superstar of his day. This was a man who had hit 59 home runs in a single season (1921) and was literally, larger than life. He had just signed a contract with the Yankees for $52,000 a year, because, said Ruth, "I've always wanted to make a grand a week…" (The next highest paid player in baseball made just $16,000!) Ruth came with teammate Bob Meusel and between the two of them, they would receive the first $2,000 of the gate receipts for each game they played. This was big dough back in the day, and it was easy to see why so many big-leaguers were anxious to make a few extra bucks during their Fall break. (In fact, the year before Ruth signed that fat contract, he actually made more money barnstorming than as a major leaguer.)

So, on October 14th, Babe and Bob played in an exhibition game at Nicollet Park. Ruth, who played first base and went 4-for-5 with a pair of homers and six RBIs, played for the "Odd Fellows," the Minneapolis amateur champions. Meusel, meanwhile, played for the "Al Dretchko's All-Stars," which lost the game, 8-5.

Two days later, Ruth wound up playing a game in little Sleepy Eye, in Southwestern Minnesota. Why Sleepy Eye? According to columnist Randy Krzmarzick, the Knights of Columbus at St. Mary's may have been involved in attracting him there. The Babe was a devout Catholic and was fond of the Knights of Columbus chapters that regularly honored him in New York, so he went out of his way to help them out. Well, the big day came, and with that, so did the Minnesota weather. It got below freezing that afternoon and even snowed. A crowd of 10,000 was anticipated, but that number didn't even come close. It was a financial disaster for the locals, but it was a dream-come-true for the kids who played hooky and got the see the great Babe Ruth. A band met him when he arrived and he was even presented a key to the city from the mayor.

During the exhibition game Ruth and Meusel played with an all-star team of sorts made up of ballplayers from the surrounding area. The lucky chap who would get to pitch to the Babe was local boy Sylvester "Sox" Schueller, a "21-year-old fireballer from Sleepy Eye's town team." Schueller, despite giving up a pair of very long homers, was able to fan the fat man — giving himself an instant "story for the grandkids." According to the New Ulm Review newspaper, Ruth played right field, then second base, and finally pitched the ninth as his team won the contest 9-7. After the game, the Babe and his entourage attended a banquet and even a dance before boarding a train that next morning for Sioux Falls, and another game the next day.

Another great story of the 1920s and '30s era is that of the Great Soo League, which featured teams from: Richmond, Watkins, Eden Valley, Paynesville, Cold Spring, Albany, Holdingford, New Munich, Melrose, Rockville, St. Anthony, St. Martin, St. Joseph, and St. Cloud. Former Senator Eugene McCarthy played for five seasons in the "Soo" for tiny Watkins, a town of just 600 souls, and later wrote about it in a classic article entitled: "My Life in the Great Soo League." According to McCarthy, "the name of the league was an amalgam of the two east-west railroad lines—the Saulte Ste. Marie (known as the Soo Line) and the Great Northern, which ran parallel to the Soo and about 15 miles to the north."

The league was a throw-back, even back then. They were against bringing in ringers, and it was just understood that if your team needed a pitcher, you had to recruit one from within your city limits. Their was also no age limit in the league either, which made it a generational thing for friends and families.

It was a different time in American history, and this was in the height of Prohibition. But, out in the sticks, moonshine was all the rage for the fans and players alike. "The drinking at the games never presented a problem," said McCarthy, "and in fact, it may have attracted some of the better umpires from Minneapolis, who otherwise, might have been reluctant to make the trip."

The teams never made any money, they just tried to break even and have fun. Between bats and balls, transportation, hotels, ballpark maintenance, umpires, an off-duty cop to patrol the joint, and maybe even an occasional pitcher from the big city, the teams rang up about $100 a week. So, between gate receipts, program ads and volunteers selling baked goods at the concession stands, the clubs did OK. Adults got in for 35¢ and kids were a quarter, so if they were able to draw a few hundred fans out to see them, they were in business.

The ballparks of the day were nothing like we know of today either. They were mostly sand infields, because the upkeep on grass was simply too difficult. And the outfield grass was mowed when the farmer was good and ready to mow it! Sometimes the players had to run the gauntlet through hay, between gopher holes and around ant hill mounds just to catch a fly ball.

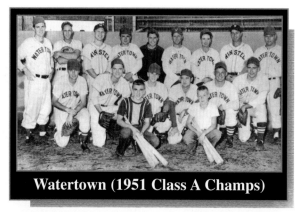
Watertown (1951 Class A Champs)

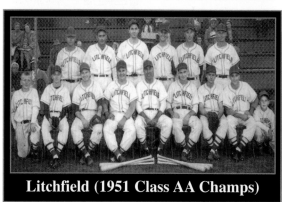
Litchfield (1951 Class AA Champs)

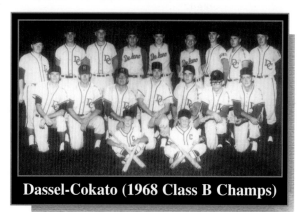
Dassel-Cokato (1968 Class B Champs)

Hamel (1987 Class B Champs)

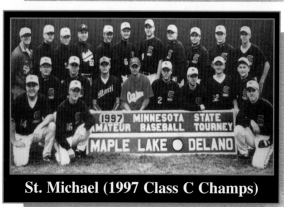
St. Michael (1997 Class C Champs)

McCarthy also talked about the difficulty of hitting home runs. "Home runs were hard to come by in the Soo League because few parks had fences," he said. "The one time I figured I had an advantage was when we played a park where there was a cemetery in the outfield. The idea was to try to hit the ball among the headstones, figuring that the left fielder wouldn't chance stepping on his grand-father's grave just to chase a ball."

Wagering, fist-fights and gopher holes were all par for the course in the old Soo, but it was old-time baseball at its purest — and just one story in a million as to why town ball is so important to Minnesota's sports heritage.

In 1930 town ball went to a two class system of A & AA. (They also had "mythical" state champions which were selected until the 1970s to determine one overall winner.) One highlight of the '30s came in 1938, when the "Splendid Splinter" himself, Ted Williams, played a town ball game in Springfield. Teddy Ballgame, who was then playing for the Red Sox AAA farm club, the Minneapolis Millers, was staying sharp before being called up to the "Show."

Town ball continued to grow in popularity throughout this era. Between 1945 and 1959 the State Tournament drew over 20,000 fans on nearly a dozen occasions. And, in 1950 alone, Minnesota had 950 amateur and semi-pro teams playing in 103 leagues. Some 35,000 fans attended that year's tourney as the Class A portion went to a paid format, while the B stayed free. It seemed like just about every town from each corner of the Land of 10,000 Lakes had fielded a team at one time or another, and more were signing up every year.

(It is also interesting to note that throughout this era, many famous Negro League players came to Minnesota either as individual "ringers-for-hire" or else as members of traveling teams which did the circuit of town ball and exhibition games on a nightly basis. Fairmont, for instance, had the great Satchel Paige play at local Martin Park as a ringer, while other teams such as the Colored Brooklyn Dodgers and even the Harlem Globetrotters Colored Team play there in the '30s as well. The teams, which were given a percentage of the gate receipts, usually let the locals get an early lead, to get the fans into it, and then come back to win. They were usually careful, however, not to win by too much — after all, they wanted to get invited back the next year! Did you know that Hall of Fame Negro League Pitcher Hilton Smith spent the summer of 1949 playing on tiny

Fulda's town ball team? For many folks in these small towns, it was their first encounter with African Americans. It was also an interesting sidebar to our amazing baseball history.)

Throughout the 1950s a pair of town team leagues stood above all the rest, the Western Minny League and the Southern Minny League. This was the era of the post-war baseball boom and the fans couldn't get enough. The pro game was also getting more and more popular, and as a result, the need for feeder programs was on the rise. Enter the Western Minny.

The Western started out as just another town team league in Sibley and Renville Counties in 1936, but after it began to completely dominate the state tournament a few years later, it started looking for some tougher competition. With that, the league made the decision to go big-time and turn pro. By 1947 the Western was a full-fledged semi-pro circuit competing in Class AA, and in 1950 it became a fully paid league.

Among the towns that fielded teams in the Western Minny over the years were: Springfield (1940-54), Fairfax (1939-42; 46-52), New Ulm (1939-54), Fairmont (1951-54), Gibbon (1939-47), Marshall (1941, 53-54), Litchfield (1954), Bird Island (1939), Mankato (1940), Redwood Falls (1947-54), Olivia (1939; 42; 50), Sleepy Eye (1945-54), Franklin (1939; 47), Willmar (1954), Winthrop (1939-42; 50-53), St. James (1943-53) and Hector (1939).

By now it had evolved into one of the

Front Row: L to R - Milt Nielsen, Harry Pritts, Don Dahlke, Herb Banton, Loyal Bloxam, Myron Hoffman, bat boy: Tom Ross. **Back Row** - Jim McNulty, Ray Rosenbaum, Jerry Ackerman, Fred Boiko, Don Neuenfeldt, Jim Lange.

The 1959 AA Champs from Fairmont
(Manager Jim McNulty led the Martins to a 224-142 lifetime record)

top professional leagues in the nation. So popular was the Western that it often out-drew the popular AAA Minneapolis Millers and St. Paul Saints. Thousands of fans lined up to see the games and the clubs were rewarding those fans with some outstanding baseball. In no time bidding wars ensued between the teams who were vying for top players. A top notch pitcher in the early 1950s made nearly $2,000 a month — bigger bucks than a lot of major leaguers were making at the time.

For seven glorious seasons the Western was the real deal. Each town had a "baseball board" which scoured the country in search of new talent. Local business owners would get the players jobs in the winter and even find host families for them to live with. It became a wonderful blend of young college players on their way up and older grizzled veterans who were on their way down. But, while many of those old guys were past their prime, they could still play. In fact, many of them were ex-major leaguers still hanging on. Some of the players liked it enough to stick around forever. What started out as a summer vacation turned into a career with a wife and kids. The glue that held it all together though, was baseball. It became a generational thing as kids couldn't wait to see their local heroes up close and personal. Sure those small town kids could listen to the Yankees or Cubbies on the radio, and even travel to the Twin Cities to see the Millers or Saints, but this was the big-time right in their own backyard — and they loved it.

By the end of the 1940s another league was making some noise, the Southern Minny League. The Southern, which had been in existence since 1912, would feature several rival teams including the Fairmont Martins (which defected from the Western Minny in 1954), the Mankato Merchants, Faribault Lakers, Winona Chiefs, Austin Packers and Owatonna Aces. The Southern was every bit as competitive as the Western in its heyday, and perhaps even better towards the end. It too was a semi-professional league that played AA teams and in the process attracted a host of future major leaguers, including: Rudy York, who went on to play with Detroit, Jerry Kindall, who played with Chicago, Cleveland and Minnesota, and Bill "Moose" Skowron, who played with Austin before going on to the bigs to play with New York and Chicago. (In addition, Gopher great Paul Giel pitched for Litchfield in the Western Minny in 1954, while waiting to be sent up to the New York Giants.)

Together these two leagues put Southern Minnesota on the map. They played 50-game schedules on Tuesdays, Thursdays and Sundays from May through September and really gave their communities a sense of pride. People drove in from miles around just to see the quality of baseball being played in the two circuits. In fact, by this time most of the players in the league had played in either A, AA, AAA or in the major leagues.

Other rules which came later on included allowing each to

ALL-TIME STATE CHAMPS

YR	CHAMPION	RUNNER-UP	CLASS
1924	St Paul Armours	Stillwater	x
1925	White Bear Lake	Pine Lake	x
1926	St Paul Armours	Ely	x
1927	Mora	St James	x
1928	Mankato	Springfield	x
1929	Albert Lea	Springfield	x
1930	Fairmont	St Paul North Pac.	A
	So. St Paul	LeSueur	B
1931	St Paul Bohn Ref.	Faribault	A
	Maple Lake	Sebeka	B
	Madelia	Lake City	C
1932	St Paul Milk Drivers	Mpls. E. Henn. Mer.	A
	Chaska	Virginia	B
	Brooten	Canton	C
1933	St Paul E.M.B.A.	St Paul Armours	AA
	St Peter	Owatonna	A
	Harmony	New Richland	B
1934	Mpls. Jerseys	St Paul Park	AA
	Willmar	Lakeville	A
1935	St Paul J.J. Kohn	No. St Paul	AA
	Red Wing	Owatonna	A
1936	St Paul Comm. Row	Maple Lake	AA
	Windom	Darwin	A
1937	Mpls. Heinies	St Paul J.J. Kohn	AA

(* J.J. Kohn went on to win the World Amateur Title)

YR	CHAMPION	RUNNER-UP	CLASS
	Austin	Sturgeon Lake	A
1938	St Paul N. St. Env.	St Paul Park	AA
	Owatonna	Cloquet	A
1939	St Paul T.H. Shoe	Mpls. Local 544	AA
	Maple Lake	Fergus Falls	A
1940	Albert Lea	No. St Paul	AA
	Shakopee	Fergus Falls	A
1941	Owatonna	St Paul Robt. Rec.	AA
	New Ulm	Delano	A
1942	Austin	Mpls. Mitby Sathers	AA
	Fairfax	Delano	A
1943	Mpls. Mitby Sathers	Albert Lea	AA
	New Ulm	Nowthen	A
1944	Alberta Lea	St Paul Nickel Joint	AA
	Springfield	Monticello	A
1945	Albert Lea	Mpls. Honeywell	AA
	Excelsior	Mayer	A
1946	Albert Lea	Mpls. Banana's	AA
	Springfield	Austin	A
1947	Albert Lea	New Ulm	AA
	Chaska	Rochester	A
1948	Albert Lea	Mpls. Banana's	AA
	Winsted	Belle Plaine	A
1949	Austin	Fergus Falls	AA
	Excelsior	Winnebago	A
	Little Falls	LaCrescent	B
1950	Fergus Falls	Austin	AA
	LeCenter	Winsted	A
	Lester Prairie	Duluth Teve's	B
1951	Litchfield	Austin	AA
	Watertown	LeCenter	A
	Soderville	Searles	B
1952	Willmar	Albert Lea	AA
	Cannon Falls	Belle Plaine	A
	Soderville	Searles	B
1953	Austin	Litchfield	AA
	Delavan	Little Falls	A
	Rollingstone	Holdingford	B
1954	Benson	Little Falls	A
	Milroy	St Joseph	B
1955	St Peter	Hutchinson	A
	Cold Spring	Granite Falls	B
1956	Mpls. Teamsters	Little Falls	A
	Bemidji	St Charles	B
1957	Waseca	St Paul Briteways	A
	Braham	Norwood	B
1958	Austin	Little Falls	A
	Pipestone	Norwood	B
1959	Fairmont	Bloomington	A
	Shakopee	Springfield	B
1960	Bloomington	St Paul Como Rec	A
	Pipestone	Fergus Falls	B
1961	Mpls. T.C. Federal	St Paul ES. Merc.	A
	St Bonifacius	Perham	B
1962	St Paul Ganzers	St Paul Park	A
	Little Falls	Gaylord	B
1963	Mpls. A&B Sports	Bloomington	A
	Braham	Pipestone	B
1964	St Paul Como Rec.	Mpls. A&B Sports	A

*(Como Rec. remains the only undefeated team)

YR	CHAMPION	RUNNER-UP	CLASS
	St Bonifacius	Caledonia	B
1965	Bloomington	Rochester	A
	St Bonifacius	Rogers	B
1966	Winona	St Paul John White	A
	Perham	Brownton	B
1967	Columbia Heights	St Paul John White	A
	Arlington	Perham	B
1968	Columbia Heights	St Paul ES. Merc.	A
	Dassel-Cokato	Miesville	B
1969	St Paul Sport Spec.	Columbia Heights	A
	Arlington	Prior Lake	B
1970	Columbia Heights	St Paul ES. Merc.	A
	Deer Creek	Cold Spring	B
1971	Chaska	Delano	B
1972	Columbia Heights	Gaylord	B
1973	Cold Spring	Dassel-Cokato	B
1974	Red Wing	West St Paul	B
1975	Prior Lake	Dundas	B
1976	Prior Lake	Dassel-Cokato	B
1977	Mpls. Mr. Roberts	St Paul Tripp Oil	A
	Bemidji	St Augusta	B
1978	Columbia Heights	St Cloud Park	A
	Miesville	Chaska	B
1979	West St Paul	Minnetonka	A
	Arlington	Granite Falls	B
1980	Richfield	West St Paul	A
	New Ulm	Dundas	B
1981	Winona	Mpls. Lakonia's	A
	Cold Spring	Dundas	B
1982	Brooklyn Center	West St Paul	A
	Dundas	Jordan	B
1983	St Paul Steichens	Mpls. Lakonia's	A
	St Cloud	Red Wing	AA
1984	St Paul Frontier Bar	St Paul Red Rooster	A
	Arlington	Burnsville	AA
1985	Mpls. Haleks	St Paul Steichens	A
	Arlington	Red Wing	AA
1986	Columbia Heights	St Paul Steichens	A
	Cold Spring	Red Wing	B
1987	Bloomington	Columbia Heights	A
	Hamel	St Cloud	B
1988	Mpls. J. Botten	St Paul Highland	A
	Dundas	Jordan	B
	Delano	Maple Plain	C
1989	Columbia Heights	Bloomington	A
	Miesville	Hamel	B
	Morris	St James	C
1990	St Paul Conquest R.	Columbia Heights	A
	Red Wing	Jordan	B
	Bovey	Hampton	C
1991	Mpls. Angels	St Paul East Side	A
	Rochester	Miesville	B
	Regal	Belle Plaine	C
1992	Mpls. Angels	St Louis Park	A
	Miesville	Hamel	B
	Sartell	Detroit Lakes	C
1993	Highland Park	Mpls. Angels	A
	Red Wing	Miesville	B
	Granite Falls	Dassel-Cokato	C
1994	Mpls. Angels	Minnetonka	A
	Jordan	Cold Spring	B
	Belle Plaine	Milroy	C
1995	St Paul Rosetown	Mpls. Adrians	A
	Miesville	Rochester	B
	Sauk Rapids	Glyndon	C
1996	Highland Park	Minnetonka	A
	Cold Spring	Dundas	B
	Plato	Gaylord	C
1997	Minnetonka	St Louis Park	A
	Hamel	Cold Spring	B
	St Michael	Regal	C
1998	Minnetonka	St Louis Park	A
	Dundas	Chaska	B
	Glencoe	Richmond	C
1999	Minnetonka	Min. Athletics	A
	Dundas	Rochester	B
	Buckman	Green Isle	C
2000	Glynn Building	Mpls. Cobras	A
	Cold Spring	Rochester	B
	Brainerd	Princeton	C
2001	Minnetonka	Glynn Building	A
	Cold Spring	Austin	B
	Watkins	Buckman	C
2002	St. Louis Park	Air Freight Unlimited	A
	Austin	Chaska	B
	Granite Falls	Lonsdale	C

Source: Brian Larson

THE TOURNAMENT'S OUTSTANDING AND MOST VALUABLE PLAYERS

From 1924 to 1936 an outstanding player award was given to the tourney's top player and was usually selected by members of the media as well as baseball scouts who were in attendance. The Most Valuable Player award followed in 1937 and was called the Governor's Cup. Minnesota's governor was even usually on hand to present the award in person.

1924 - George (Lefty) Boche — St. Paul Armours
1925 - Ade Stemig — White Bear Lake
1926 - George (Lefty) Boche — St. Paul Armours
1927 - Rube Chell — Mora
1928 - George (Lefty) Boche — Mankato
1929 - Gil Aase — Albert Lea
1930 - S Weirck — St. Paul Polish National
1931 - Franny Hall — Maple Lake
1932 - Leslie Lieverman — Chaska
1933 - Harold Solomonson — St. Peter
1934 - Marvin Denzer — Willmar
1935 - Max Molock — Red Wing
1936 - Fred Ludke — Windom
1937 - John Hulet — Austin
1938 - William Guse — Owatonna
1939 - Howard Pennertz — Maple Lake
1940 - John Menke — Albert Lea
           Francis Boll — Shakopee
1941 - Henry Nicklasson — New Ulm
1942 - Sebastian Bassie — Wagner-Fairfax
1943 - Walt Mernich — Nowthen
1944 - Jimmy Delmont — Albert Lea
1945 - Al Litfin — Excelsior
1946 - Walt Menke — Albert Lea
1947 - Gread (Lefty) McKinnis — Rochester
1948 - Maurice (Spike) Gorham — Albert Lea
1949 - Rollie Seltz — Excelsior
1950 - Ed Piacentini — Fergus Falls
1951 - Dave Spencer — Soderville
1952 - Art Grangaard — Willmar-
1953 - Rich Weigel — Delavan-
1954 - Charles Bosacker — Benson
1955 - Jack Hoppe — Cold Spring
1956 - Don Woerner — Little Falls
1957 - Vein Edmunds — Waseca
1958 - Jim Lawler — Austin
1959 - Fulton Weckman — Shakopee
1960 - Wayne Tjaden — Bloomington
1961 - Richie Allen — Twin City Federal
1962 - Robert Fenske — Little Falls
1963 - Chuck Gageby — Pipestone
1964 - Gordy Bauer — Caledonia
1965 - Dick Southard — Rogers
1966 - Al Stigman — Perham
1967 - Jim Stoll — Arlington
1968 - Joe Harmala — Dassel-Cokato
1969 - Jim Stoll — Arlington
1970 - Bill Huls — Cold Spring
1971 - Bob Mielke — Chaska
1972 - Jerry Wickman — Columbia Heights
1973 - Don Nierengarten — Cold Spring

1974 - Bob Turnbull — Red Wing
1975 - Mary Menken — Prior Lake
1976 - Bob Kelly — Prior Lake
1977 - Steve Donahue — Bemidji
1978 - Dan Carey — Miesville
1979 - Joe Driscoll — Arlington.
1980 - Terry Steinbach — New Ulm
1981 - Tom Arnold — Cold Spring
1982 - Lew Olson — Dundas
1983 - Jim Eisenreich — St. Cloud
1984 - Greg Odegaard — Arlington
1985 - Greg Odegaard — Arlington
1986 - A — Randy Moselle — Columbia Heights
           B — Matt Butala — Cold Spring
           C — Ron Beckman — Jordan
1987 - A — No Selection
           B — Rod Schafer — Hamel
           C — Tom Schleper — Chaska-
1988 - A — Steve Sagedahl — J. Botten
           B — Scott Nelson — Dundas
           C — Dave Ditty — Delano
1989 - A — Randy Moselle — Columbia Heights
           B — Jay Johnson --— Miesville
           C — Steve Selk — Morris
1990 - A — Mark Crandall — Conquest Rooster
           B — Mike Hartman — Red Wing
           C — Ray Santelli — Bovey
1991 - A — Jim Meyer — Mpls. Angels
           B — Bill Cutshall — Rochester
           C — Tim Haines — Regal
1992 - A — No selection
           B — Bill Frederick — Miesville
           C — Scott Hille — Sartell
1993 - A — Steve Berryhill — Highland Park
           B — Wade Shelstad — Red Wing
           C — Tim Knapper — Granite Falls
1994 - A — Bill Zeller — Mpls. Angels
           B — John Dolan — Jordan
           C — Barry Wohler — Belle Plaine
1995 - A — Dave Lance — Rosetown
           B — Bill Frederick — Miesville
           C — Brad Keenan — Glyndon
1996 - A — Matt Farley — Highland Park
           B — Steve Taylor — Cold Spring
           C — Dave Franke — Plato
1997 - A — Bryan Krull — Minnetonka
           B — Brian Hartmann — Hamel
           C — Grant Ketel — St Michael
1998 - A — Dave Holland — St Louis Park
           B — Aaron Erickson — Dundas
           C — Brian Jenneke — Glencoe
1999 - A — Bryan Krull — Minnetonka
           B — Brice Pleschourt — Dundas
           C — Scott Boser — Buckman
2000 - A — Glynn Building (The team was named MVP)
           B — Andy Bulson — Cold Spring
           C — Chris Studer — Brainerd
2001 - A — Matt Parrington — Minnetonka
           B — Andy Bulson — Cold Spring
           C — Bruce Geislinger — Watkins
2002   A — Matt Paulson - St. Louis Park
           B — David Meyer - Austin
           C — Tim Knapper - Granite Falls

Source: Brian Larson

Most home runs hit in a state tournament
204   Granite Falls-Marshall, 1999
178   Wadena-Perham, 1995

Most triples hit in a state tournament
39   New Ulm, 1953

Largest margin of a win
33   Hamel 33 Proctor 0 (7 innings), 1990

Most runs scored in one inning by one team
14   Maple Lake   (Maple Lake 19 - Hutchinson 17), 1989
11   New Ulm   (New Ulm 22 - Duluth 2), 1995

Longest State Tournament Game
20 innings   (Hector 4 - Stark 2), 1971
           (Cyrus 2 - Fairfax 1), 1976

Most Consecutive Championships won
5   Albert Lea   (1944-48)

Most Championships won
8   Columbia Heights
7   Cold Spring
6   Albert Lea

Most Times finishing 2nd Place
4   Dundas
    Little Falls

Most Times Finishing 3rd Place
6   Cold Spring
    Jordan
5   West St. Paul

Most Consecutive State Tournament Appearances
14   Cold Spring   1988-
10   Miesville   1987-1996
     Warroad   1949-1958

Most State Tournament Appearances
40   Cold Spring
24   Crookston

Most Hits in one State Tournament game by a player
6   Walt Menke   Albert Lea (A.L. 23-Zumbrota 2), 1946

Most Hits by a player in a State Tournament
19   Scott Boser   Buckman   1999
17   Eric Welter   Chaska   1998

Tom Schieper	Chaska	1998
Joe Siple	Rochester	1999
Ron Terres	Cold Spring	2001

Most Home Runs in one State Tournament game by a player
3   Joe Sczublewski   Upsala   (Upsala 8 - Kimball 5), 1984
    Dave Dykema   Osakis   (Osakis 7 - Vegas 3), 1988
    Ronn Van Krevelen Hamel(Hamel 9 - Prior Lake 8), 1989
    Alex Bauer   Hamel   (Hamel 12 - G.Rapids 5), 1997
    Brian Hartmann   Hamel   (Hamel 12 -G. Rapids 5), 1997
    Phil Clennon   Springfield (Spr. 10 - Red Eye 5), 1997
    Josh Loesch   Cold Spring (C.S. 18-New Ulm 10), 1997
    Brice Pleachourt   Dundas (Dun. 11 - Miesville 10), 1998
    Dave Gray   St James (St J. 13 -Monticello 12), 1999
    Josh Loesch   Cold Spring (CS 10 - New Ulm 5), 1999
    Chris Studer   Brainerd (Brain. 9 - Princeton 5), 2000
    Corey Tauer   Red Wing (CS 13 - Red Wing 8), 2001

Most Home Runs by a player in a State Tournament
8   Brian Hartmann   Hamel   1997
7   Josh Loesch   Cold Spring   1999
    Corey Tauer   Red Wing   2001

Most Stolen Bases by a player in a State Tournament
9   Corey Nelson   Luverne   1999
8   Kevin Sannes   Rochester   1995

Most RBI's in one State Tournament game by a player
8   Josh Loesch   Cold Spring (CS 18-New Ulm 10), 1997
    Brian Dorr   Princeton (Pri. 16 - Minn Lake 6), 1998

Most RBIs by a player in a State Tournament
17   Mark Kragnes   Glyndon   1995
    Scott Boser   Buckman   1999

Most Runs Scored by a player in a State Tournament
15   Steve Huls   Cold Spring   2001

Most strikeouts by a pitcher in a Nine Inning game.
21   Don Jorrisen   St. Boni (St. Boni 1 - Belgrade 0), 1959
    Jerry Vandermay Perham (Perham 7 - Pierz 0), 1967

Most Strikeouts by a pitcher in a State Tournament
54   Brian Jenneke, Glencoe   1998
41   Jerry Wickman, Columbia Heights 1972
40   Vein Edmunds, Waseca   1957

Most wins by a pitcher in a State Tournament
5   Brad Keenan   Glyndon   1995

Source: Brian Larson

team to recruit up to two "ringers," or players from opposing teams which had been eliminated from the post-season, to join their clubs during the playoffs. Soon big stadiums with lights were being built to keep up with the Jones'. The fundraising was constant too, with fundraisers raffles and banquets becoming weekly occurrences in many communities. They would also sell ads for game-programs and calendars for $25 apiece to all of the local businesses to make ends meet.

By the mid-1950s a salary cap of $7,500 a month was imposed to keep the teams under control. But the local "friends of the program" businessmen had no problem subsidizing the team if it happened to go over its budget. They got to be "big-shots" in their small towns and that was good for business. The baseball boards did whatever it took to bring in the top talent, even if it meant working with the local school boards to hire teachers who could hit.

One such teacher was a kid by the name of Don Dahlke, who

had played AAA ball in the St. Louis Cardinals organization before winding up in Fairmont, to play with the Martins. And, as luck would have it, one of those baseball board big-wigs was a furniture store owner by the name of Jay Pieser. Jay did whatever it took to make his club better. From raising money for new lights at the ball-park to handling the teams' finances, Jay was the heart and soul of that franchise. Pieser ever rec-ommended Dahlke for a teaching job to the superintendent and that ballplayer-turned-teacher has been living in Fairmont ever since. Teams like the Martins were typical in this era. They were baseball crazy and truly supported their club. They came out in droves to Martin Park, often times packing in more than 1,200 fans per outing.

But in the late 1950s attendance started to dwindle, not just in the Western and Southern Minnies, but all across America. Television, bet-ter automobiles and more disposable income were all factors for the lull. For whatever the reason, baseball was losing its popularity in big way. Locally, perhaps the fans throughout the leagues got too big for their own good. After all, it was just fun and games when the local town team was made up of kids from the neighborhood, and not a bunch of young men from California and New York — who were going to be gone that next season anyway. The league even tried to counter that by imposing a "Rookie Rule" which required each team to carry three local, unpaid players. It didn't work. The fans were spoiled by now and expected top-notch talent.

Before long the league started to feel the pinch. Smaller towns couldn't afford it and bigger ones took their place. At the end of the 1956 season local powerhouse New Ulm dropped out and decided to return to the cozy confines of amateur town ball. That next year the Western Minny was disbanded. The New Ulm Brewers then went on to win the Minnesota River Conference that next year, show-ing everyone that fun could still be had at the lower levels. The Southern hung on for a little while longer, but it too finally suc-cumbed when the arrival of the Twins gave the fans much more than they ever could. It was the end of a truly wonderful chapter of Minnesota baseball.

In 1966, the State Tournament format was changed to the present setup with the region champions and the runner-ups advanc-ing to the State Tournament. Then, in 1974, the aluminum bat was introduced. The prospect of an occasional maimed pitcher or third baseman far outweighed the cost factors when dealing with wooden bats — so it stayed.

In 1986 Minnesota went to a three tiered system, implementing a Class A, B & C format in an effort to divide the teams into a more equal level of competition. Class A would include all teams composed of players inside the 694/494 loop. (Since 1987, the big-city teams from the Minneapolis, St. Paul and the Riverview Leagues have been on their own, playing their tourney at Parade Stadium.) Class B was the crème de la crème of the non-metro teams — complete with more college guys home for the Summer. Class C, meanwhile, comprised the heart and soul of what makes town ball tick, fea-turing teams from all over the state which were categorized into leagues

with neighboring towns. In addition, the 16-team double-elimination Class C extravaganza was held at various locales over a period of three weekends at the end of the Summer, with the drama of crown-ing a champion concluding on Labor Day.

Through the 1990s town team baseball has continued to be a mainstay. Other than the recent decision by the Minnesota Baseball Association (MBA) to outlaw aluminum bats and go back to using only wooden ones, the league has been a classic example of "if it aint broke…don't fix it." Today there are 59 leagues with 308 teams playing ball. It is all about fathers and sons, brothers and uncles, and friends and family getting together to play the game. From the clas-sic old ballparks of Miesville and Red Wing, to historic Hand's Park in Fairmont, town ball is alive and well in Minnesota. Full of great traditions, history and heritage, the annual town team state tourna-ment is a culmination of countless hours of hard work from fans and volunteers alike. With their support though, town team baseball has emerged as one of Minnesota's truly sacred cows.

STATE TOURNAMENT NO-HITTERS

YR	SITE	PITCHER	SCORE
1926	St. Paul	Bill Johnson	Mpls. Bottineau 4 - Dassel 0
1929	Mankato	Bob Thompson	Springfield 12 - Osseo 0
1932	St. Paul	Jack Stans	Chaska 15 - Sleepy Eye 0
1932	St. Paul	Ron DeLa Hunt	Chaska 19 - Onamia 0
1945	Albert Lea	Roger McDonald	Excelsior 4 - Mayer 0
1947	Mankato	Don Anderson Vern Cooney	Chaska 1 - Maple Lake 0
1950	St. Cloud	Roman Bartowski	Austin 16 - St. Paul Nickel Joint 0
1951	Faribault	Dick Donnelly	Litchfield 23 - St. P. Nickel Joint 0
1951	Faribault	Dave Spencer	Soderville 17 - Pengilly 0
1959	St. Cloud	Jerry Zeliner	Bloomington 4 - Mpls. 0
1967	Alexandria	Cal Larson	Alexandria 9 - Thief River Falls 0
1972	Wadena	Greg Bigalke	Shady Brook 4 - Hinckley 1
1973	Jordan	Jerry Wickman	Columbia Heights 2 - Marshall 0
1979	St. Cloud	Duane Paulson	Lastrup 10 - Menagha 0
1992	Jordan	Tom Traen	Delano 1 - Cold Spring 0

Source: Brian Larson

Bud Grant

One of the most famous "ringers" of all time is leg-endary Minnesota Vikings Coach, Bud Grant. During his college years at the U of M, where he starred in football, basketball and baseball — earning nine let-ters from 1946-1949 — Bud used to spend his sum-mers playing town ball. Since he could pitch three days a week and bat clean-up, he would venture from town to town and play baseball for about $250 a week. Back then, that was pretty big dough for a college kid! Bud, of course, went on to play pro basketball and football before becoming a Hall of Fame coach with the Minnesota Vikings. He is without question, one of Minnesota's most beloved all-time sports figures.

THE GOLDEN GOPHERS

One of the most respected and consistently most talented baseball programs in the nation, the University of Minnesota's Golden Gophers first hit the diamond way back in June of 1876. Baseball was growing in popularity during this post-Civil War era and the University was leading the way. The team used to play local semi-pro clubs at this point, including the St. Paul Saxons and Minneapolis

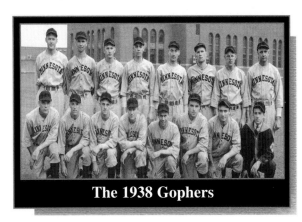
The 1938 Gophers

Unions among others. Soon, the team was playing other local college and university teams as well, with Hamline, Carleton, St. Thomas and even Shattuck Academy leading the way.

By 1891 the Gophers were finally venturing outside their borders, playing their first out-state game at Beloit (IL), winning, 10-5, and then that next night at the University Wisconsin, where they lost 5-4. The Gophers went 9-5 in 1894, highlighted by a 34-0 win over Macalaster. By now the Gophers were taking the trains to as such far away exotic locales as Michigan, Indiana, Illinois, Iowa and Nebraska.

By 1906 the team was playing in conference action. That next year the team won the Big Nine conference championship. The star of the team was the soon-to-be-legendary Bobby Marshall, who was also a star on the Gopher Football team. In 1908 the team got its first coach when Walter Wilmot took over. He would go 36-20-3 in his three year tenure in Gold Country. Wilkie Clark took over in 1911 and was replaced in 1913 with Dr. Denny Sullivan. The good Doctor would win 19 games before handing the reigns to Frosty Thomas in 1915.

The Gophers were playing good baseball through this era when all of a sudden, in the winter of 1915, the Big Nine Conference (it would be renamed as the Big 10 in a few years) voted to abolish intercollegiate baseball. The Gophers would play on an informal basis during what proved to be a seven year hiatus, scrimmaging against many local teams, especially those from the nearby MIAC. They returned to action in 1922, however, beating St. Olaf, 11-2, in their first official game back.

That next year the Gophers hired what would prove to be their first full-time

Don Tepel

coach, Lee Watrous, who would post a modest 32-39 record during his four-year tenure in Gold Country. In 1927 Potsy Clark took over and in 1928 he would be replaced with A.H. Bergman. But, Bergman would sport just a .444 winning record in his three years behind the bench, so he passed the baton to Frank McCormick in 1931.

McCormick would be the longest tenured skipper in the team's history up to this point, guiding the club to an impressive 138-89-1 record from 1931-1941. McCormick was eager to get his club into the upper tier of Big 10 Conference schools and in 1933 led the Gophs to a 6-1 record, good for its first ever Big 10 title. Then, after finishing last in 1934, the Gophers came back to win their second conference crown in 1935 with an impressive 17-3 record.

In 1942 David McMillan took over as the team's new coach. McMillan, who was also a basketball coach, would lead the Gophers to a 67-35-1 record through 1947. He did manage to lead the club to a second place finish that next year, but could not get any higher than that afterwards.

Ken Yackel

Then, in the Fall of 1947, the Gophers hired Dick Siebert to serve as their new coach. And, by the time the "Chief" would leave his post more than three decades later, he would garner 754 victories — becoming the program's all-time winningest coach.

In 1952 the Gophers were blessed with the debut of Winona native Paul Giel, who was also starring on the Gopher Football team. Siebert would later say that "Pitching Paulie" Giel was the hardest-throwing pitcher he had ever coached. Giel was incredibly named as a two-time All-American in 1953 and 1954. (Minnesota's first All-American was Second Baseman Gene Elder, who won the award in 1952.) On the mound, Giel earned 21 wins, and had the same number of complete games. He is still in the Gopher record book top-10 for the most career strikeouts, with 243, and most single season strikeouts, with 92. He finished his brilliant career with a 2.16 ERA before going on to play for Leo Durocher's New York Giants. Giel, who was also an All-American Gopher running back, finished as the runner-up for the Heisman Trophy to Notre Dame's Johnny Lattner that season as well, and was even drafted by the NFL's Chicago Bears.

The Chief struggled through the early part of the 1950s, but got serious in 1955, when his 23-9 Gophers

Jerry Thomas

finished second in the Big Ten. Then, in 1956 the Gophers made history by capturing their first national championship. It was a storybook year that saw the club breeze through its competition and coast into the Mideast Region Semifinals, which were held in Minneapolis. There, the Gophs were edged by Notre Dame, 4-3, in Game One. The Gophers recovered to win the next two games, 15-5 and 10-1, to take the series. Minnesota kept it going that next week in the Mideast Regional Finals in Athens, Ohio. There, they swept Ohio, 5-0 and 7-6, to advance to the College World Series in Omaha.

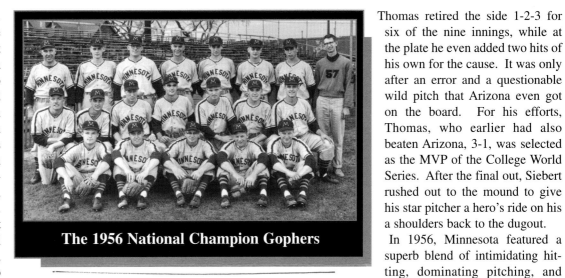

The 1956 National Champion Gophers

Gopher Pitchers Jerry Thomas, Rod Oistad and Ron Craven all made big contributions in leading Minnesota to its first national championships. Thomas, an All-American, would appear in three games during the World Series, going 1-1 with two complete games, while Oistad and Craven would each earn a complete-game victory as well. So, on June 9th, the Gophers opened up the big dance by downing the University of Wyoming, 4-0. In Game Two the Gophs, behind Pitcher Jerry Thomas' three-hit gem, topped Arizona, 3-1, and in Game Three they beat up on Mississippi, 13-5. On the fourth day of tournament play Minnesota just kept on rolling, beating Bradley, 8-3. But then, in the first game of the Finals, the Gophers finally got beat, losing to Arizona, 10-4, in the double-elimination tournament. They rebounded in that next game though, thoroughly pounding the Wildcats, 12-1, to claim their first ever NCAA championship.

The Gophers jumped out to a quick 1-0 lead in that championship game when Bill Horning led off the first inning with a single, stole second, and then scored on a Dave Lindblom double. Minnesota never relinquished the lead after that. Doug Gillen followed with another double and, before you knew it, coach Siebert's boys were up by 3-0. It became 4-0 in the fourth after two walks, plus another Horning single, and 10-0 after a six-run fifth inning where the Gopher bats really came alive. With the score 10-1 in the seventh, Horning belted his second homer of the game to put the final nail in the Wildcat coffin. Along with Horning's four hits, other Gophers who had hits in the game included Gillen, McNeeley and David Lindblom, who each had a pair, while Jack McCartan, Jerry Kindall, R. Anderson and Gene Martin, each added one apiece.

Gopher pitcher Jerry Thomas pitched masterfully, giving up only five hits en route to mowing down four Wildcats, and walking only one. Amazingly,

The 1960 National Champion Gophers

Thomas retired the side 1-2-3 for six of the nine innings, while at the plate he even added two hits of his own for the cause. It was only after an error and a questionable wild pitch that Arizona even got on the board. For his efforts, Thomas, who earlier had also beaten Arizona, 3-1, was selected as the MVP of the College World Series. After the final out, Siebert rushed out to the mound to give his star pitcher a hero's ride on his a shoulders back to the dugout.

In 1956, Minnesota featured a superb blend of intimidating hitting, dominating pitching, and smooth fielding. Led on the mound by All-American and tournament MVP Jerry Thomas, who won 12 games that season while going 5-0 in conference games, the Gophers started a string of what would be 11 Big Ten championships and three NCAA titles over coach Siebert's brilliant 31-year career. Leading the way offensively was slugger Jack McCartan, who was not only an All-American third baseman on the baseball team, but was also an All-American goalie on the John Mariucci's Gopher Hockey team. Another key member of that squad was Shorty Cochran, who stole 22 bases in 1956 as well.

The Gophers hit .320 as a team and boasted an amazing .976 fielding percentage as well. The conference championship ended an 18-year drought for the Gophers, who were typically at an arctic disadvantage geographically against the southern schools who had the luxury of having longer and more temperate practicing weather.

On winning his first NCAA crown, Coach Siebert would say: "You're always prejudiced about your own kids, but I think this was the greatest team that ever played in the College World Series. This was my greatest thrill, barring none!"

Two weeks later All-American Gopher Shortstop Jerry Kindall, who hit a record 18 home runs that year in Gold Country — a single-season record that would stand for 40 years, turned pro by signing with the Chicago Cubs. (It is interesting to note that Kindall, who would later play with the Twins, would make history some 20 years later when, as head coach of those same Arizona Wildcats, he led his teams to three national championships. In the process, he became the only person ever to play on and coach a College World Series national champion.)

Minnesota missed the post-season in 1957, but rebounded to make the Mideast Regionals in 1958. There, at Kalamazoo, Mich., Western Michigan blanked the 26-7 Gophers, 4-0, in Game One, while Notre Dame finished them off in Game Two, 11-8, to

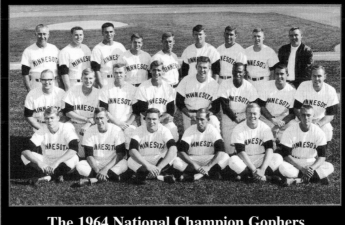

The 1964 National Champion Gophers

DICK SIEBERT

A native of Fall River, Mass., Dick Siebert began his baseball days at St. Paul Concordia High School and he later attended Concordia Junior College. From there he moved to the Concordia Seminary in St. Louis with full intentions of becoming a Lutheran minister. But the lure of baseball was too much for the calling of the pulpit, and so Dick started his pro baseball career in 1932.

Originally a pitcher, Siebert switched over to first base when he developed some arm problems. He went on to play for Ohio, Pennsylvania, and New York minor league teams, and, in 1935, he joined Buffalo in the International League. Siebert then became a member of the Brooklyn Dodgers system, and later the Chicago Cubs and St. Louis Cardinals systems until 1938, when he became a regular first baseman for the Philadelphia Athletics under the legendary Connie Mack.

Siebert played for the A's through 1945 and appeared in the 1942 All Star game. He was chosen as an all-star again in 1945 only to see the game canceled due to wartime restrictions. Siebert later recalled his greatest day in the big leagues was when he broke up a no-hit attempt by Cleveland great Bob Feller. Siebert played in 1,035 games over his big league career and finished with a respectable .282 lifetime batting average.

Siebert's pro career came to an abrupt end in 1946 due to some unfortunate contract problems with management. He simply traded in his first-baseman's mitt for a microphone when he accepted the position of sportscaster with WTCN radio in Minneapolis. But, only one year later, Siebert would get the baseball itch one more time. This time it was to take over as head coach of the Golden Gophers. (Later he would do radio and television work with WCCO as well.)

Dick took the reigns as the University of Minnesota head coach in 1947 from then-head coach David MacMillan. No one in the University's athletic department could've known it at the time, but they were creating a living legend when they hired him as head baseball coach. The "Chief" was one of the greatest coaches in college baseball history.

Siebert helped develop baseball at all levels in Minnesota. He was a pioneer and was credited with introducing the aluminum bat and designated hitter to college baseball. As a coach, he emulated many of the mannerisms of his long-time mentor, Connie Mack.

A president of the American College Baseball Coaches Association, college baseball's Coach of the Year in 1956 & 1960, and three-time winner of the NCAA Championship, Siebert would later refer to the trouncing of Arizona in the 1956 College World Series and the amazing come-from-behind win over USC in the 1960 Series as his most memorable moments in baseball. He compiled one of the most incredible records in college baseball history. Until 2001, when John Anderson broke his record, Siebert was the winningest coach in Gopher history with 754 wins against 361 losses, with a .676 winning percentage.

He is one of only a few coaches at major universities to have coached a team to more than 700 wins. He sent five different teams to the College World Series and of course, he brought home three titles. His teams also captured 11 Big Ten titles as well. Amazingly, he endured only three losing seasons. He is a member of the College Baseball Hall of Fame and was a recipient of college baseball's highest award, the Lefty Gomez Trophy, which recognizes the individual who has given the most outstanding contribution and service to the development of college baseball.

After 31 years of coaching in Gold Country, Siebert passed away on December 9, 1978, the Chief died, succumbing to numerous respiratory and cardiac illnesses. Dick was survived by his wife Marie and their children: Marilyn, Beverly, Richard, and Paul — who went on to play ball in the major leagues with the Mets and Cardinals.

In his last year of life, Siebert was quoted as saying: "I actually expected my coaching job at the U to last a few years and then I would go into business. No one in the world could have convinced me then I would still be here 31 years later. But I loved it, working with great young men and staying active in the best form of baseball I knew, the college game."

On Saturday, April 21, 1979, the University of Minnesota Baseball Stadium was officially renamed "Siebert Field," in honor of the greatest Gopher baseball coach. The entire baseball world mourned his passing, and tributes to the coach came from every corner of the baseball world.

For more than three decades, the Chief brought honor and respect to the University of Minnesota baseball program. Dick was a true ballplayer and a real throwback to another era. A tireless worker, his life was consumed with Gopher baseball. The cold weather was no match for the Chief, because he worked at his craft all-year long. Whether it was from his old Cooke Hall office, or from the fieldhouse, he was always trying to improve and help his teams to win.

He was a man who learned virtually every aspect of the game of baseball throughout his life and chose to teach others what he had to learn mostly on his own. He was a teacher, a coach, a mentor, and a friend. We appreciate coach Siebert for all these things, but also, maybe especially, for the fact that he did so much of it with local home-grown talent. He will be forever thought of as the standard to which all other coaches will be measured against.

Here is what a few of his former players had to say about him:

"He was a tremendous teacher," said Paul Molitor. "I think baseball at the University of Minnesota was successful under him because of the fact that he knew how to teach college players to be fundamentally sound. He taught us how to execute and gave us a chance to be competitive with any college team in the nation. That's why we could go from the fieldhouse to the ball field at the University of Texas and be competitive, because we were always the type of teams that wouldn't beat ourselves. We did the little things that would give us the chance to compete on a day to day basis. Personally, he was great to me and is one of the people who helped me get to where I am today. When you played for the Chief, you were playing for a man with a national reputation. He felt he never had to go out of the state to get his players, and he competed on a national scale. The Chief put a lot of pride in that Minnesota uniform for us."

"Dick Siebert was a great coach, and I really enjoyed my playing days at the University of Minnesota working with him," said Dave Winfield. "I felt that I was as good a hitter as I was a pitcher in college, but they wouldn't let me hit, insisting instead that I become specialized. My friends would come to the games and yell at him, 'Put in Winfield and let him hit, because he's the best hitter you've got!' But it didn't matter how good or bad you were, you had to get out there and work when you played for the Chief. You could be a star on his team, but he played no favorites and treated everyone alike. I learned a lot playing for him."

"Dick Siebert was just a heck of an all-around guy," said Paul Giel. "He was a very fine coach, and I had so much respect for him as a man. He knew the fundamentals of the game so well, but he had a sense of humor and made it fun for you. I learned the game from Dick, and even while I was in the majors, I still felt like he was better than most of the managers that I had. Every person on the team respected him and he got a lot out of his kids."

"When you think about Dick, you don't just think about his record at Minnesota, which is distinction enough in itself," said Jerry Kindall. "But I don't think people realize what he did for college baseball in general. Dick was one of the leaders in restoring good relations with major league baseball. There was a time when there was an antagonistic, very tense, relationship between the colleges and the pros. He overcame that. And he was the most expert of all college baseball coaches on the rules of the game. He served on virtually every committee that college baseball has instituted. I think it's safe to say - and I don't think I'm stretching it at all that Dick was the most highly respected and honored coach in collegiate baseball."

BUD GRANT

Harry "Bud" Grant was born on May 20, 1927, and raised in Superior, Wisconsin. His father Harry, was the Superior Fire Chief. He grew up playing sports and became a tremendous prep athlete. After playing football, baseball and basketball at Superior's Central High School, Bud joined the Navy in 1945 and was stationed at the Great Lakes Military Base outside Chicago. Bud continued his athletic prowess as Great Lakes played Big Ten teams under head football coach Paul Brown and head basketball coach Weeb Ewbank, both hall of famers. In 1946, Bud was discharged and enrolled at the U of M.

There, even without a scholarship (because he was in the service, the G.I. bill paid for his tuition), he would excel in three sports, earning nine letters from 1946-1949. He was a two-time All-Big Ten End on the gridiron, starred as a forward and was the team MVP on the basketball team, and also played centerfield and pitched for the baseball team, where he led the team in hitting as a freshman. Under Bernie Bierman, Bud played with Gopher greats such as Leo Nomellini, Clayton Tonnemaker, Gordie Soltau, Billy Bye, Jim Malosky and Vern Gagne. To earn spending money in the summers throughout college, Grant became creative. Since he could pitch three days a week and bat clean-up, he played baseball as a "ringer" for several small town-teams around Minnesota and Wisconsin, where he could mop up around $250 in a good week.

"Being a Gopher kind of grows on you a little bit," Bud would later say. "It wasn't anything that I felt particularly strong about when I got there, but now it means a lot. Back then, the Gophers were the only game in town, and we always played before a packed house. It was a tough time, with no scholarships and little money, but we had a lot of fun."

By 1950, Bud had finished his tenure at the U of M, and was considered by most to have been the most versatile athlete ever to compete there. (That was affirmed when he beat out Bronko Nagurski and Bruce Smith to be named as the "Top Athlete at the University of Minnesota for the First 50 Years of the Century.") From there he joined George Mikan and Jim Pollard as the newest member of the mighty Minneapolis Lakers dynasty. In joining the Lakers, Bud also became the NBA's first "hardship case," meaning he could leave college early and play professionally. (Lakers G.M., and longtime friend, Sid Hartman, petitioned the league and made it happen for him.) As a Laker, Grant averaged 2.6 points per game in each of the two years he played for the club, both of which were NBA championship teams.

Anxious to try something different, Bud then joined the NFL's Philadelphia Eagles, who had made him their number one draft pick that year. So talented was Grant, that in 1952, after switching from linebacker, where he led the team in sacks, to wide receiver, he finished second in the league in receiving and was voted to the Pro Bowl. After two years in Philly, he decided to take a 30% pay-raise and head north of the border to play for the Winnipeg Blue Bombers of the Canadian Football League. In so doing, Bud became the first player in NFL history to play out the option on his contract. He dearly missed hunting and fishing, something he figured he could readily do in up in Winnipeg, which was not that far from Minneapolis.

There, he played both ways, starting at corner and at wide receiver. He led the league in receiving for three straight years and also set a record by intercepting five passes during a single game. Then in 1957, after only four years in the league, and at the prime of his career, the front-office offered the 29-year-old the teams' head-coaching position. He accepted and proceeded to lead the Blue Bombers to six Grey Cups over the next 10 years, winning four of them.

On March 11th, 1967, Grant came home again, this time to take over the Minnesota Vikings. "I enjoyed Winnipeg very much, but coming to Minnesota was coming home for me," said Grant. It was a position that former Lakers owner, Max Winter, who now ran the Vikings, had originally offered to him, but had declined, in 1960. He took over from Norm Van Brocklin, and although he only won three games in his first season, that next year he led the Purple to the division title. In his third season the Vikings made it to the Super Bowl, and Bud was named the league's Coach of the Year. That was the beginning of one of the greatest coaching sagas in all of sports. Bud could flat out coach, and his players not only respected him, but they also liked him. Bud treated them like men, didn't work them too hard in practice, and his players always knew they could count on that post-season playoff check.

Grant, who went on to coach for 28 years, won a total of 290 regular season and post-season games, 122 as coach of the Winnipeg Blue Bombers of the CFL from 1957-66 and 168 as coach of the Vikings from 1967-83 and 1985. At Minnesota, his teams made the play-offs 12 times, and won 15 championships: 11 Central Division (1968-71, 1973-78, and 1980), one NFL (1969) and three NFC (1973, 1974 and 1976). In 1994 Bud was inducted into the Hall of Fame. With it, he became the first person ever to be elected to both the NFL and the Canadian Football League Hall of Fames. "It's something that they can't take away from you," said Bud, who was introduced at the event by his best friend, Sid Hartman. "Usually in sports there is a new champion crowned every year, but this is forever."

In 1983, Bud Grant, possibly the greatest athlete ever to play and coach in the history of Minnesota sports, retired as the head coach of the Vikings. The gray-haired, crew-cutted warrior's exit from the game signified an end of one of the greatest era's of all time.

"There were people that could run faster, jump higher, throw harder and shoot better than me, but I don't think anybody competed any harder than I did," said Grant on how he might want to be remembered. "I felt that I always had an advantage over my opponents because I never got tired. The longer we played, the stronger I got. Then I could beat you. And I applied that same theory to coaching. That was the type of player who I was always looking to get to play for me. Also, one thing that most coaches can't say, is that I've never been fired. I've always left whatever I was doing on my own accord, and I am proud of that. Every dollar I have ever made was from professional sports. I've had no other business or profession, and the only investments that I've got are six kids with college educations. Other than that, I don't have much."

Today, Bud and his wife Pat live in Bloomington. They have six children and many grandchildren. Although he still has an office at the Vikings headquarters, he is officially retired from football and spends much of his time either with his family or in the great outdoors. He has also championed the cause against commercial fishing with nets and spears on Minnesota lakes.

Jon Andreson

end their season. They made it back to the Mideast Regionals that next year, this time in South Bend, Ind. There, the 22-8 Gophs, led by All-American Left Fielder Ron Causton, exacted a little revenge over Western Michigan in Game One, winning 6-4. From there it got ugly though, as the Gophers lost to Notre Dame 12-4 and Western Michigan, yet again, 5-1, to put an end to the season.

The Golden Gophers once again made history in 1960, winning their second NCAA title in just four years. The team, which was led by All-American Pitchers Larry Bertelsen and Wayne Knapp, kicked off the post-season by crushing Notre Dame in Game One of the Mideast Regional, which was held at Midway Stadium in St. Paul. They kept on rolling in the first game of the semifinals, spanking the University of Detroit, 12-5, and then made it official when they swept Detroit again that next night, 5-4, to advance to the College World Series in Omaha.

The Gophers opened the World Series by beating the University of North Carolina in Game One, 8-3, and then followed that up with an 8-5 win over Arizona — the same team which the Gophers beat to take the title in 1956. From there the team rallied from an 11-2 seventh inning deficit to come back and beat USC, 12-11, in 10 innings. That next afternoon the Gophs edged a tough Oklahoma State squad, 3-1, to advance to the Finals. First, USC got a little revenge by winning their own extra inning ballgame over Minnesota, taking this one, 4-3, in 11 innings.

With that, the table was set for a one-game, winner-take-all title game. There, the Gophers hung on to edge those USC Trojans, 2-1, in 10-innings, to lay claim to their second NCAA championship. This thriller came down to the wire when, with the bases juiced in the bottom of the 10th, Third Baseman Cal Rolloff drew a five-pitch walk which, in turn, scored Dave Pflepsen from third to give the Gophers the hardware. Second baseman John Erickson, who played solid "D" and came up with some clutch hitting, was named as the tournament's MVP. (Another star on this team was future Men's Athletics Director, Tom Moe, who batted .333 during the season and was third on the team with 26 RBIs.) It was an outstanding year in Gold Country indeed, considering the fact that the Gopher Football Team won the National Championship as well!

The 1961 Gophers started out 1-4 but came back to put together a nice season. They won 12 of their final 14 games, losing just one series to the Illini late in the year. They wound up with a 21-8 overall record and 12-3 in the Big Ten — good for second in the conference. In addition, Pitchers Larry Bertelsen and Wayne Knapp each earned All-American honors for the

second straight season.

From there it got ugly as the team finished 10th in 1962, but they rebounded in '63 to record 24 wins — good for third — thanks to the efforts of All-American Second Baseman Jon Andreson. Then, in 1964, the team made another run to glory, winning its third NCAA title in just nine seasons. The Gophers, behind All-American Catcher Ron Wojciak, started out horribly that year, losing six of their first seven games. From that point on, however, they went 30-6, to finish in first place in the conference and win the national championship.

The team kicked off its third title run at the Mideast Regionals in Kent, Ohio, where they took care of Kent State in two straight games, 7-4 and 13-2, to advance back to the College World Series in Omaha. There, Minnesota opened the festivities by beating Texas A&M, 7-3, in Game One, and then spanking Maine, 12-0, in Game Two. From there the club edged their Finals foes from 1956, USC, 6-5, in a wild one to advance to the Semifinals. Then, the team got just one hit in a 4-1 loss to Missouri. But, they rebounded back that next night in the double-elimination tournament to avenge their loss to those same Tigers, 5-1, to win their third NCAA crown. Pitcher Joe Pollack was the real-deal in this tourney, winning three games, including the Finals — where he allowed just four hits in the big win.

After a dismal seventh place finish in 1965, Minnesota rallied to finish second in 1966 with a nice 27-10-2 record. The '67 squad was able to muster just a third place tally, but did manage to win a whopping 32 games — including an amazing mid-season stretch where they won 24 of 25. Leading the charge for this club was All-American First Baseman Dennis Zacho.

The Maroon and Gold came back in 1968 to win the Big Ten title and make their first post-season appearance in four years when they advanced to the Mideast Regionals, which were held in Minneapolis that year. One of the highlights of the season came on May 10th, when they pounded on Purdue, 15-0. With 35 wins that year the club was expected to go far, but, after beating Valparaiso, 6-4, in Game One, they lost a couple of heart-breakers to Southern Illinois, 10-9, and Ohio, 5-4, to end their season.

They did even better that next year, winning an incredible 36 games and claiming their second straight Big Ten title. The club was led by a pair of All-Americans in Center Fielder Noel Jenke and First Baseman Mike Walseth, each of whom carried the load that season. After a five game losing streak in April of that year, the club rebounded in a big way under Coach Siebert, rattling off 23 wins in a row. But, like in the previous year, the club wound up laying an egg in the Mideast Regionals, which were once again held in Minneapolis. This time, after downing Ohio, 11-8, they lost a tight one to Southern Illinois, 4-3, followed by a 4-1 loss to Ball State to end an otherwise fabulous season.

The 1970 Gophers once again won 30+ games, going 34-16 and winning their third straight conference crown. It was yet another disappointing finale for the club though, as they wound up losing in the Mideast Regionals in Columbus, Ohio, to both Ohio and Notre Dame, 6-4 & 6-2, respectively.

The team slipped just a bit in 1971, winning 28 games and finishing in second in the conference but out of the playoffs. It was more of the same in 1972 as the club started out by losing eight of its first 11 games in a hellish

Jack McCartan

Larry Bertelsen

pre-season Texas tour. They got back on track after that, but managed just 15 wins that year, tied for third in the Big Ten.

In 1973 the club came back in a big way, winning the conference crown and, after a nine-year absence, made a triumphant return to the big dance. They once again started out slow this year, even posting an ugly eight-game losing streak in May. But, they came back and won 31 games, earning yet another trip to the Mideast Regionals, which were held in Carbondale, Ill. There, the Gophers took the first over Miami, 3-2, and then swept Southern Illinois in two straight, 2-0 and 7-6, to advance onto the College World Series in Omaha.

The Gophers opened the Series against Oklahoma, where a

PAUL GIEL

As a young boy, Paul Giel grew up playing football on the sandlots of Winona during the Great Depression. There, he would often try to emulate the smooth moves of his childhood hero, Gopher Halfback Bruce Smith. Paul's imagination was refueled every Saturday morning, when he religiously listened to his beloved the Gophers on the radio. Soon he grew into an incredible prep athlete on his own right, starring in football, baseball and basketball at Winona High School. By 1950, not only was he one of the most celebrated prep football prospects in Minnesota history, he also had an opportunity to sign on with several major league baseball teams right out of high school as well. The kid was a natural, and luckily for us, he had decided long ago that he too was going to wear the maroon and gold.

Giel came in and literally took the Gopher sports world by storm. By the time he had finished his illustrious career in Minnesota, he had shattered most of Bruce Smith's records while single-handedly rewriting the record books. All in all, he rushed for 2,188 yards, caught 281 passes for 279 yards, and posted 417 return yards on both punts and kicks, for a total of 3,165 career all-purpose yards which also included 22 touchdowns — a number that still ranks eighth all-time as of the new millennium.

He was a throwback. Not only was he an unbelievable halfback, but he was also an tremendous quarterback, defensive back, punter, punt returner, kick returner, and sometimes even kicked. It is a wonder how he ever had time to come off the field to catch his breath! So successful was Giel athletically, as well as academically, that in 1954 he was awarded the prestigious Big Ten Medal of Honor. In football he was a two-time All-American halfback, the first-ever two-time Big Ten MVP, and in 1953 was named as the Player of the Year. He even finished runner-up to Notre Dame's Johnny Lattner in the Heisman Trophy race that same year, in what remains the closest balloting ever recorded.

In addition to all of that, he also starred on the baseball diamond, where, as a pitcher on Coach Dick Siebert's Gopher Baseball teams, he was simply unstoppable. Siebert said "Pitching Paulie" Giel was the hardest-throwing pitcher he had ever coached. From 1952-54, the pitcher was named to the All-American and All-Big Ten teams. On the mound, he earned 21 wins, and had the same number of complete games. He still holds the Gopher record for the most career strikeouts with 243, and remains fourth all-time for the most single season strikeouts, with 92. He finished is brilliant career with a 2.16 ERA.

So, with a resume like that, what was Paul to do after graduation? "I knew in my heart that I wanted to play baseball over football, and I was trying to be realistic about myself," said Giel. "I wondered where in the heck I would play in pro football. I mean I wasn't fast enough to be a halfback in the pros, and I couldn't have made it as a pure drop-back quarterback. So, I thought I still had a shot to make it in baseball."

His tenure as "Mr. Everything" at the U of M, however, was just a springboard for bigger and better things to come in the world of Minnesota sports. He is truly a home-grown hero in more ways than one. Despite being drafted by the NFL's Chicago Bears, Giel opted to instead try his hand at professional baseball with the New York Giants. He would make his big-league debut for legendary Manager Leo Durocher on June 29, 1954, striking out the side in the 9th inning of a 10-7 loss at home to the Pirates. It would be the beginning of a six-year major league career, interrupted only by a two-year stint to serve his country in the military. From New York he went to San Francisco, and then to Pittsburgh for two seasons before finishing up his pitching career with his hometown Twins in 1961. He would hang up the spikes for good that same year. He would finish his career with an overall record of 11-9, with an ERA of 5.39.

"Coming out of high school in Winona, I was really steeped in the tradition of the Gophers, and because of guys like Bruce Smith, I wanted to be a Gopher," said Giel. "Also, because I could play both football and baseball there, it was even better. It meant everything for me to be a Gopher."

From there he simply did it all, working first for the Vikings doing public relations and game management; followed by an eight year career as Sports Director of WCCO Radio, while also broadcasting prep, college and pro sports. In 1972 he was asked to come home, and serve as the University's Athletic Director, a position he would gladly accept and perform masterfully for more than 17 years in Gold Country. When that was up he even became a Vice President with the North Stars. Having seemingly covered every sport possible in the Land of 10,000 Lakes, in 1990 Paul settled down and took over as the Vice President of the Minneapolis Heart Institute Foundation, where he raised millions for heart health research and education. It was only fitting that a man with a heart as big as Paul's round out his illustrious career at such an appropriate place. Tragically, Paul died in the Summer of 2002, leaving behind a legacy that will never be equaled.

Paul Giel is a legend at the University of Minnesota. He was one of those players that comes around once in a millennium. He played the game like no one will again, and did it with an unpretentious demeanor, earning the respect of his teammates and his opponents alike. It has been 44 years since he first lived out his dream of playing football and baseball for the Golden Gophers. The old brick stadium is gone and so is that old baseball diamond, but memories of Paul Giel will live on forever.

Tom Moe

kid from St. Paul Central by the name of Dave Winfield took over. The six-foot-six pitcher struck our 14 Sooners that afternoon and allowed just six hits in a 1-0 Minnesota victory. The team then lost its next game of the double-elimination tourney by being shut-out 3-0 by Arizona State. The club rebounded though, and defeated Georgia Southern, 6-2, thanks to a solo home run by, you guessed it, Dave Winfield. The Gophers were headed back to the semifinals.

The next game was one that will go down as one of the most infamous in Gopher history, and for all the wrong reasons. It was against USC, where Winnie was back at it out on the mound, striking out 15 Trojan batters through eight innings. Then, with Minnesota up 7-0 and looking poised to make it into the Finals, all hell broke loose. After a controversial double play which saw a Trojan batter being called safe at first, Head Coach Dick Siebert went berserk and was ejected. As a result, the Trojans started a huge eight-run rally in the ninth thanks to a pair of errors and a passed ball. The result was a tragic 8-7 heartbreaker which left a very sour taste in the collective mouths of all Minnesotans. The All-American Winfield, however, was named as the World Series MVP, while the club received third place honors.

The Gophers made it back to the post-season in 1974 after tallying a 11-5 conference record — good for a share of the Big Ten Championship. With that, they advanced onto the regionals, which were held in Minneapolis. There, they started out strong by downing Southern Illinois, 9-4, and Miami of Ohio, 4-3. But the Salukis from Southern Illinois got their revenge in the Finals, sweeping the Gophers in two straight, 10-2 and 4-3, to knock them out of the action.

After a third place finish in 1975, Minnesota came back to finish in second place in 1976 with an outstanding 38-11 record. Highlighting the season were a trio of 13, 6 and 8-game winning streaks, which catapulted the team into the Rocky Mountain Regionals, which were held in Tempe, Arizona. There, the club, which was led by All-American Paul Molitor, started out sluggish, getting blanked by Memphis State, 6-0. But, they came back to shut-out Gonzaga, 4-0, in Game Two, and then got some payback on Memphis State, pulverizing the Tigers, 17-4. From there the Gophers got clobbered in the Finals, however, 12-5, by the hometown Arizona State Wildcats to put an end to an otherwise tremendous season.

The Gophers were back in the hunt in 1977, winning an impressive 39 games en route to reclaiming the Big Ten title. After opening the season at 2-7, the club roared back to go 33-3 down the stretch. From there they breezed through the Mideast Regionals, which were once again held in Minneapolis. There, the Gophs blanked Florida 7-0 in the first round.

Wayne Knapp

GOPHER CAREER
PITCHING RECORDS

Wins

	Name	(Years)	Wins
1.	Steve Comer	(1973-76)	30
2.	Jerry Ujdur	(1976-78)	27
3.	John Lowery	(1989-92)	26
4.	Bryan Hickerson	(1983-86)	25
5.	Bob Meyer	(1980-83)	24
6.	Dan Morgan	(1975-77)	22
	Scott Bakkum	(1990-92)	22
	A. Hammerschmidt	(1992-95)	22
9.	Paul Giel	(1952-54)	21
	Ron Craven	(1954-56)	21
	Jerry Thomas	(1955-57)	21
	Jim Francour	(1981-84)	21
	Shane Kangas	(1986-89)	21
	Justin Pederson	(1994-97)	21

ERA

	Name	(Years)	ERA
1.	Dave Cosgrove	(1968-70)	1.90
2.	Dan Morgan	(1975-77)	1.97
3.	Joe Pollack	(1963-65)	2.04
4.	Frank Brosseau	(1964-66)	2.11
5.	Jack Palmer	(1967-69)	2.12
6.	Gary Petrich	(1968-70)	2.13
7.	Paul Giel	(1952-54)	2.16
8.	Mike McNair	(1965-67)	2.17
	Jerry Ujdur	(1976-78)	2.17
10.	Ken Herbst	(1973-75)	2.18

Complete Games

	Name	(Years)	CG
1.	Steve Comer	(1973-76)	25
2.	Jerry Thomas	(1955-57)	24
	Jerry Ujdur	(1976-78)	24
4.	Scott Bakkum	(1990-92)	22
5.	Paul Giel	(1952-54)	21
6.	Joe Pollack	(1963-65)	17
	Dave Cosgrove	(1968-70)	17
	Bryan Hickerson	(1983-86)	17
9.	Ron Craven	(1954-56)	16
	Ken Herbst	(1973-75)	16

Strikeouts

	Name	(Years)	SO
1.	Paul Giel	(1952-54)	243
2.	Justin Pederson	(1994-97)	240
3.	Dave Winfield	(1971-73)	229
4.	Joe Westfall	(1993-96)	228
5.	Mike Diebolt	(1994-97)	218
6.	Bryan Hickerson	(1983-86)	201
7.	Dan Morgan	(1975-77)	198
8.	Jerry Thomas	(1955-57)	197
9.	Darren Knight	(1985-88)	195
10.	John Lowery	(1989-92)	192

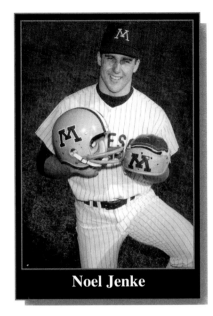
Noel Jenke

In Game Two they pounded on Central Michigan, 13-2, and then went on to beat Florida once again, 5-1, to advance to the College World Series.

There, the second seeded Gophers dropped their first game to UCLA, 7-4. They rebounded to claim a 4-3, 11-inning victory over Baylor in Game Two, but came up short in their third game of the double-elimination tournament. In that one, Minnesota jumped out to a quick 2-0 lead over the potent Arizona State Sun Devils. But ASU, which came into the game averaging over nine runs per outing, rallied to score seven runs in the next three innings. Tom Mee, who had three hits and two runs, tried to get the Gophers back into it, but they came up short. In the end, they were eliminated with an 8-4 loss, but did manage to finish with a sixth place national ranking. In addition, Molitor would receive All-American honors for the second year in a row.

The 1978 Gophers slipped back to a fifth place finish with a 7-7 record in the Big Ten in Siebert's final season. That next year was a historic one in Gold Country as Siebert was succeeded by George Thomas, who knew that it was not going to be easy retracing the footsteps of his three-time national championship winning mentor. (It should also be noted that Siebert's top assistant coach throughout his tenure was Glenn Gostick, who later went on to become one of the most highly regarded baseball historians in the nation.)

GOPHER ALL-AMERICANS

Name	Pos.	Year(s)
Paul Giel	P	1952-54
Jerry Kindall	SS	1956
Jerry Thomas	P	1956
Jack McCartan	3B	1958
Ron Causton	OF	1959
Larry Bertelsen	P	1960
Wayne Knapp	P	1960-61
Jon Andresen	2B	1963
Ron Wojciak	C	1964
Noel Jenke	OF	1969
Dennis Zacho	1B	1967
Mike Walseth	1B	1969
Dave Winfield	P	1973
Paul Molitor	SS	1976-77
Dan Morgan	P	1977
Greg Olson	C	1982
Brian Raabe	2B	1990
Dan Wilson	C	1990
Brent Gates	SS	1991
Mark Merila	2B	1993-94
Shane Gunderson	C	1995

On Saturday, April 21, 1979, the University of Minnesota Baseball Stadium was officially renamed "Siebert Field," in honor of the former Gopher coaching great. The team improved to win 12 conference games that year, but could manage just a fourth place finish in the Big 10. They returned to the 30-win club in 1980 when they finished up with a 33-13 overall record, and second in the conference with a 14-4 mark.

In 1981 the conference decided to change its post-season format and go with the newly created Big Ten Tournament. (Beginning that year the winner of the Big Ten Tournament would be named as the Big Ten champion.) The Gophers finished that season with a much-improved 37-16 record and roared into the "Big Ten's." There, they got a rude awakening when the Purdue Boilermakers spanked them, 9-0, in the opening game. They rebounded in Game Two to beat Illinois, 2-0, and then got revenge over Purdue in the semi's, 8-3. Minnesota then lost to Michigan, 10-6, in the inaugural championship game. They still got a high enough seeding to make it to the Southern Regionals, however, which were held in Coral Gables, Fla., that year. The Gophers were soundly defeated there though, getting pounded by Miami in Game One, 12-0, and then falling to Florida State 9-5, in Game Two to finish the season.

That next season former Gopher John Anderson took over as the team's new coach. Anderson, who played for the Maroon and Gold back in 1974-75, came out strong in his first season at the helm, leading his team to an 8-8 league record and a No. 4 seed in the 1982 Big Ten Tourney held in Illinois. There, after dropping their opening round game to Ohio State, 5-3, the Gophers came back to eliminate the tourney

National Award Recipients

Big Ten Player of the Year
1983	Terry Steinbach, C*
1991	Brent Gates, SS
1994	Mark Merila, 2B*
1995	Shane Gunderson, C*
1999	Robb Quinlan, 1B
2001	Jack Hannahan, 3B

Big Ten Freshman of the Year
1988	Dan Wilson, C
1991	Mark Merila, 2B

Big Ten Coach of the Year
1982	John Anderson
2000	John Anderson

Big Ten Tournament MVP
1982	Terry Steinbach, C*
1985	Jon Beckman, OF
1986	Tim McIntosh, OF
1988	Vince Palyan, OF
1992	Scott Bakkum, P
1995	Shane Gunderson, C*
1998	Mark Groebner, OF
2001	Jack Hannahan, 3B

*Denotes co-winner of award

Mike Walseth

DAVE WINFIELD

Dave Winfield is probably the greatest athlete ever to hail from the great state of Minnesota. Dave grew up in St. Paul loving sports. After a phenomenal prep career at St. Paul Central High School, Winfield opted to stay close to home and attend the University of Minnesota to pitch for legendary Coach Dick Siebert on a baseball scholarship. He was eventually "discovered" by Gopher basketball Coach Bill Musselman while playing in an intramural basketball league on campus. The Gopher junior varsity basketball team needed some tough competition to practice against, and since Winfield's intramural team, the "Soulful Strutters" were campus champs, a scrimmage was arranged. There, upon seeing Winfield's incredible athleticism, Musselman immediately made the six-foot-six forward a two-sport star at the U of M.

"I switched from a baseball scholarship to a basketball scholarship," recalled Winfield. "Baseball was only partial, so I needed a full ride. A poor kid from St. Paul… so I switched, and the rest is history."

Making the jump to the hardcourt, Winfield played two seasons with the Gopher basketball team, becoming a starter on the 1971-72 team that went 18-7 and won the Big Ten championship — the school's first in 53 years. His big break though, ironically enough, came on the heels of the now infamous "Ohio State Brawl," in which several players were suspended from the team. Thrust into the starting lineup as a member of the notorious "Iron-Five" squad, Winnie went on to average 6.9 points per game that season. Then, in 1972-73, he averaged 10.5 points per game en route to leading the Gophers to a 21-5 record — good for second in the Big Ten.

His Gopher sports career was nothing short of incredible. On the diamond Winfield was a three-time All-Big Ten pitcher and was a career .353 hitter. In 1973, he led the Gophers to the Big Ten title, and was selected as an All-American as well as the MVP of the College World Series. As a pitcher, his 19-4 career record afforded him an amazing winning percentage .826. He finished with 229 career strikeouts, second only to Paul Giel's 243, and his single season record of 109 strikeout's stood for nearly 25 years. (The University of Minnesota baseball program has since honored the former great by giving the Dave Winfield Pitcher of the Year Award, to the team's top annual hurler.) "For me, I was a baseball player first," said Winfield. "But I loved playing basketball for the Gophers as well, and I was lucky enough to play both sports. I really liked all the guys on the basketball squad, and we had a lot of good competitors on that team. Mentally and physically I thought I was ready, and each game I thought I got better. It was here and now, and we just had a good time. That's why we were successful."

"He is truly an amazing athlete and, as our captain, he was a strong team leader," recalled Dick Siebert. "I don't know of any sport he can't excel at. I remember when David asked for a half-hour off from baseball practice to compete with his buddies in an intramural track meet. He had never before high jumped, and all he did was place first, going 6-foot 6-inches while still in his baseball uniform. He may be the finest all-around athlete I have coached, or for that matter to ever compete for Minnesota. To top it all off he was also a fine student."

Upon graduating from the U of M in 1973, Winfield found himself with several post-graduate options. He is one of the few persons in the history of sports to be drafted in all three professional major sports. He was taken in baseball by the San Diego Padres, in basketball by the NBA's Atlanta Hawks as well as the ABA's Utah Stars, and in football by the Minnesota Vikings.

"In football, they drafted me strictly as an athlete," said Winfield. "I was six-foot-six and 230 with good hands, speed, and strength. The Vikings officials figured they could make me into a tight end. Who knows? It would have been great to have caught some of those Fran Tarkenton passes! There's no question that I made the right choice though, and I would have had a short career playing football."

Not surprisingly, Winfield chose baseball, going directly to the big-leagues to join the Padres, where he batted .277 his first year. (Not bad for a guy drafted as a pitcher!) In 1979, he became the first Padre voted to the All-Star Game starting lineup, and in 1980 he signed with the New York Yankees and became the richest man in professional sports. He stayed with the Bronx Bombers until being traded to the California Angels in 1990. He signed with the Toronto Blue Jays in 1991 and won a World Series with that club in 1992. Then, in 1993, he came home to join the Twins, where, on September 16th, Dave got his 3,000 hit off of Oakland's vaunted relief pitcher, Dennis Eckersley, becoming only the 19th player in major league history to achieve that mark. "It was great," said Winfield. "I was so glad to come home and to have been able to accomplish such a major milestone in front of my home crowd in the Metrodome. That was definitely a special event for me in my career, and it's something that I will always remember."

And, while he was traded that next season to the Cleveland Indians, he certainly made Minnesota proud. Spanning nearly a quarter of a century, two countries, two leagues, and six cities, Winfield has done it all. The 12-time all-star won seven Gold Gloves and six Silver Bat awards. He amassed more hits than Babe Ruth, more home runs than Joe DiMaggio, and more RBIs than both Mickey Mantle or Reggie Jackson. He is one of only five players with over 3,000 hits, 450 homers, and 200 stolen bases. In the summer of 2001, Winnie was finally given his due when he was inducted into the Baseball Hall of Fame, alongside fellow Minnesota sports icon Kirby Puckett. An all-star and fan-favorite who played hard well into his forties, Winnie will always be remembered as one of the game's great ones.

"I always looked at baseball three ways," said Winfield. "It was a game, a science, and a business. I used it as a springboard to do the other things that I am doing in life such as the Dave Winfield Foundation. I met a lot of people, traveled the world, and have done a lot of great things. I have become a role model, if you will, for a lot of young people. I think I have become someone that people listen to and they respected the way I went about my work, and I am proud of that. It seemed that the better I played, the more I was able to accomplish."

Off the field, his accomplishments are equally impressive: He served on the board of President Bill Clinton's National Service Program. He was a Williams Scholar at the U of M. He received the first Branch Rickey Community Service Award, and he was given baseball's coveted Roberto Clemente Award. Now Dave devotes much of his time to what might be considered to be his crown jewel of achievements, the Winfield Foundation — a non-profit foundation, which for more than a quarter century has been a reflection of his commitment to children. Winnie has always been a very popular athlete and role model and has given of himself long before it became fashionable. His foundation's message to kids isn't "be a superstar" but rather "be the best that you can be." His generous monetary gifts, contributions of time, creativity, and commitment are immeasurable. He has traveled coast to coast to conduct drug-prevention assemblies and seminars. His organization has generated and distributed millions of dollars, and worked with four presidential administrations, government, organizations, corporations, media, celebrities, and every-day people to bring forth grassroots programs that have touched thousands.

"It was a real pleasure to play for the Minnesota Twins," recalled Winnie. "Minnesota is a place that I really wanted to play at during some point in time over my baseball career. I just didn't know if it would ever happen, but luckily it worked out. It was easy playing and working in Minnesota, and I was really glad that I got a chance to do it."

"When I was in 8th grade, Dave was a senior in high school," said former Twin Paul Molitor. "I saw him play, but I never had a chance to play with him. I think in a lot of ways, I owe him a lot, because as a member of the Gophers when he was drafted, he opened some eyes about Minnesota baseball. That gave kids like myself a lot more opportunities to get some exposure. The parallels of our careers are somewhat remarkable in that we grew up on the same playgrounds, played for the same Legion team, competed at the same University, and we both had to go north of the border and wait until the latter stages of our careers to win a World Series championship. For two guys who grew up five blocks apart in St. Paul to end up both accumulating 3,000 hits with their hometown teams is pretty remarkable, I think. I marveled at Dave's play for many years. He was a tremendous, tremendous athlete. I consider him to be a good friend, and whenever we see each other, we always reminisce about our past and growing up in St. Paul."

"When I was a rookie, Winnie took me under his wing," added Kirby Puckett. "I'll never forget going to New York City and talking to him. I remember saying 'Hello Mr. Winfield,' and I remember him saying to me, 'I've heard a lot about you, rook.' I was just in awe. He's like 6-6 and so intimidating. Then he sent me a note in the clubhouse inviting me to dinner with him that night after the game. I remember just talking to him. He was so nice to me. That was really special to me."

One of our most precious of native sons, Dave Winfield is without question the greatest all-around athlete to ever come out of the Gopher State.

PAUL MOLITOR

One of eight children, Paul Molitor was born in St. Paul on August 22, 1956. He grew up as a Twins fan, worshipping Harmon Killebrew, and loved to play baseball as a kid. A natural athlete, his talents became apparent as a high schooler for the Cretin Raiders in St. Paul.

"I first thought of Molitor as having the potential to become a professional when he was in the ninth grade," said Bill Peterson, his high school and American Legion team coach. "He was always an exceptional player and had a very strong arm." In his senior year at Cretin High School, Molitor missed the entire regular season with mononucleosis. "He wasn't even supposed to practice," Peterson added, "but he begged and begged to hit. He must have had a month's worth of energy stored because he put on a hitting exhibition like I've never seen."

Molly rejoined the Raiders for the playoffs and led his team to a pair of Catholic League High School titles in 1973 and 1974. So, it was off to the State Tournament, where in the championship game, Paul pounded a 380-foot grand slam home run, en route to helping Cretin repeat as state champs. That same year Paul led his St. Paul Attucks-Brooks American Legion team to a state title as well. It was the second Legion title for Paul, who was just an eighth-grader on the 1968 championship team which was led by a kid named Dave Winfield.

In addition to garnering All-State honors in baseball and basketball, Paul also played football and soccer. He even caddied at Town and Country Golf Course as well to earn some extra cash.

"I always remember when I would have to leave early from the golf course to go to my baseball games and one time the caddy-master asked me 'what do you want to do — make money or play baseball?' "

At this point, Molitor had drawn the interest of both college and major league scouts, who had their eyes on Minnesota. In 1973, when the San Diego Padres drafted fellow St. Paulite Dave Winfield, it had spurned fresh interest in northern baseball. After Winfield, major league baseball scouts paid closer attention to the quality of players who had been developed in the arctic reaches of the U.S., so Molly was noticed throughout his high school career.

Paul was getting mixed reviews from the major league scouts, particularly those representing the Minnesota Twins. They thought he was too small and would have a difficult time in organized ball. However, the St. Louis Cardinals decided to take a chance on the young shortstop and selected him in the 25th round of the entry draft. The Cards offered him a $4,000 contract, which was just the kick in the rear he needed to opt for a college education instead.

"I got a partial scholarship from the Gophers," said Paul. "Coach Siebert used to offer half-scholarships to a lot of the kids, giving tuition and books to the Twin Cities kids and room and board to the out-staters, so he could double the number of kids he could get. I lived at home my freshman year and can still remember hitch-hiking to campus from my house near Summitt Avenue in St. Paul. The four grand from the Cardinals was more money than I had ever seen at that point, but I wanted to follow Dave Winfield to the U of M, and it was a great decision."

Siebert would later say that Paul had the best base-running instincts of any player he ever saw in amateur or professional baseball, and that he was, without a doubt, the best major league prospect he'd ever seen.

"Growing up in the St. Paul, as I did, I knew that the Gophers had a tremendous baseball tradition," said Paul. "Back then, it was a very rare occasion when the Chief would recruit outside the state to bring in players, so almost everyone in uniform was home-grown. I think that when you played for his teams, you realized that it wasn't just the U, but the type of baseball that Minnesota kids played, that was being represented. It carried a lot of significance for me, and it meant a great deal for me to be a Gopher."

As Paul and his teammates prepared for the 1977 College World Series, he heard the substantial news that he had been drafted by the Milwaukee Brewers. He was the third overall player chosen in the draft, after the White Sox took Harold Baines and the Expos Bill Gullickson. The Twins, who had made it clear that they were now interested in drafting him, had missed their chance at the young slugger. "It took me a little while to get down to the ground," said Paul after hearing the news. College baseball's hottest prospect, and newest cheesehead, signed with the Brewers for $85,000.

By the time Paul had become a Brewer rookie after his junior season at the U, he had established himself as one of the greatest all-around baseball players in Gopher history. He had become the Gophers' career leader in runs-scored, hits, RBI's, triples, home-runs, total bases, and stolen bases. In his three seasons, he set five single-season records and seven college-career records. The Gopher shortstop's best year was his sophomore season in which he batted a career-best .376, earning himself first-team All-American honors for the second straight season. He would finish his college baseball with an impressive career batting average of .350.

The 20-year-old Molitor was then sent to Milwaukee's Class-A farm team in Iowa to play with the Burlington Bees. After winning the batting title and leading the team to a league championship, Molly was off the "show."

Profoundly modest, Molitor doesn't care about personal accolades, rather he has always preferred to be a team player. He was an explosive athlete with an ability to attack with the sudden element of surprise, whether at bat or on the bases. He was a hitting machine, able to swing so late, stretching time until that optimum instant for contact seems to have passed. His eyes could evaluate a pitch, calculate its curve, its spin, its velocity, and then measure it, to precisely drive the ball exactly where he wants it to go, all in about the same time it would take the average person to blink. That was his signature, and his knowledge of the physics of the game allowed him to persevere.

Paul played 15 seasons with the Brewers, making it to the World Series in 1982 before losing to the Cardinals in the so-called "Suds Series." Molitor left Milwaukee to go north of the border in 1993 where he led the Blue Jays to the World Series championship and was named MVP of the Series. Following this accomplishment, many felt that Paul could have run for the position of Prime Minister in Canada, and they weren't kidding.

Then, on December 5, 1995, Paul came home to Minnesota. He fulfilled a lifelong, childhood dream by getting the opportunity to play for his hometown Twins. In 1996, he led the Twins with an outstanding .341 average and led the league in hits with 225. Then, on September 16, 1996, in a road game against the Kansas City Royals with Jose Rosado on the mound, Molly made history. With the entire state of Minnesota waiting in anxious anticipation for the big event to finally happen, Paul became the 21st player in major-league history to get 3,000 hits, as well as being the first player ever to get it on a triple. In an otherwise ho-hum Twins season, Paul Molitor had made baseball fun again.

"When the opportunity finally came up where I was available, and they had an interest, I couldn't pass up the opportunity to finally be a Twin in spite of a lot of interest from elsewhere and probably more money from some other teams," said Molly. "To have a chance to return home and to kind of complete the cycle, so to speak, was something that goes back to that dream as a kid. Now, to have it happen so far down the road was a little bit ironic, but also a real nice way to end my career. I am very content now and am excited about finishing up my career at home."

"I think at least for Dave Winfield, Jack Morris, Terry Steinbach, and I, after growing up and playing high school baseball here, we had a certain pride about being from Minnesota that maybe people from other parts of the country might not easily understand," he added. "This has to do with the lifestyle and priorities of family — it's a Midwestern thing. I'm not sure that just that on it's own would've been enough to entice us back, but when you factor the current status of the team under manager Tom Kelly, it became even more appealing. Combine that with the chance to return home to friends and family, and then to play for the team we followed as youngsters was just an irresistible package for me."

As far as how he would want to be remembered: "I hope that people will have seen in the way that I played that I had a certain passion and, yet, respect for the game. Whatever I have accomplished, I have tried to do with humility and when I failed, I tried to maintain a certain level of consistency about my demeanor. I think that's important because in a lot of ways sports reflects life. How you handle your ups and downs says a lot about your character. That's what I hope has left an impression, and particularly on young people."

Paul finally hung up the cleats in 1998. The 21-year veteran played his last game on September 27th at the Dome, where he singled and then scored in his last at-bat. The crowd went nuts. The next stop for this superstar? Cooperstown, and the Hall of Fame.

host Fighting Illini, 8-3. From there Minnesota, behind Center Fielder Pat Pohl's two-run single to center in the top of the seventh, cruised to a 7-5 victory over Ohio State to clinch the title. Leading the charge that year was future Major League All-Star Terry Steinbach, who was named as the tournament's Most Valuable Player. (And, while Steinbach would go on to become an All-Star catcher in the major leagues, he was actually an infielder for the Gophers. The actual catcher for the club was Edina's Greg Olson, who would be named to the All-American team in 1982 before going on to star for the Atlanta Braves in the big leagues.)

Next up for these Gophers was Oklahoma State, who they faced in the opening round of the Mideast Regionals. There, at the Cowboys' home field in Stillwater, Minnesota came up on the short end of a real barn-burner, losing 16-9. They came back to spank Oral Roberts, 9-0, in Game Two, but then lost to Middle Tennessee State in Game Three, 7-1, to round out their season.

After winning 18 of their final 20 games, the Gophers headed into the 1983 Big Ten's full of optimism. But, the squad lost a pair of heart-breakers to both the host Wolverines, 10-9, and then the Iowa Hawkeyes, 2-0, to end their season. It was more of the same in the '84 conference finals, where the 31-20 Gophers wound up losing to Michigan and Northwestern, 6-3 and 10-2, respectively, to round out the year.

Then, in 1985, the 33-23 Gophs made another nice run to claim their second Big Ten Tournament title. After sweeping Wisconsin in four straight to end the regular season, the Golden Gophers opened up the tourney with an 11-10 upset over host Michigan. The Wolverines, who entered the tourney with an unbelievable 51-6 record, roughed up Gopher starter Bryan Hickerson for 10 runs on 13 hits as they took a 10-8 lead after six innings. Minnesota rallied back with one run in the eighth and two in the ninth though and went on to win thanks in part to the outstanding pitching of reliever Gregg Mau, who allowed just one hit over the last three innings. From there the Gophs, behind tournament MVP Jon Beckman, defeated Ohio State twice, 8-5 & 5-3, en route to bringing home the hardware. The stunk it up at the Mideast Regionals in Oklahoma, however, as they got beat by host Oklahoma State, 8-3, in Game One, and then got crushed by Oral Roberts in Game Two, 17-8, to end it all.

The 1986 Gophers won a record 40 games that year. One

TERRY STEINBACH

Terry Steinbach was born on March 2, 1962 in New Ulm and grew up loving the Twins — especially Harmon Killebrew, Tony Oliva and Rod Carew. He went on to star as an infielder at New Ulm High School under the tutelage of Jim Senske, Minnesota's all-time winningest high school baseball coach. He then followed in his big brother Tom's footsteps and came to the University of Minnesota in 1980 on a baseball scholarship. (His brother Tim also played at the U of M in 1981 as well).

Terry lit up Gold Country like no one before him, finishing his illustrious career with a .375 average and hitting plenty of dingers to boot. The two-time All-Big Ten slugger also led his Gopher teams to a Big Ten championship and a pair of NCAA regional appearances.

"It was pretty special to be a Gopher, especially having my brother Tom there before me," said Terry. "He set the way for me there and it was a pretty neat experience. Once you get there and realize the baseball talent that they have put out over the years there, it was amazing. John Anderson was a great coach and I had a lot of great memories playing there."

From there he was drafted by the Oakland Athletics. While playing in Double-A ball, the A's converted the third baseman into a catcher. He took to it like a duck to water and has been referred to as not a hitter who catches, but as a catcher who hits. After 14 years in the A's organization, he hit .275 with 132 homers, 205 doubles, 595 RBI, and 1,144 hits. Considered by many to be one of the games' premier defensive catchers, he's gunned-down 37 percent of the runners who have tried to steal on him. He led the A's to four Western Division titles, three American League pennants, and a World Championship in 1989, where he led the team with 7 RBIs in nine post-season games. He's also played in three All-Star games, even earning MVP honors in the 1988 mid-season classic. And, in typical Steinbach fashion, he donated the van that he won for being named as the MVP to the New Ulm United Way. He also finances a college scholarship every year for a student-athlete from one of New Ulm's three high schools.

In 1996, after a career-year in Oakland, where he set a number of career batting highs — including his AL-record 34 homers as a catcher (35 total) and 100 RBI (33 more than any previous season) — Terry exercised his free-agent status and came home to sign a three-year contract with the Twins. For Steinbach, even though it meant taking a several million dollar pay cut, it was worth it. He could now be closer to his family and be able to do what he loves most, enjoy the outdoors.

The avid angler and hunter wanted to see his first Minnesota spring in over 14 years, something very important to him. He even bought his very own outdoor paradise: a 110-acre plot of land, which borders half of an 80-acre lake, near his Plymouth home. Sometimes during hunting season, he and Simon, his Brittany spaniel, come to the oasis two or three times a day to check up on things. To say he loves the outdoors might be an understatement. In 1989, after winning the World Series, Terry balked at the opportunity to visit the White House and meet President Bush because it conflicted with the opening of deer season.

Terry is one of the best baseball players ever to come from Minnesota. He is best described as a pro's pro who respects the game, plays hard, and has fun. "He's one of the most respected players in the league because of his knowledge and how he calls a game," said teammate and fellow Gopher, Paul Molitor. The Twins were lucky to get him, and have him groom in their young pitching staff, something he took great pride in. He retired in 1999 for good, finishing his three year stint with the Twins with an additional 309 hits, 30 homers and 150 RBIs. His final Major League Baseball career stats would include a lifetime .271 batting average, 1,453 hits, 638 runs, 162 homers and 745 RBIs — outstanding numbers from one of the best in the business.

Said Terry of how we would like to be remembered: "I would like my character to be thought of more than my accomplishments. I would like to be remembered as a hard worker and willing to work with everybody. I would like to thought of as someone who was always approachable and not hung up on himself, and as a guy who was respected by his peers."

Tom Steinbach

highlight for the young players came on May 5th, when they played the Minnesota Twins in an exhibition game, having a ball but losing, 12-5, nonetheless. They once again advanced to the Big Ten Tourney, which was held that year in their own back yard at Siebert Field. They opened the festivities with a 16-4 drubbing of Purdue, only to drop Game Two, 10-7, to Michigan. They rallied to beat the cheese-heads from Wisconsin in Game Three, 13-3, but then lost to those same Wolverines in the finals, 9-5, to round out the year. Despite the loss, Gopher Left Fielder Tim McIntosh was named as the tournament's Most Valuable Player.

In 1987 the 36-25 Gophers were eliminated from Big Ten Tourney action by Purdue and Michigan, 9-3 & 9-8, respectively. From there, the club advanced on to the West Regionals at Palo Alto, Calif., where they got whipped first by Stanford, 12-1, and then by Oral Roberts 7-0.

That next season Minnesota won 38 ballgames and went on to make a splash at the Big Ten's. There, they bounced back from a 10-5 loss opening round to Michigan State with four straight wins, including a pair over those same Spartans in the championship round. In the first club's first game, they pounded Michigan State, 17-4, as 10 Gophers had at least one hit. Then, in the rematch, Minnesota got four in the fourth and got outstanding pitching from future big-leaguer Denny Neagle, to earn a 5-3 win. In addition, Vince Palyan was received tourney MVP honors to boot. From there the Gophers advanced to the West Regionals in Fresno, Calif., where they proceeded to get beat by both Fresno State and Santa Clara, 10-8 & 6-3.

In 1989 Minnesota won six of its last eight conference games, but it wasn't enough to get them into the conference tourney.

In 1990 they won 36 games, but once again lost out in the Big Ten's, this time getting beat by Illinois and Ohio State, 11-5 & 6-4, respectively, to round out the year. The stars of this club were a pair of All-Americans in Catcher Dan Wilson and Second Baseman Brian Raabe — both of whom would go on to play in the big leagues.

Minnesota came back in 1991 to do some damage. Behind All-American Shortstop Brent Gates, the Gophers wound up winning 37 games that year, including a 36-7 spanking of Rutgers on March 18th. The team then

Dan Wilson

opened tournament action by beating Indiana in a wild one, 15-11, followed by Northwestern in Game Two, 7-5. But, they lost in the Finals to Ohio State, 15-5. They still were able to advance on to the West Regionals that year, which were held in L.A. There, they beat Hawaii in the opener, 5-3, only to lose their next two to Creighton and Hawaii, 8-3 & 12-9, respectively, to finish their season.

The 1992 Gophers won a record 42 games and cruised into the post-season, where they won the Big Ten Tournament in Columbus, Ohio. There, the second-seeded Gophers grabbed an opening round 5-0 victory over Michigan State, behind Pitcher Scott Bakkum, whose eight strike-out, four hit gem was good enough to earn him tournament MVP honors. They then followed that up with a 4-3, 12-inning decision over the Illini and completed the clean sweep by beating those same Michigan State Spartans, 11-5, in the championship game to take home the hardware. From there the club advanced on to the Mideast Regional in Wichita, Kan., where they lost a wild Game One to Oklahoma State, 12-11. They responded by waxing George Washington University in Game Two, 19-3, and then made it to the Finals behind a 7-6 win over Cal-State Northridge. But, Oklahoma State would have their number, as they beat the Gophers for the second straight time, 15-6, to bring an end to a pretty good season.

Minnesota was able to pound out an amazing 43 wins in 1993 and for the third straight year, enter the conference tournament as the No. 2 seed behind the regular season champs from Ohio State. There, the Gophers beat Purdue in Game One, 8-3, and then beat the Buckeyes, 11-2, in Game Two. But, Ohio State, facing elimination, came back behind five wild pitches — including a wild pitch which brought in the game-winning run, avenged its earlier loss to Minnesota with a 7-6, 10-inning victory. The Gophers then advanced to the West Regionals in Tempe, Ariz., on a technicality. You see, the winner-take-all rematch was rained out that next day, so the automatic bid to the NCAA Tournament was awarded to the Gophers, based on their 2-0 record after the second round. The Gophs stunk it up in Tempe though, losing first to Pepperdine, 4-1, and then Arizona State, 6-5, to end their year.

The 42-21 Gophers started out horribly in 1994, losing seven of their first eight games to Georgia Tech, Florida State and Miami.

Greg Olson

Denny Neagle

Robb Quinlan

DICK JONCKOWSKI

The voice of the Golden Gophers is a guy you have got to meet! One of the funniest human beings you will ever meet, Dick Jonckowski has spent a life-time making others laugh. He is also one Minnesota's biggest sports fanatics. In fact, the basement of his Shakopee home is a venerable fire hazard, because it is crammed so full of wonderful pieces of sports memorabilia. Full of signed pictures, programs and random treasures, it is a collection like no other, and truly shows the passion he has towards the world of sports.

A graduate of New Prague High School in 1961, Dick went on to play one season of professional baseball in the St. Louis Cardinals farm system, in Salisbury, NC. (I assure you, it was nothing like Doc. Moonlight Graham's infamous "cup of coffee" from the movie "Field of Dreams!") After studying at Brown Institute, Jonckowski worked for several years as a sportscaster in both Minnesota and Wisconsin.

Then, in 1967, Jonckowski joined the upstart Minnesota Muskies basketball club of the American Basketball Association, working in the team's public relations department. When the Muskies moved to Miami that off-season, Dick then became Assistant Public Relations Director for the Minnesota Pipers, yet another ABA club which immediately moved in from Pittsburgh when the Muskies left town.

Since then, the "Polish Eagle" has become one of the Midwest's top after-dinner speakers, emceeing roasts and banquets from Des Moines to Duluth along the way. In addition, he has gained much notoriety as the voice of Gopher baseball, football and basketball, serving as the team's long-time public address announcer. He has also hosted a radio program called "The Coaches Round Table" for some 35 years as well.

"Sports and laughter are the center of my universe," says Dick. "Ever since I was a kid, sports were the only thing I cared about. Laughter is so important, I just love to see people happy."

A true living legend, (Hey, just ask him…), Dick is a true Minnesota Sacred Cow!

American Catcher Shane Gunderson, who was named as the tournament's MVP, led the offensive charge. Minnesota wound up losing big to the Buckeye's in the final two games though, 19-13 & 11-6, to finish out of the money.

The Gophers struggled in both 1996 and 1997, and despite winning 30+ games in each season, wound up with a pair of fifth place finishes in the conference and out of the post-season. They rebounded in 1998, however, and after finishing with a record 45 wins, went on to capture their sixth conference tournament title.

The Golden Gophers entered the Big Tens' as the winners of 16 of their last 18 games and their solid play would continue against Ohio State in the opening round. There, Minnesota jumped out to a quick 4-0 lead en route to a 10-3 victory. Senior Left Fielder Mark Groebner parked a pair of two two-run homers in this one, while Pitcher Ben Birk (the brother of Vikings All-Pro Center Matt) tossed an eight hitter for the "W." The Gophers then rallied to score a record 10 runs in the sixth inning in a 14-5 win over Penn State in Game Two. From there they cruised to the championship round, where they met up with the host Illini. Illinois had an 8-5 lead heading into the seventh in this one, but the Gophers rallied to come up with four runs in the eighth and ninth to win, 9-8. Right Fielder Craig Selander hit a two-run dinger in the eighth, while tournament MVP Mark Groebner drove in what proved to be the game winner when he smacked a two-out, bases-loaded single in the bottom of the ninth to give Minnesota the title.

From there the Gophs headed west, to Stanford, Calif., where they met up with Alabama in the opening round of the West Regionals. The Crimson took care of them though, 8-2, as did host Stanford that next day, 19-1, to send the Maroon and Gold packing for home.

In 1999 Minnesota won an amazing 46 games, and wound up entering the Big Ten's as the No. 2 seed. The Gophers opened the tourney with a 12-9 loss to Illinois, thus sending them to the losers bracket to face the regular season champs from Ohio State. There, a freshman phenom by the name of Jason Kennedy stole the show by drilling three home runs out of the park while driving in seven RBIs en route to a 10-1 win. Next up was a rematch against Illinois, and this time the Gophers hung on to avenge their earlier loss, winning the game, 9-3. From there Minnesota went on to defeat Michigan, 13-10, setting up a winner-take-all rematch game that next day. This one was a heart-breaker too, as Gopher Reliever Frank Wagner gave up a game-winning single to Michigan's Bobby Scales in the bottom of the ninth to give the Wolverines a heart-breaking 12-11 victory. They did get invited to the Regionals, however, which were held that year in Waco, Texas.

They settled down though and put together a nice season after that. Leading the way was two-time All-American Second Baseman Mark Merila, who was simply awesome both on the field and behind the plate. Minnesota wound up winning their first game of the Big Ten's over Michigan, 8-1, only to lose their next two to Ohio State and Michigan, 6-5 & 4-2, respectively. They did manage to receive a bid to the Atlantic Regionals in Miami, Fla., though, where they opened the post-season by beating up on both Kent and Florida, 11-6 and 12-2, to advance on to the next round. Their old nemesis from Miami was waiting for them in that next round, however, and the Hurricanes got the best of them once again, winning this time by the final score of 11-3. Minnesota then tried to get back to the College World Series by beating Florida, but came up on the wrong side of a 4-1 ballgame to end their season.

The next year the Gophers went 16-12 in Big Ten play and ended up beating Northwestern, 9-8, in the first round of the conference tourney. They then went on to absolutely spank Purdue in Game Two, 26-3, as All-

Jack Hannahan

Brent Gates

BATTING AVERAGE

	Name	(Years)	Avg.
1.	Mark Merila	(1991-94)	.393
2.	Brent Gates	(1989-91)	.387
3.	Robb Quinlan	(1996-99)	.381
4.	Greg Olson	(1980-82)	.375
	Terry Steinbach	(1981-83)	.375
6.	Matt Scanlon	(1997-99)	.373
7.	Tim McIntosh	(1984-86)	.366
8.	Bob Fenwick	(1966-67)	.364
9.	Jay Kvasnicka	(1986-88)	.362
10.	Shane Gunderson	(1993-95)	.359

HITS

	Name	(Years)	Hits
1.	Robb Quinlan	(1996-99)	345
2.	Ryan Lefebvre	(1990-93)	271
3.	Mark Merila	(1991-94)	269
4.	Brian Raabe	(1987-90)	264
5.	Charlie Nelson	(1991-94)	255
6.	Brent Gates	(1989-91)	249
7.	Jason Kennedy	(1999-02)	245
8.	Jeff Monson	(1988-91)	225
9.	Matt Scanlon	(1997-99)	224
10.	Jeff Goergen	(1985-88)	223
	Josh Holthaus	(1998-01)	223

HOME RUNS

	Name	(Years)	HR
1.	Robb Quinlan	(1996-99)	55
2.	Tom Steinbach	(1980-83)	45
3.	Jason Kennedy	(1999-02)	39
4.	Darren Grass	(1992-94)	36
5.	Craig Selander	(1996-98)	33
6.	Alex Bauer	(1983-86)	31
	Shane Gunderson	(1993-95)	31
7.	Jack Hannahan	(1999-01)	27
	Josh Holthaus	(1998-01)	27
8.	Mark Groebner	(1995-98)	26

TOTAL BASES

	Name	(Years)	TB
1.	Robb Quinlan	(1996-99)	617
2.	Jason Kennedy	(1999-02)	428
3.	Brent Gates	(1989-91)	385
4.	Mark Merila	(1991-94)	376
5.	Tom Steinbach	(1980-83)	362
6.	Josh Holthaus	(1998-01)	361
7.	Charlie Nelson	(1991-94)	357
8.	Jack Hannahan	(1999-01)	351
9.	Ryan Lefebvre	(1990-93)	349
10.	Matt Scanlon	(1997-99)	348

RUNS SCORED

	Name	(Years)	Runs
1.	Robb Quinlan	(1996-99)	249
2.	Charlie Nelson	(1991-94)	224
3.	Jason Kennedy	(1999-02)	213
4.	Mark Merila	(1991-93)	201
5.	Ryan Lefebvre	(1990-93)	195
6.	Gary Jost	(1979-82)	188
7.	Brain Raabe	(1987-90)	168
8.	Bill Piwnica	(1980-83)	166
9.	Tom Steinbach	(1980-83)	157
10.	Matt Scanlon	(1997-99)	153

RBIs

	Name	(Years)	RBI
1.	Robb Quinlan	(1996-99)	230
2.	Jason Kennedy	(1999-02)	182
3.	Mark Merila	(1991-94)	181
4.	Tom Steinbach	(1980-83)	175
5.	Darren Grass	(1992-94)	166
6.	Terry Steinbach	(1981-83)	165
7.	Brent Gates	(1989-91)	163
8.	Josh Holthaus	(1998-01)	161
9.	Matt Scanlon	(1997-99)	156
10.	Alex Bauer	(1983-86)	154

STOLEN BASES

	Name	(Years)	SB
1.	Charlie Nelson	(1991-94)	93
2.	J.T. Bruett	(1986-88)	77
3.	Jason Kennedy	(1999-02)	68
4.	Vince Palyan	(1986-89)	61
5.	Ryan Lefebvre	(1990-93)	53
6.	Paul Molitor	(1975-77)	52
7.	Bob Fenwick	(1966-67)	50
8.	Wes Denning	(1994-95)	49
9.	Mark Merila	(1991-94)	47
10.	Brian Raabe	(1987-90)	42

There, the Gophers kicked off the festivities by beating Arizona, 4-3, but lost that next night to Baylor, 6-4. They rebounded in a big way for their third game, beating Eastern Illinois, 15-10, but got spanked in the semi's by Baylor, 22-6, to round out the season.

The 38-24 Golden Gophers earned the right to host the 2000 Big Ten Tournament after clinching the regular-season title for the first time since 1977. The No. 1 seeds jumped out to a good start in the tourney as well, beating Northwestern, 8-4, in the opening round. Leading the charge for the Gophs were Pitcher Mike Kobow, who got his sixth complete-game victory of the season; freshman Luke Appert, who added a pair of home runs; and Mike Arlt and Scott Welch, who each knocked one out too. Minnesota came up short against Purdue

in the second round though, getting just four hits in the 6-1 loss to the Boilermakers. Then, later that day, the Gophers stranded 12 runners on base and wound up being upset by Penn State, 5-2, to get eliminated from the tournament.

The team did get to host the Midwest Regionals though, and wound up getting off on the right foot when they beat Wichita State, 10-7, in the first round. But, from there the wheels came off, as they lost to both Nebraska and those same Shockers, 4-1 & 5-1, respectively, to end their year on a downer.

The 2001 Gophers finished with an outstanding record of 39-21 and went on to win the Big Ten's, which were held in Columbus, Ohio, that year. There, the Gophers beat Penn State, 4-2, in the open-

JOHN ANDERSON

A graduate of Nashwauk-Keewatin High School in northern Minnesota, John Anderson came to the University of Minnesota as a player hoping to catch on as a pitcher for legendary Coach Dick Siebert. After suffering an arm injury that ended his playing career, however, Anderson opted instead to become the team's student coach. So well liked was Anderson that in 1977 he was voted Team MVP by the players.

After receiving his degree from Minnesota, Anderson began his coaching career as a graduate assistant under Siebert in 1978. After Siebert's death later that year, Anderson was promoted to assistant coach under then head coach George Thomas. Upon Thomas' resignation after the 1981 season Anderson, at just 26 years of age, was named as the 13th coach in Gopher history. Two decades later he is the second-longest tenured coach in the entire Athletic Department.

With 760 wins, Anderson has, like his mentor before him, become a legend. Now the winningest coach in Big Ten Conference history, Anderson has twice been honored with the Big Ten Conference Coach of the Year Award, and his teams have made appearances in the Big Ten Tournament in 17 of his 20 seasons, winning six championships. He has led Minnesota to 12 NCAA post-season appearances. In addition, Anderson has sent some 60 players on to professional baseball, including seven currently in the major leagues

Aside from being a players-coach, he is also a great recruiter of top-notch student-athletes. During his tenure in Gold Country, Anderson has coached more than Academic All-Big Ten selections and more than 150 University of Minnesota Scholar-Athlete Award winners. And, as it is said in his bio, he is "Known for his fairness in dealing with his players, Anderson believes in providing student-athletes with the best opportunities for education both on and off the field, a hallmark that has been a staple of Minnesota baseball for generations."

advance to the Big Ten Tournament Championship game against Ohio State. Senior Jason Kennedy and junior Luke Appert combined to drive in nine of the 11 runs. Then, against the Buckeyes, the Gophers fell, 6-3, to finish at 2-2 in the tournament and out of the post-season hoopla. DH Ben Pattee finished the game with a home run and two RBIs, while Luke Appert was named to the all-tournament team as the top second baseman.

Since the Big Ten Conference Tournament's inception back in 1981, Minnesota has led the way with a league-leading 20 appearances. This, from a team that has to contend with brutal cold weather for much of the year — often discouraging young pitchers from venturing north. But, the Gophers have aspired. Not only do they have one of the finest facilities in the country in Siebert Field, but they are also fortunate to be able to move indoors for early season competition with the use of the Metrodome. All in all, Gopher Baseball is rock solid. Coach Anderson is one of the best in the nation, and is now the program's all-time leading winner. The program is also continuing to produce a ton of major leaguers as well.

In 2002 alone, Right Fielder Jason Kennedy was selected in the 20th Round by the Detroit Tigers, becoming the 14th Golden Gopher to be selected in Major League Baseball's Amateur Draft during the past five years. In fact, there were four former Gophers on Opening Day major league rosters in 2002: Kerry Ligtenberg (Atlanta), Denny Neagle (Rockies), Dan Wilson (Mariners) and Jim Brower (Reds). Many others are just a moment's notice away from getting to the show, including former All-American Third Baseman Jack Hannahan of St. Paul, who is close to being called up by Detroit.

Today, the Gophers are leading the way in the Big Ten and aren't looking back. They are also enjoying a tremendous home-field advantage at Siebert Field, where, over the past seven seasons, they have posted an amazing 100-29 (.775) record there. Even so, the team is poised to get the necessary funding for the construction of a new on-campus stadium, which will make the program even stronger.

All in all, the program continues to graduate its kids and get them on to the next levels of baseball, and that is what it is all about. Not only does this program have one of the best attended and participated alumni games, with dozens of former major leaguers coming home to support their alma-maters each year, they also have a lot of corporate help as well. In fact, local sponsorship of this team has always been great. From the Wheaties Tournament of Champions years ago to the Hormel Foods Classic of today, they have all been there to help this team get better and better.

Let's just hope the next 130 years of Gopher Baseball are just half as great as the first. With Coach

er, and then kept on cruising from there. Next up were the Illini, whom Minnesota beat, 15-11, followed by a 6-5 win over Ohio State to reach the Finals. The championship game was a barn-burner, as the Gophers hung on to beat Michigan, 3-2, to bring home the hardware yet again.

With that, the team headed south, to Baton Rouge, La, where they opened the NCAA Regionals with a tough 10-9 loss to LSU. They then came back that next afternoon and got beat by California, 9-3, to miss their chance at the College World Series. It was a tough ending to a great season.

The 2002 Gophers went on to win the regular season Big Ten championship with a 14-5 record and from there advanced to the Big Ten Tourney, which was held at Siebert Field. The top-seeded Gophs, winners of a first-round bye, were then upset in the opener by Northwestern, 5-2. Minnesota rallied back to beat Michigan State, 6-0, in Game Two though, as Pitchers Jay Gagner and Matt Loberg allowed just six hits in nine shutout innings, while Junior Ben Pattee led the way offensively, going 3-for-4 with a run and an RBI. Minnesota then defeated Northwestern, 11-5, to

Mark Merila

Shane Gunderson

Anderson steering the ship, these Gophers are poised to get back to the College World Series and bring the University its fourth National Championship — and, who knows, maybe more!

ALL-TIME GOPHER MAJOR LEAGUERS

Player	Team(s)
Ralph Capron	Pittsburgh (1912-13)
Harry Elliott	St. Louis (NL) (1953, 1955)
Paul Giel	NY (NL) (1954-55), San Fran (1958) Pitt. (1959-60), Minn. (1961), KC(1961)
Jerry Kindall	Chicago (NL) (1956-58, 60-61) Cleveland (1962-64), Minn. (1964-65)
George Thomas	Detroit (1957-58, 1961) LA (AL) (1961-63), Detroit (1963-65) Boston (1966-71), Minnesota (1971)
Fred Bruckbauer	Minnesota (1961)
Bill Davis	Cleveland (1965-66), San Diego (1969)
Frank Brosseau	Pittsburgh (1969, 1971)
Bobby Fenwick	Houston (1972), St. Louis (1973)
Mike Sadek	San Francisco (1973, 1975-81)
Dave Winfield	SD (1973-80), NY (AL) (1981-90), Calif. (1990-91), Tor. (1992), Minn. (1993-94), Clev. (1995)
Steve Comer	Tex. (1978-82), Phil. (1983), Clev (1984)
Paul Molitor	Mil.(1978-92),Tor.(93-95),MN (96-98)
Jerry Ujdur	Detroit (1980-83), Cleveland (1984)
Brian Denman	Boston (1982)
Terry Steinbach	Oakland (1986-96), Minn. (1997-99)
Greg Olson	Minnesota (1989), Atlanta (1990-93)
Tim McIntosh	Mil.(1990-93), Mon.(1993), NY (1996)
Bryan Hickerson	San Francisco (1991-94), Chicago (NL) (1995), Colorado (1995)
Denny Neagle	Minnesota (1991), Pittsburgh (1992-96) Atlanta (1996-98), Cinc. (1999-2000) New York (AL) (2000), Colorado (2001)
J.T. Bruett	Minnesota (1992-93)
Dan Wilson	Cinc. (1992-93), Seattle (1994-2001)
Brent Gates	Oakland (1993-96), Seattle (1997) Minnesota (1998-99)
Brian Raabe	Minn. (1995-96), Seattle & Col. (1997)
Jeff Schmidt	California (1996)
Kerry Ligtenberg	Atlanta (1997-98, 2000-01)
Jim Brower	Cleveland (1999-2000), Cinc. (2001)

Gophers In The Major League Draft

Year	Name	Franchise	Round
2001	Jack Hannahan	Detroit	3rd
	Mike Kobow	Detroit	27th
2000	Ben Birk	Florida	24th
	Rick Brosseau	Toronto	16th
	Andy Persby	Minnesota	18th
1999	Brad Pautz	Philadelphia	4th
	Robb Quinlan	Anaheim	10th
	Matt Scanlon	Minnesota	8th
	Frank Wagner	Milwaukee	12th
1998	Jason Dobis	Oakland	27th
	Kai Freeman	Chicago (AL)	12th
	Craig Selander	Minnesota	27th
	Mark Groebner	Montreal	NA
1997	Mike Diebolt	Detroit	7th
	Bryan Guse	San Francisco	23rd

1998	Steve Huls	Minnesota	15th
1995	Wes Denning	Montreal	17th
	Shane Gunderson	Minnesota	6th
	Brian Mensink	Philadelphia	10th
	Andy Hammerschmidt	San Diego	14th
1994	Jim Brower	Texas	6th
	Darren Grass	San Diego	10th
	Mark Merila	San Diego	33rd
	Bill Mobilia	Philadelphia	21
1993	Ryan Lefebvre	Cleveland	19th
1992	Scott Bakkum	Boston	29th
	George Behr	Milwaukee	18th
	Tom Doyle	Montreal	20th
	Keith Krenke	Colorado	30th
	Jeff Schmidt	California	1st
1991	Brent Gates	Oakland	1st
1990	Dan Wilson	Cincinnati	1st
	Brian Raabe	Minnesota	41st
1989	Denny Neagle	Minnesota	3rd
	Vince Palyan	San Francisco	42nd
1988	J.T. Bruett	Minnesota	11th
	Jay Kvasnicka	Minnesota	8th
1986	Pete Bauer	New York (NL)	8th
	Tim McIntosh	Milwaukee	3rd
	Bryan Hickerson	Minnesota	7th
1985	Mike Clarkin	Boston	5th
1984	Jack Schlichting	Los Angeles	13th
	Bill Cutshall	Montreal	11th
	Doug Kampsen	Cincinnati	9th
1983	Terry Steinbach	Oakland	9th
	Tom Steinbach	Seattle	19th
	Barry Wohler	Los Angeles	14th
1982	Greg Olson	New York (NL)	7th
	Ronn Van Krevelen	Minnesota	28th
1978	Brian Denman	Boston	1st
	Jerry Ujdur	Detroit	4th
1977	Tim Loberg	Minnesota	25th
	Paul Molitor	Milwaukee	1st
	Tom Mee, Jr.	Atlanta	12th
	Dan Morgan	Montreal	15th
1975	Joe Kordosky	Minnesota	17th
	Jim Moldenhauer	Oakland	11th
1974	Bruce Gustafson	New York (NL)	22nd
1973	Dave Winfield	San Diego	1st
	Tim Grice	New York (AL)	16th
1971	Steve Chapman	Boston	18th
	Dave Carey	Montreal	4th
1970	Phil Flodin	Minnesota	36th
	Bob Nielsen	New York (AL)	39th
	Al Kaminski	Detroit	17th
1969	Noel Jenke	Boston	1st
	Mike Walseth	Atlanta	7th
1968	Russ Rolandson	Minnesota	21st
1967	Jerry Wickman	New York (AL)	20th
	Bob Fenwick	San Francisco	1st
1966	Steve Schneider	California	3rd
	Gary Hoffman	Minnesota	31st

M.I.A.C.
Minnesota Intercollegiate Athletic Conference

Most of the current MIAC schools began playing organized baseball around the time of the late 1800s. Among them was Carleton, which has roots reaching back to 1876. According to the book "Carleton: The First Century," here is how that school's first ever game went down:

"On June 13, 1876, a special meeting of the faculty was called to consider a request from the Base Ball nine to be excused from duty on Wedns. afternoon, June 14th, to play with the club from Shattuck School of Faribault."

During this era games were played somewhat regularly between Carleton's "Boss Nine" team, as they were known, and Northfield High School, Pillsbury Academy of Owatonna, Shattuck Military School, Seabury Seminary and the Minnesota School for the Deaf of Faribault. Carleton also played the University of Minnesota.

"A short time ago," reported the Carletonia of September, 1882, "the Carleton boys sent to the University (of Minnesota) a challenge to play a game of baseball. In response to this challenge on Monday, Sept. 25, a motley crew composed of two or three University students, several black-balled professionals, a barber, and a few Minneapolis bummers came down to Northfield and represented themselves as the University nine. The match was played in the afternoon of the same day resulting in a score of 13-9, in favor of the 'University' boys." No doubt this was a flagrant but by no means isolated example of the casual standards of the beginning years of Carleton sports competition."

In the late 1890s many of the local college and universities in the Midwest began forming athletic conferences. Among them was the "Southern Minnesota Intercollegiate Baseball League," which included Carleton, St. Olaf, Shattuck, and Pillsbury. A few years later the circuit was renamed as the "Minnesota Athletic Conference," and among its members were Hamline, Macalester, St. Olaf and St. Thomas.

Around this same time the first recorded baseball game was played at St. John's, as the Johnnies beat the local St. Cloud "Crackers," 15-7. And, while the school had been playing the game on an intramural basis since the 1870s, the competition was still fierce among the locals. The local

St. Thomas' Angie Giuliani

paper, the "Record," covered the game and reported: "We advise the home club to do a little more practicing and a little less mouthing if they want to invert the score"

In the early 1900's the organization and control of most sports was for the most part student-centered. Issues such as eligibility restrictions, scheduling procedures, awarding championships, and the establishment of consistent rules and regulations were sporadic at best. As a result, conferences and associations became more and more common in an attempt to formalize athletic competition.

One such organization was the Tri-State Conference, which was made up of colleges from both Minnesota and the Dakotas. In 1919, after a heated debate between the two state factions regarding rule changes and eligibility, the Minnesota contingent broke away and formed its own conference called the Minnesota Intercollegiate Athletic Conference. The MIAC's first charter members included: Carleton College, Gustavus Adolphus College, Hamline University, Macalester College, St. John's University, St. Olaf College and the University of St. Thomas.

The first ever MIAC season got underway just as World War I was coming to a close in 1920. St. Thomas won the inaugural championship that year, only to see St. Olaf take two-in-a-row in 1921 and '22. Concordia College in Moorhead was then admitted to the conference in 1921. The Tommies responded by claiming a pair of their own titles in 1923 & 1924, as Augsburg College was admitted to the league that year as well. The Oles answered by claiming two more crowns in the following two seasons while St. Mary's University in Winona was also admitted that season, bringing the total number of teams in the MIAC to an even 10 by 1926. The Gusties, behind Coach George Mirum, kept with tradition and won two of their own in '27 & 28, while St. Olaf came back to lay claim to the last title of the Roaring '20s in 1929.

Gustavus and St. Thomas dominated the 1930s, winning or sharing eight of the 10 titles that decade. A couple of the stars of the this era for the Tommies was Angie Giuliani, who went on to play major league ball with St. Louis, Washington and Brooklyn, and Pitcher Johnny Rigney, who played for eight seasons in the bigs with Chicago.

St. John's first intercollegiate baseball championship, 1919 (Minnesota-Dakota Intercollegiate Conference). From left, seated: John Daleiden (Fr. Charles, O.S.B.), Leo Witzleben, Matthew Barry (captain), Leonard Kapsner (Fr. Oliver, O.S.B.), August Kapsner (Fr. Roland, O.S.B.), Standing, from left: William (Bart) Rooney, John Cullen, Mathias Weber, Coach Edward Flynn, George Reuter, Francis (Hans) Wagner, Leo Reger.

The 1919 Johnnies

MIAC AWARD WINNERS

Year	MVP	Team
1985	Tim Anderson	Concordia
1986	Joe Meyer	St. Thomas
1987	Tim Piechowski	St. Mary's
1988	Jeff Ernste	St. Olaf
1989	John Nielson	Carleton
1990	Kyle Leske	St. Mary's
1991	John Nielson	Carleton
	Marvin Stoltz	Carleton
1992	Josh Gilbert	Bethel
1993	Chris Coste	Concordia
1994	Chris Coste	Concordia
1995	Chris Coste	Concordia
1996	Kevin Truax	Hamline
1997	Ryan Roder	St. John's
1998	Buzz Hannahan	St. Thomas
1999	Brian Sprout	St. Olaf
2000	Brian Sprout	St. Olaf
2001	Brian Sprout	St. Olaf
	Jake Mauer	St. Thomas
2002	Brad Mazer	Gustavus

MIAC BATTING LEADERS

Year	Avg.	Player	Team
1983	.549	Tom Gothmann	Hamline
1984	.510	Mark Nelson	Concordia
1985	.533	Clay Anderson	St. Olaf
1986	.512	Nick Whaley	St. Thomas
1987	.543	Nick Whale,	St. Thomas
1988	.537	Matt McDonald	St. Olaf
1989	.500	Tim Schwartz	Gustavus
1990	.477	Nat Halstead	St. Olaf
1991	.478	Adlai Kunst	Carleton
1992	.534	Dave Hultgren	Gustavus
1993	.596	Jon Dold	St. John's
1994	.520	Kevin Berger	St. Mary's
1995	.485	Chris Coste	Concordia
1996	.458	Jesse Bryant	St. Thomas
1997	.585	Ryan Roder	St. John's
1998	.524	Matt Bergstrom	Concordia.
1999	.473	Brian Sprout	St. Olaf.
2000	.507	Brian Sprout	St. Olaf
2001	.500	Derek Dormanen	Concordia
2002	.458	Tom Carroll	St. Thomas

In 1950 the University of Minnesota-Duluth Bulldogs joined the MIAC. That same year Macalester came out of nowhere and won the MIAC championship. More than a half-century later, it remains

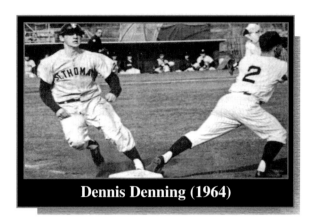

Dennis Denning (1964)

as their lone crown. While St. Thomas took the 1951 title, this decade was all about St. John's and St. Mary's, which each won or shared five conference titles during this period. So dominant were the Johnnies during this era that in one game, during the 1955 season, they crushed Augsburg 27-8!

St. Thomas laid claim to the 1956 crown behind Catcher Chuck Hiller, who went on to play eight seasons in the big leagues with San Francisco and New York. The Tommies also took co-honors in 1959 and then claimed it outright in 1960. The Auggies then took charge in 1961 and got back to the top of the MIAC in a big way. (One star of this era was a kid by the name of Jim Senske, who played for Hamline before going on to become the winningest high school coach in Minnesota history at New Ulm.) The Cobbers from Concordia and the Hamline Pipers finally got into the fray in 1962, sharing the title in a three-way split with St. Thomas that season.

From there on, St. Mary's and St. Thomas exchanged titles, with only Augsburg (1963) and St. John's (1969) overtaking them throughout the rest of that decade.

By the 1970s baseball was booming in Minnesota. More and more kids were moving on to the next levels and schools were reaping the benefits of better talent, better coaching and better fan support. St. Mary's took the 1970 title while St. Thomas and Gustavus each posted matching 11-3 records in '71 to share the crown. Denny Raarup's Gusties went down to the wire in the 1971 season, as a five hit shutout by Pitcher Doug Brinkman in a 2-0 win over St. Mary's sealed the deal for the team's first title in 31 years. Gustavus then went on to lose to Winona State in the NAIA district play-off, two games to none.

The Tommies would share it again in 1972, this time with St.

Augsburg, which won it in 1931, and St. John's, which won it outright in 1936 and shared it with Gustavus in 1937, were the only other schools to grab championships during this era. In the 1939 season alone, Gustavus had six all-conference players: Orris Atkinson, Bud Lutz, Duane Rippel, Ronnie Speibrink, Jerome Webster and Bill Young.

St. Thomas, St. Mary's, St. John's and Augsburg won the first four titles of the 1940s. The Johnnies even posted a perfect 11-0 record in 1942, one of the first clubs to do so. But then everything came to a screeching halt. By 1944 World War II was in full force and most of our boys were being sent overseas to serve their country. As a result, the MIAC was shut down for two seasons from 1944-45. Play resumed in 1946 with St. Thomas jumping back into the conference drivers

Gustavus Career Hitting Records

Batting Average	.400	1999-Present	Brad Mazer
Home runs	21	1999-Present	Brad Mazer
RBI's	107	1999-Present	Brad Mazer
Hits	166	1996-99	Chris Swansson

seat. The Auggies made a mini-run in 1947, winning a pair, only to see the Oles knock them off their perch in 1949.

By this time high school baseball was growing by leaps and bounds in the Land of 10,000 Lakes. The state tournament was three years old by 1950 and more and more kids were getting opportunities to showcase their talents to the masses. As a result, the college ranks were being filled with the state's top-notch kids who wanted to play the game at the next level. The MIAC would prosper greatly from the newly formed tourney and watch its level of competition get even better.

Concordia's Career Hitting Records

Batting Average	.442	1993-95	Chris Coste
Runs	126	1982-85	Kent Kuball
Hits	162	1993-95	Chris Coste
Home Runs	19	1993-95	Chris Coste
RBI's	110	1993-95	Chris Coste
Stolen Bases	100	1982-85	Kent Kuball

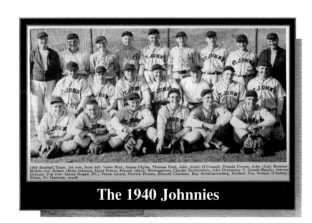

The 1940 Johnnies

HOWIE SCHULTZ

One of the stars of th 1940s was Hamline's Howie "Stretch" Schultz (Class of '45), who was regarded by many as Hamline's greatest all-time athlete. A baseball and basketball star for the Pipers, Shultz went on to play pro baseball with Grand Forks in the Northern League before signing with his hometown St. Paul Saints in 1942. That next summer he was called up by the Brooklyn Dodgers, where he played for five seasons before losing his roster spot to a guy named Jackie Robinson. In 1947 Howie was sold to the Phillies, where he played for two more seasons.

He returned to Minnesota in 1951 and then began playing with the NBA's Minneapolis Lakers. Prior to that he had been playing pro basketball with the Anderson Packers and Fort Wayne Pistons. (Schultz would play pro basketball for three seasons, but during the summer would play townball. He first played for Willmar in the West-Central League, before moving on to play with Faribault of the old Southern Minny. He finally hung up his spikes in the late 1950s, but not before becoming one of the state's al time top sports figures.)

Howie (right) with legendary Hamline Coach Joe Hutton

Mary's, only to see Augsburg take the 1973 and 1975 titles. (Incidentally, Bill Nelson, the present head coach at Carleton, was the top pitcher on that Auggies' 1973 MIAC championship team.) The Johnnies would grab it in 1974, while the Oles came back to take the 1976 title with a 13-5 mark. That same year the UM-Duluth Bulldogs, behind their star Terry Egerdahl, finished sixth in the MIAC before making the jump to the Northern Sun Intercollegiate Conference.

In 1977 St. John's won the MIAC but St. Olaf was the team to beat in the post-season, advancing on to the NCAA D-III Playoffs. Gustavus went 16-2 and 15-3, respectively, in 1978 and 1979, advancing on to the NCAA D-III Playoffs in 1978 as well. Leading the charge for the men of St. Peter were Pitcher Brian Engel, who won six games, and Jim Mortinson, who led the league in batting with a .499 average. Others Gusties who hit over .300 included Jim Swanson, Brad Baker, Ron Starke, and Jay Soule. The Gusties missed the cut in 1979, but St. Olaf, behind their star pitcher Dave Ario, who won 13 ballgames that season, made it to the NCAA D-III Playoffs as well.

Gustavus and St. Olaf shared the MIAC title in 1980 and each advanced on to the NCAA D-III Playoffs that year. In addition, Gustavus' Bill Soule had an amazing .987 slugging percentage that year, tops in the nation. Led by tri-captains and all-MIAC recipients Steve Swansson, Jay Soule, and Brad Baker, the Gusties beat St. Cloud State 6-2 and 4-3 in NAIA district play, but then missed out on going to the Nationals by losing to Wis.-Parkside, 6-4, and Briar Cliff, 9-8.

The Oles would share conference honors four of the next five seasons, and advance on to the NCAA's post-season party each time. The Tommies and Cobbers shared it in 1983 with the Cobbers, behind All-MIAC Pitcher Howard Berglund,

Dennis Denning

getting an invite to the big dance that year as well.

In 1986 the Tommies grabbed a share of the MIAC with an impressive 18-2 record. The Auggies were right there with them though thanks to Pitchers John Nelson and Jeff Dainty, who led their club to the post-season along with St. Thomas.

The Auggies won it in 1987, but it was the Oles who wound up going on to the big dance. They then went on to win back-to-back MIAC titles in 1988 and 1989 and again made it back to the NCAA D-III Playoffs in each of those seasons as well. In addition, Carleton won 13 games in 1989 and was led by All-American John Nielson.

St. Mary's notched top honors in 1990 while Carleton and St. Olaf shared them in 1991. (That 1991 Carleton squad won 24 games, more than any team in school history.) Each of those clubs made it to the NCAA's post-season extravaganza that year, while the Oles did it again in 1992. St. Mary's, which shared top honors in '92, was right there in '93 as well, along with Concordia. And, while St. Mary's and Concordia each advanced on to the NCAA's, it was the Johnnies' Jon Dold who led the entire nation in batting that year with a whopping .562 percentage. (In fact, it was fourth highest single-season batting average in NCAA D-III history.)

Macalester Career Hitting Records

Batting Average	.446	1988-89 Scott Sheehy
Runs	150	1996-99 Matt Kessler
Hits	178	1998-01 Keenan S.
Home Runs	26	1994-97 Kawika Alo
RBI's	152	1996-99 R.T. Luczak
Steals	72	1994-97 David Young

St. Thomas pulled away from the pack from here on out. They shared the crown with the Johnnies in 1994, and, after Concordia won it in 1995 behind All-American Pitcher Chris Coste, they went on to win seven championships in a row from 1996-2002. The 1996 club even posted an incredible 19-1 conference mark, while going 38-5 overall. They became mainstays at the NCAA Division III Playoffs and simply became the team to beat in the entire Midwest. (It should also be noted that in 1997 St. John's Ryan Roder led the nation with a .540 batting average.)

In 1998 and 1999 the Tommies were led by All-American Buzz Hannahan as well as Pitcher Bryan Toov, who had an unbeliev-

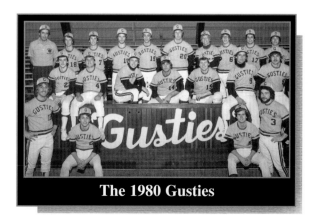

The 1980 Gusties

able .064 ERA. That next season Pitcher Chris Olean was named to the All-America team after giving up just six runs in 16 games to post an amazing .60 ERA. The 1999 club also won 19 games, and in 2000 the Tommies finally did some damage in the NCAA Division III Playoffs where they finished as the National Runner-Ups. They finished up as the No. 2 team in the nation yet again that next year, until 2001, when they made history by becoming the first Minnesota D-III team ever to win the National Championship. In 1999 and 2000, however, the Tommies finished the season better than 354 NCAA Division III institutions.

ALL-TIME MIAC BASEBALL CHAMPS

Year	Champion	Year	Champion	Year	Champion
1920	St. Thomas	1951	St. Thomas	1975	Augsburg
1921	St. Olaf	1952	St. John's	1976	St. Olaf
1922	St. Olaf	1953	St. Mary's	1977	St. John's
1923	St. Thomas	1954	St. John's	1978	Gustavus
1924	St. Thomas		St. Mary's	1979	Gustavus
1925	St. Olaf	1955	St. John's	1980	Gustavus
1926	St. Olaf	1956	St. Thomas	1981	St. Mary
1927	Gustavus	1957	St. John's		St. Olaf
1928	Gustavus		St. Mary's	1982	St. Thomas
1929	St. Olaf	1958	St. John's	1983	St. Thomas
1930	Gustavus		St. Mary's	1984	St. Olaf
1931	Augsburg	1959	Augsburg	1985	Concordia
1932	Gustavus		St. Thomas		St. Olaf
1933	Gustavus	1960	St. Thomas	1986	St. Thomas
1934	St. Thomas	1961	Augsburg	1987	Augsburg
1935	Gustavus	1962	Concordia	1988	St. Olaf
1936	St. John's		Hamline	1989	St. Olaf
1937	Gustavus		St. Thomas	1990	St. Mary's
1938	Gustavus	1963	Augsburg	1991	Carleton
	St. John's	1964	St. Mary's	1992	St. Olaf
1939	Gustavus	1965	St. Thomas	1993	Concordia
1940	St. Thomas	1966	St. Mary's		St. Mary's
1941	St. Mary's	1967	St. Thomas	1994	St. John's
1942	St. John's	1968	St. Mary's	1995	Concordia
1943	Augsburg	1969	St. John's	1996	St. Thomas
1944	No Champion	1970	St. Mary's	1997	St. Thomas
1945	No Champion	1971	Gustavus	1998	St. Thomas
1946	St. Thomas		St. Thomas		St. John's
1947	Augsburg	1972	St. Mary's	1999	St. Thomas
1948	Augsburg		St. Thomas	2000	St. Olaf
1949	St. Olaf	1973	Augsburg	2001	St. Olaf
1950	Macalester	1974	St. John's	2002	St. Olaf

In January of 2000 the Tommies made history when they traveled to Havana, Cuba, to play a series of exhibition games versus the University of Havana. As a result, they became the first college baseball team to play in the country since 1986. And, when the Cuban team came to the Twin Cities for a return trip that May, it marked just the second Cuban college team ever to play in the U.S. in the last four decades.

The 36-14 Toms would lose to Montclair State (N.J.) in the College World Series that season, but would learn from that experience to come back that next year. That 2000 squad was led by All-American Second Baseman Jake Mauer, from Cretin, and outfielder Tony Wolverton, from Fairmont. Both were voted to the College World Series All-Tournament team that year as Mauer batted .458 with five RBIs, while Wolverton batted .583 with three runs.

The 2001 season was a real roller-coaster ride for the 39-10 Toms. The club opened their season by being no-hit and from there they grabbed onto the No. 1 national ranking in April. They slumped in May to finish third in the MIAC, but then rebounded to win 10 of 12 post-season games.

After beating St. Mary's 10-2 in the MIAC Playoffs, the Toms beat St. Olaf, 8-3, to advance to the NCAA Midwest Regionals in Oshkosh, WI. There, they beat Edgewood, 9-8, in an 11-inning thriller, in Game One, and then eliminated UW-Steven Point, 5-1, in Game Two. St. Thomas then advanced on to Appleton, Wis., for the Division III Championships. There, the Tommies lost the opening game of the double-elimination tournament, 6-4, to Ripon. They rebounded that next afternoon, however, to beat Ripon, 10-3. Next up was Illinois Wesleyan, and the Toms blanked them, 7-0, behind Right Fielder Tony Wolverton's three hits and three RBIs. From there the

Gustavus' Brad Mazer

MIAC TITLES
WON OR SHARED (1920-2002)

School	No.	Last Title
University of St. Thomas	22	1999
St. Olaf College	17	2002
St. Mary's University	14	1993
Gustavus Adolphus College	13	1980
St. John's University	13	1998
Augsburg College	10	1987
Concordia College	4	1995
Carleton College	1	1991
Hamline University	1	1962
Macalester College	1	1950

Ryan Benson

team got serious, crushing SUNY-Cortland, 17-5, behind Catcher Kyle Olson's six RBI, followed by Montclair State, 8-5. But the Toms got stung in their next game against Marietta College (Ohio), losing 8-6. They rebounded back that next day at the Appleton, Wis., stadium though, to beat that same Marietta club in the College World Series Finals, 8-4, to win it all.

That last game was a real thriller. Senior Brad Bonine was the hero in this one, going 3-for-5 with four RBIs, including a two-run homer, while scoring three runs to lead the Tommies to the 2001 NCAA Division III Baseball Championship. Junior Brian Whinnery tossed a complete-game as well, allowing just six hits while fanning six, and even pitched out of a bases-loaded jam in the eighth to spoil a Marietta rally. In addition, Matt Buzzell had an RBI double in the sixth and an RBI triple in the seventh. Other Tommies with at least a pair of hits in the team's 14-hit attack were Nate Sundberg, Luke Sather and Jake Mauer, the All-American who finished the season with an amazing .449 batting average and went on to sign with the Twins. (Jake's brother Joe was also drafted by the Twins, except he was just a high school senior at the time when he was selected as the No. 1 overall selection in the 2001 Amateur Draft.)

When it was all said and done, the 39-10 Tommies, who also won the coveted NCAA Division III batting crown that year with an unconscious team average of .372, had completed a dream season. And, they were now just the second team in Minnesota history to win a national championship. (The Gophers won three in 1956, 1960 & 1964.) In addition, Dennis Denning was named as the D-III National Baseball Coach of the Year to boot. In his seven seasons behind the

Tommy bench, his teams have posted the third-best won-loss record in all of Division III baseball at 255-69 (.787). Denning, who posted a 378-76 record at Cretin High School prior to coming to STU, was also 126-24 in all games vs. MIAC foes as well — making the Toms the team to beat in the conference these days.

Other highlights of this era included St. Olaf's Brian Sprout being named as an All-American in 2000, while Second baseman Joel Brettingen became Macalester's first NCAA Division III All-America baseball player ever in 2002 as well. He was joined by Gustavus Catcher Brad Mazer as the only MIAC players honored with All-America status that year. Other things to look for in the near future of MIAC baseball include the 500-win watch for long-time St. John's Jerry Haugen, who, with a career record of 471-397, is among the top 25 winningest active coaches in all of Division III baseball.

Recognized as one of the toughest and most prestigious NCAA Division III intercollegiate athletic conferences in the country, today, the MIAC sponsors championships in 23 sports — 12 for men and 11 for women. And, because its members are all private undergraduate colleges, none of them can offer athletic scholarships to its student-athletes. So it really is about the kids, good sportsmanship, fun and good ol' fashioned baseball.

The 2001 National Champs

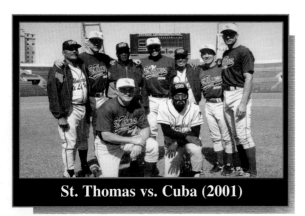

St. Thomas vs. Cuba (2001)

ALL-TIME MIAC INDIVIDUAL SEASON RECORDS

Batting:

At-Bats:	78	Brian Sprout	St. Olaf	2002
Hits:	67	Brian Sprout	St. Olaf	2000
		Ryan Roder	St. John's	1997
Home Runs:	10	Nick Beissel	St. Olaf	2001
		Barry Midthun	Bethel	1988
		Doug Dainty	St. Olaf	1986
		Kyle Aug	Hamline	1985
Doubles:	13	Jeremy Belisle	Bethel	1999
		Nick Belde	St. Mary's	1988
Triples:	7	Brian Sprout	St. Olaf	2000
		John Mayer	Augsburg	1988
RBIs:	38	Kyle Aug	Hamline	1985
Runs:	33	Brian Sprout	St. Olaf	2000
Average	.596	Jon Dold	St. John's	1993

Pitching:

Wins:	8	Mike Honsa	St. Thomas	1999
		Tim Piechowski	St. Mary's	1987
Innings:	63.3	Tim Piechowski	St. Mary's	1987
Strikeouts:	75	Tim Piechowski	St. Mary's	1987
ERA:	0.66	Charlie Rudd	St. Olaf	2002

Widely acclaimed as one of the top NCAA Division II athletic conferences in the nation, the North Central Conference has a strong tradition which dates back to the Fall of 1921 when the groundwork was laid to create the new circuit. Originally called the North Central Intercollegiate Conference, the league featured seven original members including: the College of St. Thomas, South Dakota State College, Des Moines College, Creighton University, North Dakota Agricultural College (now NDSU), University of North Dakota, and Morningside. By 1932 several of the teams had dropped out, including St. Thomas, which had defected to the MIAC. That same year the circuit was renamed as the Northern Teacher's Athletic Conference and a decade later it would become known as the State Teacher's College Conference of Minnesota.

Over the next several years many teams would come and go including Northern Iowa, Augustana College and Omaha University (later known as University of Nebraska-Omaha), among others. In 1962 the league switched its name to the Northern Intercollegiate Conference (NIC) and in 1968 Mankato State, which had previously been in the Northern Sun Conference (NSIC), came into the league as well. The Mavs won NSIC titles in both 1960 and 1968 before making the jump to the new league. Then, in 1981, St. Cloud State University, which had also previously played in the NSIC, defected to the league. (Mankato State, which would later change its name to Minnesota State, Mankato, briefly left the NCC in 1978 to re-join the NSIC, where they would remain until 1981, before returning for good.)

MSU's Dean Bowyer

The nine-team conference, renamed in 1982 as the North Central Conference (NCC), continues to provide countless opportunities for young men and women throughout the Midwest in one of the nation's truly elite NCAA Division II athletic conferences.

Since joining the league in 1981, Minnesota State, Mankato has dominated the NCC, winning an amazing 19 titles in that span. Here is that school's story: In 1868 Mankato Normal School first opened its doors in the picturesque river valley town of Mankato, with its primary role

St. Cloud State Coaches:
(L-R) Jim Stanek (1968-78), John Kasper (1950-67),
Al Brainard (1946-49), Denny Lorsung (1979-present)

being to train teachers for work in rural schools throughout Southern Minnesota. In 1921 the school became Mankato State Teachers College and was authorized by the State to offer a four-year curriculum. The school began playing baseball on an informal basis from around the turn of the century, primarily against local high school teams, and later against regional college teams from around the state.

Mankato finally started to play organized baseball in 1936, in the Northern Teacher's Athletic Conference. The team went 2-6 that next year under legendary coach C.P. Blakeslee, the namesake for the present football stadium on campus. From there they would go on to play in the NIC and NSIC before finally settling down in

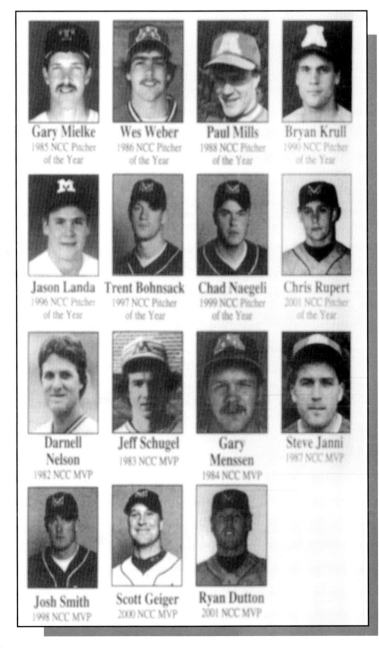

Gary Mielke
1985 NCC Pitcher of the Year

Wes Weber
1986 NCC Pitcher of the Year

Paul Mills
1988 NCC Pitcher of the Year

Bryan Krull
1990 NCC Pitcher of the Year

Jason Landa
1996 NCC Pitcher of the Year

Trent Bohnsack
1997 NCC Pitcher of the Year

Chad Naegeli
1999 NCC Pitcher of the Year

Chris Rupert
2001 NCC Pitcher of the Year

Darnell Nelson
1982 NCC MVP

Jeff Schugel
1983 NCC MVP

Gary Menssen
1984 NCC MVP

Steve Janni
1987 NCC MVP

Josh Smith
1998 NCC MVP

Scott Geiger
2000 NCC MVP

Ryan Dutton
2001 NCC MVP

MSU's Jerry Terrell

MSU Baseball Records

Individual Hitting Records

At Bats
Season - 209, Mike Carroll (1980)
Career - 533, Josh Smith (1996-99)

Hits
Season - 81, Mike Carroll (1980)
Career - 192, Josh Smith (1996-99)

Average
Season - .467, Tom Ashley (1993) (min. 50 ab)
Career - .400, Tom Lepel (123/307, 1985-88)
(minimum 200 at bats)

Singles
Season - 54, Bryan Zollman, (1996)
Career - 128, Josh Smith (1996-99)

Doubles
Season - 19, Scott Geiger (2000)
Career - 37, Tim Huber (1997-01)

Triples
Season - 6, Mike Carroll (1980)
Career - 11, Mike Carroll (1978-80)

Home Runs
Season - 16, Jason Pfingsten (1996)
Career - 29, Josh Smith (1996-99)

Runs
Season - 58, Joe Marchese (1986)
Career - 134, Eric Lonnquist (1999-SA)

Hitting Streak
30 games, Darnell Nelson (1982)

Consecutive Hits
10, Jason Pfingsten (1996)

RBI
Season - 59, Jason Pfingsten (1996)
Career - 141, Dave Whiteford (1984-87)

Stolen Bases
Season - 32, Gene Glynn (1978)
Career - 82, Gene Glynn (1976-79)

Sacrifice Hits
Season - 11, Bill Wildman (2000)
Career - 16, Ron McCann (1978-81)

Walks
Season - 41, Richard Austin (2000)
Career - 83, Dave Whiteford (1984-87)

Individual Pitching Records

Appearances
Season - 19, Mike Landkammer (1999)
Keith Meyers (2000)
Career - 43, Kory Kosek (1992-95)

Innings
Season - 86.6, Blake Everson (1980)
Career - 210.0, Mike Kanter (1984-87)

Strikeouts
Season - 100, Chris Hart (1996)
Career - 227, John Rulmyr (1967-70)

Victories
Season- 10, Chris Rupert (2000)
Career - 23, Mike Kanter (1984-87)

Earned Run Average
Season - 0.00, Greg Langevin (1969) (30 inn.)
1.05, Jim Hahn (1979) (50 inn.)
Career - 0.67, Jim Hahn (1978-79)

Saves
Season - 10, Todd Revenig (1990)
Career - 12, Todd Revenig (1988-90)

Individual Fielding

Putouts
Season - 400, Mike Carroll (1980)
Career - 829, Mike Carroll (1978-80)

Assists
Season - 152, Eric Lonnquist (2000)
Career - 421, Eric Lonnquist (1999-SA)

Fielding Average
Season - 1.000, Mike Carroll (227, 1979)
Ken Blumberg (188, 1972 & 1974)
Dan O'Brien (147, 1975)
Career - .998, Ken Blumberg (min 250)
(1971-74)

Mike Carroll
1978-80

Gene Glynn
1976-79

Team Records

Games Played	57	(1980)
Wins	36	(1980, 1996, 2000)
Consecutive Wins	19	(1970)
At Bats	1,711	(1980)
Runs	426	(1986)
Batting Average	.344	(1995)
Hits	581	(1980)
Doubles	114	(2000)
Triples	22	(1980)
Home Runs	60	(1997)
Runs Batted In	365	(1980)
Sacrifices	37	(2000)
Base on Balls	267	(1986)
Total Bases	859	(1980)

Team Fielding

Double Plays	44	(2000)
Putouts	1,191	(1980)
Assists	661	(1982)
Fielding Pct	.962	(1972, 1996)

Single-Season Hitting Top Ten
(Minimum 75 at bats)

1. Tom Ashley (1993)		.467
2. Joel Hayford (1983)		.463
3. Josh Smith (1998)		.438
4. Fritz Polka (1984)		.435
5. Ryan Dutton (2001)		.432

6. Jeff Schugel (1983)		.426
7. Tim Huber (2001)		.421
8. Joel Hayford (1981)		.420
9. Darnell Nelson (1982)		.417
10. Bob Breshnahan (1980)		.413
11. Jason Pfingsten (1995)		.411
12. Chris Urbain (1990)		.408
12. Bryan Zollman (1996)		.408

Mike Kanter
1978-80

Dave Whiteford
1976-79

Josh Smith
1996-99

Scott Geiger
1998-00

MSU's Lonnquist

titles in 1982 and 1983, and then from 1985-1990. They slowed down in the early '90s but then picked up right where they left off in 1996, when they won back-to-back titles in 1996-97. Then, after losing out to Northern Colorado in 1998, the Mavs went on a tear, claiming four straight NCC Crowns from 1999-2002. One of the premier teams in the entire Midwest, this program has simply been awesome.

In that most recent year, 2002, the Mavs went 31-16 and then got an invitation to play in the four-team, double-elimination NCAA Division II Central Regionals in Warrensburg, Mo. There, the Mavericks downed Nebraska-Omaha, 17-16, in the opener and then upset top-ranked Central Missouri State, 12-11, that next day. From there, however, Central Missouri State rebounded to beat MSU 7-3 and 10-6 to end their season. For the tourney, junior outfielder Donnell Boyer hit a team-high .600, Junior infielder Aaron Olson hit .533 and senior outfielder Josh Hinson hit .500 as well.

MSU's Heitzman

The Mavs have been outstanding in the post-season since joining the NCC, making 24 NCAA Division II Tournament appearances — the third most in the nation. The Mavericks stand at 40-51 overall in NCAA post-season play (including D-II College World Series games), while their record in regional action is 36-41.

The man responsible for this amazing success is long-time coach Dean Bowyer, who, with more than 800 career coaching victories, is among the top five winningest NCAA Division II active coaches. Simply put, he is real legend in Minnesota baseball. The Ada, Minn., native, who played profes-

the NCC for good. The Mavs won NIC titles in 1960 and again in 1968 before defecting to the NCC.

MSU, now under the tutelage Coach Jean McCarthy, won its first titles in 1970 and 1971, and then added three more in 1974, 1976 and 1977. Coach McCarthy would conclude his career in Mankato with an impressive 250-127 record from 1964-76, before handing the reigns to Dean Bowyer. The Mavs would make a brief return to the NIC from 1977-81, taking a pair of titles once again in 1979 and 1981 before coming back yet again to the NCC — this time for good. In the '80s the Mavs simply took over under Coach Bowyer, winning

JIM EISENREICH

Jim Eisenreich was drafted by the Twins in 1980 in the 16th round. He played sporadically with the team over the next couple of years until voluntarily retiring from the game in 1984, due to a nervous disorder known as Tourette's Syndrome. He made his triumphant comeback three years later though, in 1987, when he joined the Kansas City Royals. He spent four full seasons in KC before signing as a free-agent in 1993 with the Philadelphia Phillies. Jim batted .361 in 1996 with Philly, and also reached the 1,000-hit plateau that same year. Eisenreich would appear in two World Series over his illustrious career, winning the title in 1997 with the Florida Marlins.

ST. CLOUD HITTING RECORDS

At Bats

Season:	192	Mike McKinney	1999
Career:	651	Mike McKinney	1996-99

Runs

Season:	60	John McFarland	1988
	60	Mike McKinney	1999
Career:	151	Mike McKinney	1996-99

Hits

Season:	69	John McFarland	1988
Career:	227	Mike McKinney	1996-99

Home Runs

Season:	12	Mike McKinney	1997
	12	Jim Schlieman	1999
Career:	33	Mike McKinney	1996-99

RBI's

Season:	52	Jim Schlieman	1999
Career:	119	Mike McKinney	1996-99

Stolen Bases

Season:	26	Charlie Eisenreich	1985
Career:	61	Mike McKinney	1996-99

Total Bases

Season:	122	John McFarland	1988
Career:	380	Mike McKinney	1996-99

Batting Average

Season:	.467	Bob Altuvilla	1948-49
Career:	.454	P.J. Hanson	1988-89

PITCHING RECORDS

Complete Games

Season:	9	Josh Vorpahl	1998
	9	Pete Pratt	1988
Career:	19	Wayne Parks	1965-69

Victories

Season:	8	Josh Vorpahl	1998
	8	Mike Morehead	1988
	8	Brock Kiecker	1972
	8	Jim Tomozik	1971
Career:	23	Wayne Parks	1965-69

Saves

Season:	6	Mike Hammer	1989
Career:	8	Mike Hammer	1988-89

Strikeouts

Season:	81	Larry Vergin	1963
Career:	187	Dan Jensen	1968-71

ERA

Season:	0.61	Jack Peterson	1968
Career:	1.63	Jack Peterson	1966-68

sionally in the Baltimore Orioles organization, was actually an all-conference football player at Mayville State, where he also played baseball and basketball. He is a an 11-time NCC Coach of the Year, and a three-time NCAA Midwest Region Coach of the Year as well.

Under his tutelage, MSU baseball teams have played in NCAA post-season competition 17 out of his 25 years, and have won at least 30 games in 16 out of those same 25 years. Of Bowyer's 18 NCAA post-season appearances, three of his teams made it all the way to the NCAA Division II College World Series. The most recent trip to the big dance came in 1986 when the Mavericks racked up an impressive 35-15 record and finished fourth at the Series. The other two trips came in 1980, when the Mavericks won a school-record 36 games and took third, and in 1979, when MSU went 26-22-1 and was ranked seventh in the nation.

Now in his 30th year behind the bench, Bowyer's success can be attributed to his ability to recruit and develop talent. In addition to two All-Americans and countless all-region and all-conference selections, more than three dozen of his former players have signed professional contracts. Among the most recent major league draftees include Pitcher Chris Rupert, who won a school-record 25 games over four years before signing as a free agent with Philadelphia in 2002. In addition, four other MSU players were drafted and signed by major league teams that year as well: Pitcher Aaron Heitzman (19th round by Houston), Pitcher Jason Cierlik (23rd round by Baltimore), Pitcher Adam Steen (29th round by Philadelphia) and Shortstop Eric Lonnquist (34th round by Kansas City). In addition, two Mavs have made it to the "Show," Todd Revenig, who was drafted and signed with Oakland in 1990, and reliever Gary Mielke, a St. James native who played briefly with the Texas Rangers in the late 1980s.

St. Cloud State is the other Minnesota team to play in the NCC. Originally founded in 1896, St. Cloud State University was first known primarily as a teacher's college. The school began playing baseball around that same time on an informal basis, primarily

MSU's Individual Award Recipients

MSU Baseball All-Americans	Year
Wes Weber	1986
Fritz Polka	1986

NCC Most Valuable Pitchers	Year
Gary Mielke	1985
Wes Weber	1986
Paul Mills	1988
Bryan KruII	1990
Jason Landa	1996
Trent Bohusack	1997
Chad Naegeli	1999
Chris Rupert	2001

NCC MVP Winners	Year
Darnell Nelson	1982
Jeff Schugel	1983
Gary Mensten	1984
Steve Janni	1987
Josh Smith	1998
Scott Geiger	2000
Ryan Dutton	2001

St. Cloud's Larry Miller

Mavericks Who Have Signed Contracts With Major League Baseball Organizations

Team	Player
Athletics	Wes Weber
	Todd Revenig
Astros	Aaron Heitzman
Braves	Jeff Matthews
Orioles	Larry Woodall
	Jason Cierlik
Cubs	Bob Will
	Jeff Sjoberg
Dodgers	Keith Meyers
Expos	Mike Carroll
	Joel Lepel
	Gene Glynn
	Mike Fier
	Ryan Van Gilder
Mets	Fritz Polka
Phillies	Kory Kosek
	Chris Rupert
	Adam Steen
Rangers	Gary Mielke
	Mark Young
	Larry Ogden
	Brian Seesz
	Kevin Wozney
Reds	Chuck Engle
	Larry Jensen
	Mike Landkammer
Red Sox	Ty Herman
	Joe Marchese
Royals	Jerry Terrell
	Eric Lonnquist
Tigers	Dave Lottsfeldt
Twins	Jay Bombach
	Bob Bresnahan
	Mike Hartman
	Randy Heidman
	Steve Johnson
	Sam Terrell
	Jeff Schugel
	Gary Menssen
	Monte Dufault
Yankees	Darnell Nelson

MSU's Gary Mielke

NCC MEMBERS

St. Cloud State
Minnesota State, Mankato
Augustana
Nebraska-Omaha
North Dakota
North Dakota State
Northern Colorado
South Dakota
South Dakota State

Reformatory. In 1932 the league changed its name to the Northern Teacher's Athletic Conference and the Huskies responded by taking the Minnesota State Championship. Then, in 1944 it would become the Northern Intercollegiate Conference (NIC). (In the 1940s and 1950s the Huskies won a handful of "Bi-State" tournaments as well, taking those crowns in 1947, 1956, 1957 & 1958.) As members of the NIC the club has been outstanding, winning titles in 1964, 1965, 1967, 1969, 1970, 1971, 1976 and 1978. In 1981 SCSU left the NSIC to join the NCC, where they have remained ever since.

Early on the Huskies played a mixture of MIAC and NSIC teams, but always fielded tough teams. One of the stars of the 1950s was Rip Repulski, who went on to play in the major leagues from 1953-61 with the Cardinals, Phillies, Dodgers and Red Sox. He garnered 830 hits, 106 homers, 416 RBIs and hit .268 over his career.

In 1957 the Huskies played in the NAIA Regionals and that next year the Huskies, under Coach John Kasper, received an invitation to play in the first annual NAIA National Baseball Tournament, in Alpine, Texas. There, Pipestone native Jack Kelly led the team to a third place finish at the NAIA World Series. In that third place game against Creighton, the Huskies rallied with two outs in the bottom of the ninth from a 5-1 deficit to get the big win. Steetar homered to tie it and the Huskies won it in the 10th inning on a suicide squeeze bunt.

The 1969 club, behind Pitchers Wayne Parks and future Twin Greg Thayer, would also finish third at the NAIA World Series as well, under Coach Stanek. In 1971 the Huskies played in the NCAA Midwest Regionals. Perhaps the biggest stars of the program, however, came through the Granite City in the early 1980s, under Coach Dennis Lorsung. The first was an outfielder by the name of Jim Eisenreich, who would flirt with .400 during his tenure at SCSU, and the other was a pitcher from Sleepy Eye by the name of Dana Kiecker. Both of these players would go on to star in the major leagues.

After wining the North Division of the NCC in both 1988 and 1989, the 20-

Dana Kiecker pitched for the Boston Red Sox during the 1990 and 1991 seasons, posting a career ERA of 4.68 with a 10-12 record and 114 strike-outs. Today the Sleepy Eye native is a broadcaster for the St. Paul Saints.

against local high schools. In fact, the school's first ever game was against St. Cloud High School in 1896. The team played again in 1897 but then dropped the program on and off until 1918. This was the height of World War I, so the game was still sporadic, but it did get going a few years later.

St. Cloud State first began playing baseball on an organized basis in 1924, going 2-4 that season as members of the Northern Intercollegiate Conference. Under Coach Zeleny the team got wins over both St. John's and of the Year in three Minnesota conferences during his career. (He was named the MIAC Coach of the Year in 1977 while leading St. John's University. He then earned NIC Coach of the Year honors in 1980, as well as NCC Coach of the Year honors in both 1991 and 2001 while at St. Cloud State.) He is one of Minnesota's very best.

St. Cloud State's 1991 Title Team

Both Minnesota State, Mankato and St. Cloud State have both done Minnesota proud and continue to represent the state well throughout the ranks of Division II baseball.

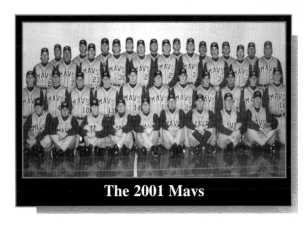

The 2001 Mavs

16 Huskies roared back in 1991 to win their first and only NCC crown. They would advance on to make a National Tournament Appearance that year, playing in the coveted NCAA North Central Regionals as well.

The man behind the team's success was long-time Coach Dennis Lorsung, who is now in his 25th season at St. Cloud and 28th overall. And, with more than 500 wins, he is still going strong — even garnering 2001 NCC Coach of the Year honors after posting a 19-13 record. Since Lorsung took over in 1978, his teams have appeared in North Central Conference post-season play 13 times, winning the NCC Championship in 1991. In addition, his Huskies were conference runner-ups in the 1986, 1989, and 1999 seasons as well. Incredibly, Lorsung, who also led the Huskies to the 1980 Northern Intercollegiate Conference title, has been named the Coach

THE NSIC

While most of the NSIC schools have a rich tradition of playing baseball in the modern era, a few of the schools have a history that goes way back to the turn of the century. Among them is the University of Minnesota – Duluth, which, known then as the Duluth State Teachers College "Peds" (short for Pedagogues, or teachers), played as far back as 1885. The school played on an informal basis at that time, mostly against northern schools, but they also traveled to the Twin Cities to play the local college and university teams there as well. Moorhead State and Winona State were also playing baseball during this era of the late 1800s

GARY GROB

By the time Gary Grob had finally retired after 35 seasons at Winona State University, they had to completely rewrite the record books. Grob surpassed legendary Gopher Coach Dick Siebert in 1994 to become Minnesota's all-time leader in collegiate coaching victories. In fact, he is only the sixth NCAA Division II baseball coach to reach 1,000 career victories and just the 30th in all of NCAA baseball to reach the milestone. Grob's involvement and career at Winona State spans over six decades and in the past 43 years Grob has spent 40 years as a Winona State University student, coach and instructor. He first came to the university as a student in 1959 after a stint in the U.S. Marine Corps. As a player he would lead the Warriors to the 1961 and 1962 NAIA World Series. Grob became the program's head coach in 1965 and simply dominated along the way. During his illustrious career at WSU, Grob posted a 1,020-563-10 record, good for a gaudy .643 winning percentage. Over that span he won 15 conference championships, produced 161 All-Conference players, and saw 16 of his players sign professional baseball contracts. Three times his teams advanced to the NAIA World Series (1972 , 1988 and 1992 — where they finished 3rd), and when the team became an NCAA Division II member in 1995, Grob sent two teams on to the NCAA II regional tournaments. The first came in 1998, when the Warriors opened the NCAA Playoffs with a 5-1 loss to Northern Colorado but rebounded to beat Pittsburgh State, Kan., 7-5, followed by Northern Colorado, 16-11, to advance on to the Region Finals — where they were beaten soundly by Central Missouri State, 15-3. They made it back in 2000, only to lose a pair to Rockhurst, Mo., 8-7, and Central Missouri State, 13-1. Simply a legend, in addition to 15 NAIA District 13 Coach of the Year awards and three NSIC Coach of the Year awards, Coach Grob is also a member of both the NAIA and American Baseball Coaches' Association Halls of Fame as well.

UMD Coach Scott Hanna

too, primarily against neighboring amateur and high school teams. And, while many of these teams would begin playing into the 20th century, it wasn't until after the first world war that they all got together to create a league.

In 1923 a junior college sports conference was organized in Minnesota, consisting of the state's teacher colleges (Winona, Mankato, St. Cloud, Moorhead, Bemidji and Duluth), as well as its junior colleges (Duluth, Virginia, Hibbing, Itasca and Rochester), with the purpose of placing the two on an equal basis regarding eligibility of athletes, scholastic require-

ments, length of participation of athletes, and regulation of transfer students. It was called the Northern Intercollegiate Conference (NIC). Then, in 1932, the league changed its name to the Northern Teacher's Athletic Conference (NTAC). Charter members of the new circuit included Bemidji State, Mankato State, Minnesota-Duluth, Moorhead State, St. Cloud State and Winona State. In 1944 the NTAC became the newly-named Northern Intercollegiate Conference (NIC).

Then, after a two-year pause for World War II, NIC baseball got a big boost thanks to a big batch of crusty service veterans who came

St. Scholastica's Ben Sickler

UMD's 1999 NSIC Title Team

SWSU's Travis Irwin

NSIC SCHOOLS

Team	Nickname	Location	Joined NSIC
Bemidji State	Beavers	Bemidji	1932
MSU-Moorhead	Dragons	Moorhead	1932
Northern State	Wolves	Aberdeen, S.D.	1978
Southwest State	Mustangs	Marshall	1969
Minn.-Duluth	Bulldogs	Duluth	1932/1975
Minn.-Morris	Cougars	Morris	1966
Winona State	Warriors	Winona	1932
Wayne State	Wildcats	Wayne, Neb.	1998
Minn.-Crookston	Golden Eagles	Crookston	1999
Concordia-St. Paul	Golden Bears	St. Paul	1999

REGULAR SEASON TEAM TITLES WON OR SHARED

School	No.	Last Title
Winona State University	21	2001
Southwest State University	4	2002
University of Minnesota-Duluth	3	1999
Bemidji State University	3	1997
Minnesota State, Moorhead	2	1983
Northern State University	1	1993
University of Minnesota-Morris	1	1970

home from overseas and wanted to play some ball. The league featured some outstanding baseball through the 1950s and '60s and established itself as one of the nation's elite.

In 1950 the University of Minnesota-Duluth Bulldogs left the league to play in the MIAC. In 1966 the University of Minnesota-Morris joined the conference, followed by Southwest State in 1969. Then, in 1976, UM-Duluth returned to the NIC, where it has remained ever since. Meanwhile, Mankato State, which had left the league back in 1968 to join the North Central Conference, came back to the NIC for a four year stint, from 1978-82, until returning back to the NCC for good that same year. In addition, St. Cloud State withdrew from the NIC that year as well to also join the NCC. Northern State (Aberdeen, S.D) was added to the league in 1978, however, giving the conference some new blood into the Dakotas.

UMD's Jeff Kaldor

UMD's Matt Joesting

UM-DULUTH'S ALL-TIME RECORDS

Career Hitting Stats

Runs	150	Mike Petrich	(1986-90)
Hits	161	Mike Petrich	(1986-90)
Home Runs	34	Jeff Kaldor	(1988-91)
RBIs	137	Jeff Kaldor	(1988-91)
Batting Avg.	.397	Scott Gerten	(1994-97)
	.397	Mike Petrich	(1986-90)
Stolen Bases	53	Mike Petrich	(1986-90)

Career Pitching Stats

Innings Pitched	206	Brian Zadro	(1987-90)
Appearances	51	Chris Swiatkiewicz	(1996-99)
Games Won	20	Brian Zadro	(1987-90)
	20	Chris Swiatkiewicz	(1996-99)
Complete Games	19	Chris Swiatkiewicz	(1996-99)
Saves	12	Brian LaShomb	(1990-93)
Strikeouts	247	Chris Swiatkiewicz	(1996-99)
ERA	1.39	Jason Malec	(1982-84)

BULLDOGS IN THE PROS

Name	(Years at UMD)	Pos.	Team
Pat Berquist	(1985-87)	OF	Kansas City Royals
John Engen	(1979)	P	Detroit Tigers
Jason Malec	(1982-84)	P	Minnesota Twins
Mike Petrich	(1986-88, 90)	OF	Houston Astros (Drafted)
Chris Swiatkiewicz	(1995-99)	P	New York Yankees
Brett Tucker	(1991-92)	P	Houston Astros
Mark Wilson	(1989-91)	P	St. Paul (Northern League)

UMD's Matt Johnson

WINONA'S ALL-AMERICANS

NAIA All-Americans
1962   Lance Johnson (OF) 1st Team
1963   Jon Kosidowski (P/OF) 1st Team
1970   Todd Spencer (SS) Honorable Mention
1972   Terry Brecht (P) Honorable Mention
1973   Doug Sauer (3B), Jeff Youngbauer (OF), Terry Brecht (P), Lee Boettcher (P) Honorable Mention
1974   Jeff Youngbauer (OF) 2nd Team
1975   Howie Strey (1B), Dick Sauer (SS), Jeff Youngbauer (OF), Jeff Kroschel (P) Honorable Mention
1976   Howie Strey (1B), Jeff Fleck (OF) Honorable Mention
1977   Mike Huettl (OF) 2nd Team
1978   Spin Williams (1B) Honorable Mention
1981   Robin Rusch (P), Bob Bosche (1B), Clint Faas (OF) Honorable Mention
1983   Rich Meier (OF) Honorable Mention
1984   Dan Walseth (SS) Honorable Mention
1985   Jon Wisecup (P), Warren Sbragia (SS), Dean Schulte (2B), Duane Vike (OF) Honorable Mention
1986   Dan Walseth (2B) Honorable Mention
1987   Brian Hellenbrand (SS), Dave Repinski (P) Honorable Mention
1988   Scott Wanshura (DH) 1st Team, Scott Cozad (OF), Chris Shimek (2B),
       Dean Barkey (SS), John Costello (P) Honorable Mention
1989   Scott Wanshura (DH) 2nd Team, Brad Lange (P), Dan Galvin (C) Honorable Mention
1992   Jeremy Kendall (OF) Honorable Mention
1993   Jeff Maschka (3B) Honorable Mention
1994   Chris Gove (OF), Pat Holmes (P) Honorable Mention

Rawlings/ABCA All-Americans
1998 Aaron Braund (DH) First Team

GTE/Version All-Americans
1998   Aaron Braund (C) Third Team
2001   Travis Zick (1b) Third Team

Then, in 1992 the NSIC was formed from the merger of the Northern Intercollegiate Conference (NIC), which was the men's conference, and the Northern Sun Conference (NSC), which was the women's. Three years later the conference switched its national affiliation from the NAIA to the larger, more prestigious NCAA. That next year the conference adopted an annual tournament, which gave the bottom teams hope for pulling off an upset to crack the post-season. In 1999 the NSIC would expand from seven teams to a 10-team league when Wayne State College (Neb.), the University of Minnesota-Crookston and Concordia-St. Paul — which is led by Coach Mark "Lunch" McKenzie, were all added to the mix. Today the 10-team NSIC is among the top Division II conferences in the country, producing many elite players and providing countless opportunities for kids to play ball at the next level.

Let's take a look at just a few of the highlights from the past several decades, starting in 1960, when Mankato State claimed its first NIC crown. Winona State then simply took over the league, winning outright titles in 1961 and 1962, before sharing the crown in 1963 with Moorhead State. St. Cloud State took it in 1964, only to see Winona storm back to share the honors with them in 1965. Winona took it alone in '66 and then saw the Huskies from St. Cloud take it in 1967. Mankato State took the NSIC crown in 1968 before defecting to the NCC, while St. Cloud State came back to take three in a row from 1969-71 — sharing the 1970 crown with Minnesota-Morris. Winona State was at it again in 1972 and 1973, winning back-to-back titles, only to see the newcomers from Southwest State get into the mix in 1974. SWST would go on to earn the NAIA District 18 title that year as well. Winona and St. Cloud went back and forth from 1975 to 1978, each taking a pair of titles. Mankato, back yet again to the NSIC, won a couple in 1979 and 1981, sandwiched in between by another St. Cloud State title in 1980.

Bemidji State made its presence felt in 1982, and then made it all the way to the NAIA Baseball World Series — where they lost out in the first round. Moorhead State finally got on the board by winning its first crown that next season. But for the rest of the decade of the 90's, it was all Coach Gary Grob's Winona State Warriors, who won an amazing eight straight outright conference titles from 1984-91 — sharing just one with Bemidji State in 1988. In 1992 the Winona Warriors won a record 61 games, but it was the boys from Minnesota-Duluth who wound up with the hardware. UMD would then share the honors that next season along with Northern State to make it two in a row.

Southwest State took it in 1994 and then, that next year, the league adopted an annual tournament which would see its winner be declared as the conference champion. Winona State took the inaugural NSIC Tourney crown that 1995 season and, as a result, earned an invitation to the NCAA Division II Central Regional Tournament. Southwest State then came back to reclaim their hardware in 1996, posting a 24-17

SWSU's Jeff Jonckowski

UMD's Brett Spaeth

record en route to taking the NSIC regular season & tournament championships. Bemidji State made it happen in 1997, only to see Winona State come back strong in 1998.

Led by Pitcher Chris Swiatkiewicz and Center Fielder Matt Joesting, the 1999 NSIC Player of the Year, Minnesota-Duluth got back into the action in 1999. The title also earned NSIC Coach of the Year honors for Scott Hanna, who is presently nearing the coveted 500-win plateau. Winona then continued its dominance by claiming a pair of titles in 2000 and 2001. Winona's legendary Coach Gary Grob retired after 35 years behind the Warriors' bench that season, making room for assistant Kyle Poock.

The 31-19 Southwest State Mustangs, under Coach Paul Blanchard, finally rounded out the festivities by regaining the top spot in 2002. Even more impressive was the fact that the team did it without NSIC Player of the Year, Matt Tiggas. The Mustangs did have, however, Travis Irwin, who just broke SSU's single season home run (17) and RBI (62) records that year. Overall, SSU has been one of the league's top clubs over the past five years, averaging 28 wins per season, three NSIC Tournament championships, and five straight top eight regional finishes.

Overall, our small colleges have been among the best in the nation with regards to producing top talent and providing countless kids the opportunity to play the game at the next level. From the community colleges to the JUCOs and from to the Division II's to the IIIs, Minnesota is a fantastic place for young men to learn and play the game of baseball.

UMD's Chris Swiatkiewicz

UMD's Brian Zadro

UMD's Ryan Skubic

UMD's Mike Petrich

MINNESOTA COMMUNITY COLLEGE CONFERENCE

The Minnesota Community College Conference is also an important circuit for the development of kids wanting to play at the next level. The league, which falls under the jurisdiction of the National Junior College Athletic Association (NJCCA), gives countless kids an opportunity to get an education while still being able to play an extremely good quality of baseball. (Other schools in the conference such as, Minneapolis Community College and Rainy River Community College, in International Falls, also feature athletic programs, but just not baseball.)

Minnesota Community College Conference Teams

Northern Division

Fergus Falls Community College	(Fergus Falls)	Spartans
Central Lakes College	(Brainerd)	Raiders
Hibbing Community College	(Hibbing)	Cardinals
Itasca Community College	(Grand Rapids)	Vikings
Mesabi Range Comm. & Tech. College	(Virginia)	Norsemen
Northland Comm. & Tech. College	(Thief River Falls)	Pioneers
Vermilion Community College	(Ely)	Ironmen
Dakota County Technical College	(Rosemount)	Blue Knights

Southern Division

Anoka-Ramsey Community College	(Coon Rapids)	Golden Rams
Bethany Lutheran College	(Mankato)	Vikings
Minnesota West Comm. & Tech. College	(Worthington)	Blue Jays
North Hennepin Community College	(Brooklyn Park)	Norsemen
Ridgewater College	(Willmar)	Warriors
Riverland Community College	(Austin)	Blue Devils
Rochester Comm. & Tech. College	(Rochester)	Yellow Jackets

THE UPPER MIDWEST ATHLETIC CONFERENCE

Originally started in 1972 as the Twin Rivers Conference, the Upper Midwest Athletic Conference is today an affiliate of the National Association of Intercollegiate Athletics (NAIA). The UMAC is also affiliated with the National Christian College Athletic Association (NCCAA) and recently voted to change its status to NCAA Division III. There are now seven institutions in the UMAC: College of St. Scholastica (Duluth, MN), Crown College (St. Bonifacius, MN), Martin Luther College (New Ulm, MN), North Central University (Minneapolis), Northland College (Ashland, WI), Northwestern College (Roseville, MN), and Presentation College (Aberdeen, SD). In addition, the University of Minnesota Morris will be leaving the NCAA Division II Northern Sun Conference and moving to the UMAC in 2003.) Several of the schools located in Minnesota also play various MIAC schools, and provide countless kids the opportunity to play ball at the next level.

One program, however, has stood head and shoulders above the rest in this league, and that is the College of St. Scholastica, which has simply dominated the UMAC over the years. In fact, since 1995 the team has posted an amazing 230-86 record. The school has sent a host of squads on to the NCAA Tournament as well, with the most recent trip coming in 1999. That next year, 2000, saw the Saints win their first regional championship, host their first-ever Super Regional, and surpass the 40-win plateau for the first time. Following that season All-American shortstop and NAIA Region Player-of-the-Year Leland Swenson signed with the Texas Rangers, becoming the first Saint to sign a professional contract.

St. Scholastica went 13-0 in the UMAC in 2001 and kept on cruising that next year as well. One of the highlights of that 2002 season came against the eventual national champs from St. Thomas, where Six-foot-eight lefthander Brett Nyquist tossed a no-hitter amidst a horde of major league scouts.

Through the years several other players have gone on to the pro ranks, including Centerfielder Chris LePine, Pitcher Corey Kemp and Second Baseman Jeff Lahti, who played with the Northern League's Duluth-Superior Dukes in 2001. Others to play in the Northern include pitchers Kevin Kuklis and Joe Wicklund, who played with the Sioux City Explorers and Albany-Colonie Diamond Dogs, respectively.

UMAC SCHOOLS

College of St. Scholastica	(Duluth, MN)
Crown College	(St. Bonifacius, MN)
Martin Luther College	(New Ulm, MN)
North Central University	(Minneapolis, MN)
Northwestern College	(Roseville, MN)
Presentation College	(Aberdeen, SD)

Minnesota's high school baseball history has roots that can be traced back for more than 130 years. Some of those first teams which fielded teams back in the late 1800s included Shattuck, Pillsbury Academy, Northfield, Minneapolis Central, St. Paul Central, St. Cloud and Stillwater. Some of those squads' earliest competition included the University of Minnesota, the Minneapolis Millers and St. Paul Saints — teams which the prepsters often beat.

It wasn't until 1947, however, that the Minnesota State High School League (MSHSL) got involved and made the event official. Prior to that, teams from neighboring schools would play ball via house rules — primarily to let the kids to have fun. The genesis of how the MSHSL got involved goes back to 1947. Up until that point the American Legion had been running successful summer baseball programs. The MSHSL initially approached both the national and state Legion officers to discuss a proposed program, but the Legion officials encouraged them to develop their own program. The Legion, which primarily catered to 15 and 16 year-olds, thought that a high school program would stimulate competition and increase the participation for older kids — thus creating a stronger and more effective program for both institutions.

With that, the MSHSL adopted a set of conformed rules and set out to host its first season of organized baseball. That first season was thought to be a test of sorts, taking place during the "Summer Program of Activities." So, that June, the first-ever state tournament was held on the campus of the University of Minnesota, and here is how it all went down:

1947: St. Cloud Tech vs. Glencoe

Duluth Denfeld topped Melrose in the opener, 4-3, followed by St. Cloud annihilating Crookston in Game Two, 18-0. The onslaught continued in the afternoon games as well with Glencoe blanking Westbrook, 6-0, and St. Paul Washington steamrollering Faribault, 17-0. The semifinals were much closer contests as St. Cloud got past Denfeld in the first game, 3-2, and Glencoe rallied back to beat St. Paul Washington, 5-2, to advance to the Finals. There, St. Cloud Tech won the inaugural title by edging Glencoe, 6-5.

Overall, the tournament was viewed as a moderate success. Some 1,060 fans showed up for the three day event, giving the MSHSL reason to believe that this sport could hold its own as a regular Spring event.

TECH HIGH SCHOOL, ST. CLOUD
First row (left to right): Leroy Saatzer, Leroyd Court, Wayne Haupt, Bob Nyberg, Roy Wengert, Jim Kiffmeyer, Harvey Heurung, Fred Durand, and Mel Koshiol.
Second row: Coach Dale Daugherty, Don Schmid, Bob Obermiller, Al Hansen, Bill Campbell, Dean Daugherty, Gene Cashman, and Coach Tim Turner.
Bat boys in front: Jack Bergren and Walter Wifall.

St. Cloud Tech — 1947

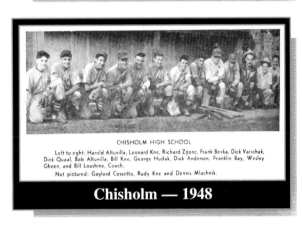

CHISHOLM HIGH SCHOOL
Left to right: Harold Altuvilla, Leonard Kne, Richard Zgonc, Frank Bevka, Dick Varichak, Dick Quaal, Bob Altuvilla, Bill Kne, George Hudak, Dick Anderson, Franklin Bay, Wesley Gheen, and Bill Loushine, Coach.
Not pictured: Gaylord Cossetta, Rudy Kne and Dennis Mlachnik.

Chisholm — 1948

(Left to right) First Row: Burkland, Warhol, Cybyske, Schleisman, Uchanski.
Second row: Rog, Dank, Koziol, Elhardt, Cloutier.
Third row: Harlien, Gonsior, Dreger, Vorpe, Anderson, Dziediec, Coach Pete Guzy.

Minneapolis Edison — 1949

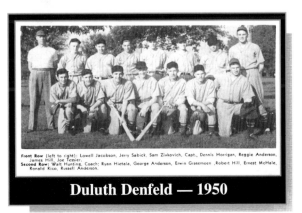

Front Row (left to right): Lowell Jacobson, Jerry Sabick, Sam Zivkovich, Capt., Dennis Horrigan, Reggie Anderson, James Hill, Joe Tessier.
Second Row: Walt Hunting, Coach; Ryan Hietala, George Anderson, Erwin Grassmoen, Robert Hill, Ernest McHale, Ronald Rico, Russell Anderson.

Duluth Denfeld — 1950

1948: Chisholm vs. Springfield

In 1948 the State High School Baseball Tourney was moved to Glencoe with undefeated Chisholm edging Austin, 10-7, in the opener. Game Two saw St. Paul Washington beat Mankato, 4-3, while Little Falls topped Bemidji, 10-6 in Game Three and Springfield upended Delano in Game Four, 1-0. Chisholm edged Washington, 3-1, in the first semifinal, while Springfield hung on to beat Little Falls, 7-6, in the other. Then, in the Finals, Chisholm outlasted Springfield, 13-8, to take the title. Wohlrabe pitched well but took the loss for Springfield as Chisholm belted out 17 hits in the Finals. Anderson and Hudak carried the pitching load for Chisholm, striking out 10 and 9 batters throughout the tourney, respectively.

1949: Edison vs. St. Paul Washington

The third annual state high school baseball tournament was played in Duluth that August with the Finals resulting in another 'Twin City Championship" affair between Minneapolis Edison and St. Paul Washington. The event opened with tiny Wheaton upsetting Austin, 4-3, followed by Edison pounding Westbrook, 10-0, in Game Two. Washington then out-slugged Springfield, 16-12, in the third game of the day, followed by Eveleth beating Bemidji, 9-4, in the last quarterfinal contest. Edison kept rolling into the Finals be topping Wheaton, 12-8, while Washington hung on to top Eveleth, 2-0, in the other semifinal. Edison then went on to beat Washington, 6-3, to capture its first state tournament title.

1950: Duluth Denfeld vs. Buffalo

Rain was the big story at the fourth state tourney, this time held in Detroit Lakes. While storms interrupted five of the six sessions and the weather at times was pretty cold, the three day tournament proved to be exciting and full of great action.

Rochester opened the festivities by blanking Halstad, 5-0, followed by Duluth Denfeld edging Mankato, 5-4, in Game Two. The third quarterfinal of the day featured Melrose outlasting Glencoe, 3-2, while Buffalo beat Elk River, 5-2, in Game Four. Then, in the first semifinal, Denfeld hung on to beat Rochester, 8-7, while Buffalo breezed past Melrose in the other semi with ease, 5-0, to advance to the Finals. There, Duluth Denfeld rallied to beat Buffalo in spectacular fashion, 6-5, to earn their first state championship.

1951: Redwood Falls vs. Melrose

The fifth annual tournament was held in Owatonna with Redwood Falls opening it up with a big win over Duluth Central, 3-1. Bill Henke scored a pair of runs in this one and Pitcher Laurie Slocum struck out 10 in the victory. Mankato, behind Darrell Theissen's game-winning run in the 11th inning, topped Alvarado, 9-8, in Game Two. Game Three then saw Austin beat Shakopee, 2-1, behind third baseman Dayle Rasmussen's two hits and two runs. The last quarter-final of the day saw Melrose, behind Ken Hanson and Leo Jackel's late runs, top St. Paul Washington, 3-1, in a 10-inning thriller. Melrose Pitcher Edgar Meyers struck out 20 in the win.

Redwood Falls then pounded Mankato in the first semifinal 11-0. First Basemen Chuck Burmeister led the charge by knocking out a pair of hits and scoring a trio of runs while Right Fielder Richard Fowler added a pair of his own. Melrose then edged Austin in the other semi, 1-0, behind Right Fielder Jerome Schulte's first inning single that resulted in the game's only run.

Pitcher Laurie Slocum fanned 19 en route to leading his Redwood Falls club past Melrose, 1-0, in the Finals. Third baseman Bob Wolf's dramatic homer in the eighth sealed the deal in this one as the Cards hung on to take the crown. Melrose Pitcher Edgar Meyers struck out 11 in the loss.

1952: Halstad vs. Austin

The 1952 state tournament was played in Owatonna late that June with St. Paul Monroe taking Game One, 12-2, over Eveleth. Game Two saw Austin spank Bricelyn, 9-0, behind Hastings and Arnold's homers. St. Louis Park then doubled up Melrose, 10-5, in the third quarterfinal as Stone, Hammel and Norren each scored a pair of runs in this one. Then, in Game Four, Halstad beat New Ulm, 5-2, behind Johnson and Hesty's three hits and two runs.

Austin, behind a pair of dingers from Anderson and Hastings, advanced to the Finals by edging St. Paul Monroe, 7-5, in the first semifinal. The other semi then saw Halstad upset St. Louis Park, 7-4, to advance to the Finals. Alrosen and Holm each scored a pair of runs in the victory. The Finals were supposed to feature mighty Austin rolling to victory, but tiny Halstad had other ideas as they went on to crush the Packers, 9-2, and cruise to their first state title. Leading the charge for Halstad was Pitcher Morris Holm, who pitched 22 of his teams 23 innings, allowing a total of just 11 hits and 10 walks, while striking out 35 batters.

1953: St. Paul Washington vs. Austin

Held in Little Falls, the 1953 Tourney opened with Eveleth blanking Minneapolis Washburn, 3-0. Richard Tomassoni, Mike Castellano and Tommy

Modec each scored runs for the Golden Bears. Austin then beat the previously undefeated Granite Falls Granites, 1-0, thanks to Garry Underhill's third inning score in Game Two. Wells, behind Center Fielder Phillip Deulaf's two runs, topped Moorhead, 2-1, in Game Three. Finally, St. Paul Washington crushed Cass Lake, 11-0, in the final quarter of the day. Leading the charge in this one was future Gopher and Minnesota Twin Jerry Kindall, who tallied three hits and three runs in the blow-out.

Austin rolled over Eveleth, 8-0, in the first semi, thanks to a six-run first inning barrage which grew from there. Washington then got past Wells in Game Two, 3-2, behind Richard Hoffman and Randy Tollefson — who each had a pair of hits in the win. In the Finals is was Washington running past Austin, 6-1, to earn its first title in five state tourney appearances. Washington got a pair of runs in the third and then added three more in the eighth to seal the deal. Randy Tollefson had two hits and struck out nine in the complete game performance.

1954: Austin vs. Duluth Denfeld

The 1954 State Tourney quarterfinals got underway in St. Cloud with Duluth Denfeld edging Melrose, 6-4, in the opener. Gene Bradt and Dick Gillen led the charge in this one by tallying a pair of runs each in the win. Edina-Morningside, behind Harry Wilson's two hits, blanked Cass Lake in the late morning game, 6-0. In Game Three it was Norwood-Young America shutting out Lakefield, 3-0, on runs by Roland Latzig, Duane Wolff and Maynard Rolf. Finally, in Game Four, Austin outlasted Montgomery, 1-0, thanks to Shortstop Jerry Hatch's sixth inning hit and run.

By the time the semifinals rolled around the skies opened up with rain and hail — turning the schedule into a real mess. Games had to be postponed and rescheduled, resulting in some contests being played with nearly no fans in the stands. The show went on however, and with that Duluth Denfeld advanced to the Finals by edging Edina-Morningside, 3-1. Erickson and Chivotte did the damage in this one, each smacking out a pair of hits and scoring a run each as well. Then, in the other semi, Austin, despite getting just one hit in the game, topped Norwood-Young America, 2-1. Greenmeyer scored the game-winner in the seventh to seal the deal in this one.

Then, in the Finals, Austin rallied from a 2-0 deficit to beat Duluth Denfeld, 3-2, in the ninth inning. Scoring for the Pack were Smith, Luksik and Ploof — who also added three hits of his own in the dramatic victory. After a pair of runner-up finishes, Austin, playing in its fourth consecutive tournament and in the sixth of the eight played, had finally won its first title.

Redwood Falls — 1951

Front Row (left to right): Chuck Burmeister, Dick Barnes, Gary Richey, Neil Young, James Auna.
Back Row: Jerry Richey, coach; Bill Henke, Dick Fowler, Dennis Stoffel, John Stoffel, Laurie Slocum, Ronnie Skillman, Chuck Kelly, Bob Wolf, Bob Gray.

Halstad — 1952

Front Row: Dale Serum, Gerald Hesby, Don Lervold and George Johnson.
Second Row: Wallace Oien, Don Hanson, Darrel Hesby, Curtis Johnson, Jerry Anderson.
Back Row: Marlan Aasenson, Jim Akaton, Morris Holm, Alden Holte.
Not pictured—Chuck Bernhagen.

St. Paul Washington — 1953

ST. PAUL WASHINGTON HIGH SCHOOL
Front Row—Milo Fuller, Randy Tollefson, and Dick Hoffmann. Center Row—Mike Daulton, John Erickson, Jim Rantz, Dennis Klark, Joe Unger, and Dick Hassel. Mgr. Back Row—Roger Pietrus, Ralph Fagen, Tony Gruber, Al Madigan, H. Nelson (Coach), Jerry Kindall, Waye Kindall, John Bubasta, John Laporat.

Austin — 1954

Front Row: Charles Louk, Ken Smith, Jerry Hatch, Dean Lommen, Bob Mathias, Dale Beckel, Dan Greenemeyer.
Back Row: Dick Seltz, Coach; Terry Meyer, Dave Ploof, Gary Underhill, Larry Arnold, Frank Luksik, Louis Lenz.
Not Pictured: Gary Morem who left for the Navy.

1955: Minneapolis Washburn vs. St. Paul Wilson

Held in Rochester, the Twin City champs from St. Paul Wilson kicked off the Tourney by blanking Mankato, 3-0, thanks to runs by Schreiber, Causton and Zell. Little Falls pounded Thief River Falls in Game Two, 9-4, behind Bailey, Adelmeyer and Kerich, who scored six runs between them. Austin kept on rolling in Game Three, shutting out International Falls, 4-0. Arnold and Beckel combined for five hits, while Underhill struck out seven in the win. Finally, in Game Four, Mpls. Washburn beat Springfield, 6-2, thanks to a pair of runs each from Sweeney and Sachs.

St. Paul Wilson kept it rolling in the first semi be edging tough Little Falls team, 4-3. The Falls rallied to pull ahead in this one early in the third, only to see Wilson rally behind Causton's run, followed by Peterson's homer in the sixth to put the final nail in the coffin. The other semi saw Washburn upset the defending champs from Austin, 2-0. The star of this game was Pitcher Gordie Sundin, who whiffed 10 batters and added a hit en route to the big win.

The Finals were a blow-out as Ray Ross' Minneapolis Washburn squad pummeled their Twin City brethren, St. Paul Wilson, 11-0. Washburn pounded out 12 hits in this one, and were led by a quartet of All-Tournament players: Outfielder Jon Spolum, Second Baseman Dave Wiggins, First Baseman Stu Hanson and Pitcher Gordie Sundin. Many of the team's players starred on the school's state championship basketball team as well.

1956: St. Paul Washington vs. Bemidji

The '56 Tourney moved to the newly constructed Metropolitan Stadium, home of the Minneapolis Millers, in Bloomington this year, drawing record crowds along the way. Bemidji opened the tourney by edging fellow Northerner Hibbing, 3-2. The Lumberjacks rallied late in this one, getting a pair of runs in the sixth from Mayer and Johnson to pull ahead for good. Game Two saw tiny Benson upset Austin, 4-2, thanks to a three-run fifth inning rally. Game Three had St. Paul Washington beating Fairfax, 5-1, on a four-run fifth inning surge highlighted by Rantz and Erickson, who each got a pair of hits. Then, in the final quarterfinal contest of the day, Edina-Morningside crushed Mankato, 11-0. Future Gopher star Tom Moe led the charge in this one, knocking out three hits and driving in four runs.

Bemidji got past Cinderella Benson in the first semi, 3-1, on a trio of sixth inning runs scored by Fortier, Mayer and Anderson. Washington then spanked Edina-Morningside in the other semi, 5-0, on John Erickson's three RBI's.

Washington then went on to become the first school to win more than one state title in the 10 years of the tourney's history when they edged Bemidji, 4-2. Despite Johnson's two-hit, 12 strike-

out gem, Washington hung in there thanks to the efforts of John Erickson, Jim Rantz and Milo Fuller — all of whom earned All-Tourney honors.

1957: Little Falls vs. Mankato

Little Falls won the opening game of the tournament, beating Tracy, 1-0. Little Falls was able to grab just four hits and one run off of Pitcher Merlin Mickelson, but it was enough to get the "W." Meanwhile, Pitcher Tony Kerick fanned 14 while allowing just one hit in the big win. Game Two saw Austin blank Bemidji, 4-0, thanks to Pitcher Ron McKay, who, in addition to throwing a six-K shut-out, added a pair of hits as well. Mankato then topped International Falls, 3-2, in Game Three thanks to a thrilling three-run seventh inning which saw Lynn Gallop, Jeryl Jackson and Bill Anderson each touch the plate. Edina-Morningside spanked St. Peter in the final quarterfinal, 9-2, in a game which saw the Hornet's first four hitters: John Freudenthal, Don Meyers, Tom King and Roy Bostock score eight runs between them.

In the semifinals against Austin, Little Falls pounded out 10 hits, six of which were for extra bases, in an 8-5 win. Once again it was Tony Kerick who was the hero. In addition to his two hits and two runs, he struck out nine batters. In the other semifinal, Mankato rallied back to edge Edina-Morningside, 2-1, behind Lee and Peterson's pair of late runs.

The Finals were an exciting affair as Little Falls, led by the hitting of Jerry Foltmer and Tom Adelmeyer, squeaked past Mankato, 3-2, to give Coach Lou Filippi's Flyers their first state championship. The strong right arm of Pitcher Tony Kerick, who struck out 10 and scored the game-winning run, proved again to be the difference in this wild one which went into extra innings. Mankato Pitcher Herb Stangland was also outstanding on the mound, but his team came up short when Little Falls scored the winning run with one out in the last of the eighth.

1958: St. Paul Johnson vs. Minneapolis Washburn

In the opening game of the tournament St. Paul Johnson got three runs in the sixth to defeat the defending champs from Little Falls by a score of 8-6. Jerry Evenson, Mark Skoog and Greg Ostedt each rapped out a pair of hits in the win. Game Two saw Mankato blank Ada, 4-0, behind Pitcher Herb Stangland, who, in addition to striking out six, added three hits as well. Grand Rapids, behind Norm Card's two hits, then snubbed Minneota, 4-0, in the third game. Game Four had Minneapolis Washburn edging Austin, 1-0, on Jim Saman's fourth inning score

Minneapolis Washburn — 1955

Top Row: Les Kjos, Gordin Sundin, Jack Hastings, Jerry Hedin, Jon Spolum, John Councilman, Ed Munson, Coach Ray Ross.
Middle Row: Tom Dubay, Bob Ristow, Jack Medcalf, Tom Woldum, Dick Kohlan, Mike Murphy.
Front Row: Jim Spetz, Clyde Smith, Dave Wiggins, Pat Sweeney, Bob Anderson, Bruce Sachs.

St. Paul Washington — 1956

Front Row: Richard Frieberg, Keith Kryszaniak, Bruce Tollefson, Mike Gerdts, Jim Schwartz, Dick Wells, Dick Ulring.
Back Row: William Dammon, Jim Rantz, Milo Fuller, George Christea, Tom Sager, Jim Gibbons, Don Kieger, Ernest Kendig, Tom Daulton, Bob Schneider, John Erickson, Harry Nelson—Coach.

Little Falls — 1957

Front Row, left to right: Jay Bailey, Tom Adelmeyer, Tony Kerick, Quentin Fabro, Loring Michaelis.
Back Row, left to right: Stu. Mgr. Larry Helmerick, Jerry Foltmer, Alan Nelson, Louie Eich, Claire Deering, Roger Adelmeyer, Jerry Trafas, Dorian Sprandel, Dennis Sprandel and Jim Zak.

St. Paul Johnson — 1958

Front Row: Dave Brooks, Glen Marien, Leo Reck, Jerry Evenson, Dave Linnerooth, Gary Ostedt, Nick DeMike, Charles Davidson, Louie Torinus. Back Row: Coach Pete Kramer, Mike Payton, Brian Johnson, Sam Forsythe, Ray Wolf, Harold Vinnes, Mark Skoog, Gary Schmaltzbauer, Bryan Jarvinen, Dick Soderquist.

which proved to be the game-winner.

The first semifinal game saw Johnson destroy Mankato, 19-2. Glen Marrion and Mark Skoog each had four hits, while Harold Vinnes and Jerry Evanson each added three of their own in the lopsided win. The second semi then saw Washburn, behind Howie Tyson's four hits, overtake Grand Rapids, 3-0, to advance to the Finals. Pitcher Stan Carlson added seven strike outs as well.

With a 6-2 win over Washburn, Johnson kept it rolling in the title game and got Coach Pete Kramer his first state crown. Johnson jumped out to a quick 2-0 first inning lead and never looked back. Leading the charge for Washburn were a quartet of All-Tourney players in: John Collier, Howie Tyson, Bob Romfo and Gerry Gustafson.

1959: Minneapolis Washburn vs. Austin

The 13th annual tournament kicked off with St. Paul Washington blanking Greenway-Coleraine, 2-0, thanks to a couple of key hits by Donny Norqual and Ernest Kendig and a pair of first inning runs by George Christea and Bob Olson. Game Two then saw Austin crush Mankato, 11-0, behind Clayton Reed's three hits and three runs, and Daryl Richardson's two hits and three runs. New Ulm beat up on Thief River Falls in Game Three, 7-2, as Pitcher Nels Iverson tossed a three-hitter and struck out five for good measure. In the final quarterfinal game of the day, Washburn got past Little Falls, 5-2, behind Pitcher Harlan Anderson's 15 strike-outs. In addition, Left Fielder John Collier had a pair of hits and a pair of runs in the win.

Austin, behind Richardson's nine K's, spanked St. Paul Washington, 6-1, in the first semifinal. Washburn then got past New Ulm, 4-1, in the other semi. John Collier, James Salmon and John Oster each had a pair of hits in the big win.

Washburn then got over on Austin, 7-2, in the Finals to take the crown. They jumped out to a quick 4-0 lead in the first and never looked back. John Collier and Bill Hartupee each scored a pair of runs in the win and Pitcher Harlan Anderson was once again dominant as he struck out 10 in the victory.

1960: Minneapolis Washburn vs. Little Falls

Minneapolis Washburn began its journey of defending its title by beating Greenway-Coleraine, 5-0, in the first quarterfinal game of the 1960 state tournament. John Simus, John Oster and Bill Cartwright each scored in the first inning as the team cruised from there. The skies opened up on that first day though and this one was called after just five innings. The other games were all postponed until the next day. Then, Crookston outlasted North St. Paul in a nine-inning marathon which was decided when Deane Knox, Alden Hermodson and Stew Uggen each scored in the last frame to seal the deal. Game Three saw Little Falls down St. James, 7-1, thanks to Werner and Adelmeyer's pair of runs. The final quarterfinal of the opening round saw Hutchinson squeak past Austin, 2-1, behind runs from Paul Skrien and Jeff Miller. In addition, Pitcher Richard

Mielke struck out eight batters in the big win.

Washburn kept it rolling in the semis when they breezed by Crookston, 5-1, behind John Oster, Bill Hartupee and John Collier, who each had two hits. Pitcher Earl Hacking also struck out seven en route to throwing a one-hit gem as Coach James Cosgrove's Washburn squad now stood just one game from back-to-back state titles. The other semi saw Little Falls pummel Hutchinson, 11-1, as Jim Werner, Bob Adelmeyer and Louis Eich all had multiple hit afternoons.

Pitcher Earl Hacking struck out nine and was once again simply outstanding as his Washburn team scored three huge runs in the top of the sixth to break a 1-1 tie and put this one away, 4-1. Leading the charge for the offense was Catcher James Salmon, who had four hits and a key RBI in the win.

1961: North St. Paul vs. Minneapolis Washburn

The 1961 baseball tournament opened in St. Cloud but after a whole bunch of soggy rain, the Finals, which featured a pair of Twin City area teams, were moved back to Midway Stadium in St. Paul. Game One saw Springfield annihilate Pipestone, 14-3, behind Brad Ames, who struck out nine in the win. Offensively, in addition to Mike Renner's four runs, Dennis Hammerschmidt, Chris Christianson, Brad Ames and Dennis Dysart all had multiple hits for Springfield. Game Two saw Minneapolis Washburn double up on Bemidji, 6-3, thanks to Left Fielder Jerry Pryd's four hits and two runs — including

Front Row: Managers — Robert Ferris and Richard Schmidt. Second Row: John Simus, James Salmon, Wayne Wesala, Richard Montgomery, Harlan Anderson and Rolf Svendsen. Back Row: Earl Hacking, Thomas Anderson, William Hartupee, Michael Grossman, Thomas Potter, John Sipple, John Collier, John Oster, Jon Curwen and Coach James Cosgrove.

Minneapolis Washburn — 1959

a lead-off score to score the first run of the game. Game Three saw North St. Paul edge Rochester, 2-1, behind Pitcher Jack Riley's 12 strike-outs and First Baseman Steve Gustafson's fourth inning game-winning run. The last quarterfinal then saw Fergus Falls top Hinckley, 1-0, on Pitcher Barry Johnson's fourth inning game-winning run. Johnson also K'd 16 batters as well.

Washburn kept it going into the semis with an impressive 5-0 win over surprising Springfield, 5-0. Leading the charge in this one was Pitcher David Kern, who struck out nine and scored a run for good measure. Jerry Pryd also added a pair of runs and a hit as well. The other semi saw North St. Paul edge Fergus Falls, 5-3. Fergus rallied to score three in the fifth, but came up short when Jim Zueg scored his second run of the game shortly thereafter. Pitcher Jack Riley struck out 15 in this one, and he scored a pair of runs to boot.

First Row: Donald Johannson, Gerald Pryd, Gerald Stahl, John Simus, James Salmon, Wm. Cartwright. Second Row: John Sipple, Kenneth Hanson, Thomas Anderson, Wm. Hartupee, John Oster, Leonard Stream. Third Row: Kenneth Erickson—Std. M., John Flood—Std. M., Geoffrey Carlson, Nathan Mitchell, Earl Hacking, Mike Welbaum, James Cosgrove—Coach.

Minneapolis Washburn — 1960

The Finals were all about North St. Paul as they blanked their cross-town rivals from Washburn — who were on a quest to three-peat as state champs. Pitcher Don Arlich was particularly impressive, striking out 16 batters and allowing just one hit en route to posting the shut-out. The Polars jumped out to a quick 2-0 lead in the first on runs from Jim Friberg and Steve Gustafson in this one and never looked back. Leading the charge for North St. Paul were Jack Riley, Gustafson, John Jents and Arlich — all of whom earned All-Tournament honors.

Front Row: Edward Pistel, student manager; John Jents, Pat Crawley, Bill Springborn, Bruce Johnson, student manager. Second Row: Bob Carlson, Jack Riley, Jon Oace, Jim Friberg, John Rafferty, Jim Zeug. Back Row: Mr. Larry Hartman, faculty representative; Ron Pearson, Steve Hanner, Don Arlich, Steve Gustafson, Clyde Doepner, Joe Alfonso, Mr. John Groven, coach.

North St. Paul — 1961

1962: Richfield vs. Austin

The Tourney moved to Midway Stadium this year, and would stick around in the quaint St. Paul neighborhood for the next 13 years. Austin kicked off the 1962 games by beating Pine City, 3-1. The Pack rallied to get two runs in the sixth and pull ahead for good in this one. Game Two saw Little Falls edge Bemidji, 2-1. The Flyers, behind Ken Bentler and Larry Vernon, rallied from a 1-0 deficit to score the game-tying and winning runs in the sixth. Richfield pounded Springfield in the third quarterfinal, 9-2, on the strong play of Dick Hoffman, Ken Smith and Mike Sadek. St. Paul Central topped St. James in Game Four, 6-1, thanks to a strong third and fourth inning which produced five runs. Leading the charge were Second Baseman Jim Nelson and First Baseman Craig Mathies, who played solid ball.

Austin kept it going in the first semifinal, beating Little Falls, 6-0. The Pack had five runs on the board by the second, and never looked back. Norm Heuton, Steve Schmitt, Tim Schmitt and Terry Ball all scored in the game. The other semi was a barn-burner as St. Paul Central edged Richfield, 5-3, in a dramatic 12-inning thriller. John Wells, Bob Lary and Ken Smith provided the heroics to seal the deal in this one.

Richfield kept the momentum going into the Finals when they outlasted a tough Austin team, 4-3, to win their first state title. This one was a nail-biter as well, as it went 10 innings before determining a winner. Richfield scored three runs in the fourth, only to see the Pack tie it up in the fifth. From there it went into extra innings before Smith, Drury, Wheeler, Nord and Thoreson put together a late rally.

1963: Minneapolis Washburn vs. Hibbing

Washburn, behind runs from Jerry Clark and Dave French, advanced to the semifinals with a 2-0 first round win over Fairmont. Game Two saw Hibbing edge Thief River Falls, 5-4, behind Garry Novak's solid pitching and Roger Mattson's game-winning run in the sixth. Springfield then blanked Anoka in Game Three, 6-0, as Pitcher Mike Davidson struck out 11 and allowed just two hits. Austin edged Brainerd in the last quarterfinal, 2-0, behind Al Berg and Norm Heuton's fifth inning scores.

Washburn kept it going in the first semifinal game, edging Austin 1-0, to advance to the Finals. Second Baseman Jerry Clark's third inning score proved to be the difference in this one. Hibbing then pounded Springfield in the other semi, 8-3. The Blue Jackets got four runs in the first and cruised from there as Second Baseman Gary Gambucci, Third Baseman Roger Mattson, Center Fielder John Steffan and Pitcher Garry Novak all played outstanding in the win.

The Finals were all Washburn, however, as the Minneapolis school proceeded to destroy Hibbing, 9-1, to take its fourth State High School Baseball Championship. Washburn got five runs in the third and added three more in the seventh for good measure in this one. Third Baseman Bruce Berry, Catcher Phil Lang and Center Fielder Bob Straka each scored a pair of runs in the win, while Pitcher

Dave Kern struck out five and kept em' guessing on the mound.

(Incidentally, in the third place game, Springfield Pitcher Mike Davidson went on to strike out 19 in a 4-0 no-hitter win over Austin!)

1964: Austin vs. Minneapolis West

Austin, a veteran team with almost the same lineup as its 1963 tourney team, came out smoking in the opening round of the 1964 tournament by whipping Halstad, 6-2. Pitcher Dave Hartman K'd nine, while Outfielders Charles Granholm and Lynn McAlister each had multiple hits in the win. Game Two saw mighty Fairmont rally late to beat Ely, 2-1, thanks to a pair of runs by Dave Swift and Clark Rieki in the last half of the seventh. The third quarterfinal game saw Benson rally late to upset New Ulm, 4-0, thanks to four sixth inning runs from Jerry Gallagher, Jim Hanson, Spencer Thompson and Mike Walsh. Game Four was a tight one as Minneapolis West eked out a 2-1 victory over West St. Paul. Minneapolis West Pitcher Dave Baldridge struck out 24 batters and gave up three hits while West St. Paul Pitcher Mark Johnson struck out 15 and allowed three hits over 13 innings before West was able to break the 1-1 tie and take the game, 2-1.

Austin advanced to the Finals by doubling up on Fairmont, 6-3. The Cardinals were ahead in this one but Austin, led by Catcher Al Berg, scored three runs in the sixth and added two more in the seventh to take it. West then kept it rolling by beating Benson, 9-0, in the other semi. West jumped out to a quick 5-0 lead in the first and never looked back as Gordy Morrill, Dave Baldridge and Ted Nixon each scored a pair of runs in the win.

The Packers then went on to win their second state title by beat West, 3-0. Although out-hit 5-2, Austin's strong defense and timely hitting proved to be the difference in this one. First Baseman Steve Schmitt and Left Fielder Lynn McAlister each tallied in the second for the Pack, while Pitcher Dave Hartman struck out nine to seal the deal.

1965: Richfield vs. St. Paul Humboldt

Virginia opened the 1965 state tournament with a 16-4 shellacking of Norwood Young America. Bob Carlson, (future UM-Duluth Hockey Coach) Mike Sertich, Mike Norlander and Mike Wirtanen all had multiple hits and runs in this one. Game Two was a much closer affair as St. Paul Humboldt edged Brainerd, 3-2. Brainerd jumped out to a 2-1 lead in this one, only to see Humboldt rally behind a pair of John Prow runs in the fourth and sixth innings to ice it. The third quarterfinal was a shut-out as St. James, behind runs from Steve Wolner, Roger Thies and Mike Peterson, blanked Bemidji, 3-0. Game Four was another blow-out as Richfield pounded on Northfield, 13-3. Leading the charge in this one were Jerry Peterson, Bill Kendall, and Barry and Bob Bishop, who, between them, had eight hits and scored an amazing 11 runs.

Humboldt kept it going in the semis, edging Virginia, 6-4. Humboldt

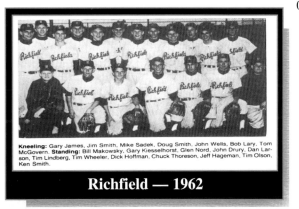

Kneeling: Gary James, Jim Smith, Mike Sadek, Doug Smith, John Wells, Bob Lary, Tom McGovern. **Standing:** Bill Makowsky, Gary Kiesselhorst, Glen Nord, John Drury, Dan Larson, Tim Lindberg, Tim Wheeler, Dick Hoffman, Chuck Thoreson, Jeff Hageman, Tim Olson, Ken Smith.

Richfield — 1962

First Row: Bob Keegan, Student Mgr., Dave French, Jan Heining, Bob Straka, Phil Lang, Bruce Berry, Paul Heim, Dave Kern, Mike Perry, Student Mgr. **Second Row:** Steve Runkel, Jim Erickson, Gerry Clark, Craig Lien, Roger Kramer, Dan Cybyske, Steve Perlman, Brian Love, Jeff Arnold, Jim Cosgrove, Coach.

Minneapolis Washburn — 1963

Front Row: John Morrison, Mike King, Charles Granholm, Jeff Williams, Lynn McAlister, Randy Tigner, Lonnie Williams, Steve Russell, Harry Roberts, Paul McAlister. **Back Row:** Dick Seltz, Mike Hause, Larry Faber, Steve Schmitt, Jay Best, Al Berg, Dave Hartman, Bob Richardson, Howie Streg.

Austin — 1964

went up 3-1 after one, and added three more in the second and third to seal the deal. Robin Eggum and George Augst each tallied a pair in the win, while Pitcher Chip Schwartz K'd 11 as well. The other semifinal had Richfield scoring four early and hanging on for a 4-3 win over St. James. Second Baseman Jerry Peterson scored a pair of runs and added a key stolen base, while Pitcher Al Payne K'd 13 and allowed just three hits in the win.

Richfield kept its 24-0 record intact as they edged St. Paul Humboldt in an extra-inning thriller, 2-1. Both teams scored a run in their first at bat and then sat idle until Richfield Shortstop Dean Lambert scored the winning run in the last half of the eighth. Humboldt tried to pull ahead in this one but had three potential game-winning runs cut off at home plate. Richfield was led by a quartet of All-Tourney selections in Bob Bishop, Scott Stien, Jerry Peterson and Al Payne.

1966: Bloomington Kennedy vs. Hastings

Bloomington Kennedy Pitcher Bob Mielke kicked off the 1966 tourney by throwing a four-hit gem in a 5-1 victory over Melrose. Catcher Jim Wanshura and Left Fielder Mike Esterley each pitched in with a pair of runs as well. Game Two saw New Ulm double up on Roseau, 6-3, thanks to a pair of hits each from: Left Fielder Steve Bloedel, Right Fielder Chuck Christiansen and Catcher Doug Hitzeman. Game Three had Hastings downing International Falls, 3-1, behind Right Fielder Kirk Pederson, who scored a pair of runs and a pair of RBIs on a homer and a triple. The last quarterfinal contest of the day saw Albert Lea squeak by Wells, 1-0, on Center Fielder Louis Gueltzow's game-winning run.

New Ulm was spanked by Kennedy in the first semifinal, 7-0, as New Ulm committed seven errors in the loss. Leading the charge for Bloomington was Dennis Kruse who had a first inning three RBI dinger, followed by Second Baseman Tom Herron and Shortstop Rick Martin, who each tallied a pair of runs as well. The other semi saw Hastings get over on Albert Lea, 6-1, thanks to Pitcher Dan Carey, who K'd 16 and allowed just two hits in the win.

The Finals were all Kennedy as they came out and scored a pair of runs in the third and fourth to blank Hastings, 2-0, and take the title. Incredibly, despite Hastings' Pitcher Dan Carey throwing a no-hitter, a couple of walks and three errors allowed Kennedy to win the game. Left Fielder Mike Esterley and Shortstop Rick Martin scored what proved to be the winning runs for Kennedy, while Pitcher Bob Mielke K'd 13 in the win.

1967: Hastings vs. Austin

Richfield, behind the two-hit performances of both First Baseman Doug Kingsriter and Right Fielder Tom Dallman, opened

the tourney with a 2-1 win over Hibbing. Pitcher Tim Denman added 10 Ks for good measure as well. Hastings then blanked the Region Eight champs from Baudette in Game Two, 1-0, on First Baseman Kevin Keene's second inning run. Game Three saw Mankato pound on Moorhead, 12-2, as Phil Meyer, Jim Rademacher, Rich Stotka, Jim Roy and Rick Eckstrom each had multiple hits in this one. The final quarterfinal contest had Austin downing New Ulm, 5-1, thanks to Pitcher Rich Heard's 11 strike-outs — including the final six batters he faced.

Hastings kept it rolling in the semifinals, doubling up on Richfield, 4-2, to advance to the Finals. The score was tied going into the bottom of the sixth inning in this one when Pitcher Dan Carey led off with a double. Left Fielder Greg Gardell was then hit by a pitch and Right Fielder Bob Bathrick singled to load the bases. Successive walks to Catcher Kirk Johnson and First Baseman Kevin Keene followed giving Hastings the two run win. Austin then edged Mankato, 4-3, in the other semi. Mankato was ahead 3-1 in this one until the Packers rallied behind sixth inning runs from First Baseman Gary Morgan, Catcher Rich Heard and Right Fielder Tim Keller.

Hastings, behind Mike Hartung and Dan Carey, jumped out a quick 2-0 first inning lead in the championship game and never looked back, adding another two runs later in the sixth to make it a 4-0 shut-out victory over Austin. Hastings got strong pitching from Joe Peterson, Dan Carey and Kirk Pederson throughout the tourney. Austin, however, managed to get runners on base in every inning but failed to score. Perhaps they were just too tired — you see this was their second game of the day as they were forced to make up the rained out Thursday evening game the afternoon of the Finals.

1968: Edina vs. Hibbing

Austin edged St. Paul Highland Park in the opening game, 5-4. Austin, behind Center Fielder Ron Riley, scored three runs in the second only to see Highland rally right back to make it 4-3 later in the inning. Austin's First Baseman Gary Morgan and Second Baseman Dave House added the game-tying and game-winning runs in the sixth and seventh to seal the deal. Game Two saw Edina pound Bemidji, 8-0, behind Pitcher Bob Firth's two-hit gem. Game Three had the Cardinals of Fairmont shutting out Glencoe, 4-0, on runs from Shortstop Rog Drobinski, Catcher Doug Bancks, Right Fielder Brian Riedesel and First Baseman Cal Gould. The Final quarterfinal had Hibbing smashing Moorhead, 10-1. Second Baseman Nick Novak, Third Baseman Kerry Taylor and First Baseman Gary Southgate rapped out eight hits and scored eight runs between them.

Edina Pitcher Mark Untiedt

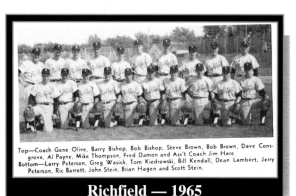

Top—Coach Gene Olive, Barry Bishop, Bob Bishop, Steve Brown, Bob Brown, Dave Consgrove, Al Payne, Mike Thompson, Fred Damon and Ass't Coach Jim Hare.
Bottom—Larry Peterson, Greg Wasick, Tom Kiedrowski, Bill Kendall, Dean Lambert, Jerry Peterson, Ric Barrett, John Stein, Brian Hagen and Scott Stein.

Richfield — 1965

First Row: Dave Hohag, Dale Rossette, Dennis Kruse, Jim Block, Tom Herron, Jerry Englholm, Rick Martin, John McNally.
Back Row: Thomas Selim, Ass't. Coach; Al Hoffman, Harvey Ratzloff, Ed Hoffman, John Wanshura, Don Skoy, Mike Esterley, Bob Mielke, Marshall Radebach, Coach.

Bloomington Kennedy — 1966

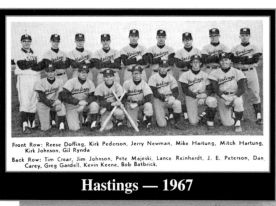

Front Row: Reese Doffing, Kirk Pederson, Jerry Newman, Mike Hartung, Mitch Hartung, Kirk Johnson, Gil Rynda
Back Row: Tim Crear, Jim Johnson, Pete Majeski, Lance Reinhardt, J. E. Peterson, Dan Carey, Greg Gardell, Kevin Keene, Bob Batbrick.

Hastings — 1967

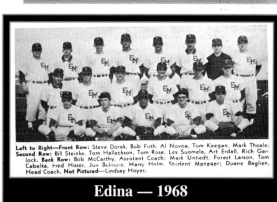

Left to Right—Front Row: Steve Dorek, Bob Firth, Al Novoa, Tom Keegan, Mark Thoele. Second Row: Bill Steinke, Tom Halleckson, Tom Rose, Les Suomela, Art Erdall, Rich Garlock. Back Row: Bob McCarthy, Assistant Coach; Mark Untiedt, Forest Larson, Tom Cabalka, Fred Huser, Jon Delmore, Harry Holm, Student Manager; Duane Baglien. Not Pictured—Lindsay Hoyer.

Edina — 1968

pitched a no-hit 1-0 shut-out in the first semifinal, a game which was called after four innings because of rain. Catcher Lindsay Hoyer had both of Edina's hits off of Austin Pitcher Nick Lindgren in the win. Hibbing then crushed Fairmont in the other semifinal, 9-0. Pitcher William Techar tossed a two-hitter in this one while Right Fielder Mike Jerulle, Second Baseman Nick Novak, Third Baseman Kerry Taylor and First Baseman Gary Southgate all had multiple hits as well.

The Finals were all Edina as Coach Duane Baglien's Hornets hammered Hibbing, 12-4, to take the title. Edina jumped out to a 5-0 lead in the first and never looked back. Edina Pitcher Bob Firth allowed only six hits and four runs while his teammates collected a total of 13 hits. Leading the charge were Center Fielder Mark Thoele, Third Baseman Al Novoa, Left Fielder Fred Huser and Catcher Lindsay Hoyer all had multiple hits in the win.

1969: Minneapolis Washburn vs. Albert Lea
Albert Lea got runs from Third Baseman Lynn Hebel and Second Baseman Ron Brackey as they edged Greenway-Coleraine, 2-1, in the opener. Bemidji pounded Fergus Falls in Game Two, 7-1, behind Pitcher Tom Hill's 12 K's. Offensively, First Baseman Gary Sargent (a future Minnesota North Star), Second Baseman Don Dokken and Hill, each had a pair of hits for the Lumberjacks. South St. Paul took Game Three by topping Pipestone, 4-0, behind Catcher Tony Kallas' three RBIs. Appearing in their eighth state tournament, Minneapolis Washburn blanked Norwood Young America in Game Four, 2-0, behind the solid pitching of Rolf Baglien, who K'd 12 and allowed just two hits in the win.

Albert Lea kept it going in the first semi, edging Bemidji, 5-4. First Baseman Jay Gustafson, Third Baseman Lynn Hebel and Pitcher Larry Brandt each had a pair of hits in this one as Albert Lea got three runs in the fourth and held off a late Lumberjack rally. The other semifinal game found Washburn taking advantage six South St. Paul errors to win 5-3. Incredibly, none of their runs were earned. Third Baseman Jim Dougherty led the way for Washburn with a pair of runs while Right Fielder Robert Edwards added a pair of hits as well.

Pitcher Rolf Baglien allowed six hits and struck out seven in the championship game as his Washburn club played tough defense and hung on to beat Albert Lea, 5-1. Shortstop Dennis Berry opened the game with a first inning hit and run while First Baseman Jim Hatlestad and Second Baseman Dale May each had a pair of hits in the win.

1970: Albany vs. New Ulm
Cinderella Albany, playing in its first state high school baseball tournament, opened the 1970 festivities with a 7-5 come-from-behind win over Windom. Center Fielder Loren Schiffler and Catcher Jack Hasbrouk each had a pair of hits in the win, while Pitcher Dick Glatzmier allowed just six hits along the way. Austin had no trouble with Morris in the second

game, winning, 4-1, thanks to Right Fielder Rick Knutson's two hits and two RBI's. Eveleth got past Bemidji in Game Three, 5-3, behind Third Baseman John Gevik and Pitcher Bob Novak's pair of RBI's. Also adding a hit was future Hockey Hall of Famer, Doug Palazzari. Game Four was a barn-burner which saw New Ulm's Center Fielder Dan Alwin score the game-winner in the ninth.

Albany had no problem with Austin in the first semifinal, winning easily, 7-0. Dick and Jim Glatzmaier each had a pair of hits in this one, as did Loren Schiffler, Mike Stovlil and Tim Terres. New Ulm then got a trio of runs from Dan Alwin, Scott Backer and Steve Martinka in the twelfth inning to edge Eveleth 3-0.

Albany then defeated a strong New Ulm team in the Finals, 1-0, in a twelve inning thriller to win their first title. Breaking the 0-0 tie in the 12th was Right Fielder Gordy Meyer, who scored after Second Baseman Tim Terres and Jim Glatzmaier both reached on errors, followed by a walk from Center Fielder Loren Schiffler. For New Ulm, who had each of their three games go into extra innings, the loss was devastating.

1971: Richfield vs. Faribault
The mighty Fairmont Cardinals kicked off the 1971 tourney by spanking Hibbing, 4-0. Scoring for the Cards were First Baseman Steve Hinrichs, Left Fielder Bruce Grabau, Center Fielder Dick Pritts and Pitcher Lynn Betts — who also tossed a three-hitter in the win. Faribault got four runs in the second from Dick Grass, Dave Schake, Larry Hafemeyer and Stu Spicer to double up Bemidji in Game Two, 4-2. Little Falls had no problem with Montevideo in Game Three as the Flyers won easily, 9-2. Pitcher John Dengel tossed a three-hitter and also knocked out three hits and a pair of RBI's to boot. Richfield blanked Anoka in the final quarterfinal match, 5-0, thanks to a four-run third inning which was sparked by Cather Jim Moldenhauer's two hits and two RBI's.

Faribault then edged Fairmont, 7-6, in the first semifinal. Faribault got three in the first and then added four more in the fifth to ice this one. Center Fielder Dick Grass led the charge, going 2-4 and scoring a pair of runs. The other semi was a blow-out as Richfield crushed Little Falls, 7-0, behind a pair of runs each from Cather Jim Moldenhauer and Center Fielder Jim Strommen. Pitcher Rick Peterson struck out seven and allowed just five hits in the win.

Amazingly, Richfield then completed their three game tournament series without allowing a run to be scored against them by blanking Faribault, 5-0. It was the Spartans' third championship in the past 10 years. Leading the charge in this one were Jim Moldenhauer and Left Fielder Dave Johnson who each had a pair of hits in the big game. Pitcher Brad Christensen struck out 10 en route to a one-hit masterpiece.

1972: Richfield vs. Anoka
Richfield picked up right where it left off in the first game of the 1972 tourney.

Minneapolis Washburn — 1969

1st Row: Robert Halvorson, William Meadowbrook, Dennis Berry, Richard Newberry, Robert Pearson, Edward Bush.
2nd Row: James Hatlestad, Robert Edwards, Peter Sovell, Rolf Baglien, David Spiedel, Dale May, James Dougherty.
3rd Row: William Elscham, David Lovejoy, Richard Alagna, Douglas Rivers, Allen Hendrickson, David Bunker, James Cosgrove, Coach.

Albany — 1970

1st Row: Standing: Head Coach John Nett, Asst. Coach Paul Ebnet, Kneeling: Don Glatzmaier, Jim Glatzmaier, Tim Terres, Craig Baggenstoss, Dick Glatzmaier.
2nd Row: Jeff Neutzling, Loren Schiffler, Neil Neuwirth, Mike Stovlil, Jack Hasbrouck, Gordon Meyer, Steve Blenker.

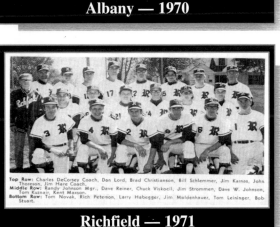

Richfield — 1971

Top Row: Charles DeCorsey Coach, Dan Lord, Brad Christianson, Bill Schlemmer, Jim Karnas, John Thoreson, Jim Hare Coach.
Middle Row: Randy Johnson Mgr., Dave Reiner, Chuck Viskocil, Jim Strommen, Dave W. Johnson, Tom Kuznair, Kent Maxson.
Bottom Row: Tom Novak, Rich Peterson, Larry Habegger, Jim Moldenhauer, Tom Leininger, Bob Stuart.

The defending champs made easy work of Lake City, winning 9-2 thanks to a seven-run first inning. Shortstop Dave Reiner, First Baseman Dan Lord, Pitcher Chuck Viskocil, Second Baseman Bob Stuart and Catcher Mike Sirany each had multiple hits in this one. Cloquet doubled up on Marshall in Game Two, 6-3, as Second Baseman Keith Johnson and Right Fielder Rick Wahtera each had a pair of hits in this one. Bemidji absolutely annihilated Luverne in Game Three, 17-3. The Lumberjacks were up 10-0 by the second inning and never looked back as they rattled out 19 hits. Leading the charge were Center Fielder Mike Malmquist, First Baseman Gary Sargent, Catcher Dave Drown and Left Fielder Charlie Meyers, who each had at least three hits in the blow-out. Anoka rounded out the quarterfinals by beating Alexandria, 4-1. Shortstop Jerry Castle and Center Fielder Bill Lester each had a pair of hits in this one, while Pitcher Mike Leadens added 11 K's as well.

Richfield edged a tough Cloquet squad in the first semi, 2-0, on runs from Shortstop Dave Reiner and Second Basemen Jeff Kendall — each of whom had a pair of hits in the win. Anoka took the other semifinal contest, beating Bemidji, 9-3. The Tornadoes jumped out to a quick 2-0 lead in the first and never looked back as both Center Fielder Bill Lester and Cather Rick Johnson each had a pair of hits in the win.

The Finals came down to the last of the seventh, when Second Baseman Bob Stuart scored the game-winner for Richfield on Center Fielder Bob Lace's second hit of the afternoon. Pitcher Chuck Viskocil K'd 8 and allowed just four hits in the win.

1973: Bemidji vs. Winona
Winona opened the 1973 tourney in grand fashion by whipping Blue Earth, 12-2. Third Baseman Karl Kreuzer, Second Baseman Gary Ahrens and Center Fielder Greg Scarborough each crossed the plate more than once in this one while Pitcher Greg Zaborowski K'd 11 and allowed just three hits in the win. Game Two saw St. Cloud Apollo double up on Benson, 6-3, thanks to Left Fielder Mike Carr, who had three hits and a pair of runs in the win. Game Three saw Bemidji edge Glencoe, 1-0, when Pitcher Earl Sargent drove in Shortstop Charlie Meyers early in the first inning. Meyers was awesome from the mound as well, striking out 13 Glencoe batters and not allowing them a single hit. Park Center took the fourth quarterfinal contest by beating a tough Duluth East squad, 2-0. Incredibly, it was the second straight no-hitter as Pitcher Tom Hall struck out 10 Greyhounds and didn't allow them a hit all day. Meanwhile, Third Baseman John Kahler had a pair of hits and scored the game-wining run in the fifth.

Winona beat St. Cloud Apollo in the first semifinal, 5-0, thanks to yet another no-hitter, this one by Pitcher Jim Lee, who fanned six along the way. Leading the charge offensively for Winona were Karl Kreuzer, Greg Scarborough, Kelly Scoffield and Lee, who each had multiple hits. The other semi saw Bemidji take care of Park Center, 5-2. The Jacks got two runs in the first and never looked back in this one as Pitcher Andy Kannenberg allowed just four hits on the day. Left

Fielder Dave Drown and Second Baseman Don Degerman each had a pair of hits in this one.

Bemidji kept it going into the Finals, topping a tough Winona squad, 3-1, to capture their first state title. Winona jumped out to a quick 1-0 lead on Second Baseman Gary Ahrens' run early in the first, only to see the Jacks tie it up on Right Fielder Bob Johnson's score in the third. From there Bemidji got two more runs from Shortstop Charlie Meyers and Catcher John Buckanaga to seal the deal. Pitcher Andy Kannenberg allowed just four hits in the win.

1974: Owatonna vs. Willmar
Willmar topped Grand Rapids, 7-4, in the opening round of the 1974 tourney, thanks to the efforts of Left Fielder Scott Swanson, Shortstop Bob Carlson and First Baseman Dennis Jacobson, who each had a pair of RBIs in the win. Morris crushed Jasper in Game Two, 14-4, behind Pitcher John Mullin's two hits and three runs, not to mention his nine K's from the mound. Catcher Larry Schmidt and Third Baseman Steve Kent added three hits and three runs, respectively. Game Three was an offensive slug-fest as Harding knocked off the defending champs from Bemidji, 10-7. Harding got a pair of runs each from Second Baseman Bob Wittman and Catcher Tim Jones, while Shortstop Reed Hess, Third Baseman Tim Pariseu and Jones each drove in two RBI's as well. Bemidji Cather John Buckanaga went 4-4 with a pair of RBI's and a pair of runs in the loss. The final quarterfinal saw Owatonna blank Glencoe, 1-0, on First Baseman Dan Horecka's fourth inning game-winning run. Pitcher John Herrman struck out nine and allowed just two hits in the win.

Willmar whitewashed Morris in the first semi, 6-0. Leading the charge in this one were Scott Swanson, Dean Kaihoi, Bob Carlson, Dennis Jacobson and Peter Smith, who each scored in the team's five- run third inning. The other semifinal then saw Owatonna double up on Harding, 4-2, thanks to a three-run sixth inning which proved to be the difference in this one. Third Baseman Dan Hartle, Right Fielder Jon Kuntz and Gary Hortop each crossed the plate that inning to seal the deal.

Owatonna and Willmar, both newcomers, then met in the championship game with Owatonna jumping out to a quick lead and then hanging on for a 6-5 win. Shortstop Ron McCann was the offensive hero in this one, going 2-4 and scoring three runs in the team's victory. Also adding fire-power was First Baseman Dale Horecka, who went 3-4 and scored a pair of runs as well. Pitcher John Herman was outstanding in this one, allowing just three hits in the win.

1975: Bloomington Kennedy vs. Fairmont
Set back a day because of heavy rain, Bloomington Kennedy came out smoking in the opening quarterfinal game at Midway Stadium, spanking Crookston, 9-2. Kennedy got seven runs in the fourth, highlighted by Shortstop Mike Kelley's two hits and three RBI's.

Back Row: Coach Jim Hare, Bob Stewart, Jeff Kendall, John Hedrix, Mike Sirany, John Vogelbacher, Brian Denman, Brad Redman, Bob Lace, Mike Bruss, Greg Carlson, Asst. Coach Chuck DeCorsey. **Middle Row:** Mike Carney, Steve Voit, Dan Lord, Chuck Viskocil, Co-Capt., Dave Reiner, Co-Capt.; John Thoreson, Craig Anderson, J.D. Walker. **Front Row:** Mgrs. Mark Gillick, Scott Olson, Randy Johnson, Pete Hoversten.

Richfield — 1972

Back Row: Head Coach Chuck Grillo, Randy Beck, Dave Berg, Perry Dreyer, John Buckanaga, Joe Weltzin, Bob Olson, Mgr. Tom Schwartz, Brad Nelson, Bob Johnson, Pete Maus, Mike Fairchild, Asst. Coach Des Sagedahl. **Front Row:** Andy Kannenberg, Jim Conway, Charlie Meyers, Mike Malmquist, Dave Drown, Earl Sargent, Don Wackowitz, Dan Degerman. **Sitting:** Maria Maglio, Sharon Gennes and Theresa Ashley (bat girls)

Bemidji — 1973

Front Row: Gary Hortop, Jeff Baud, Mark Kottke, Captain Dan Horecka, Duane Perkins, Mark Buss, Jon Kuntz, Ron McCann. **Back Row:** Ass't Coach Dale Timm, Brad Vought, Dan Hartle, Jack Kralick, John Herrmann, Randy Christey, John Jungbluth, Curt Anderson, Steve Nelson, Head Coach Hugh Miller.

Owatonna — 1974

Game Two saw St. Peter double down on Northfield, 4-2, thanks to a four-run sixth inning which saw Catcher Mark Zallek, Left Fielder Ron Bresnahan, Pitcher Brad Baker and Right Fielder Chuck Gardner all cross the plate. Fairmont needed eight innings to finally beat Montevideo, 5-3, thanks to a pair of late runs from Center Fielder Lon Miles and Pitcher Paul Dahlke. The last game of the day only went five innings as Cloquet was afforded the 10-run-rule in eliminating Alexandria, 10-0. The Lumberjacks got seven runs in the fifth as Pitcher Dean Levinksi, Third Baseman Tom Marciniak and Catcher Dennis Super each had a pair of RBI's in the win.

Bloomington Kennedy kept it on cruise control in its first semifinal, winning yet another 10-run-rule game, 11-1, over St. Peter. This five inning affair was highlighted by a seven-run fifth inning which saw Catcher Gregg Gaughran and Second Baseman Phil Jonnson each knock in a pair of runs, while Left Fielder Tom Bauer added three hits as well. The other semifinal saw Fairmont knocking off Cloquet, 4-3, behind a four-run first inning which had Catcher Scott Gudahl, Center Fielder Lon Miles, Pitcher Mark Hillmer and Third Baseman Tom Schweiger each touch home plate. Hillmer allowed just five hits in the win while striking out seven for good measure.

The Finals were all Bloomington Kennedy, however, as Coach Buster Radebach's squad scored its 30th runs of the tourney against the Fairmont Cardinals. The 10-4 match had Kennedy jumping out to a 3-0 lead, only to see the Cards rally in the fourth to take a 4-3 advantage. The Eagles came right back though behind multiple hit games from Rick Anderson, Tony Bauer, Steve Soleck, Mike Kelly and Phil Johnson to seal the deal.

1976: Hill-Murray vs. Marshall (CLASS AA)

The 30th annual State High School Baseball Tournament was held for the first time in a two class format this year. Under the new format, quarterfinal games in each class were played at various sites throughout the state and semifinals, finals and third place games were played at St. Cloud's Municipal Stadium.

Little Falls opened the AA tourney with a 2-0 shut-out of Proctor. Leading the way for the Flyers were Center Fielder Doug Fregin and Catcher Milo Backowski. Game Two had Marshall blanking Rochester Mayo, 1-0, behind Second Baseman Randy Galbraith and Left Fielder Craig Miller. The third game had Hill-Murray beating up on Kellogg, 6-1. The Pioneers score two in the second and then added four in the fifth to ice it. First Baseman Mike Hurt led the way with three hits and a pair of RBI's in the win. Game Four then had Park Center topping Bloomington Kennedy, 4-1, behind Second Baseman Charlie Head's pair of first and second inning runs. Pitcher Don Noland was outstanding on the mound, allowing just one hit while striking out nine for the "W."

Marshall hung on to beat Little Falls, 1-0, in the first semifinal game. Second Baseman Randy Galbraith scored the game's only run in the fifth as Pitcher

Brian Kern did the rest in holding the Flyers scoreless. The other semi saw Hill-Murray blank Park Canter, 2-0, thanks to Pitcher Ed Rech, who mowed down 13 Park batters while allowing just two hits along the way. Scoring for the Pioneers were Shortstop Jeff Whistler and Left Fielder Mike Hurt — who added a pair of hits for good measure.

It took eight innings, but the inaugural Class AA championship went to Hill-Murray as they edged Marshall, 1-0, to win it all. Marshall had a chance, but couldn't recover when their ace pitcher, Pat Buschard, who pitched 21 scoreless innings in the tournament, was lifted in the championship game because of the 14 inning pitching rule. Hill-Murray won impressively, giving up only one run in three games. Doing the damage in the title tilt was Shortstop Jeff Whistler, who scored the game-winner in the eighth. Pioneer Pitcher Joe Tamble was awesome, striking out eight and allowing just three hits in the win.

1976: Babbitt vs. Sleepy Eye (CLASS A)

St. Cloud Cathedral, behind the strong play of Left Fielder Dan Williams and Shortstop Kurt Hardee, opened the Class A tourney with a 3-1 win over Audubon. Sleepy Eye got solid play out of Left Fielder Al Riederer as well as the two Augustin's: Brian and Brad, to edge out a tough Arlington-Green Isle team in Game Two, 6-5. Game Three had Babbitt topping Roseau, 4-3, as Center Fielder Joe Boffa and Shortstop Mike Eide had solid games. The final quarterfinal featured Plainview beating Windom, 7-4, thanks to the strong play of Center Fielder Chuck Kruger and Catcher Dan Klassen.

Sleepy Eye knocked off St. Cloud Cathedral, 3-2, in the first semifinal. Sleepy Eye got a pair of runs from Shortstop Phil Johnson while Pitcher Dean Deibele struck out seven for good measure. Cinderella Babbitt advanced to their first Finals when they doubled up on Plainview, 6-3. Plainview went up 3-1 in the third in this one only to see Babbitt rally to score three runs in the fourth to take the lead for good. Leading the charge were First Baseman Randy Rosett, Third Baseman Chuck Evancevich and Left Fielder Terry Podloger, who all scored during that rally.

In the Finals it was the Babbitt Knights who rallied to produce four last inning runs to overcome Sleepy Eye, 6-5, to take home the hardware. Scoring for Babbitt on that amazing rally were Mike Eide, Jeff Krensing, Randy Rosett and Grant Boisner. Leading the way for Sleepy Eye was Right Fielder Mike Augustin, who went 2-4 at the plate and scored two runs in the loss.

1977: St. Peter vs. Edina East (CLASS AA)

Minneapolis Roosevelt, behind runs from Left Fielder Jeff Brown and Pitcher Brian Anderson, who also tossed a one-hitter, opened the 1977 tourney by blanking St. Cloud Apollo, 2-0. Game Two saw St. Peter double up on St. Thomas Academy, 6-3, as Catcher Bob Bresnahan and Right

1st ROW L-R — Paul Zilka, Mike Kelly, John Sorenson, Tim Christensen, Steve Saleck, Bob Graden, Rick Anderson, Phil Johnson, Terry Squire, Marty Vaurosky. 2nd ROW L-R — Assistant Coach Steve Strommen, Tim Goodmanson, Tom Bauer, Gregg Gaughran, Gary Wiley, Ron Koval, Gary Vinje, Mgr. Jon Thurston, Head Coach Buster Radebach.

Bloomington Kennedy — 1975

Front Row, L-R — Bill Schmitt (mgr.) and John Yarusso (stat). Middle row, L-R — Dean Milan, Jeff Langevin, Ed Stroebel, Gary Jost, Mark Smith, Jay Scokness. Back Row, L-R — Coach Terry Skrypek, Mike Rydel, Bruce Hoheisel, Ed Rech, John Wurm, Joe Tamble, Mike Hurt, Dan Rogers, Joe Stadler, Mario Cocchiarella, Jeff Whisler.

Hill Murray (Class AA) — 1976

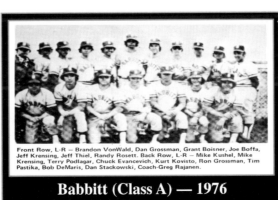

Front Row, L-R — Brandon VonWald, Dan Grossman, Grant Boisner, Joe Boffa, Jeff Krensing, Jeff Thiel, Randy Rosett. Back Row, L-R — Mike Kushel, Mike Krensing, Terry Podlagar, Chuck Evancevich, Kurt Kovisto, Ron Grossman, Tim Pastika, Bob DeMaris, Dan Stackowski, Coach-Greg Rajanen.

Babbitt (Class A) — 1976

Fielder Dan Bowles each had a pair of hits in the win. Spring Lake Park took Game Three by the same 6-3 score over Red Wing as Left Fielder Keith Ballstadt and Center Fielder Willie Sharp had two hits apiece in the victory. Edina East got six runs in the first and never looked back in their 6-0 win over Grand Rapids in Game Four. Gordy Nevers, Brad Burley, Steve Ramler, Jon Flor, Greg Olson and Jim Swanson all touched home plate in this one.

St. Peter annihilated Roosevelt in the first semi, 8-1, behind the clutch hitting of Ron Hill, Dan Bowles and Jeff Baker, who each had a pair of hits in the win.

Edina East continued to roll in its semifinal game, beating Spring Lake Park, 11-5, to advance to the Finals. The Hornets rallied from two down and came up with a five-run second inning to ignite an offensive explosion. Leading the way were Gordy Nevers, Bill Peterson and Greg Olson, who all had multiple hits in the game, while Brad Burley, Steve Ramler and Nevers all scored a pair as well.

The Title game was all St. Peter, however, as the Saints swatted the Hornets big time, 11-1. This one was so lopsided that the game had to be shortened to five innings because of the 10-run rule. Doing most of the damage from behind the plate was First Baseman Dan Bowles, who had four RBI's to go along with his two hits and two runs. Shortstop Ron Hill and Pitcher Bob Bresnahan each scored a pair of runs as well. In addition, Bresnahan K'd four and allowed just four hits in this one as the Saints went on to win their first crown.

1977: St. Cloud Cathedral vs. Staples (CLASS A)

Staples opened the Class A tourney by blanking Roseau, 2-0, behind a pair of third inning runs from Right Fielder Mike Fleisher and Center Fielder Randy Peterson. Morgan, behind a pair of runs each from Second Baseman Bill Bohn and Shortstop Glen Zimmerman, then took Game Two with a 6-2 win over Wanamingo. The third game was a thriller as St. Cloud Cathedral edged Hermantown, 4-3, in nine innings. Then, in the last quarterfinal of the day, Pipestone rallied back to beat Farmington, 4-1, behind Shortstop Dean Hess' two hits and one RBI.

The first semifinal of the tourney had Staples topping Morgan, 3-2, as Pitcher Duane Miller allowed just three hits while fanning five. Catcher Bob Nurnburger scored what proved to be the game-winning run in the fourth. The other semi had St. Cloud Cathedral blanking Pipestone, 1-0, as Pitcher Dan Meyer not only scored the game-winning run in the third, he also K'd 11 and allowed just three hits in the win.

St. Cloud Cathedral just kept on rolling from there. After a rain delay postponed the festivities, the Crusaders came out and scored a pair of first inning runs against Staples and held on to win their first title, 2-1. Touching home plate for Cathedral were Dan Meyer and Kurt Haider. Getting the game-winning RBI was Jim Pryzbilla, who drove in Haider with a clutch double.

1978: Grand Rapids vs. Cooper (CLASS AA)

Grand Rapids opened the Class AA Minnesota State High School Baseball Tournament by beating Columbia Heights, 5-1. Senior righthander Jim Jetland tossed a one-hitter in this one as the Indians cruised into the semis. New Ulm easily took Game Two, beating North St. Paul, 9-2, behind the Steinbach brothers, Tom and Terry, who had four hits and two runs between them. Winona shut out St. Paul Johnson in Game Three, 3-0, behind Pitcher Tom Holubar's six K's and four-hits while Catcher Rick Lilla added three hits for the Winhawks as well. Game Four was all Cooper, as the Hawks downed St. Cloud Apollo with ease, 5-1, to advance onto the next round.

Pitcher Jim Jetland not only tossed a two-hitter for Grand Rapids in the opening semifinal contest, but he also scored the game-winning run as the Indians hung on to beat New Ulm, 1-0, and advance to the Finals. Leading the way for Grand Rapids was Catcher Dave Salminen, who drove in Jetland with a clutch single in the sixth to ice it. The other semi was all Cooper, which downed Winona, 9-3. The Hawks got three in the third and another six in the sixth and seventh to win this one going away. Center Fielder Ronn VanKrevelen and First Baseman Steve Ferry each had three hits and three runs apiece in the win.

The Finals were once again all about Pitcher Jim Jetland, who tossed a one-hitter against Cooper to lead his team to a 2-0 victory. Jetland, who would go on to star as a goalie for the Hockey Gophers, was simply awesome on the mound, while Third Baseman Roger Bishop had a pair of hits and a run in the win.

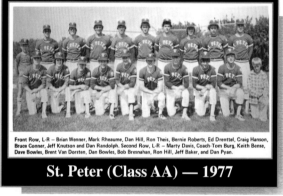

Front Row, L-R – Brian Wenner, Mark Rheaume, Dan Hill, Ron Theis, Bernie Roberts, Ed Drenttel, Craig Hanson, Bruce Conner, Jeff Knutson and Dan Randolph. Second Row, L-R – Marty Davis, Coach-Tom Burg, Keith Bense, Dave Bowles, Brent Van Dorsten, Dan Bowles, Bob Bresnahan, Ron Hill, Jeff Baker, and Dan Pyan.

St. Peter (Class AA) — 1977

Front Row, L-R – Paul Daniel, Dennis Schleper, Dan Hagen, Kurt Haider, Steve Faber, Bob Lahr, Al Primus, Roger Korte, Neal Binsfeld. Second Row, L-R – Asst. Coach Marty Rosen, Jeff Muntifering, Andy Fish, Pete Loehr, Dick Krippner, Rick Primus, Dan Meyer, Duane Voight, Jim Pryzbilla, Mike Justin, Head Coach Bob Karn.

St. Cloud Cathedral (Class A) — 1977

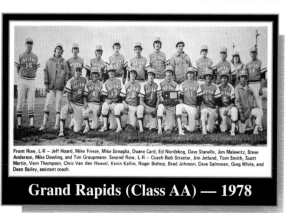

Front Row, L-R – Jeff Hoard, Mike Frieze, Mike Sonaglia, Duane Card, Ed Nordskog, Dave Stanelle, Jim Malawitz, Steve Anderson, Mike Dowling, and Tim Graupmann. Second Row, L-R – Coach Bob Streetar, Jim Jetland, Tom Smith, Scott Martin, Vern Thompson, Chris Van den Heuvel, Kevin Kellin, Roger Bishop, Brad Johnson, Dave Salminen, Greg White, and Dean Bailey, assistant coach.

Grand Rapids (Class AA) — 1978

1978: Plainview vs. Benson (CLASS A)

Bagley kicked off the Class A Tourney by hanging on to beat Holy Angels Academy, 6-4. Benson then blanked Truman, 1-0, in Game Two, followed by Greenway downing Perham, 3-2, in Game Three. The final quarterfinal then saw the Plainview Gophers outlast Jordan, 4-2, in an 11-inning thriller.

The first semifinal had Benson spanking Bagley, 6-0, behind Third Baseman John Rustad, First Baseman Jim Gosson, Catcher Pat Collins and Shortstop Dave Martin — who each had two hits apiece in the win. Plainview took the other semi, doubling up on Greenway, 4-2. Plainview jumped out to a 3-0 first inning lead in this one and never looked back. Scoring for the Gophers were Pitcher Brent Wohlers, First Baseman Bill Kruger and Right Fielder Doug Folkert. Wohlers K'd nine and allowed just four hits in the win.

The Finals were all Plainview as they scored three in the first and kept on rolling, beating Benson, 5-2, to earn their first state title. Wohlers, Third Baseman Ed Jacobs and Right Fielder Doug Folkert each touched home plate once, while Second Baseman Dave Arnett touched it twice in the win.

1979: Little Falls vs. Minnetonka (CLASS AA)

Little Falls opened the Class "AA" MSHSL State Baseball Tournament held at St. Cloud's Municipal Stadium with a 6-3 win over the defending champs from Grand Rapids. St. Paul Highland Park edged Mounds View in Game Two, 2-1, on a pair of first inning runs from Shortstop Jim Goldman and Center Fielder Dan Nayman. Game Three had Shakopee beating Rochester Mayo, 4-1, followed by Minnetonka blanking Minneapolis Edison in Game Four, 5-0. Skipper Shortstop Bill Piwnica led the way with three hits, including a triple, and two runs in the win. Pitcher Jeff Grewell tossed a two-hitter in this one while striking out eight.

Little Falls won its semifinal game by topping Highland Park, 2-1, thanks to a pair of runs in the top of the third scored by Shortstop Roger Henze and Second Baseman Roger Fregin. Pitcher John Shea allowed just three hits in the big win while striking out seven. The other semi was a blow-out as Minnetonka hammered Shakopee, 7-0. The Skippers got four runs in the second and never looked back in this one. Shortstop Bill Piwnica and Catcher Mark Brand had a pair of hits and a pair of runs, respectively, in this one while Pitcher Ken Smith tossed a three-hitter and struck out seven in the win.

Little Falls, making their tenth tournament appearance, then won its second ever title (the first was in 1957) with an exciting 5-4 victory over Minnetonka. Trailing 4-0 going into the bottom of the seventh, the Flyers scored five runs (Shea, House, Fregin and Czech), courtesy of seven walks, to tie the game, and then got a game-winning run off of a dramatic suicide squeeze bunt from First Baseman Steve Hamm, which scored Center Fielder Tom Kinsella.

1979: St. James vs. Fertile-Beltrami (CLASS A)

St. James opened the tourney by smashing Wanamingo, 10-0, in Game One. Game Two was much closer as Wadena got by Delano, 4-2, followed by Le Sueur beating Sleepy Eye St. Mary's, 8-5. The final quarterfinal then saw Fertile-Beltrami blank Eveleth, 7-0, to advance to the semis.

St. James kept it rolling in its first semifinal by scoring six second inning runs to blitz Wadena, 6-0, and reach the Finals. Pitcher Jim Veglahn threw a one-hit masterpiece in this one, while First Baseman Jay Esser led the charge on offense by tallying three hits and a run. The other semi had Fertile-Beltrami edging a tough Le Sueur squad, 4-3, thanks to a dramatic sixth inning run scored by Center Fielder Randy Faul. Right Fielder Dale Sannes and Shortstop Craig Simmons each had a pair of hits as well. Pitcher Ron Sannes allowed just three hits while fanning six in the win.

St. James finally allowed someone to score on them in the tourney, but it was too little too late, as they went on to crush Fertile-Beltrami, 10-2, and win their first championship in several tries. The

Saints scored three in the first and four more in the third to ice this one early on. Leading the way was Pitcher Todd Schmidtke, who, in addition to allowing just two hits, also had three hits of his own and scored two runs in the win. Center Fielder Gary Menssen also had a trio of hits and a pair of runs as well.

1980: Coon Rapids vs. St. Cloud Apollo (CLASS AA)

Held at Midway Stadium in St. Paul, the AA Tourney kicked off with Coon Rapids, behind Mike Carter's two RBI's, blanking St. Peter, 3-0. New Prague then shut-out Cretin, 1-0, in Game Two, thanks to Pitcher Dale Lapic's two-hit gem. The third game had St. Cloud Apollo edging Osseo, 1-0, on Todd Hubbard's suicide squeeze. While Game Four had Bloomington Kennedy, behind Pitcher Tom Dubay's three-hitter, topping Grand Rapids, 4-3.

The first semifinal had Coon Rapids blanking New Prague, 2-0. The Cardinals scored both of their runs off oosing pitcher Paul Kamish in the second inning, while Coon Rapids Pitcher Todd Herman struck out five in the shut-out victory. The other semifinal then saw St. Cloud Apollo edge Bloomington Kennedy, 5-4, to advance to the Finals. Lefthander Ben Skilling got the "W" for Apollo, striking out seven en route to tossing a one-hitter.

In their first ever state tourney appearance, the Coon Rapids Cardinals did something that had never been done before in the 33-year history of the state tourney — they won all three of their games via shutouts. The Final game was even more lopsided than the first two, with the Cards blanking St. Cloud Apollo, 5-0, to take home the hardware. Mike Mensen's sac-fly in the first drove in Jeff Kahl, who had gone to third on John Yelle's double. Then, in the fourth, Kevin Farrington singled home Mike Carter to make it 2-0. Carter added another RBI in the fifth, while Pitcher Jay Olson came in to strike out two of the final three batters in this one as Apollo cruised.

1980: St. Cloud Cathedral vs. Sleepy Eye (CLASS A)

Brooklyn Center, behind Pitcher Jack Schlicting's three-hit, 9-K outing, opened the Class A Tourney at Municipal Stadium in St. Cloud, by beating St. James, 5-3. Game Two had hometown St. Cloud Cathedral, behind Pitcher Dan Harlander, beating Fertile-Beltrami, 5-2, while Greenway-Coleraine, behind Pitcher Eric Gager's one-hitter, edged Morris, 2-1, to take Game Three. The last quarter was all Sleepy Eye St. Mary's, as the Knights beat Winona Cotter, 3-1, to advance to the next round.

The first semi had St. Cloud Cathedral slamming Brooklyn Center, 8-0. The Crusaders scored three runs in the

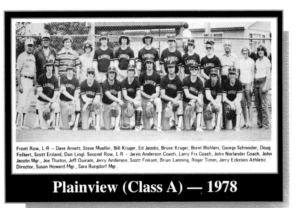
Plainview (Class A) — 1978

Front Row, L-R – Dave Arnett, Steve Mueller, Bill Kruger, Ed Jacobs, Bruce Kruger, Brent Wohlers, George Schneider, Doug Folkert, Scott Ersland, Dan Lingl. Second Row, L-R – Jarvis Anderson Coach, Larry Fix Coach, John Norlander Coach, John Jacobs Mgr., Joe Tlustos, Jeff Ouiram, Jerry Anderson, Scott Fiskum, Brian Lanning, Roger Timm, Jerry Eckstein Athletic Director, Susan Howard Mgr., Sara Burgdorf Mgr.

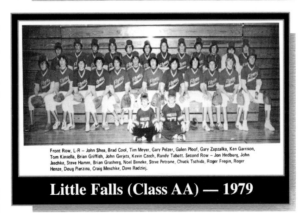
Little Falls (Class AA) — 1979

Front Row, L-R – John Shea, Brad Cool, Tim Meyer, Gary Pelzer, Galen Ploof, Gary Zapzalka, Ken Garrison, Tom Kinsella, Brian Griffith, John Gerjets, Kevin Czech, Randy Tabatt. Second Row – Jon Hedburg, John Jaschke, Steve Hamm, Brian Grasberg, Noel Beneke, Steve Petrone, Chuck Tschida, Roger Fregin, Roger Henze, Doug Pierzina, Craig Meschke, Dave Radziej.

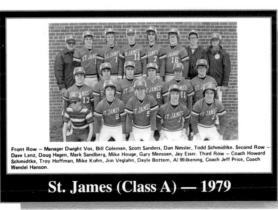
St. James (Class A) — 1979

Front Row – Manager Dwight Vos, Bill Coleman, Scott Sanders, Dan Nessler, Todd Schmidtke. Second Row – Dave Lenz, Doug Hagen, Mark Sandberg, Mike Houge, Gary Menssen, Jay Esser. Third Row – Coach Howard Schmidtke, Troy Hoffman, Mike Kohn, Jim Veglahn, Dayle Bottem, Al Wilkening, Coach Jeff Price, Coach Wendel Hanson.

Coon Rapids (Class AA) — 1980

Front Row, L-R – Jim Lowe, Todd Herrmann, Kevin Farrington, Mike Mensen, Todd Trick, Mark Heil, Frank Feland. Second Row – Dean Piquette, John Orth, Mike Carter, Brad Hank, Mike Weekley, Steve Novak, Jeff Kahl, Scott Peters. Third Row – Todd Morrissette, Bruce Carson, Jay Olson, Craig Johanns, Mark Plombon, Brian Picotte, John Yelle.

fourth and added five more in the fifth. Pitcher Pat Opatz, who threw a six-hitter, also had a key double in this one as well. The other semi was a barn-burner as Sleepy Eye St. Mary's hung on to beat Greenway-Coleraine, 11-9, in a real wild one. Dan Sellner's game-winning double proved to be the difference though, as both teams battled until the end.

The Finals were all St. Cloud Cathedral as the Crusaders sidelined Sleepy Eye St. Mary's, 7-0, to win their second state title in four seasons. Shortstop Paul Muenzhuber drove in the first three runs of the game off of a single and double to get things started. But Bill "Willie" Janson was the hero in this one, tossing a one-hitter with some 1,200 local fans cheering him on. Janson also drove in a pair of runs on a bases-loaded single in the sixth. In addition, Janson also scored two runs while adding a spectacular diving catch in right field in the seventh as well.

1981: Cretin vs. Waseca (CLASS AA)

Held at Siebert Field on the campus of the University of Minnesota and also at Parade Stadium, in Minneapolis, the Class "AA" tourney opened with Grand Rapids, behind Shortstop Mike Sonaglia's three runs, spanking Brainerd, 11-4. Game Two saw Waseca getting over on Osseo, 5-1, thanks to Shortstop Randy Matejcek's fifth inning homer. Cretin, behind Pitcher Joe Paatalo's 10-strike-out, three hitter, then topped Coon Rapids, 6-1, in Game Three. The fourth quarterfinal then had Edina East out-slugging Burnsville, 11-7. Left Fielder Pat Carroll had three hits and scored a pair in this one en route to leading his team to the semis.

Waseca beat Grand Rapids, 5-1, in the first semi. Pitcher Todd Ellis, who allowed just four hits in this one, helped his own cause by scoring a pair of runs as well. Cretin then doubled up on Edina East to take the second semifinal, 4-2. The Raiders got two runs in the second and added two more in the fourth to ice this one. Leading the charge were Pitcher Joe Paatalo and Right Fielder John Bannigan, who each had a pair of hits in the big win.

The Finals were all Cretin, as the Raiders crushed Waseca, 11-0, in a game shortened to five innings because of the 10-run rule, and won their first title. Pitcher Bryan Bowlin tossed a one-hit gem in this one, striking out six for good measure. Third Baseman Greg Whaley, Shortstop Mark Grogan, Left Fielder Kevin Murphy and Second Baseman Tim Gormley each had a pair of hits in this one, while Whaley and Murphy each scored a trio of runs apiece as well.

1981: Sleepy Eye vs. Winona Cotter (CLASS A)

This rain-delayed Class A Tourney kicked off at St. Cloud's Municipal Stadium with St. James shutting-out Norwood-Young America, 4-0, to take Game One. Pitcher Dean Roeglin allowed just four hits and K'd five in the win. Game Two had Winona Cotter, behind Pitcher Bob Polus' one-hitter, edging Greenway-Coleraine, 3-1, while Sauk Centre 10-run-ruled Crookston Mount St. Benedict, 12-2, in Game Three. Shortstop Robbie Essler, Left Fielder Tom Moritz, Right Fielder Don Kleinschmidt, Third Baseman John Haskamp and Catcher John Peters each scored a pair of runs in this one. Game Four then had Sleepy Eye squeak past St. Cloud Cathedral, 3-2, behind a pair of hits and a key run from DH Rick Cook, to advance to the next round.

The first semifinal had Winona Cotter beating up on St. James, 14-7. Shortstop Mike Waldorf, First Baseman Bob Polus, Center Fielder Mark Czaplewski and Second Baseman Doug Mark each had multiple hits in this wild one which saw Cotter rally from a 6-4 deficit. The other semi had Sleepy Eye edging Sauk Centre, 4-3. The Indians got runs from DH Rick Cook, Third Baseman Stott Krueger as well as the Krzmarzick's — Kip (Catcher) and Jay (Shortstop). This one was tied until Left Fielder Willie Schauman drove in Kip Krzmarzick in the seventh to seal the deal.

The Finals were a thriller as Sleepy Eye got past Winona Cotter, 4-1, in a 10-inning slug-fest to win their first championship. Cotter got on the board first in this one when Shortstop Mike Waldorf smacked a dinger to make it 1-0. Sleepy Eye answered in the fifth, however, on Stott Krueger's sacrifice. From there it went into overtime, with Sleepy Eye finally ending it all on a pair of runs from the Krzmarzick boys, who both walked but came in to score thanks to Willie Schauman's game-winning RBI's. First Baseman Dean Mathiowetz added one more score later that inning to seal the deal..

1982: Cretin vs. Hill-Murray (CLASS AA)

The Class "AA" tournament was held at Chaska this year with Hill-Murray opening the festivities by edging Osseo, 5-4, behind Nick Belde's three hits. Bemidji blanked Winona in Game Two, 3-0, on Pitcher Craig Johnson's two-hitter, while Grand Rapids got past St. Peter in the third game, 3-1. Game Four was all Cretin, as the defending champs got a two-hitter from Pitcher Greg Whaley and four RBI's from Catcher Nick Whaley en route to 10-run-ruling the Minnetonka Skippers, 10-0.

Hill-Murray then beat up on Bemidji, 11-5, in the first semifinal. Jeff Borndale and Mark Krois had three hits and three RBI's, respectively, for the Pioneers in this one, while Pitcher Mark Kleinschmidt allowed just six hits as well. Bemidji Center Fielder Jim Toninato, a future UMD Hockey star, scored a run and drove in another for the

St. Cloud Cathedral (Class A) — 1980
Front Row, L-R — Dan Borgert, Mark Faerber, Kevin Hengel, Dan Supan, Greg Mavis, Chris Kalla, Harry Simon, Kurt Lommel. Second Row — Dan Raden, Clarence White, Joe Hanson, Al Supan, Jeff Steichen, Dale Meyer, Bill Hess, Ken Lund, Andy Hollenkamp, Brian Hagen. Third Row — Ass't. Coach Jeff Mergen, Ass't. Coach Pete Hess, Pat Opatz, Dan Schleper, Bill Janson, Paul Muenzhuber, Mike Streit, Steve Kalthoff, Bill Plafcan, Dan Harlander, Head Coach Bob Karn.

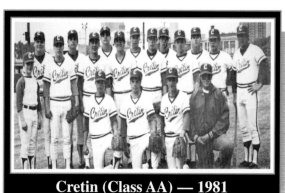
Cretin (Class AA) — 1981

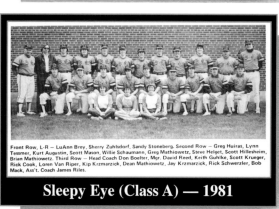
Sleepy Eye (Class A) — 1981
Front Row, L-R — LuAnn Brey, Sherry Zuhlsdorf, Sandy Stoneberg. Second Row — Greg Huiras, Lynn Tessmer, Kurt Augustin, Scott Mason, Willie Schaumann, Greg Mathiowetz, Steve Helget, Scott Hillesheim, Brian Mathiowetz. Third Row — Head Coach Don Boelter, Mgr. David Reed, Keith Guhlke, Scott Krueger, Rick Cook, Loren Van Riper, Kip Krzmarzick, Dean Mathiowetz, Jay Krzmarzick, Rick Schwerzler, Bob Mack, Ass't. Coach James Riles.

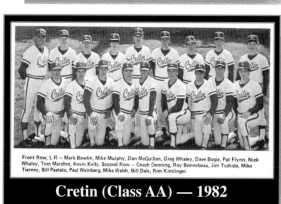
Cretin (Class AA) — 1982
Front Row, L-R — Mark Bowlin, Mike Murphy, Dan McQuillan, Greg Whaley, Dave Bogie, Pat Flynn, Nick Whaley, Tom Marchio, Kevin Kelly. Second Row — Coach Denning, Ray Bonnebeau, Jim Tschida, Mike Tierney, Bill Paatalo, Paul Weinberg, Mike Walsh, Bill Dale, Ron Kimlinger.

Beavers in the loss. The other semi was also a rout as Cretin got over on Grand Rapids, 10-2. Nick Whaley and Left Fielder Dan McQuillan had three hits and three RBI's, respectively, for the Raiders.

Cretin, with a predominantly underclassmen roster, kept rolling into the Finals, beating Hill-Murray, 8-3, for all the marbles. Greg Whaley, First Baseman Paul Weinberg, Right Fielder Mike Murphy and Third Baseman Ron Kimlinger each had multiple hits in the win. By winning it all, the Raiders became the first school since Richfield (1971-72) to claim back-to-back championships — and they did it by outscoring their foes, 28-5.

1982: Sauk Centre vs. Delano (CLASS A)

The Hermantown Hawks opened the 1982 Class A Tourney by downing Red Lake Falls, 3-1, thanks to Shortstop Keith Eisenminger's pair of runs. Game Two saw Delano beat St. James, 3-2, on Pitcher Dave Ditty's seventh inning run. The third game was all about Brooklyn Center, who beat Benson, 7-5, behind a pair of runs each from Catcher Bill Block and Pitcher Brad Jackson. Game Four then featured Sauk Centre out-scoring Wabasha-Kellogg, 12-9, in a wild one. Up 7-4 in the sixth, Wabasha-Kellogg rallied to score six runs to take the lead. Sauk Centre hung in there though, and rallied back behind a pair of Shortstop Robbie Essler runs to take it.

Delano held off Hermantown, 6-5, to win the first semifinal. The Hawks were up 5-3 in the third until Delano rallied behind runs from Third Baseman Steve Eilen, DH Joe Kvasnicka and Left Fielder Brian Diem to take it. The other semi then had Sauk Centre doubling up on Brooklyn Center, 4-2, thanks to runs from Shortstop Robbie Essler, Right Fielder Don Kleinschmidt, Third Baseman John Haskamp and Catcher Steve Schneider.

The Finals had the Sauk Centre Mainstreeters taking out Delano, 4-2, to win their first title. Delano jumped out to a 2-0 lead in this one only to see the Mainstreeters rally back behind runs from Essler, Kleinschmidt, Haskamp and Right Fielder Tom Moritz. It was Sauk Centre's first title.

1983: Edina vs. St. Cloud Apollo (CLASS AA)

The 37th annual MSHSL State Baseball Tournament opened at the new Municipal Stadium in St. Paul with Edina, behind right Fielder Paul Kemble's fifth inning homer, pounding Stillwater, 11-1, in five innings. Grand Rapids then got past Kellogg, 8-7, thanks to Center Fielder Todd Cleveland's three runs, in Game Two, while St. Cloud Apollo hammered Shakopee, 10-0, in Game Three. In addition to going 2-for-4 at the plate, Pitcher Pete Pratt also allowed just three hits while fanning six in this one. The Final quarterfinal contest had Holy Angels outlasting Burnsville, 11-7, as Stars' First Baseman Fred Breitling went 4-for-4 and score a pair of runs in this one.

The Semifinals were both romps as Edina cruised in the first one, 8-0, over Grand Rapids. Leading the charge for the

Hornets were First Baseman Pat Donohue and Third Baseman Rob Wassenaar, who each had a trio of hits in the big win. Pitcher Rick Raether allowed just two hits in this one while fanning nine. The other blow-out had St. Cloud Apollo destroying Holy Angels, 10-0. Right Fielder Mike Kerfeld and Shortstop and Skillingstad each had a pair of hits in the win, while Pitcher Paul Gross knocked out three hits and drove in a pair of runs to boot. Gross also allowed just three hits while striking out five in the win.

In the title game, the Edina Hornets rallied from a 6-2 deficit in the fourth inning by scoring six of their own to overcome St. Cloud Apollo, 9-6. Leading the charge for Edina was Pitcher Rob Wassenaar, who scattered nine hits while fanning eight in the finale. In addition, Shortstop Tim McGovern, who had three hits and scored a pair of runs in what proved to be the Hornets second ever baseball title.

1983: Staples vs. Windom (CLASS A)

The Class "A" tourney opened in St. Cloud with Austin Pacelli crushing Roseau, 10-2, in the opener. First Baseman Tom Wiechmann and Pitcher Mark Larkoski each scored a pair of runs in this one. Game Two saw Windom come from behind to beat Greenway-Coleraine, 8-7, in a nine-inning thriller which saw Center Fielder Dan Flatgard score the game-winning run off of Catcher Joel Frederickson's sac-fly. Dassel-Cokato out-dueled Montgomery-Londsdale in the third game, 11-7, thanks to the three-run performances of Center Fielder Jim Carlson, First Baseman Ryan Nelson and Shortstop Brent Rice. Game Four then saw Staples edge out Montevideo, 3-2, behind Pitcher Dave Hagenson's two-hit, seven K outing.

The first semifinal saw Windom jump all over Austin Pacelli, 10-2. The Eagles jumped out to a quick 5-0 lead in the first and added five more in the fourth for good measure. Shortstop Mark Olson, Third Baseman Tim Gronseth, Second Baseman Richard Hanson and DH Kent Elness each score a pair of runs in this one. In the other semi Staples scored seven unearned runs in a 9-7 triumph over Dassel-Cokato. The Cardinals got four runs in the fourth, followed by two more each in the sixth and seventh to seal the deal in this one. Center Fielder Jerry Volesky, First Baseman Dave Hagenson and Second Baseman Jeff Dravis each touched home plate twice in the game, while Pitcher Tom Hollister had nine K's as well.

The Finals saw the Staples Cardinals beat Windom, 7-5, thanks to five unearned runs. Catcher Randy Card was the hero in this one, scoring three runs, and adding an RBI to boot. The Cards got five runs in the fourth and never looked back as the rallied to a thrilling victory.

1984: Grand Rapids vs. Hopkins (CLASS AA)

Grand Rapids opened the 1984 Class AA Tourney in style as Pitcher Mark Sonaglia tossed a no-hit, 15 strike-out masterpiece in a 4-0 white-washing of

Sauk Centre (Class A) — 1982

Front Row, L-R – Craig Sunderman, Ron Moritz, Pat Haeny, Billy Brown, Randy Leukam, Curt Sorenson. Second Row – Jim Otte, Paul Froseth, Robbie Essler, Don Kleinschmidt, John Peters, John Haskamp, Mgr. David King. Third Row – Head Coach Joe Kleinschmidt, Tom Moritz, Steve Winters, Jason DuBois, Steve Schneider, Ron Spier, Dean Moritz, Ass't. Coach Jim Super.

Edina (Class AA) — 1983

Front Row, L-R – Brian Hill, Bob McGarry, Mike Halloran, Tim McGovern, Paul Kemble, Carl Ramseth, Pat Egan, Mark Hoffman, Pat Hurley, Brett Lamb, Jim Williams. Back Row – Coach Phil Finanger, Ted Cadwell, Andy Venell, Doug Montgomery, Tom Bjork, Robert Wassenaar, Pat Donohue, Pat Finley, Brian Martinson, Dan Carroll, Rick Raether, Coach Jim Luther.

Staples (Class A) — 1983

Front Row, L-R – "D.J." Anderson, Darrell Card, Batboy Roger Bienusa, Jeff Dravis, Brian "Shag" Miller, Randy Card. Second Row – Mike Lauer, Co. Captain Dave Hagenson, Mike Miller, Dennis Shequen, Tom Hegre, Tom Hollister. Third Row – Coach Jerry Riewer, Bernie Volesky, Gene Peet, Co. Captain Jerry Volesky, Kevin Dosmann, Mark Lauer, Joel Rengel, Dean Jennissen. Not Pictured – Ass't Coach George Warn.

Anoka. Game Two had Cretin pummeling St. Cloud Apollo, 16-2, behind First Baseman Paul Weinberg and Left Fielder Steve Walsh (a future NFL star), who each scored three runs apiece in the big win. New Ulm, behind Catcher Aron Allen's three hits and four RBI's took Game Three by beating Rochester Mayo, 7-5. The final quarterfinal had Hopkins doubling up on Holy Angels, 4-2, thanks to a pair of hits each from Second Baseman Josh Mack and Third Baseman Jeff Cox.

The first semifinal had Grand Rapids crushing Cretin, 10-2, behind a pair of three RBI performances each from Shortstop Tom Streetar and Pitcher Bill Kinnunen. Left Fielder Chris Nielson also added a pair of hits and a pair of runs as well. Cretin committed five errors and stranded 11 men on base in the loss. The other semi featured Hopkins edging New Ulm, 11-9, in a real barn-burner. While New Ulm got a pair of hits and a pair of runs from future Twin, Second Baseman Brian Raabe, this one came down to the wire. New Ulm jumped out to a 6-4 lead after two, only to see Hopkins rally to make it 8-6 after six. Each team scored three in the seventh, but New Ulm came up short. Leading the charge for the Royals was Right Fielder Dan Schmidt, who had three RBI's and a pair of runs in the win.

The Finals were a blow-out as Grand Rapids 10-run-ruled Hopkins in five innings to win the crown. Pitcher Dan Renner allowed just three hits in this one and helped his own cause by tallying three hits of his own. Center Fielder Todd Cleveland also touched home on two occasions as eight of nine starters scored at least one run in the lopsided victory.

1984: Windom vs.
Winona Cotter (CLASS A)
Springfield beat Hermantown, 4-0, while Windom topped Roseau, 7-4. Perham, behind Third Baseman Jim Hanson's two hits and three RBI's, then out-lasted Montgomery-Lonsdale, 6-3, in Game Three. Winona Cotter edged Delano, 3-1, behind Pitcher Don Peshon's fourth inning home run to tie the game. Cotter got runs from Shortstop Jim Galkowski and Center Fielder Scott Jerowski to seal the deal.

Windom rallied back to beat Springfield, 6-5, in the other semifinal. Windom was down 5-3 going into the seventh inning, when Pitcher Chad Lindaman, Shortstop Tim Gronseth and Second Baseman Tim Hayenga each touched home plate to ice it for the Eagles. The other semi saw Winona Cotter down Perham, 3-0, behind three sixth inning runs from Right behind Tom Pasykiewicz, Left Fielder Todd Kukowski and Second Baseman Rick Coshenet.

The Finals were all Windom as the Eagles went on to shut-out Winona Cotter, 2-0, to earn its first state title. Pinch-hitter Mitch Kaiser and First Baseman Jeff Olson each scored in the sixth, while Pitcher Tim Gronseth allowed five hits while fanning seven..

1985: St. Cloud Apollo vs.
Fridley (CLASS AA)
Fridley commenced the 1985 state tourney by downing Duluth East, 5-1, behind Pitcher Scott Kaul, who, in addition to smacking two hits and driving in a run, also struck out 11 in the win. Cretin edged Rosemount, 3-2, in Game Two thanks to Second Baseman Chris Gnetz's game-winning run in the seventh. Game Three was all St. Cloud Apollo as the Eagles crushed Irondale, 10-3, behind Shortstop Jeremy Mendel's two hits and two RBI's, as well as Center Fielder Sean Moe's two hits and three RBI's. The final quarterfinal had Bloomington Jefferson taking out New Ulm, 5-1. Leading the charge for the Jaguars was Left Fielder Jeff Holforty, who knocked in three runs off of a pair of doubles and a single.

The first semifinal featured Fridley knocking off Cretin, 3-2, to advance to the Finals. Cretin went up 2-0 in this one, only to see the Tigers rally back to get three runs in the fifth to ice it. Leading the charge were Center Fielder Bob Storevik, Shortstop Todd Boone and Left Fielder Trent Van Hulzen, who each scored runs in that great comeback. The other semi had St. Cloud Apollo edging Bloomington Jefferson, 5-3. Jefferson went up 2-0 in this one, only to see Apollo rally to get four runs in the fifth and sixth innings to seal the deal. Center Fielder Sean Moe's RBI triple in the fourth started the rally, while Second Baseman Denny Yoerg's two hits and one run kept it going. Pitcher Mitch Fuecker tallied nine strike outs in the win as well.

The Finals were an eight-inning affair that saw St. Cloud Apollo take out Fridley, 7-4, behind an 11-hit attack from the Eagles. Shortstop Jay Sannes, Left Fielder Mitch Fuecker and Pitcher Dan Athmann each had a pair of hits in this one, while First Baseman Neil Hubbard added a pair of key RBI's too. The win was Apollo's first state title.

1985: Windom vs.
Eden Valley-Watkins (CLASS A)
Eden Valley-Watkins opened the Class A Tourney by downing undefeated Frazee, 3-2. Second Baseman Allan Wortz and Third Baseman Bob Dockendorf each scored runs in the sixth to ice this one for the Eagles. Game Two had Silver Bay out-dueling Jordan, 9-6, behind a pair of runs each from Second Baseman Stu Taylor and First Baseman Tom Bott. The third quarterfinal had Windom edging past Plainview, 3-2. Both teams scored a pair of runs in the first, but it wasn't until Center Fielder Jeff Schmidt singled in the fifth and was brought home by three straight walks that the game was decided. Tracy then pummeled Lake of the Woods-Baudette in Game Four, 12-1. Leading the way in the offensive showing were Third Baseman Steve Mickelson, Second Baseman Bryan Koopman, Pitcher Doug Hatch, First Baseman Jim

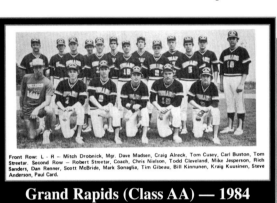
Front Row: L - R — Mitch Drobnick, Mgr. Dave Madsen, Craig Alreck, Tom Cusey, Carl Buston, Tom Streetar. Second Row — Robert Streetar, Coach, Chris Nielson, Todd Cleveland, Mike Jesperson, Rich Sanders, Dan Renner, Scott McBride, Mark Sonaglia, Tim Gibeau, Bill Kinnunen, Kraig Kuusinen, Steve Anderson, Paul Card.
Grand Rapids (Class AA) — 1984

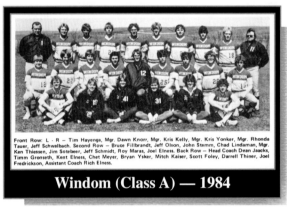
Front Row: L - R — Tim Hayenga, Mgr. Dawn Knorr, Mgr. Kris Kelly, Mgr. Kris Yonker, Mgr. Rhonda Tauer, Jeff Schwalbach. Second Row — Bruce Fillbrandt, Jeff Olson, John Stemm, Chad Lindaman, Mgr. Ken Thiessen, Jim Sotebeer, Jeff Schmidt, Roy Maras, Joel Elness. Back Row — Head Coach Dean Jaacks, Timm Gronseth, Kent Elness, Chet Meyer, Bryan Ysker, Mitch Kaiser, Scott Foley, Darrell Thiner, Joel Fredrickson, Assistant Coach Rich Elness.
Windom (Class A) — 1984

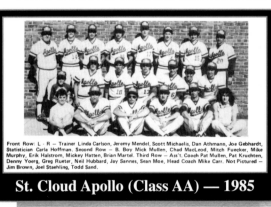
Front Row: L - R — Trainer Linda Carlson, Jeremy Mendel, Scott Michaelis, Dan Athmann, Joe Gebhardt, Statistician Carla Hoffman. Second Row — B. Boy Mick Mullen, Chad MacLeod, Mitch Fuecker, Mike Murphy, Erik Halstrom, Mickey Hatten, Brian Martel. Third Row — Ass't. Coach Pat Mullen, Pat Kruchten, Denny Yoerg, Greg Rueter, Neil Hubbard, Jay Sannes, Sean Moe, Head Coach Mike Carr. Not Pictured — Jim Brown, Joel Staehling, Todd Sand.
St. Cloud Apollo (Class AA) — 1985

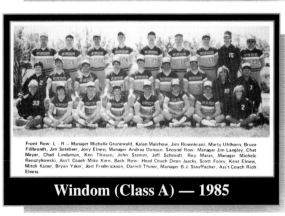
Front Row: L - R — Manager Michelle Grunewald, Kalan Malchow, Jim Rosenkranz, Marty Uhlhorn, Bruce Fillbrandt, Jim Sotebeer, Joey Elness, Manager Andrea Duncan. Second Row — Manager Jim Langley, Chet Meyer, Chad Lindaman, Ken Thiesen, John Stemm, Jeff Schmidt, Roy Maras, Manager Michele Renzrykowski, Ass't Coach Mike Kern. Back Row — Head Coach Dean Jaacks, Scott Foley, Kent Elness, Mitch Kaiser, Bryan Ysker, Joel Frederickson, Darrell Thiner, Manager B.J. Stauffacher, Ass't Coach Rich Elness.
Windom (Class A) — 1985

West and Right Fielder Rale Van De Wiele, who each scored a pair of runs in the win.

The first semi had Eden Valley-Watkins topping Silver Bay, 2-1, thanks to a pair of last-minute seventh inning runs from Second Baseman Bruce Geislinger and Pitcher Allan Wortz. The other semi-final game had Windom pounding Tracy, 10-0, in a game that was shortened to just five innings. All of the damage in this one came in the fifth inning, when, believe it or not, it was tied 0-0, until Windom's bats woke up. All nine starters reached base that inning, while Left Fielder Chet Meyer, Right Fielder Jim Sotebeer and Third Baseman Bryan Ysker each scored twice to make it official. The real hero in this one though, was Pitcher Chad Lindaman, who tossed a seven-strike-out no-hitter for the huge win as Windom successfully defended its title.

1986: Cretin vs. Bemidji (CLASS AA)

With the semis and finals now taking place in the Metrodome, Cretin took care of Chaska in the Tourney's opening round, 1-0, thanks to Pitcher Steve Schneider's 12 strike-out no-hitter. Left Fielder Jeff Lester scored the only run of the game in the fifth. Game Two had Hill Murray edging Rochester Mayo, 2-1, behind DH Mike Hurley's two hits and two runs. The third quarterfinal had Bloomington Kennedy topping Duluth East, 7-5, as Second Baseman Joe Decker and Third Baseman Chuck Stevenson each tallied a pair of hits in this one. Bemidji advanced to the semifinals by narrowly escaping past Park Center, 6-5, thanks to a pair of seventh inning runs scored by Right Fielder Mark Runnigan and Left Fielder Len Henry to seal the deal.

The first semifinal had Cretin beating Hill Murray in a real barn-burner, 10-6. Shortstop John Tschida, Center Fielder Pat Scanlon, First Baseman Dan Cummings, DH Mike Magnuson and Left Fielder Steve Mooney all had multiple hits in this one with Scanlon scoring three runs to boot. The other semifinal then saw Bemidji get past Bloomington Kennedy, 3-2, to advance to the Finals. Left Fielder Scott Jallen, Right Fielder Mark Runnigan and Second Baseman Scott Eichstadt each touched home plate in this one, while Shortstop Corey Boyer had a pair of hits as well.

The Finals were a blow-out as Cretin crushed Bemidji, 13-2, in a 10-run-ruled, six inning game. Leading the Raiders was Pitcher Jeff Lester, who K'd eight and allowed just two hits in the win. Offensively, Cretin was led by Scanlon, Cummings, Magnuson, Schneider and Tshida, who each had either multiple hits or multiple runs in the big win.

1986: Greenway-Coleraine vs. Park Rapids (CLASS A)

Two-time defending champion Windom kicked off the 1986 Class A Tourney by downing Cyrus/Hancock, 1-0, in a nine-inning thriller. Pitcher Chad Lindaman allowed just four hits in this one while First Baseman Chet Meyer scored the game winner in the ninth off of Second Baseman Joel Elness' double to end the

game. Game Two saw Park Rapids defeat Arlington-Green Isle, 5-2, thanks to a four-run fifth inning sparked by singles from Bill Magnuson, George Schmaus, John Peterson, Jack Ainley and Doug Sanders. The third game of the tourney saw Clarkfield edge La Crescent, 2-1, thanks to a pair of third inning runs from First Baseman John Livermore and Pitcher Troy Jurgenson. Game Four featured Greenway-Coleraine shutting-out Pierz, 4-0, thanks to future NHLer Kenny Gernander's three hits and two runs to seal the deal.

Park Rapids took care of Windom in the first semifinal, 7-6. Windom jumped out to a 5-2 lead in the fourth, only to see the Panthers roar back to score four in the fifth. Windom answered in the sixth to tie it up at 6-6, forcing the game into extra innings. Then, in the ninth, Catcher George Schmaus, who had two hits on the afternoon, scored what proved to be the game-winner — thus sending Rapids into the Finals. The other semi saw Greenway-Coleraine pummel Clarkfield, 13-4. Left Fielder Craig Miskovich led the way in this one by going 2-5 and scoring four runs in the process. Also contributing were Shortstop Derek Vekich, Kenny Gernander and Pitcher Rick Torkkola, who each touched home plate twice.

Greenway-Coleraine kept rolling in the Finals, beating Park Rapids, 5-3, in an eight inning thriller to win the state championship. Greenway went up 1-0 in the first, only to see Park rally to a 2-1 lead in the second. The Raiders tied it in the third, and then took a one run lead in the sixth on Vekich's run. In the seventh, Park Catcher George Schmaus singled and eventually scored to tie it up and send it into extra innings. Then, in the eighth, Pitcher Kris Miller singled, as did Pinch Runner Jeff Haiskanen (who was

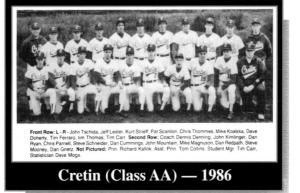

Front Row: L - R - John Tschida, Jeff Lester, Kurt Strieff, Pat Scanlon, Chris Thommes, Mike Koalska, Dave Doherty, Tim Ferraro, tim Thomas, Tim Carr. Second Row: Coach Dennis Denning, John Kimlinger, Dan Ryan, Chris Parnell, Steve Schneider, Dan Cummings, John Mountain, Mike Magnuson, Dan Redpath, Steve Mooney, Dan Gnetz. Not Pictured: Prin. Richard Kallok, Asst. Prin. Tom Collins, Student Mgr. Tim Carr, Statistician Dave Moga.

Cretin (Class AA) — 1986

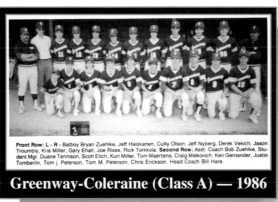

Front Row: L - R - Batboy Bryan Zuehlke, Jeff Haiskanen, Cully Olson, Jeff Nyberg, Derek Vekich, Jason Troumbly, Kris Miller, Gary Ehalt, Joe Risse, Rick Torkkola. Second Row: Asst. Coach Bob Zuehlke, Student Mgr. Duane Tennison, Scott Elich, Kurt Miller, Tom Maertens, Craig Miskovich, Ken Gernander, Justin Tomberlin, Tom j. Peterson, Tom M. Peterson, Chris Erickson, Head Coach Bill Hare.

Greenway-Coleraine (Class A) — 1986

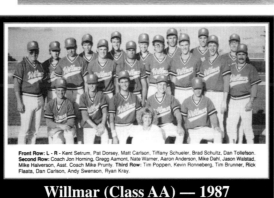

Front Row: L - R - Kent Setrum, Pat Dorsey, Matt Carlson, Tiffany Schueler, Brad Schultz, Dan Tollefson. Second Row: Coach Jon Horning, Gregg Aamont, Nate Warner, Aaron Anderson, Mike Dahl, Jason Walstad, Mike Halverson, Asst. Coach Mike Prunty. Third Row: Tim Poppen, Kevin Ronneberg, Tim Brunner, Rick Flaata, Dan Carlson, Andy Swenson, Ryan Kray.

Willmar (Class AA) — 1987

running for First Baseman Rick Torkkola). Catcher Justin Tomberlin then reached on a fielder's choice, scoring both runners along the way.

1987: Willmar vs. Hopkins (CLASS AA)

The 41st annual State High School Baseball Tournament got underway with Willmar downing Anoka, 3-2, in an extra inning thriller. Shortstop Tim Poppen scored the game-winner off of Right Fielder Dan Carlson's clutch RBI. Game Two had Park of Cottage Grove edging Holy Angels Academy, 2-1, thanks to Left Fielder Sean Berry's RBI double. The third game had Hopkins topping Bemidji, 5-4, behind Second Baseman Matt Miller's two hits and two runs. The final quarterfinal then saw Apple Valley double up on Grand Rapids, 8-4, as Pitcher Brett Holum and Catcher Brad Rasmussen each had a pair of hits in this one.

Willmar got past Park in the first semifinal, 4-1, thanks to Right Fielder Dan Carlson's fourth inning homer. Carlson finished with a pair of RBI's, as did Shortstop Tim Poppen, who also had a pair of hits to boot. Hopkins spanked Apple Valley in the other semi, 12-5, thanks to First Baseman Shawn Doherty's fourth inning dinger. Doherty had four RBI's on the day, while Shortstop Todd Steiner added three runs of his own in leading the Royals into the Finals.

Surprise entry Willmar, with a

record of just 11-9, rallied for five runs in the final inning to defeat Hopkins, 5-4 in the Finals. It was Willmar's first boys state team championship in any sport. Leading the way for the Cardinals were Pat Dorsey, Dan Carlson, Gregg Aamot, Matt Carslon and Kent Setrum, who all scored in that final rally. Pitcher Tim Brunner allowed six hits while tallying six K's in the win.

1987: Greenway-Coleraine vs. St Cloud Cathedral (CLASS A)
The defending champion Greenway-Coleraine Raiders opened state tournament play with a 4-3 triumph in an eight-inning game against Long Prairie. Shortstop Derek Vekich tallied the game-winner off of Catcher Justin Tomberlin's RBI sac-fly. Game Two had Windom edging Cottonwood, 3-2, in another eight inning thriller, thanks to First Baseman Kalan Malchow's game-winning RBI which drove in Left Fielder Mark Evers. Game Three saw Waseca blank Norwood-Young America, 3-0, behind a pair of hits each from Center Fielder Derrick Harmon and Second Baseman Brian Earle. The last quarter of the day featured St. Cloud Cathedral doubling up on Roseau, 6-3. Down 3-2, the Crusaders rallied back behind Shortstop Mike Simone's triple and Center Fielder Paul Laverman's double to seal the deal.

Greenway-Coleraine kept rolling in the first semifinal, beating Windom, 3-1. Windom went up 1-0 in the first only to see the Raiders rally for three late runs from Second Baseman Kenny Gernander and DH Gary Gustason. Pitcher Tom Maerten's allowed six hits and struck out seven in the win. The other semi had St. Cloud Cathedral edging Waseca, 3-2, behind Shortstop Mike Simones two runs. Second Baseman Tracy Langer added a pair of hits as well, while Pitcher Tom Meyer allowed just three hits in the win.

Greenway-Coleraine made it two titles in a row in the Finals, out-dueling St. Cloud Cathedral in a wild one, 14-11. Leading the charge for the Raiders were First Baseman Kris Miller and Catcher Justin Tomberlin who each had a pair of hits and a trio of runs, while Third Baseman Jeff Nyberg, who had a seventh inning dinger in this one, and Pitcher Kurt Miller each added a pair of runs of their own in the big win. Center Fielder Paul Laverman scored three runs, while Pitcher Tracy Langer, Left Fielder Leon Stockinger and First Baseman Rick Bancroft each had a pair of hits and a pair of runs of their own for St. Cloud Cathedral in the loss.

1988: Owatonna vs.
Grand Rapids (CLASS AA)
Grand Rapids kicked off the 1988 Class AA Tourney by crushing Rocori, 12-2. Pitcher Brett Holum went the distance for Grand Rapids, giving up five hits with six strikeouts and six walks. New Ulm scored two runs in the sixth and seven in the seventh to blank Park Center in Game Two, 9-0. The third quarterfinal was all Cretin, as the Raiders, behind their star third baseman Jeff Rosga, rocked Coon Rapids All-Metro Pitcher Tom Benson, 10-3. The final quarterfinal of the afternoon had Owatonna spanking Hopkins, 14-3. Chad

Wiley and Jon Springer hit back-to-back, two-run singles in this one, while Right Fielder Rich Zak went 3-for-3 with a double, a triple and an RBI. Pitcher Chuck Wiley allowed just one hit in the win.

The first semi had Grand Rapids doubling up on New Ulm, 8-4. Grand Rapids advanced to the semis on a 12-hit attack, highlighted by a 385-foot homer to right field by Brett Holum, who went 3-for-4, with four RBI. The other semi saw Owatonna down top ranked and once-beaten Cretin-Derham Hall, 4-0, in the Metrodome. Owatonna, paced by the Wiley twins, Chuck and Chad, who allowed a total of eight hits and just one earned run while striking out 31 in the tourney, beat Grand Rapids, 6-1, for their second state title in as many years. Chad got the "W" in this one, however, giving up only two hits while striking out 11 Raiders.

The Finals then saw Owatonna down Grand Rapids, 6-1. This time it was Pitcher Chuck Wiley's turn to shine as he had 10 strikeouts and gave up just four hits en route to leading his Indians to the Class AA title. Down 1-0 in the second, Owatonna rallied to take a 2-1 lead in the bottom of the inning on Rich Zak's RBI triple and Steve Smith's RBI single. They added four more in the fifth to ice it, and take home the hardware.

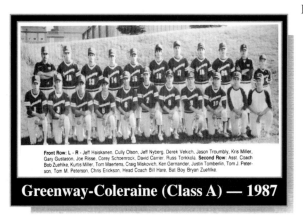
Front Row: L - R - Jeff Haiskanen, Cully Olson, Jeff Nyberg, Derek Vekich, Jason Troumbly, Kris Miller, Gary Gustason, Joe Risse, Corey Schoenrock, David Carrier, Russ Torkkola. Second Row: Asst. Coach Bob Zuehlke, Kurtis Miller, Tom Maertens, Craig Miskovich, Ken Gernander, Justin Tomberlin, Tom J. Peterson, Tom M. Peterson, Chris Erickson. Head Coach Bil Hare, Bat Boy Bryan Zuehlke.
Greenway-Coleraine (Class A) — 1987

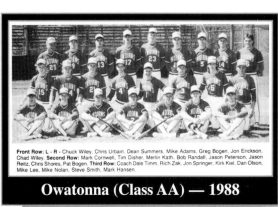
Front Row: L - R - Chuck Wiley, Chris Urbain, Dean Summers, Mike Adams, Greg Bogen, Jon Erickson, Chad Wiley. Second Row: Mark Cornwell, Tim Disher, Merlin Kath, Bob Randall, Jason Peterson, Jason Reitz, Chris Shores, Pat Bogen. Third Row: Coach Dale Timm, Rich Zak, Jon Springer, Kirk Kiel, Dan Olson, Mike Lee, Mike Nolan, Steve Smith, Mark Hansen.
Owatonna (Class AA) — 1988

1988: St. Cloud Cathedral vs.
Waseca (CLASS A)
Arlington took care of Luverne in the opening quarterfinal game, 8-3, behind a pair of RBI's each from Right Fielder Pat Keeger and First Baseman Mike Weinand. Game Two had St. Cloud Cathedral pounding on Redwood Falls, 8-1, thanks to DH Cory Bittner's homer as well as Second Baseman Tom Meyer's three runs. The Third quarterfinal saw Waseca stop two-time defending champion Greenway, 13-3, ending their state record 31-game winning streak in the process. Waseca did most of the damage in the third, when nine batters touched home plate. Shortstop Monte Dufault, Pitcher Chris Case and DH Troy Holtz each knocked in three RBI's in this one as well. The final game of the day had Warroad edging Wadena, 9-7, behind Shortstop Chad Erickson's three hits and two runs.

The first semifinal had St. Cloud Cathedral beating Arlington, 9-3. The Crusaders cruised behind the pitching of Tom Meyer and the hitting of Right Fielder Matt Zenner. Meyer went the distance, giving up four hits and striking out seven, while Zenner went 4-for-4 with a pair of RBI's and two runs scored.

The second semi saw Waseca roll over Warroad, 13-6. The Blue Jays rallied from a 3-0 first-inning deficit to get into the Finals in this one. Waseca Pitcher Joel Tveite not only pitched a complete game, striking out 10 and walking two, he was the offensive leader as well, going 3-for-4 with three runs and three RBI's. First baseman Troy Holtz also pitched in by going 3-for-4 with two runs and an RBI. Pitcher Chad Erickson took the loss for Warroad, which committed six errors.

Then in the Finals, St. Cloud

Row 1-L to R: Brian Kuborst, Doug Dingman, Mike Simones, Joe Bauer, Scott Lauerman, Craig Ahlstrand, Eric Loch, Kevin Feddema. Row 2: Paul Wenner, Bob Matz, Derek Holman, Scott Johnson, Jeff Torborg, Tom Meyer, Shawn Nahan, Cory Buettner, Steve Ahlstrand, Rob Mettenburg, Matt Zenner, Mark Scholtes, Head Coach-Bob Karn.
St. Cloud Cathedral (Class A) — 1988

Cathedral and Waseca met for a second year in a row. (In 1987 Cathedral beat Waseca, 3-2, in the semis.) This year was no different as St. Cloud Cathedral won again, 6-3, this time in eight innings before about 1,500 fans at the Metrodome. It was Cathedral's third championship in six state tourney appearances. The two teams were tied at two apiece after five innings, and then made it 3-3 through seven. With one out, Cathedral's Matt Zenner tripled to right field, while Craig Ahlstrand then walked and stole second base. Cory Buettner then hit a grounder to Waseca Third Baseman Chad Schumacher, who threw home wildly, thus giving Cathedral a 4-3 lead. Later that inning, Mike Simones drove home Ahlstrand, while Buettner also touched home plate on a fielding error by Left Fielder Mike Ruhland.

1989: Cretin-Derham Hall vs. Hibbing (CLASS AA)

Brainerd beat Burnsville, 3-1, to open the 43rd annual State Tourney behind Shortstop Todd Vanek's pair of game-winning hits, runs and RBI's. Game Two saw Hibbing upset top-rated and previously unbeaten New Ulm, 2-1, thanks to Third Baseman Bill Bussey's ninth inning game-winning RBI single to seal the deal. Cretin advanced to the semis by taking out Wayzata, 8-5, as Right Fielder Mike Vogel, Shortstop Jeff Rosga and Third Baseman (and future Heisman Trophy winner) Chris Weinke each scored a pair of runs. The final quarterfinal contest had Hill-Murray whipping Holy Angels, 6-1, behind Third Baseman Dave Muetzel's three hits and three RBI's.

The first semifinal had Hibbing blanking Brainerd, 2-0. Lead-off hitter Todd Krollman scored early in the first and then Second Baseman Tim Kemp iced it when he scored on Bill Bussey's sixth inning RBI. Pitcher Bob Nichols struck out four and allowed five hits in the win. The other semi was a blow-out as the Raiders of Cretin pounded the Pioneers of Hill-Murray, 8-2. Cretin got three in the first and added four more in the second to breeze to victory. Mike Vogel led the hit barrage in this one by grabbing a pair of singles and scoring a trio of runs along the way. Chris Weinke was also solid, knocking in four runs and adding a homer for good measure as well.

Coach Dennis Denning's Cretin-Derham Hall Raiders then went on to win their fourth championship of the 1980's, with a 4-3 win over surprising Hibbing at Municipal Stadium in St. Paul. Mike Vogel scored in the first to make it 1-0, and First Baseman Mark Wagner made it 2-0 in the fourth. The Blue Jackets rallied though, and got three runs in the fourth to take a 3-2 lead on scores from Right Fielder Todd Krollman, First Baseman Jason St. John and Second Baseman Tim Kemp. Cretin came back in the seventh, however, to seal the deal on a pair of runs from DH Bert Sager and Shortstop Jeff Rosga. Pitcher Sean McCauley added 8 K's as well as the Raiders proved they were the team of the decade.

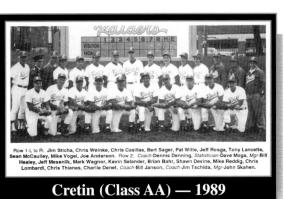

Row 1-L to R: Jim Sticha, Chris Weinke, Chris Casillas, Bert Sager, Pat Witte, Jeff Rosga, Tony Lancette, Sean McCaulley, Mike Vogel, Joe Anderson. Row 2: Coach-Dennis Denning, Statistician-Dave Moga, Mgr-Bill Healey, Jeff Mesenlik, Mark Wagnor, Kevin Selander, Brian Bahr, Shawn Devine, Mike Reddig, Chris Lombardi, Chris Thienes, Charlie Denet, Coach-Bill Janson, Coach-Jim Tschida, Mgr-John Skahen.

Cretin (Class AA) — 1989

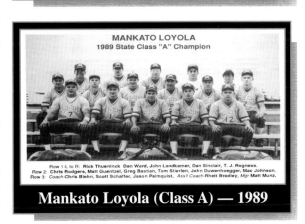

MANKATO LOYOLA
1989 State Class "A" Champion

Row 1-L to R: Rick Thueninck, Dan Ward, John Landkamer, Dan Sinclair, T. J. Rogness.
Row 2: Chris Rodgers, Matt Guentzel, Greg Bastian, Tom Stierlen, John Duwenhoegger, Mac Johnson.
Row 3: Coach-Chris Biehn, Scott Schaffer, Jason Palmquist, Ass't Coach-Rhett Bradley, Mgr Matt Munz.

Mankato Loyola (Class A) — 1989

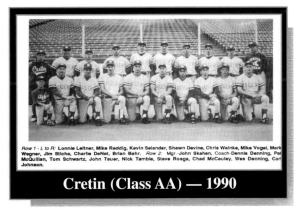

Row 1 - L to R: Lonnie Leitner, Mike Reddig, Kevin Selander, Shawn Devine, Chris Weinke, Mike Vogel, Mark Wegner, Jim Sticha, Charlie DeNet, Brian Bahr. Row 2: Mgr- John Skahen, Coach-Dennis Denning, Pat McQuillan, Tom Schwartz, John Tauer, Nick Tamble, Steve Rosga, Chad McCauley, Wes Denning, Carl Johnson.

Cretin (Class AA) — 1990

1989: Mankato Loyola vs. Sauk Rapids (CLASS A)

The Byron Bears got four runs in the first and held on to edge Sauk Centre, 5-4, in the first Class "A" tournament quarterfinal held at Dick Putz Stadium in St. Cloud. Sauk Rapids took Game Two over Luverne, 3-1, behind Third Baseman Craig Braun's two hits. Then, in the third quarter game, Mankato Loyola snuck past Sleepy Eye, 4-3, thanks to Center Fielder Chris Rodgers' game-winning run in the seventh. Game Four was a barn-burner, as Greenway-Coleraine hung on to outlast Crookston, 14-12. This one had it all. Greenway scored six in the fifth only to see Crookston answer with six of their own in the sixth. Greenway scored four in the seventh to ice it behind Right Fielder Pat Kane's three hits and four runs.

Sauk Rapids advanced to the semis over Byron, 5-2, behind Second Baseman Greg Benjamin's two hits and Catcher Mike Moilanen's two RBI's. The Indians got two in the third and added two more in the fourth to wrap this one up. Pitcher Brad Kenning allowed five hits and K'd five as well in the win. The other semi saw Mankato Loyola edge Greenway-Coleraine, 2-1, behind runs from Shortstop Matt Guentzel and First Baseman Scott Schaffer. Third Baseman Rick Thueninck knocked in the game-winning RBI in this one while Pitcher Chris Rodgers allowed just four hits in the victory.

The Finals went down to the wire as first-time entrant Mankato Loyola won its first ever state championship in any MSHSL sport. The Crusaders, who finished with an overall mark of 20-3, beat top-rated Sauk Rapids, 6-5, thanks to a four-run sixth inning rally. Second Baseman Dan Sinclair led the way in this one with three hits and three RBI's. Pitcher John Duwenhoegger was awesome on the mound, mowing down 15 batters along the way.

1990: Cretin-Derham Hall vs. Austin (CLASS AA)

Austin opened the 1990 Class AA Tourney by blanking Osseo, 5-0, thanks to a pair of hits each from Left Fielder Troy Schaefer and First Baseman Ryan Rasmussen — while Right Fielder Matt Cano added a pair of RBI's as well. New Ulm won its quarterfinal game by topping Moorhead, 4-1, on a pair of runs each from Left Fielder Mike Wenninger and DH Darrin Poss. Game Three had Cretin edging Grand Rapids, 3-2, thanks to Chris Weinke's 420-foot home run while Shortstop Steve Rosga score the game-winner in the fifth. The last quarterfinal was a blow-out as Hill Murray spanked Bloomington Kennedy, 10-3, on an eight-run first inning tirade. First Baseman Steve Washenberger led the way in this one with three hits and a pair of runs.

The first semifinal featured Austin downing New Ulm, 4-1, on runs from Shortstop Bob Peters, DH Jason McClary, Catcher Jason Wellman and Third Baseman Rick Schwab. The other semi was a wash as Cretin rolled over Hill Murray, 12-4. Second Baseman Jim Sticha led the way with two hits and three RBI's, while Mike Vogel, Chris Weinke and Steve Rosga each added a pair of hits as well.

The Finals then saw Cretin-Derham Hall successfully defend its Class AA championship by blanking Austin, 2-0. The Raiders were led by Chris Weinke, a 6-4, 205-pound senior who would go on to play professionally for several years in the Toronto Blue Jays system, only to later play in the NFL as a quarterback with the Carolina Panthers. Weinke hit a key double into the right field corner during the third inning of this title tilt which yielded what proved to be the two game-winning runs. Pitcher Brian Bahr also threw a three-hit shutout while fanning eight of Austin's hitters in the win.

1990: Waseca vs. Sleepy Eye (CLASS A)

Waseca opened the 1990 Tourney by trouncing on Red Lake, 11-0, in six innings. The Blue stole a team-record 13 bases in the win. Game Two featured Luverne downing Eveleth-Gilbert, 6-1, thanks to Pitcher Terry VanEngelenhoven's 11 strike-outs. In the third quarterfinal, Sleepy Eye, despite committing five errors, edged Morris Area, 7-4. Senior Shortstop Brooks Helget had a couple of game-saving defensive gems in this one. Game Four then saw Annandale get by Gibbon-Fairfax-Winthrop, 10-6, in a real wild one. Down 1-0, the Cardinals rallied back behind a pair of two-run doubles by junior Eric Raisenen and senior Matt McAlpin.

The first semifinal had Waseca beating up on Luverne, 9-1. Sluggers Tom Holtz and Barry Dufault combined to go 5-for-5 with seven RBI to lead their Bluejays past the Cardinals and into the Finals. The other semi saw Sleepy Eye defeating Annandale, 11-6, to advance to the Finals. The first seven Indians reached base and six scored against Annandale Pitcher Brad Fobbe. But the Cardinals rallied to make it 7-6 after three. But the Indians tallied four runs in the fourth, highlighted by senior Ken Hauser's big two-run single to seal the deal.

Waseca then won the Class A title when Sleepy Eye Pitcher Kevin Logue walked in the game-winning run in the bottom of the seventh to give the Bluejays a 4-3 victory. Waseca scored three unearned runs in the third inning, and held on to that lead until the sixth inning, when several errors, coupled with some timely hitting, led to a tie game. Senior Steve Moeller's two-out, bases-loaded walk in the seventh then propelled Waseca past Sleepy Eye for the Bluejays' first state title.

1991: Stillwater vs. Osseo (CLASS AA)

The 1991 Tourney opened with Osseo doubling up on Hopkins, 4-2, thanks to Shortstop Brian Zaun's pair of RBI's. Bemidji made it to the semis by downing Park, Cottage Grove, 3-1, behind a pair of hits each from First Baseman Troy Depew and Right Fielder Aaron Tank. Game Three was a wild one as Stillwater outlasted Hibbing, 11-6, thanks to a homer each from Right Fielder Steve Walters and Shortstop Josh Campbell. The last game of the day had New Ulm beating Winona, 9-3, as Second Baseman Mike Syverson, First Baseman Mike Wenninger and Catcher Kurt Moelter each had a pair of

RBI's.

The opening semifinal was a blow-out as Osseo cut down the Lumberjacks of Bemidji, 14-0. Right Fielder Jason Thornberg, Catcher Brian Roberts, Pitcher Shon Burns and Second Baseman Rob Kinderman each knocked in a pair of runs in this one, while First Baseman Dan Vreeman added a dinger for good measure as well. The other game was much closer as Stillwater edged New Ulm, 1-0, thanks to First Baseman Eric St. Martin's seventh inning triple. He later scored on Pitcher Don Harvieux's game-winning RBI single to ice it. Harvieux struck out five and allowed just four hits in this one.

Stillwater cruised in the Finals, spanking Osseo, 10-0, in five innings to take the crown. Shortstop Josh Campbell belted out a three-run blast in this one to put an exclamation point on an outstanding season. In addition, DH Brian Scheel added three hits and an RBI as well.

1991: Greenway-Coleraine vs. Rocori, Cold Spring (CLASS A)

Madelia/Truman kicked off the Class A Tourney by edging Middle River/Marshall County Central, Newfolden, 2-1, on Pitcher Colby Vogt's dramatic game-winning home-run with two outs in the bottom of the seventh. Game Two was a blow-out as Greenway-Coleraine spanked Kerkhoven-Murdock-Sunburg, 14-2. Leading the charge in this one were Right Fielder Chris Bellefy and Catcher Chris Tok, who scored four and three runs, respectively, while First Baseman Tom Savaloja knocked in five RBI's as well. Game Three was all Brooklyn Center, as the Centaurs pounded Frazee, 12-1, thanks to First Baseman Tim West's homer and three RBI's, and Second Baseman Derek Hageman's two hits and four RBI's. The last quarterfinal game was also a lopsided affair as Rocori, Cold Spring beat up on Pine Island, 11-5, to advance to the semis. Right Fielder Josh Loesch, First Baseman Ben Griffen and Shortstop Steve Huls each scored a pair of runs in this one.

Greenway-Coleraine kept rolling in the first semi, beating Madelia/Truman, 5-1, thanks to First Baseman Tom Savaloja's RBI homer and two runs scored. Second Baseman Mike Chupurdia added two hits of his own and also touched home plate. The other semi had Rocori, Cold Spring hammering Brooklyn Center, 10-1, thanks to a pair of runs each from Right Fielder Joel Loesch and Pitcher Todd Steil. Steil went on to allow no hits in this one while striking out five for good measure as the Spartans cruised to the Finals.

The Finals saw Greenway-Coleraine clinch its third state title when Right Fielder Chris Bellefy knocked a two-out, bases-loaded single into center field in the bottom of the seventh to edge Rocori of Cold Spring, 6-5. Rocori went up 3-0 in the second in this one, only to see the Raiders rally back behind a pair of runs each from DH Jason Elmes and Second Baseman Mike Chupurdia.

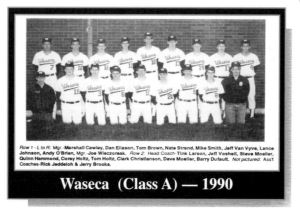

Row 1 - L to R: Mgr.-Marshall Cawley, Dan Eliason, Tom Brown, Nate Strand, Mike Smith, Jeff Van Vyve, Lance Johnson, Andy O'Brian, Mgr.-Joe Wieczoreak. Row 2: Head Coach-Tink Larson, Jeff Voshell, Steve Moeller, Quinn Hammond, Corey Holtz, Tom Holtz, Clark Christianson, Dave Moeller, Barry Dufault. Not pictured: Ass't Coaches-Rick Jeddeloh & Jerry Brooks.

Waseca (Class A) — 1990

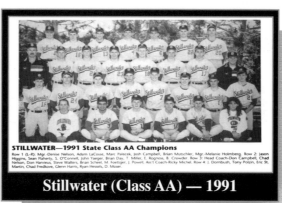

STILLWATER—1991 State Class AA Champions
Row 1 (L-R): Mgr.-Denise Nelson, Adam LaCosse, Marc Palecek, Josh Campbell, Brian Mutschler, Mgr.-Melanie Holmberg. Row 2: Jason Higgins, Sean Flaherty, S. O'Connell, John Yaeger, Brian Day, T. Miller, E. Rogness, B. Crowder. Row 3: Head Coach-Don Campbell, Chad Nelson, Don Harvieux, Steve Walters, Brian Scheel, M. Foettger, J. Powell, Ass't Coach-Ricky Michel. Row 4: J. Dornbush, Tony Polzin, Eric St. Martin, Chad Fredkove, Glenn Harris, Ryan Hessels, D. Moser.

Stillwater (Class AA) — 1991

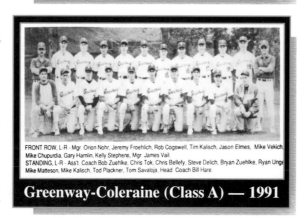

FRONT ROW, L-R - Mgr. Orion Nohr, Jeremy Froehlich, Rob Cogswell, Tim Kalisch, Jason Elmes, Mike Vekich, Mike Chupurdia, Gary Hamlin, Kelly Stephens, Mgr. James Vail. STANDING, L-R - Ass't. Coach Bob Zuehlke, Chris Tok, Chris Bellefy, Steve Delich, Bryan Zuehlke, Ryan Unge, Mike Matteson, Mike Kalisch, Tod Plackner, Tom Savaloja, Head Coach Bill Hare.

Greenway-Coleraine (Class A) — 1991

1992: Cretin-Derham Hall vs. Osseo (CLASS AA)

Played at both Dick Siebert Field on the University of Minnesota's campus and also at Municipal Stadium in St. Paul, the Class AA Tourney opened with Cretin blanking Apple Valley, 7-0, while Game Two had Irondale edging Little Falls, 5-4. Game Three was a blow-out as Minnetonka pounded Mankato West, 11-1. Center Fielder Jay Mikenas, Catcher Mike Simonson and Right Fielder Chris Kasid each had a pair of RBI's in this one. The last quarter was a close one as Osseo snuck past Forest Lake, 4-3, behind Shortstop Brian Zaun's three hits, two runs and one RBI to advance to the semis.

The opening semifinal was a wild one as Cretin outlasted Irondale, 13-9. Scoring a pair of runs each in this one were: Pitcher Steve Rosga, Right Fielder Chris Walsh, Left Fielder Chris Schwab and Center Fielder Tom Salmen. In addition, Catcher Dan Bryan drove in three runs while Rosga managed to strike out seven batters in just three innings of pitching. The other semi had Osseo edging out Minnetonka, 3-2, thanks to Pitcher Shon Burns' six strike-out, three hitter. Leading the way for the Orioles were Center Fielder Matt Wojtowich and DH Matt McDonough, who each had a hit, scored a run and drove in an RBI in this one.

The Finals were all Cretin, as the Raiders capped their school's sixth Class AA tournament title, a new record, with a five-inning drubbing of Osseo. The 15-5 score was also a record for the most runs scored in a title game. Left Fielder Chris Schwab and Third Baseman Tim Smith each had two hits, two runs and three RBI's in this one, while Brien, Heather and St. Martin each knocked in a pair of runs as well.

1992: Rocori of Cold Spring vs. Greenway-Coleraine (CLASS A)

Played at both Rocori High School and at Dick Putz Field in St. Cloud, the Class A Tourney opened with Pine Island blanking LeCenter, 10-0. Pitcher Chad Schroeder, Center Fielder Dan Drazan, Left Fielder Craig Muenkel and Third Baseman Scott Kunz each scored a pair of runs in this one. Greenway, behind DH Bob Zuehlke's four RBI's and Shortstop Gabe Troumbly's trio of hits, runs and RBI's, earned the right to defend its title with a 12-2, five-inning defeat of Brooklyn Center in Game Two. Game Three had Slayton shutting out New York Mills, 4-0, behind Pitcher Stuart Lang's two RBI's and run scored. Finally, in the last quarterfinal of the day, Rocori, behind Right Fielder Josh Loesch's three hits, three runs and five RBI's, opened its tournament title bid with a 14-4, six-inning defeat of Minnewaska Area.

The first semifinal had Greenway-Coleraine downing Pine Island, 3-1, thanks to a three-run second inning which saw Pitcher Mike Vekich, Catcher Tim Kalisch and Third Baseman Gary Hamlin each touch home plate. Vekich allowed just three hits in the win. The other semi was a blow-out as Rocori pounded Slayton, 11-1, in five-innings. Leading the charge in this one were Pitcher Troy Stein, Shortstop Steve Huls, and First Baseman Scott Fuchs, who each touched home plate twice. Stein allowed six hits while striking out six in this one.

The Finals were all Rocori of Cold Spring, which avenged its 1991 championship loss to Greenway-Coleraine, by downing the Raiders, 4-1. The Spartans got two in the fourth and added two more in the sixth to ice this one. Right Fielder Josh Loesch, Third Baseman Ben Griffen, Pitcher Greg Drontle and Catcher Marcus Bergner each touched home plate in this contest, while Drontle K'd six and allowed just three hits in the big win.

1993: Coon Rapids vs. Forest Lake (CLASS AA)

Due to heavy rains, the 1993 Tourney not only forced the cancellation of the third-place and consolation games, it also saw the games moved indoors to be played in the Metrodome. There, in Game One, Coon Rapids scored four in the first and rolled over Rosemount, 7-0. Pitcher Jeff Pelkey not only tossed a shut-out, he also got three hits, scored three runs and drove in three RBI's as well. Game Two saw Park of Cottage Grove defeat Chaska, 5-3, behind Third Baseman Adam Bestel's two hits and two RBI's. The third quarterfinal had Little Falls edging Osseo, 6-4, thanks to a dramatic four-run seventh inning rally and Pitcher Jason Dobis' pair of hits and runs. Game Four was a shut-out as Forest Lake blanked Minnetonka, 2-0, thanks to a pair of fifth inning runs from Catcher Matt Joesting and Center Fielder Ryan Poepard.

Coon Rapids defeated Park, 7-3, in the first semifinal game, thanks to an amazing seven-run, sixth inning explosion. Leading the charge were Left Fielder Jim Peregrin and Catcher Nick Izzo, who each drove in a pair of runs. The other semi was a blow-out as Forest Lake snubbed Little Falls, 6-0. The Rangers scored two in the first and added four more in the fourth to ice this one. The Poepards, Shortstop Scott and Center Fielder Ryan, each had a pair of hits to help propel their squad to the Finals.

The Finals were a wild one as Coon Rapids doubled up on Forest Lake, 4-2, to win the title. Up 3-2 in the fifth, Cardinals' Left Fielder Jim Peregrin ice it when he scored on an inside-the-park home run. The Rangers rallied in the seventh though. After Rangers' Left Fielder Aaron Wilborn led off with a single, his third of the game, Scott Gerten drove a fastball deep to right field — only to see Coon Rapids Right Fielder Brandon Groebner come up with a spectacular leaping catch at the wall to kill the rally. Cardinals' Pitcher Jeff Pelkey then struck out the side for the victory.

Cretin (Class AA) — 1992

CRETIN-DERHAM HALL—1992 State Class AA Champion

Rocori, Cold Spring (Class A) — 1992

ROCORI, Cold Spring—1992 State Class A Champion

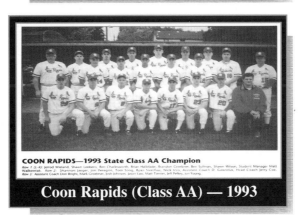

COON RAPIDS—1993 State Class AA Champion

Coon Rapids (Class AA) — 1993

1993: Greenway-Coleraine vs. Fairmont (CLASS A)

Dick Putz Field in St. Cloud was the site of the first two rounds of the 1993 Tourney where Mt. Lake/Butterfield-Odin defeated Pine Island, 7-3, in the opener. Left Fielder Levi Sanders scored a pair of runs in this one while Center Fielder Shane Marcy and Catcher Matt Buller each added a pair of hits. Game Two had Fairmont crushing Sauk Centre, 8-3, thanks to a five-run fourth inning tirade. Shortstop Jay Katzenmeyer, Pitcher Andy Nelson and First Baseman Kyle Siefert each had multiple hits in this one, while Siefert added four RBI's as well. Game Three saw Sebeka defeat Sibley East, 5-1, thanks to Right Fielder Greg Lillquist's two hits and two runs. Finally, in Game Four, Greenway pounded St. Michael-Albertville, 11-3, behind Center Fielder Jeremy Froehlich's two-run homer in the fifth.

Fairmont then advanced to the title game with an 8-4 drubbing of Mt. Lake/Butterfield-Odin in the first semifinal. Shortstop Jay Katzenmeyer led off the game with a dinger and First Baseman Kyle Siefert added three RBI's for good measure as the Cardinals cruised. The other semi featured Greenway edging Sebeka, 4-3, thanks to a dramatic game-winning two-run single by Second Baseman Bryan Zuehlke with two outs in the bottom of the seventh. Just prior to that, Third Baseman Tim Kalisch hit a homer to get the score to 3-2.

In the Finals, at the Dome, Fairmont jumped out to a 3-0 lead, only to see the Raiders rally to score four in the sixth and seventh to win the title. The dramatic game-winner came on a suicide squeeze bunt by Greenway's Jeremy Gernander to end the game and give the Raiders their fourth state title. The play was somewhat controversial because Gernander actually had two chances at the suicide squeeze. You see, his first attempt failed, but was quickly nullified by the first base umpire who had called time prior to the play because of an errant ball which had rolled onto the field from the Cardinals bullpen area. So, with the runners returned to their bases, he made good on his second chance. Gernander laid down the bunt and Bryan Zuehlke beat the throw to the plate. Greenway pitcher Mike Vekich finished the game with 11 strikeouts and finished his tremendous season at 12-0.

1994: Henry Sibley vs.
New Ulm (CLASS AA)
Rosemount opened the 1994 Class AA Tournament by doubling up on Cambridge, 6-3, thanks to a pair of hits each from Left Fielder Marc Kjeldsen and First Baseman Ryan Feezer. New Ulm blasted Irondale in Game Two, 11-6, behind DH Brady Ranweiler's five RBI. The third game of the day had Henry Sibley beating Mpls. Washburn, 5-2, on a pair of hits each from Right Fielder Rob Danneker, Center Fielder John Seidl and Third Baseman Kent Doffing. Game Four then saw Minnetonka get by Brainerd, 8-5, thanks to a seven-run first inning. DH Jim Meyer led the way in this one with a pair of hits and a pair of RBI's.

The first semifinal featured New Ulm doubling up on Rosemount, 8-4. Second Baseman David Galum, Center Fielder Brad Weber and DH Brady Ranweiler each had multiple hits in this one while Pitcher Mike Schlottman struck out five while allowing seven hits in the win. For New Ulm, it was back to the Finals. The Eagles were making their 14th tournament appearance, 12 under coach Jim Senske, who now had 515 victories — an amazing total exceeded by no one in Minnesota high school baseball history.

The other semi had Henry Sibley squeaking past Minnetonka, 4-3, despite a late Skipper rally which produced a pair of seventh inning runs. First Baseman Dan Novak, Left Fielder Corey Hessler and

Center Fielder John Seidl each had a pair of hits in this one, while Hessler also touched home plate on two occasions as well.

The Finals were as exciting as could be, and not without their share of controversy. Coach Senske, still without a state title at this point in his illustrious career, was crushed to see his boys commit two throwing errors in the top of the eighth inning which scored the two game-winning unearned runs. Here's how the 4-2 ballgame went down: Reliever Jared Visker was brought in for New Ulm in the third, and responded by retiring 10 straight batters. But in the eighth, a walk, a sacrifice bunt, another walk and then the first error — led to one run and two runners in scoring position. Then, an attempted pick-off by the Eagles catcher led to another run. New Ulm tried to rally in the last half of the inning, but went down 1-2-3 to give the title to Henry Sibley. The Warriors were led by Second Baseman Jeff Kuntz, who had a pair of hits, scored a run and added a key RBI in the win.

1994: Sibley East vs.
Sauk Centre (CLASS A)
Sibley East opened the 1994 Class A Tourney by pounding on Rochester Lourdes, 9-1, as Steve Peik tossed a two-hitter, while Matt Magers drove in three runs as well. Game Two saw Springfield outslug Faribault Acadamies, 9-6, as Catcher Jay Gostonczik's tag on a diving Ian Tyson for the controversial third out ended a four-run rally by Faribault Academies. Game Three was a real wild on with Red Lake Cty. edging Becker, 14-13. Tied at 13-13 after six innings, RLC junior Scott Lorenson drove in the winning run with a double in the top of the seventh. Game Four then saw Sauk Centre use some big innings, first with a six-run fifth and five-run sixth, to defeat Greenway, the defending champion, 12-3. Sauk Centre's Ben Dirkes and Ben Dold each had two-run singles in the fifth, while Zach State went 3-for-3, and added a two-run homer for Greenway in the loss.

Sibley East 10-run-ruled Springfield, 10-0, in a five inning semifinal contest. Wolverines Pitcher Matt Magers was awesome in this one, tossing a five-inning no-hitter to lift his squad into the Finals. Magers also went 2-for-3 with a double and two RBI's as well. The other semi had Sauk Centre downing Red Lake County, 8-5, thanks to junior Gabe Thieschafer, who went 2-for-4 with two RBI's. The Mainstreeters took the lead with a five-run third inning, and then watched Pitchers Neil Schlagel and Ben Dirkes mop it up.

The Finals then saw the Sibley East Wolverines, which fielded players from Arlington, Gaylord and Green Isle, defeat Sauk Centre, 8-6, for the 1994 Class A championship. Sibley East got five in the second to pull ahead of Sauk Centre, 7-0, and hung on to take the title. Sauk Centre rallied with five runs of their own in the bottom half of the second and added another in the third to make it, 7-6. That was as close as the Mainstreeters could get though, as the Wolverines added a final run in the seventh to clinch the victory. Reliever Steve Peik struck out five of the six batters he faced in the

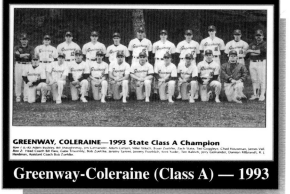

GREENWAY, COLERAINE—1993 State Class A Champion
Row 1: (L-R): Adam Buckley, Bill Shaughnessy, Jim Gernander, Adam Carlson, Mike Vekich, Bryan Zuehlke, Zach State, Ted Goggleye, Chad Houveman, James Vail. Row 2: Head Coach Bill Harju, Gabe Trisombly, Bob Zuehlke, Jeremy Tamm, Jeremy Froehlich, Kent Yoder, Tim Kalisch, Jerry Gernander, Damian Fillbrandt, R. J. Herdman, Assistant Coach Bob Zuehlke.

Greenway-Coleraine (Class A) — 1993

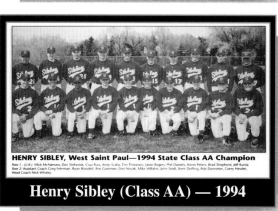

HENRY SIBLEY, West Saint Paul—1994 State Class AA Champion
Row 1: (L-R): Mick McNamara, Dan Stefaniak, Cruz Ruiz, Andy Scalia, Tim Thornton, Jason Rogers, Phil Daniels, Kevin Peters, Brad Shepherd, Jeff Kuntz. Row 2: Assistant Coach Greg Fehrman, Ryan Blaisdell, Roy Gutzman, Dan Novak, Mike Willahrt, John Seidl, Kent Doffing, Rob Danneker, Corey Hessler, Head Coach Nick Whaley.

Henry Sibley (Class AA) — 1994

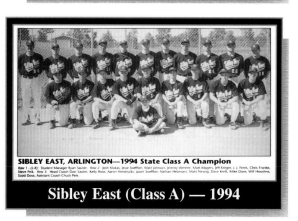

SIBLEY EAST, ARLINGTON—1994 State Class A Champion
Row 1: (L-R): Student Manager Ryan Sauter. Row 2: Josh Klukas, Jesse Soeffker, Matt Johnson, Jeremy Werner, Matt Magers, Jeff Kreger, J.J. Ferris, Chris Franke, Steve Peik. Row 3: Head Coach Don Sauter, Kelly Rose, Aaron Hendrycks, Jason Soeffker, Nathan Helsman, Matt Newvig, Dave Krell, Mike Dose, Will Hoosline, Scott Dose, Assistant Coach Chuck Peik.

Sibley East (Class A) — 1994

final two innings to ice this one.

1995: Brainerd vs. Rosemount (CLASS AA)

Rosemount first defeated Minnetonka, 7-6, in extra innings, while New Ulm downed Park Center, 3-1, in Game Two. The third game of the day had Cretin blowing past Anoka, 11-1, and in Game Four, Brainerd got past Forest Lake, 7-2.

Junior lefthander Dan Hegberg allowed just three hits en route to leading Rosemount past New Ulm, 8-2, in the first semifinal game. Hegberg was also the man with the bat, going 3-for-4 and scoring three runs, while First Baseman Lance Iverson drove in a pair of runs as well in this one. The other semifinal contest saw Brainerd defeat six-time state champion Cretin-Derham Hall, 5-4, to advance to the finals. DH Todd Anderson was the hero in this one, driving in Jade O'Brien for the game-winning run in the bottom of the seventh. In addition, the Warriors got a pair of homers from Jestin Kieffer and Jake Vincent.

The Finals were tight as the Brainerd Warriors opened the scoring with Jade O'Brien's home run in the first. In the third Rosemount sent eight batters to the plate and scored three runs, making it 3-1. Then, in the fifth, Brainerd tied it up on Josh Smith's bases loaded single which score a pair of runs to make it 3-3. Now, with one out in the top of the seventh, Wade Haapojoki stepped up and hit the game-winner — scoring Justin Kieffer scored from third. The Irish were unable to score in the bottom of the inning, giving the Warriors their 20th straight victory and first Class AA title.

1995: Crookston vs. Brooklyn Center (CLASS A)

Goodhue edged out International Falls, 9-8, in the Class A opener, while Brooklyn Center, behind All-State Pitcher Justin Dudinsky's two-hit, 12-strike-out gem, blanked Mankato Loyola, 5-0, in Game Two. Game Three saw Luverne top St. Cloud Cathedral, 6-4, and the last quarterfinal contest had Crookston outlasting Melrose, 9-7, to advance to the semifinals.

The first semifinal saw Brooklyn Center continue to roll, posting its second straight shutout — this one a 6-0 pasting of Goodhue. Pitcher Aaron Halvorson allowed just four hits and K'd nine in this one, while Mike Richter had three hits including a key two-run single in the Centaur's four-run fourth. The other semifinal had Crookston tripling up on Luverne, 9-3. First Baseman Chris Bruggeman hit his second homer of the tournament, this one a three-run shot down the left field line in the fifth inning to help his team rally from a 2-1 deficit. Pitcher Bobby Shimpa threw a six-hit complete game to get the win in this one.

The Finals were a wild one as extra-innings, replacement pitchers and errors were all key factors in Crookston's 4-3 victory over Brooklyn Center. A 3-3 tie at the end of seven innings put this one into extra innings. As a result, the rule limiting pitchers to only 14 innings in a three-day period took effect. Brooklyn Center Pitcher Justin Dudinsky, who fin-

ished with 12 strikeouts, was replaced by Aaron Halvorson, while Crookston Pitcher Bobby Shimpa left for Chris Bruggeman. With both pitchers settled down, the play got hot in the 10th, when Crookston's Mike Richter hit a grounder past the second baseman. The ensuing error then allowed Marty Aubol to score from third base to seal the deal.

1996: Cretin-Derham Hall vs. Brainerd (CLASS AA)

The first Class AA game, held at the U of M's Siebert Field, was a wild one as Brainerd downed Rosemount, 16-10. Down 6-2 after four, Brainerd, behind Chris Studer's three-run homer, rallied for two runs in the sixth and an amazing 12 in the top of the seventh to come back and win. Game Two was also a thriller, when, in the top of the 11th, Grand Rapids' First Baseman Paul Kuschel hit a two-run homer to give his Thunderhawks a 6-4 win. Game Three featured Cretin, behind Pitcher Ben Birk's two-hitter, beating Minnetonka, 5-2, as Second Baseman Jake Mauer drove in two runs off the Raiders. The last quarterfinal of the day, at Midway Stadium, had Osseo capitalizing on eight Mounds View errors to win, 13-10, and advance to the semifinals. Right Fielder Ben Tangen had three hits and five RBI's for the Orioles, while Center Fielder Olaf Wick had three hits and scored three runs as well.

Defending champion Brainerd blanked Grand Rapids, 3-0, in the first semifinal. Pitcher Luke Weiland threw just 85 pitches in earning the shut-out. All-State Shortstop Jade O'Brien drove in a pair of runs while Second Baseman Mike Bjerkeness had two hits and scored a run as well. The other semi was a blow-out as Cretin hammered Osseo, 10-1. Pitcher Mike Honsa was awesome in this one, throwing five shut-out innings while also going 4-4 with four RBI's at the plate to boot.

The Finals were tight as Cretin hung on to beat the defending champs from Brainerd, 6-4, in a rematch of the previous year's semifinal game that Brainerd won, 5-4. A third inning Jon St. Aubin single followed by a Jake Mauer hit scored three runs and gave the Raiders their first lead of the game. But a fourth-inning Jade O'Brien homer tied it up, followed just moments later by a Chris Studer home run to give the Warriors the lead. Cretin went on to score four runs than inning to make the score 6-3. Warriors' Third Baseman Jeff Barrett then scored in the fifth inning to cut the deficit to two, but Pitcher Ben Birk closed out the game in style. The seventh inning was a nail-biter, though, as Jade O'Brien popped up to shortstop Jon Guion with the bases loaded to end the game. It was Cretin's seventh championship title in 17 years — the most-ever in state tournament history.

1996: Rochester Lourdes vs. Orono (CLASS A)

The Class A Tourney opened with Rochester Lourdes shutting out Sauk Centre thanks to Pitcher Joe Siple's three-hitter and Russ Dylla's three hits. Game Two saw Pitcher Brian Jenneke

BRAINERD—1995 State Class AA Champion
Row 1 - (L-R): Jake Vincent, Mike Shogren, Josh Smith, Al Barkley, Aaron Eide. Row 2: Jade O'Brien, Tony Whitlock, Jeff Barrett, Chas Bertram, Ryan Thiesse, Joe Browning, Mike Bjerkeness. Row 3: Head Coach Lowell Scearcy, Todd Anderson, Brad Streff, Wade Haapojoki, Luke Weiland, Justin Kieffer, Jason Beyer, Student Manager Mark Malinowski. Not pictured: Assistant Coach Keith Peterson.

Brainerd (Class AA) — 1995

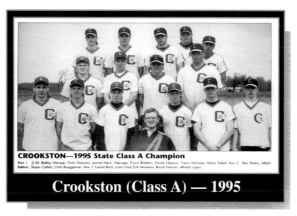

CROOKSTON—1995 State Class A Champion
Row 1 - (L-R): Bobby Shimpa, Chris Peterson, Jerrod Hann, Manager Travis Brekken, David Clauson, Travis Nicholas, Marty Aubol. Row 2: Ben Parkin, Mitch Bakken, Shaun Corbin, Chris Bruggeman. Row 3: Garret Rock, Justin Paul, Erik Monteen, Brock Hanson, Alfredo Lopez.

Crookston (Class A) — 1995

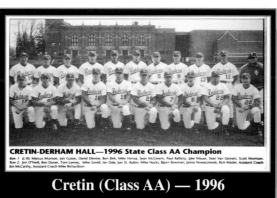

CRETIN-DERHAM HALL—1996 State Class AA Champion
Row 1 - (L-R): Marcus Munson, Jon Guion, David Devine, Ben Birk, Mike Honsa, Sean McGovern, Paul Rafferty, Jake Mauer, Sean Van Gemert, Scott Morrison. Row 2: Jon O'Neill, Ben Doran, Tom Lemey, Mike Sowell, Ian Dale, Jon St. Aubin, Mike Hocks, Bjorn Bowman, Jamie Nowaczewski, Rich Mader, Assistant Coach Jim McCarthy, Assistant Coach Mike Richardson.

Cretin (Class AA) — 1996

strike out 11 while allowing just six hits in Glencoe-Silver Lake's 3-1 win over Mankato Loyola. Orono, behind a pair of three-run homers each from Tommy John and Adam Gregg, advanced to the semis with a 15-4 trouncing of Montevideo in the third game. Then, in Game Four, Wadena-Deer Creek beat up on Hermantown, 8-2, behind a pair of hits each from seniors Jason Mahlen and Todd Wright.

Four double plays sparked Rochester Lourdes past Glencoe-Silver Lake, 6-1, in the first semifinal game. Lourdes capitalized on five Glencoe-Silver Lake errors in this one to advance to the Finals. In the other semifinal contest, Orono rallied to beat Wadena-Deer Creek, 8-7, in a real classic. Wadena-Deer Creek took an early 6-0 lead, but watched it slip away behind Orono infielder Tommy John's two clutch hits. Down 7-4 in the seventh, Orono got singles from John Hildelink, Brandon Schlinz and Tommy John to make it 7-5. Pat McPherson then drove in the tying run and they got the game-winner on a wild pitch by Corey Eckhoff to end it.

In their second tournament appearance, Rochester Lourdes won their first-ever Class A baseball title by defeating Orono in another wild one, 12-11. In what turned out to be the second-highest scoring game in tournament history, the top-ranked Lourdes scored seven fifth inning runs on only three hits to build what seemed like a safe 12-5 lead. Orono rallied though, but came up just short in the end. Lourdes was led by Joe Siple and Mike Hohberger, who each had two-run doubles in this one. When it was all said and done, 23 runs were scored on 15 hits, 12 errors, 11 walks, three wild pitches, three hit batters, one balk and one batter reaching first base after striking out.

1997: Cretin-Derham Hall vs. Coon Rapids (CLASS AA)

St. Cloud Tech downed Chaska, 4-1, in Game One behind Shortstop Aaron Sakkinen's two hits and three RBI's. Seven runs in the first three innings propelled Coon Rapids past Hopkins, 8-6, in Game Two, as Brent Hamilton went deep in this one with a two-run homer. Game Three saw Park Center get past Rosemount, 5-1, behind Outfielder Scott Reimann and Catcher Matt Mann, who each had a pair of hits. The last quarterfinal featured the defending champs from Cretin out-dueling Cold Spring, 9-6, to advance to the Finals. Jake Mauer, Jamie Nowaczewski and Rich Mader each had two hits apiece in this one.

Coon Rapids rolled in the first semifinal, 9-4, over St. Cloud Tech. Junior Pitcher Doug Groebner got the "W" in this one, retiring 15 of the final 16 batters he faced. First Baseman Drew Dehnicke's two-run single gave Coon Rapids a 6-4 lead and the Cards never looked back. Second Baseman Cameron Nelson followed that with a two-run double to seal the deal. The other semifinal had Cretin getting over on Park Center, 9-5, thanks to future big-leaguer Jack Hannahan's three runs. Pitcher Keith Arnold got the win as he threw strong down the stretch.

Cretin then won its third consecutive Class AA baseball title, this time with a shortened five inning, 10-0, shut-out at

Midway Stadium in St. Paul. It was the Raiders' eighth championship. The Raiders scored four runs on four hits in the first inning and added four more runs on three hits in the second. Pitcher Brian Whinnery led the Raiders from the mound, while Catcher Scott Morrison added three RBI's in the win. Future Twins draftee Jake Mauer's fifth inning single scored the 10th run to drive the final nail in the coffin.

1997: Cherry vs. Melrose (CLASS A)

Cannon Falls opened the 1997 Class A Tourney by downing Wadena-Deer Creek, 5-2, thanks to Pitcher Keith Meyers, who tossed a five-hitter and also drove in a run. Game Two had Melrose tripling up on Benson, 9-3, as Mike Wuertz hit a three-run homer in the sixth to rally his Dutchmen to victory. The third game of the day had Cherry-Iron beating Lake Crystal-Wellcome Memorial, 7-1, Pitcher Eric Goerdt tossed a three-hitter and also went 2-for-4 with a pair of doubles. The last quarter of the day was a blow-out as Brooklyn Center bombed Sartell, 9-0, thanks to Pitcher Mike Dubois' one-hit gem. Centaur Third Baseman Brad Weappa added a double, homer and four RBI's as well.

Melrose hammered Cannon Falls in the opening semifinal game, 14-0. This one was cut short as Melrose scored 14 runs on eight extra base hits before the start of the fourth inning. Second Baseman Jeremy Berscheit led the charge offensively with a pair of hits and three RBI's, while Catcher Eric Spanier also added a towering two-run homer as well. The other semi had Cherry-Iron outlasting Brooklyn Center, 10-7, thanks to a seven-run third inning. First Baseman Eric Goerdt went 3-for-4 and added a pair of runs in this one, while Brooklyn Center Shortstop Bob Skarset took one over the fence in the loss.

Just three years after starting a baseball program, Cherry shut out Melrose, 3-0, to claim the Class A state title. Leading the charge for the Dutchmen was Pitcher Corey Kemp, who had four hits and a run in the huge victory. Josh Bernard scored following his double, as did Eli Anderson, who scored on a double steal. Strong defense was the key in this one as Melrose star Eric Spanier was thrown out at home in the first inning, while Aaron Aimonetti made a pair of spectacular diving catches to preserve the shut-out.

1998: Cretin-Derham Hall vs. Eden Prairie (CLASS AA)

The opening quarterfinal of the 1998 Class AA Tourney opened with Champlin Park scoring six runs in the first two innings and then holding off the late charging Duluth East Greyhounds to win, 6-5. The Rebels were led by Second Baseman Andy Trocke, who hit a three-run homer in the top of the second, as well as Pitcher Ryan Semans, who struck out nine in the victory. Game Two saw Eden Prairie blank Maple Grove 4-0, as Eagle Pitcher Chris Hartshorn allowed just two hits while striking out nine.

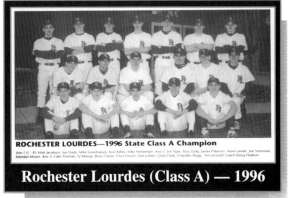

ROCHESTER LOURDES—1996 State Class A Champion
Row 1 (L - R): Matt Jacobson, Joe Dudas, Mike Goodnature, Kyle Kelley, Mike Hohberger. Row 2: Joe Siple, Russ Dylla, James Peterson, Mark Lawler, Joe Sorenson, Brendan Moore. Row 3: Colin Thomas, Ty Murray, Brian Turner, Chris Yocum, Dan Lawler, Chad Clark, Chandler Hegg. Not pictured: Coach Doug Hudson.

Rochester Lourdes (Class A) — 1996

CRETIN-DERHAM HALL — 1997 State Class AA Champion
Row 1 (L-R): Brian McQuillan, Nick Birk, Jamie Nowaczewski, Rich Mader, Keith Arnold, Mike Sovell, Ryan Donnelly, Blair Henry, Ian O'Connell, Bjorn Bowman. Row 2: Mike Richardson, Scott Morrison, Nick Birk, Luke Vogel, Dean Greenwood, Jack Hannahan, Brian Cornick, David McMahon, Jake Mauer, Brian Whinnery, Jim O'Neill.

Cretin (Class AA) — 1997

CHERRY, Iron — 1997 State Class A Champion
Row 1 (L - R): Andy Asuma, Tim Luukkonen, Bryan Ellis, Brian Constantine, Chad Greenly, Ryan Auffman. Row 2: Coach Brian Bailey, Aaron Aimonetti, Matt Asuma, Brian Kemp, Dustin Pittman, Mark Goerdt, Josh Bernard, Assistant Coach Roger Auseng. Row 3: Mike O'Brien, Ken Peterson, Kevin Koskela, Eric Goerdt, Corey Kemp, Eli Anderson.

Cherry, Iron (Class A) — 1997

Meanwhile, Justin Netzer and Erik Winegarden both tallied home runs in the win as well. Game Three was all Cretin as senior pitcher Keith Arnold tossed a three-hit gem en route to a 6-1 win over Brainerd. The last quarterfinal had New Ulm, in its 16th tournament appearance, out-dueling Rosemount, 4-1, behind Senior Pitcher Aaron Heitzman, who tossed a four-hitter while striking out 10.

The first semifinal saw Eden Prairie roll over Champlin Park, 9-4, as Pitcher Ben Cole retired 14 of the last 18 batters to lead his Eagles to victory. The Eagles got started early in this one as Greg Forsberg hit a towering three-run dinger over the center-field wall in the first inning. The other semifinal saw two-time defending champion Cretin advance to the title game with a 9-2 win over New Ulm. Cretin First Baseman Luke Vogel hit a pair of 400-foot home runs in this one, his 18th and 19th of the season, to lead the Raiders to victory. The Raiders blew open the game with six runs in the sixth inning and hung on to take the win.

The Finals were tight, but Cretin hung on to edge Eden Prairie, 2-1, to successfully defend its Class AA title — their record ninth overall and third consecutive crown. In the process, the Raiders became the sixth team in state history and the first since 1965 to finish the season undefeated. The two hour rain delay didn't deter Raiders Pitcher Brian Winnery from showing his stuff. The senior lefthander gave up only one run and two hits in the first five innings, while Jack Hannahan came in to mop up and earn the save. With the game tied at 1-1, Cretin's Brian Gornick led off the sixth inning with a walk. First Baseman Luke Vogel then sent Gornick to third on a long single. Then, Pitcher Jayson Lenz's third strike curve ball to Mark Runyon got away from Eagles Catcher Erik Winegarden, and Gornick alertly came in to score what proved to be the game-winner. Coach Jim O'Neil had himself a dynasty.

1998: Sibley East vs. Melrose (CLASS A)

McLeod West of Brownton opened the Class A Tourney by edging Chatfield, 2-1, thanks to an eighth inning rally highlighted by Eric Schuette's clutch single which scored Ray Greiner for the game-winner. Game Two saw Sibley East destroy Perham, 12-1, in five innings — thanks to an eight-run third inning tirade. The third game of the tournament saw Melrose downing St. Agnes, 3-1, behind Pitcher Eric Meyer's five-hit complete game. In Game Four, Tracy-Milroy/Balaton out-dueled Greenway-Coleraine, 11-6, behind Brian Dolan's two hits and two RBI's.

The first semifinal was much closer than the score would indicate, as Sibley East topped McLeod West, Brownton, 16-6. Tied at six apiece, this one was suspended after five innings due to rain. So, play resumed that next morning with Sibley East scoring 10 runs in its first at bat to end it. Seven Wolverine players drove in at least two runs in this one. Eric Schuette had three RBI's and a homer in the loss. When the rain finally subsided, the other semi featured Melrose defeating Tracy-Milroy/Balaton, 3-2, behind Right Fielder Mike West's two RBI's. This one came down to the wire,

but thanks to Center Fielder Craig Meyer's throwing out a Panthers runner at the plate in the bottom of the seventh, they hung on to win.

Sibley East then captured its second Class A state title in its third state tournament appearance by downing Melrose, 3-2. Ryan Sauter led the Wolverines on the mound, giving up just six hits, while Nick Schatz led the Wolverines at the plate, driving in a pair of clutch RBI's. Brad Hundt and Jeremy Berscheit each scored for Melrose, while Ryan Sauter and Nick Schatz each tallied for Sibley in the first. Sibley East won 25 consecutive games to finish its championship season with an impressive 26-2 record.

1999: Hastings vs. Maple Grove (CLASS AA)

The 1999 Tourney kicked off with Eden Prairie edging a tough New Ulm squad, 3-1, as All-Metro Pitcher Chris Hartshorn tossed a two-hitter and also smacked two hits and drove in two runs as well. Maple Grove defeated the first-time qualifiers from St. Francis, 5-2, in Game Two, as Jon Dubel and Caleb Marx each had RBI singles for the Crimson. The third game saw Hastings beat Rochester Mayo, 7-2, as Adam Gerlach had four RBI for the Raiders, while Matt VanDerBosch had two hits, including a homer. Game Four then saw Little Falls edge Mounds View, 3-2, thanks to Aaron Hennes, who stole home in the top of the seventh to score the game-winner for the Flyers.

The first semifinal featured Hastings roughing up Little Falls, 10-3. The Flyers committed four errors in this one, three of which led to Hastings runs. The Raiders' four-run second was sparked by back-to-back infield singles from Dan Welch and Adam Gerlach. Then, the Raiders scored six runs in the bottom of the fifth, led by a two-run homer by Third Baseman Ben Tharp.

The other semi then saw Maple Grove edge Eden Prairie in a nine inning thriller, 3-2. Pitcher C.J. Woodrow gave up only four hits and two unearned runs in this one as Maple Grove hung on to advance to the Finals. Maple Grove got a scare in the seventh when Eden Prairie Second Baseman Nick Hanson hit a single that drove in John Cornell, tying the score at 2-2. Now, in the top of the ninth, the Crimson loaded the bases. First Baseman Jeremy Oligmueller then hit a sacrifice fly to left field, scoring David Bullen for the winning run.

In the Finals, Hastings scored three runs on a trio of hits in the fourth inning to beat Maple Grove, 4-2. Hastings took a 1-0 lead in the bottom of the second Right Fielder Adam Gerlach tripled to right and scored on a grounder. The Crimson tried to rally, scoring a pair of runs in the fifth, but the Raiders hung on to take home the hardware. Wade Johnson, who went five innings and allowed just two runs, got the victory for the Raiders. Incredibly, Hastings' Ben Tharp and Jeff Taffe, each went on to play Gopher Hockey, and were later drafted into the NHL.

(It is interesting to note that Hastings also made history earlier in the year when they upset the nationally ranked Cretin-Durham Hall squad,

CRETIN-DERHAM HALL — 1998 State Class AA Champion
Row 1 (L-R): Brian McQuillan, J. P. Gagne, Dom D'Valle, Matt Domarus, Lonny Leitner, Mark Runyon, Brian Corcoran, Josh Howard, Ryan Block, David McMahon. Row 2: Jim O'Neill, Brian Gornick, Brian Whinnery, Luke Vogel, Jack Hannahan, Keith Arnold, Dean Greenwood, Bill Mauer, Jon Marzolf, Dan Salmen, Mike Richardson, Nick Birk, Snap Leitner

Cretin (Class AA) — 1998

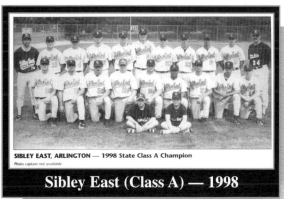

SIBLEY EAST, ARLINGTON — 1998 State Class A Champion
Photo caption not available

Sibley East (Class A) — 1998

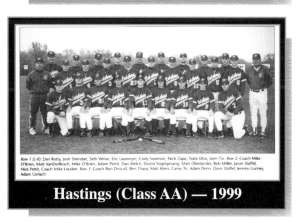

Row 1 (L-R): Dan Rotty, Josh Sheridan, Seth Weise, Eric Laumeyer, Cody Swanson, Nick Zajac, Nate Otto, John Trix. Row 2: Coach Mike O'Brien, Matt VanDerBosch, Mike O'Brien, Adam Pettit, Dan Welch, Dustin Vogelgesang, Matt Oberlander, Bob Miller, Jason Stoffel, Nick Pettit, Coach Mike Louden. Row 3: Coach Ron Driscoll, Ben Tharp, Matt Klein, Carey Trix, Adam Denn, Dave Stoffel, Jeremy Gurney, Adam Gerlach

Hastings (Class AA) — 1999

breaking up their 66-game winning streak — the second longest in high school baseball history — along the way.)

1999: Montgomery-Lonsdale vs. Breck (CLASS A)

Montgomery-Lonsdale, behind Senior Brian Vosejpka's five-hit shutout, blanked LaCrescent, 4-0, in the opening quarterfinal contest. Game Two was tight, as the Breck Mustangs, who trailed Greenway-Coleraine, 6-1 in the top of the seventh, rallied for six runs behind John Bean's thrilling game-winning three-RBI double in the final inning to seal the deal. Game Three saw Tracy-Milroy/Balaton/Prairie Home Academy crush Frazee, 12-1, in five innings, as senior Josh Holiway led the Panthers with three RBI's while Pitcher Brendan Rokke gave up three hits. St. Cloud Cathedral then downed Melrose, 5-3, in Game Four as the Crusaders rallied for three runs against the Dutchmen in the top of the seventh, highlighted by Nate Baraga's two-run double to right.

In the first semifinal, the Montgomery-Lonsdale Redbirds slid by Saint Cloud Cathedral 2-1. The Crusaders led 1-0 until the bottom of the fourth in this one. That's when both Mark Miller and Jirik each drove in an RBI apiece for the Redbirds to propel their squads into the Finals. Junior Chris Ziskovsky and senior Brian Vosejpka combined a one-hitter in this one. Then, in the other semi, Breck snuck past Tracy-Milroy/Balaton/Prairie Home Academy, 4-3, when David O'Hagen scored on an unearned run in the second inning. The run proved to be the game-winner as Breck hung on from there to get into the title game.

In the Finals, Montgomery-Lonsdale pounded on Breck, 15-5, to claim the crown. Breck jumped out to an early 2-0 lead in this one, only to see the Redbirds roar back with seven runs on four hits in the second inning. From there the Redbirds never looked back as Pitchers Mike Jirik and Brian Vosejpka held Breck to just three more runs. Leading the charge for Montgomery-Lonsdale were Chris Ziskovsky, who went 3-for-3 with a pair of RBIs, and Chad Vosejpka, who went 2-for-4 with two RBI's of his own. (The Vosejpka cousins: Brian, Chad and Brad, accounted for six runs, three hits and four RBI in this one.)

2000: Brainerd vs. Lakeville (CLASS AAA)

In the year 2000, the Tourney's format was once again changed — this time to a three-class system of AAA, AA and A.

With that, the opening round of the AAA tournament kicked off with Maple Grove topping Mankato East, 5-1. In Game Two, Lakeville, behind Justin Ancel's three-hitter, beat Bloomington Kennedy, 5-1. Third Baseman John Arlt led Lakeville with two RBIs. Brainerd defeated Elk River Area, 5-4, in the third quarterfinal as Ty Adams singled and eventually scored the game-winner on an unearned run to break a 4-4 tie on the fifth inning. Game Four then saw Mounds View cruise past the perennial champs from Cretin, 5-1, to advance to the semis.

In the first semifinal game, Lakeville edged Maple Grove, 7-4. Flash-forward to the sixth inning, when the Panthers loaded the bases on a pair of walks and a single. That's when Mark Czerniak got beaned while Bryant Rogness and Adam VanGrinsven, the next two batters, both walked, to bring in two more runs and ice it. The other semi was a wash as Brainerd blanked Mounds View, 4-0. The Warriors allowed just four hits in this one to advance on to the Finals.

The title tilt was all Brainerd as the Warriors defeated the first-time qualifiers from Lakeville, 4-1. Brainerd jumped out to an early lead in this one when Nathan Thomas reached on a walk, advanced to third on Kevin Ericson's double, and then scored on Left Fielder Chris Macy's grounder. Lakeville tied it up in the bottom of the second when Ash Larson scored on a pair of Brainerd errors. The Warriors came right back in the third though behind Tim Siekas' lead-off single which was followed by Kyle Berg's deep fly ball that was dropped, which allowed Siekas to score. Brainerd scored their last two runs in the fifth inning on a two-out single by Chris Macy to seal the deal and bring home the hardware.

2000: St. Michael-Albertville vs. Montgomery-Lonsdale (CLASS AA)

In the opening quarterfinal St. Michael-Albertville notched an 11-7 victory over Perham, while Jackson County Central defeated Blue Earth Area, 7-1, in Game Two. The other quarterfinals then featured Montgomery-Lonsdale squeaking by Byron, 5-4, in 9 innings, while Esko beat Minnewaska Area of Glenwood, 5-0, as well.

In the first semifinal, St. Michael-Albertville beat the first-time qualifiers from Jackson County Central, 6-3. Pitcher Derek Brant tossed a complete game five-hitter and added seven strike-outs for good measure en route to leading the Knights into the title game. The other semi featured the Montgomery-Lonsdale Redbirds beating up on the newcomers from Esko, 10-0. Montgomery-Lonsdale went up 3-0 in the first when Brad Vosejpka hit an inside-the-park home run. The Redbirds added two more runs in third, and an additional five in the fourth to seal the deal.

In the Class AA title game, the Knights of St. Michael- Albertville defeated the defending Class A champs from Montgomery-Lonsdale, 8-5, to win their first championship. The Knights jumped out to a quick 1-0 lead when Eric Kolles hit a 360-foot opposite-field homer in the bottom of the second. Then, in the fourth, St. Michael-Albertville's Randy Dehmer drove in a pair of runs off of a double to the gap to give his Knights a 4-3 lead. St. Michael-Albertville went on to score three more runs in the fifth, while Knights' Pitcher Jesse Scherber hung tough down the stretch to bring the title home.

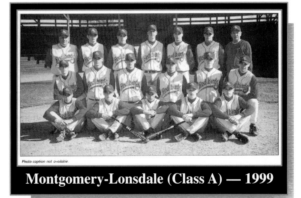

Photo caption not available.

Montgomery-Lonsdale (Class A) — 1999

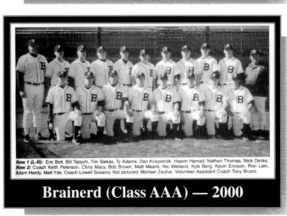

Row 1 (L-R): Eric Bolt, Bill Tadych, Tim Siekas, Ty Adams, Dan Kirkpatrick, Hason Hamad, Nathan Thomas, Nick Dircks. Row 2: Coach Keith Peterson, Chris Macy, Bob Brown, Matt Means, Nic Weiland, Kyle Berg, Kevin Ericson, Ron Lien, Adam Hardy, Matt Yde, Coach Lowell Scearcy. Not pictured: Michael Zauhar, Volunteer Assistant Coach Tony Bruno.

Brainerd (Class AAA) — 2000

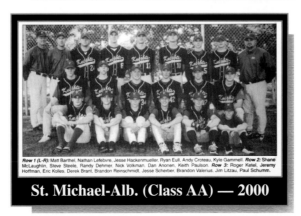

Row 1 (L-R): Matt Barthel, Nathan Lefebvre, Jesse Hackenmueller, Ryan Eull, Andy Croteau, Kyle Gammell. Row 2: Shane McLaughlin, Steve Steele, Randy Dehmer, Nick Volkman, Dan Anonen, Keith Paulson. Row 3: Roger Ketel, Jeremy Hoffman, Eric Kolles, Derek Brant, Brandon Reinschmidt, Jesse Scherber, Brandon Valerius, Jim Litzau, Paul Schumm.

St. Michael-Alb. (Class AA) — 2000

2000: Sleepy Eye vs. Lester Prairie (CLASS A)

Ely, behind Nick Levar's stellar play, blanked Hinckley-Finlayson, 3-0, in the opening round of Class A Tourney play. Sleepy Eye stomped on Bertha-Hewitt, 11-1, in the second quarterfinal as the Indians scored nine unearned runs in the fifth to break this one open. Game Three went down to the wire as Lester Prairie defeated Badger-Greenbush-Middle River (BGMR), 7-5, to advance to the semis. BGMR had the bases loaded in the bottom of the seventh, when Lester Prairie Pitcher Andy Ross struck out the final two batters to seal the deal. Then, in Game Four, Dover-Eyota, behind Jacob Zamrow's solid play, edged out Kerkhoven-Murdock-Sunberg, 3-2.

In the first semifinal, Sleepy Eye crushed Ely, 11-0. Indians Pitcher Jim Eckstein had nine strikeouts in five innings, while Steve Geschwind scored a pair of runs to boot. The other semi then saw Lester Prairie defeat the first-time qualifiers from Dover--Eyota, 2-0, to advance to the Finals.

The Finals were a wash, as Sleepy Eye cruised to its second overall title by blanking Lester Prairie, 4-0, to take the inaugural Class A crown. Lester Prairie Pitcher Josh Eckstein kept the Indians in check in this one until the fifth, when Sleepy Eye Right Fielder Bryce Belseth led off the inning with a double, and then advanced to third on a wild pitch. Second Baseman Loren Havemeier then drove him home with a single to make it, 1-0. Havemeier later scored on First Baseman Bryan Weiss' sacrifice fly to make it 2-0. Then, in the seventh, Havemeier and Catcher Mike Nachreiner each scored to put the Indians ahead for good. Sleepy Eye pitcher Cole Deibele was awesome on the mound, allowing just three hits while fanning seven.

2001: Cretin-Derham Hall vs. Rochester Mayo (CLASS AAA)

The 2001 Glass AAA Tournament, which was played at both Midway Stadium in St. Paul and at Dick Siebert Field at the U of M, opened with Cretin-Derham Hall blanking Forest Lake, 6-0. Pitcher Tony Leseman tossed a three-hitter while Outfielder Mark Dunnigan and Shortstop Cale Leiviska each went 2-for-3 and drove in one run apiece as the Raiders cruised. In the other quarterfinal games, Brainerd shut-out New Ulm 1-0, Holy Angels, behind the solid play of Gory Garven and Dominic Lawrence, beat Stillwater Area 1-0, and Rochester Mayo topped Maple Grove 7-3.

The first semifinal was a classic as Cretin rallied from 4-1 deficit to defeat the defending champs from Brainerd, 5-4. Down 1-0, Brainerd tied it up when Cretin Pitcher Sean Spencer walked in the first run. The Warriors' Adam Hardy then drove in two more runs on a bouncing liner. Cretin, trailing 4-1 in the fifth, then had Joe Mauer come to the plate with both Rob Runyon and Kim Sarin on first and second. That's when Mauer, the three sport All-American who was taken by the Twins as the No. 1 pick in the major league draft the week before the tournament, stepped up and hit a 390-foot homer to right-center field to tie it up. Then, in the bottom of the fifth, Mauer

replaced Leseman on the mound — striking our nine barters and only allowed one hit over what proved to be the next five innings. The Raiders finally iced it when First Baseman Matt Egan hit a fly ball that was caught, but the ensuing throw to the plate was high, giving them the win. The other semi then had Rochester Mayo downing Holy Angels, 8-2, to set up a solid Finals.

In the Finals, Cretin rolled over Rochester Mayo, 13-2, in five innings to claim their 10th championship in their 16th tournament appearance. The Raiders were ahead 5-2 heading into the fourth and they drove in eight more runs that inning as well. Rob Runyon, Satin, and Dunnigan each hit consecutive singles, while Mauer, Egan, Gale Leiviska and Daren Richardson each doubled, followed by another Runyon single. By now, the Spartans were on their third pitcher, and the Raiders were in the midst of a good ol' fashioned blow-out. When the smoke had cleared, Mauer was 3-for-3, with a triple and two singles, while Egan and Runyon each drove in three runs, and added a pair of RBIs.

"Over the last decade and a half Dennis Denning and Jimmy O'Neil have really made Cretin the No. 1 baseball school in the state," said Cretin alum Paul Molitor. "I mean they haven't won them all but they have certainly been at the doorstep almost every year. They just have such a great program from top to bottom there. And, when you talk about losing kids to other sports, they just have not had that problem at all. Their coaching staff is great and they have created a winning attitude that is just outstanding. They have summer camps and even wind up with like three freshman teams because so many kids want to try out. I follow them and am really proud of them."

2001: St. Cloud Cathedral vs. Luverne (CLASS AA)

The 2001 Class AA Tournament was played in St. Cloud at both Dick Putz Stadium and the adjacent Joe Faber Field. There, the opening round opened with Hermantown defeating Rochester Lourdes 1-0. In Game Two, St. Cloud Cathedral knocked off Perham, 6-3, behind a pair of RBI's each from Brian Mathiasen and Charlie Hoffman. Luverne beat the first-time qualifiers from Atwater-Cosmos-Grove City 6-3 in its quarterfinal game, while Blue Earth Area, behind Todd Rasmussen's hot bat, got past Mora, 7-3, to advance to the semis.

In the first semifinal, St. Cloud Cathedral snuck past Hermantown with a 4-3 victory. Hermantown scored one run in the first, and two more in the third, but the Crusaders rallied to make it 3-2 when Tony Dingmann hit a two-run double in the bottom of the third. Cathedral then tied the game in the fourth on an error, and took the lead for good in the fifth on Dingmann's second double of the game. The other semi, meanwhile, saw Luverne defeat Blue Earth Area, 9-3, to advance to the Finals.

The title game was tight, but St. Cloud Cathedral hung tough and won its fourth championship with a 6-4 victory over Luverne. The Crusaders built a 6-1 lead going into the seventh, when things started to fall apart on account of a whole

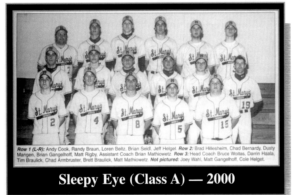

Row 1 (L-R): Andy Cook, Randy Braun, Loren Beltz, Brian Seidl, Jeff Helget. Row 2: Brad Hillesheim, Chad Bernardy, Dusty Mangen, Brian Gangelhoff, Matt Rigby, Assistant Coach Brian Mathiowetz. Row 3: Head Coach Bruce Woitas, Darrin Haala, Tim Braulick, Chad Armbruster, Brett Braulick, Matt Mathiowetz. Not pictured: Joey Wahl, Matt Gangelhoff, Cole Helget.

Sleepy Eye (Class A) — 2000

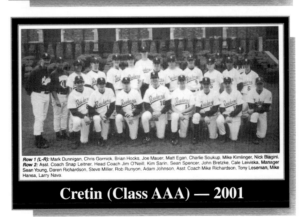

Row 1 (L-R): Mark Dunnigan, Chris Gornick, Brian Hocks, Joe Mauer, Matt Egan, Charlie Soukup, Mike Kimlinger, Nick Biagini. Row 2: Asst. Coach Snap Leitner, Head Coach Jim O'Neill, Nick Sarin, Sean Spencer, John Bretzke, Cale Leiviska, Manager Sean Young, Daren Richardson, Steve Miller, Rob Runyon, Adam Johnson, Asst. Coach Mike Richardson, Tony Leseman, Mike Hansa, Larry Nava.

Cretin (Class AAA) — 2001

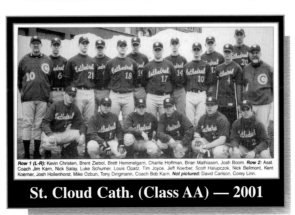

Row 1 (L-R): Kevin Christen, Brent Ziebol, Brett Hemmelgarn, Charlie Hoffman, Brian Mathiasen, Josh Boom. Row 2: Asst. Coach Jim Karn, Nick Salay, Luke Schumer, Louis Opatz, Tim Joyce, Jeff Koerber, Scott Halupczok, Nick Bellmont, Kent Koerner, Josh Hollenhorst, Mike Ozbun, Tony Dingmann, Coach Bob Karn. Not pictured: David Carlson, Corey Linn.

St. Cloud Cath. (Class AA) — 2001

bunch of errors. Luverne started hitting the ball as well, and before you knew it, the Cards were right back in it. Then, after scoring three runs and getting the tying run on first base, Pitcher Brett Hemmelgarn came in for Josh Hollenhorst and struck our final batter. Game over. Hemmelgarn had two hits and three runs in this one, while Tony Dingmann chipped in with three RBI's. Jon Jarchow led the Cardinals with a pair of hits and a pair of runs in the loss.

2001: St. Agnes vs. Sleepy Eye St. Mary's (CLASS A)

The 2001 Class A Tournament was played at both Shakopee's Tahpah Park and the Mini Met in Jordan. The opening quarterfinal got underway with St. Agnes blanking Chatfield, 3-0. In addition to knocking out a two-run double, Pitcher Adam Flaherty gave up just two hits while fanning nine in this one. In other quarterfinal action Badger/Greenbush-Middle River beat up on Eden Valley-Watkins, 7-1, Sleepy Eye St. Mary's topped Murray County Central of Slayton 7-5, and Nashwauk-Keewatin, behind the hot bats of Bob DeNucci and Sam Marrire, downed Menahga 6-2.

The first semifinal game had St. Agnes beating Badger/Greenbush-Middle River, 5-2. Pitcher Mike Valento gave up one earned run on seven hits in this one while fanning six as well. The game got off to a bang, literally, when Paul Barrett got the Aggies on the board by tattooing the first pitch of the game over the wall. Second Baseman Mike Kroona also added a pair of RBI's as the Aggies cruised into the Finals. The other semifinal was tight, but Sleepy Eye St. Mary's hung in there to edge the first-time qualifiers from Nashwatik-Keewatin, 3-2.

The Finals were all St. Agnes as the Aggies pounded Sleepy Eye St. Mary's, 16-6, to bring home their first ever state title. St. Mary's actually jumped out to a 4-0 lead in this one, only to see the Aggies roar back with six runs on a couple of key errors in the second. All told, the Knights committed eight errors in the game. Leading the offensive charge for St. Agnes were Mike Valento, who went 2-for-3, scored three runs and knocked in a pair of runs, and Dave Berthiaume, who also pitched in with a pair of runs and RBI's as well. Meanwhile, Andy Konz led Sleepy Eye St. Mary's with two runs and two RBI's in the loss.

2002: New Ulm vs. North St. Paul (CLASS AAA)

The Class AAA version of the 2002 state tourney opened with Park Center edging North St. Paul, 4-3, thanks to Jordan Roering's game-winning three-run homer in the top of the seventh. Game Two saw Pitcher Marcus McKenzie toss a three-

hitter and fanned eight en route to leading his Minnetonka Skippers past the Roseville Area Raiders, 4-0. Northfield edged Fergus Falls, 2-1, in Game Three thanks to Pitcher Kory Foss' eight strikeout gem. Finally, in Game Four, New Ulm went ballistic on St. Francis. When the smoke finally cleared in this one the scoreboard read 17-3 in five innings. Leading the way for the Eagles were Jamie Hoffmann and Jace Marti , who each had three RBI's.

The first semifinal saw North St. Paul down Minnetonka, 7-3. Kyle Richardson went 3-for-4 with three RBI and Robb Ross was 3-for-4 with two RBI to lead the Polars into the Finals. The other semi saw New Ulm rally for a 8-6 win over Northfield. Jace Marti had three hits and a RBI, Eric Austwold had two hits and three RBI's and Isaac Forstner had two hits and two RBI's for the Eagles while Chris Cariveau pitched six innings of one run, two hit relief to seal the deal. Down 5-0 after two innings of play, New Ulm got six in the third to get to the Finals.

The title game was all New Ulm, who, after 19 state tournament appearances, finally exorcised the demons with a 12-4 win over North St. Paul. Jamie Hoffmann went 4-for-4 while Dusty Fleck had two hits and three-RBI's in New Ulm's 15-hit attack. The Eagles scored six each in the first and third innings to ice this one, while Ryan Petersen went 4-for-4 for North St. Paul in the loss. For New Ulm coaching legend Jim Senske, who's coached for more than four decades, the win was oh-so-sweet!

2002: Rochester Lourdes vs. Blue Earth Area (CLASS AA)

St. Anthony Village held off a late charge by Jackson County Central to claim a dramatic 9-8 win in the opening quarterfinal game of the 2002 Class AA Tourney. Pitcher Dan O'Malley not only got the win, he also had three hits and three RBIs on a triple and home run. Game Two saw Blue Earth Area jump out to a quick 10-1 lead, only to see Paynesville Area rally back. T.J. Stallman had five RBI's for BEA, including a homer, while Wes Lieser had three hits and a pair of RBI's for Paynesville. Game Three saw Hermantown score two runs in the fourth and two more in the seventh to beat Pelican Rapids, 6-2. Brandon Swartz had three hits and four RBI's in the win. Game Four was all Rochester Lourdes, who crushed the defending champs from St. Cloud Cathedral, 11-1, in five innings. Adam Dahl had three hits, two runs and two RBI's, while Pitcher Ted Garry allowed five hits while fanning four.

The first semi had Blue Earth Area smacking St. Anthony, 10-2, behind a pair of hits each from Todd Rasmussen and Jim Grant. Lee Hodges got the "W" for BEA with four hits allowed and four strikeouts. The other semifinal saw

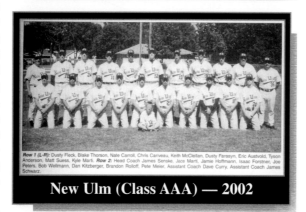

Row 1 (L-R): Kyle Quinn, Brad Rapacz, Adam Flaherty, Paul Barrett, Nick Walters, Mike Adams. Row 2: Coach Ryan Collins, Kris Nichols, John Schmit, Mike Kroona, Coach Greg Hoernke, Dave Berthaume, Mike Valento, Bill Madigan, Robbie Menne, Jordan Bauer, Greg Pepin, Coach Keith Johnson, Tim Norberg.

St. Agnes (Class A) — 2001

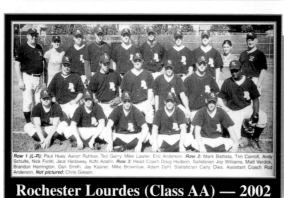

Row 1 (L-R): Dusty Fleck, Blake Thorson, Nate Carroll, Chris Cariveau, Keith McClellan, Dusty Farasyn, Eric Austvold, Tyson Anderson, Matt Suess, Kyle Marti. Row 2: Head Coach James Senske, Jace Marti, Jamie Hoffmann, Isaac Forstner, Joe Peters, Bob Wellmann, Dan Kitzberger, Brandon Rolloff, Pete Meier, Assistant Coach Dave Curry, Assistant Coach James Schwarz.

New Ulm (Class AAA) — 2002

Row 1 (L-R): Paul Huey, Aaron Ruhlow, Ted Garry, Mike Lawler, Eric Anderson. Row 2: Mark Battista, Tim Carroll, Andy Schulte, Nick Forliti, Jace Hadaway, Kolo Adafin. Row 3: Head Coach Doug Hudson, Statistician Joy Williams, Matt Verdick, Brandon Harrington, Dan Smith, Jay Kasner, Mike Brownlow, Adam Dahl, Statistician Carly Oles, Assistant Coach Rod Anderson. Not pictured: Chris Giesen.

Rochester Lourdes (Class AA) — 2002

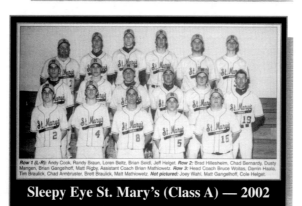

Row 1 (L-R): Andy Cook, Randy Braun, Loren Beltz, Brian Seidl, Jeff Helget. Row 2: Brad Hillesheim, Chad Bernardy, Dusty Mangen, Brian Gangelhoff, Matt Rigby, Assistant Coach Brian Mathiowetz. Row 3: Head Coach Bruce Woitas, Darrin Haala, Tim Braulick, Chad Armbruster, Brett Braulick, Matt Mathiowetz. Not pictured: Joey Wahl, Matt Gangelhoff, Cole Helget.

Sleepy Eye St. Mary's (Class A) — 2002

Rochester Lourdes gain entry to the title game with an 8-3 victory over Hermantown. Lourdes scored three in the fourth and two more in the fifth to seal the deal in this one. Paul Huey had a pair of hits and a pair of RBI's in the win, while Pitcher Mike Lawler went the distance — allowing four hits while adding seven K's.

Rochester Lourdes jumped all over Blue Earth Area in the Finals, cruising to a 15-0, 5-inning, laugher. Jay Kasner tossed a one-hit shutout that included six K's, while Mike Lawler added two hits, three RBIs and three runs for Lourdes. Right Fielder Ted Garry added three hits and a pair of RBI's as well.

2002: Sleepy Eye St. Mary's vs. Menahga (CLASS A)
The 2002 Class A Tourney kicked off with Royalton beating Adrian in Game One, 12-5. Third Baseman Josh Goedderz, Second Baseman Chris Fussy and Center Fielder Mike Wenner each had three RBI's for the Royals in the win. Game Two saw Menahga's Jamie Burkman drive in the winning run in the bottom of the fifth to give his Braves a 6-3 win over the Patriots of Win-E-Mac. In Game Three Babbitt-Embarrass/Tower-Soudan (BEST) blanked Chatfield, 8-0, on Second Baseman Joel Dostert's three hits. Pitcher Nick Herberg allowed just three hits in this one while striking out five. Game Four had St. Mary's beating Mayer Lutheran, 7-4, behind Chad Armbruster's three-run homer with two outs in the bottom of the seventh.

The first semifinal saw Menahga beat Royalton, 4-2, to advance to the Finals. Right Fielder Jamo Burkman and Shortstop Zach Etter each had a pair of RBI's in this one, while Pitcher Pete Marjamaa struck out seven in the big win. Sleepy Eye St. Mary's then topped BEST, 5-3, in the other semi. Pitcher Chad Armbruster and Third Baseman Brett Braulick each had a pair of RBI's in this one, while Shortstop Matt Mathiowetz had a couple of hits as well.

In the Finals it was Sleepy Eye St. Mary's topping Menahga, 9-8, in a barn-burner. A seven-run out-burst by the Braves to take the lead in the bottom of the fourth inning was the difference in this one.

The Knights scored three runs on four hits in the first and added two more on a pair of hits and an error to take a 5-0 lead. Menahga rallied though, and hung in there to make it interesting. Knights Left Fielder Dusty Mangen and Pitcher Darrin Haala each went 3-for-4 with two RBI's, while Shortstop Matt Mathiowetz and Right fielder Randy Braun each had a pair of hits as well. Zach Etter led the Braves with three RBI's in the tough loss.

Incidentally, the 2002 Tourney winners were credited as being from the "Highway of Champions." New Ulm (3A), Rochester Lourdes (2A) and Sleepy Eye St. Mary's (1A), are all connected by a mere 120-mile stretch along Highway 14 throughout southern Minnesota.

STATE TOURNEY ALL-TIME RECORDS (1947-2002)

Most Championships	10	Cretin-Derham Hall
Most Runners-Up	6	Austin
Most Third Place	7	New Ulm
Most Consolations	5	New Ulm
Most Appearances	19	Austin
Most Games Won	36	Cretin-Derham Hall
Most Games Lost	26	Bemidji

ALL-TIME STATE HIGH SCHOOL TOURNAMENT WINNERS

Year	Champion	(Record)	Runner-Up	Score
1947	St. Cloud Tech.	(14-1)	Glencoe	6-3
1948	Chisholm	(16-0)	Springfield	13-8
1949	Mpls. Edison	(15-2)	St. Paul Washington	6-3
1950	Duluth Denfeld	(14-1)	Buffalo	6-5
1951	Redwood Falls	(14-2)	Melrose	1-0
1952	Halstad	(13-0)	Austin	9-2
1953	St. Paul Washington	(15-2)	Austin	6-1
1954	Austin	(15-0)	Duluth Denfeld	3-2
1955	Mpls. Washburn	(17-2)	St. Paul Wilson	11-0
1956	St. Paul Washington	(16-3)	Bemidji	4-2
1957	Little Falls	(15-0)	Mankato	3-2
1958	St. Paul Johnson	(16-2)	Mpls. Washburn	6-2
1959	Mpls. Washburn	(15-3)	Austin	7-2
1960	Mpls. Washburn	(16-3)	Little Falls	4-1
1961	North St. Paul	(20-3)	Mpls. Washburn	2-0
1962	Richfield	(17-3)	Austin	4-3
1963	Mpls. Washburn	(19-1)	Hibbing	9-1
1964	Austin	(17-5)	Mpls. West	3-0
1965	Richfield	(25-0)	St. Paul Humboldt	2-1
1966	Bloom. Kennedy	(21-3)	Hastings	2-0
1967	Hastings	(17-1)	Austin	4-0
1968	Edina	(16-5-1)	Hibbing	12-4
1969	Mpls. Washburn	(18-2)	Albert Lea	5-1
1970	Albany	(15-3)	New Ulm	1-0
1971	Richfield	(24-1)	Faribault	5-0
1972	Richfield	(19-4)	Anoka	1-0
1973	Bemidji	(18-4)	Winona	3-1
1974	Owatonna	(22-4)	Willmar	6-5
1975	Bloom.Kennedy	(23-1)	Fairmont	10-4
1976	AA - Hill-Murray	(20-2)	Marshall	1-0
	A - Babbitt	(21-3)	Sleepy Eye	6-5
1977	AA - St. Peter (20-2)	Edina East	11-1	
	A - St. Cloud Cath.	(23-1)	Staples	2-1
1978	AA - Grand Rapids	(22-1)	Cooper	2-0
	A - Plainview	(20-3)	Benson	5-2
1979	AA - Little Falls	(14-7)	Minnetonka	5-4
	A - St. James	(21-2)	Fertile-Beltrami	10-2
1980	AA - Coon Rapids	(19-5)	St. Cloud Apollo	5-0
	A - St. Cloud Cath.	(17-6)	Sleepy Eye	7-0
1981	AA - Cretin	(25-1)	Waseca	11-0
	A - Sleepy Eye	(20-3)	Winona Cotter	4-1

Year	Champion	(Record)	Runner-Up	Score
1982	AA - Cretin	(22-2)	Hill-Murray	8-3
	A - Sauk Centre	(21-3)	Delano	4-2
1983	AA - Edina	(22-1)	St. Cloud Apollo	9-6
	A - Staples	(17-6)	Windom	7-5
1984	AA - Grand Rapids	(21-1)	Hopkins	10-0
	A - Windom	(21-3)	Winona Cotter	2-0
1985	AA - St. Cloud Ap.	(19-6)	Fridley	7-4
	A - Windom	(21-2)	Eden Valley-Watkins	8-1
1986	AA - Cretin	(25-1)	Bemidji	13-2
	A - Greenway, Coler.	(20-2)	Park Rapids	5-3
1987	AA - Willmar	(14-9)	Hopkins	5-4
	A - Greenway, Coler.	(22-3)	St. Cloud Cathedral	14-11
1988	AA - Owatonna	(23-3)	Grand Rapids	6-1
	A - St. Cloud Cath.	(21-3)	Waseca	6-3
1989	AA - Cretin	(24-2)	Hibbing	4-3
	A - Mankato Loyola	(20-3)	Sauk Rapids	6-5
1990	AA - Cretin	(27-3)	Austin	2-0
	A - Waseca	(21-6)	Sleepy Eye	4-3
1991	AA - Stillwater	(22-5)	Osseo	10-0
	A - Greenway, Coler.	(24-4)	Rocori, Cold Spring	6-5
1992	AA - Cretin-Derham	(25-5)	Osseo	15-5
	A - Rocori, Cold Spr.	(25-1)	Greenway, Coler.	4-1
1993	AA - Coon Rapids	(23-5)	Forest Lake	4-2
	A - Greenway, Coler.	(23-3)	Fairmont	4-3
1994	AA - Henry Sibley	(21-7)	New Ulm	4-2
	A - Sibley East	(25-2)	Sauk Centre	8-6
1995	AA - Brainerd	(23-3)	Rosemount	4-3
	A - Crookston (22-5)		Brooklyn Center	4-3
1996	AA - Cretin	(26-2)	Brainerd	6-4
	A - Rochester Lou.	(26-4)	Orono	12-11
1997	AA - Cretin	(26-2)	Coon Rapids	10-0
	A - Cherry-Iron	(21-3)	Melrose	3-0
1998	AA - Cretin	(29-0)	Eden Prairie	2-1
	A - Sibley East	(26-2)	Melrose	3-2
1999	AA - Hastings	(25-5)	Maple Grove	4-2
	A - Montgomery-Lon	(22-1)	Breck School	15-5
2000	AAA - Brainerd	(25-5)	Lakeville	4-1
	AA - St. Michael-Al.	(24-6)	Montgomery-Lon.	8-5
	A - Sleepy Eye	(26-3)	Lester Prairie	4-0
2001	AAA - Cretin	(26-1)	Rochester Mayo	13-2
	AA - St. Cloud Cath.	(22-5)	Luverne	6-4
	A- St. Agnes	(20-7)	Sleepy Eye St.Mary's	16-6
2002	AAA - New Ulm	(27-3)	North St. Paul	9-8
	AA - Roch. Lourdes	(30-1)	Blue Earth Area	15-0
	A - Sleepy Eye St. M	(20-8)	Menahga	12-4

AMERICAN LEGION BASEBALL

Chartered by Congress in 1919 as a patriotic, mutual-help, war-time veterans organization, the American Legion is committed to America's youth. In fact, they have sponsored youth baseball in this country since 1925. The goals of American Legion Baseball are the development of team discipline, individual character and leadership development qualities in young people. Legion Baseball is the oldest and largest, nationwide baseball program in America, having served more than eight million teenagers since its inception. Today, some 5,000 teams with more than 90,000 players, ages 15 to 18, are registered for National tournament play — and that number grows every year. American Legion Posts also support and sponsor some 2,500 younger age teams which are registered with Little League, Babe Ruth, Pony and Dixie, among others. Incredibly, more than 65% of all Major Leaguers and nearly 75% of all college players played American Legion Baseball as a teenagers. (In addition, some 40 American Legion alums are enshrined in the Baseball Hall of Fame.)

Continually growing and expanding, Legion Ball is the real deal. Since 1988 the American Legion National Championship Game has been televised nationally. Incredibly, over $17 million is spent annually by the American Legion's 3.1 million members to sponsor local athletic teams. In addition, the American Legion National Headquarters spends approximately $1,200,000 annually to operate and host 64 teams that qualify for the National Tournament — which includes some 1,400 players and coaches on 64 teams that compete at eight Regional Tournaments. Major League Baseball has supported the program since 1926 and currently contributes $25,000 annually (3% of the National budget), to help offset expenses.

In Minnesota, Legion ball goes way back to the beginning, 1926 — making us just one of three states in the nation that has held a tournament every year since the programs national inception. In 1959, Minnesota moved into first place in American Legion Baseball by having more registered teams than any other state. The state held this position for nine years until Pennsylvania bumped us into second, where we have remained ever since. Since its inception in Minnesota, more than 21,000 teams, involving an estimated 310,000 players, have been registered. Today, over 330 teams with more than 6,000 players are in registered programs. In addition, there are approximately 10,000 players, aged 8 through 18, who also play baseball under sponsorship of American Legion community programs, though not in its official program.

State champs are determined by a system that has been in place for decades. The District Champions, some runners-up and host teams from Division I play in the annual "American Legion Double Elimination Tournament" to determine the State Champion. A Division II Single-Elimination Tournament is also held annually. These National Playdowns are a series of tournaments in the eight National Regions. There, a host team, the state champions, along with runners-up from five states, make up the 64 teams that compete in the eight-team pool play regional tournaments. Those winners go on to represent the Eight Regional Champions and the winners go on to compete in the World Series to determine the National Champion. Some 5,300 teams start the season and just one is left standing at the end. (Minnesota's Champion and Runner-up in Division I both go on to compete in National Regional Playdowns because of the large number of registered teams in the state. Minnesota also sends a Division II team to regional national Division II play as well.) Minnesota has produced three national champions: Richfield in 1943, Edina in 1983 and New Brighton (Tri-City Red) in 1999. In addition, the 2002 team from Excelsior made it all the way to the Finals before losing to a team from Mississippi to finish as the national runner-ups.

(Also, Dick Jonckowski, the legendary voice of the Gophers, is the public address announcer at the annual World Series out in Danville, Va.)

Year	Champion (Division-I)	Runner-Up	Year	Champion (Division-I)	Runner-Up
1926	Crosby	St. Paul Navy-Marine	1965	Rosetown Memorial	Brooklyn Center
1927	St. Paul John de Parcq	Cambridge	1966	North St. Paul	St. Paul Park
1928	St. Paul John de Parcq	St. Cloud	1967	St. Paul Attucks-Brooks	Richfield
1929	Cottonwood	St. Paul Post Eight	1968	St. Paul Attucks-Brooks	Richfield
1930	Mpls. North Side	Parkers Paine	1969	Edina	Moorhead
1931	Winona	Mpls. North Side	1970	Winona	Mpls. Gophers
1932	Mpls. North Side	Duluth	1971	North St. Paul	Winona
1933	Post Eight, St. Paul	Mpls. Kyle	1972	Richfield	Moorhead
1934	New Ulm	Cokato	1973	Richfield	St. Louis Park
1935	St. Paul Christie de Parcq	Mpls. Laidlaw	1974	St. Paul Attucks-Brooks	Bemidji
1936	Mpls. North Side	St. Paul Christie de Parcq	1975	Grand Rapids	White Bear Lake
1937	Railroad, St. Paul	Cokato	1976	St. Cloud	White Bear Lake
1938	St. Paul Midway	Cokato	1977	St. Cloud	Edina
1939	Mpls. Fire and Police	Blackduck	1978	New Ulm	Bloomington
1940	Mpls. Fire and Police	Waverly	1979	St. Paul Arcade-Phalen	St. Cloud
1941	New Ulm	Mpls. Courthouse	1980	Richfield	St. Paul Arcade Phalen
1942	St. Paul Hamline	Robbinsdale	1981	Rochester, William McCoy	Hastings
1943	*Richfield	South St. Paul	1982	Edina	Richfield
*(National Champions)			1983	*Edina	New Ulm
1944	Richfield	St. Paul TCF	***(National Champions)**		
1945	Mpls. Fire and Police	Winona	1984	Waite Park	Willmar
1946	St. Paul Christe de Parcq	Stillwater	1985	St. Paul Jacobsen	Hutchinson
1947	St. Paul Christe de Parcq	St. Cloud	1986	Waite Park	Rochester
1948	Austin	St. Cloud	1987	St. Louis Park	Apple Valley
1949	St. Paul North End	Winona	1988	Moorhead	Rochester
1950	St. Paul North End	Richfield	1989	Apple Valley	New Ulm
1951	St. Cloud	Austin	1990	St. Paul Hamline	Duluth Lakeview
1952	St. Paul, North End	Melrose	1991	Excelsior	Apple Valley
1953	Austin	St. Paul North End	1992	New Ulm	Cold Spring
1954	St. Paul North End	St. Cloud	1993	Tri-City Red (New Brighton)	Osseo
1955	Edina	Mpls. Camden	1994	Tri-City Red (New Brighton)	Anoka
1956	St. Paul North End	Mpls. Grain Exchange	1995	New Ulm	Osseo
1957	Mankato	St. Paul North End	1996	Rochester A's	Excelsior
1958	Mpls. Grain Exchange	Duluth Wisted	1997	Tri -City Red (New Brighton)	St. Paul Hamline
1959	Mpls.-Richfield	Granite Falls	1998	Excelsior	South St. Paul
1960	Fergus Falls	Norwood	1999	*Tri -City Red (New Brighton)	Bloomington Blue
1961	Richfield	St. Paul Christie de Parcq	***(National Champions)**		
1962	St. Paul Christie de Parcq	Duluth	2000	Tri -City Red (New Brighton)	Waite Park
1963	St. Paul Christie de Parcq	Austin	2001	Coon Rapids	New Ulm
1964	Mpls. Grain Exchange	Austin	2002	Apple Valley	*Excelsior
			*(National Runner-Up's)		

AMERICAN LEGION DIVISION II CHAMPIONS & RUNNERS-UP

	Champions	Runners-Up
1988	Swansville	Karlstad
1989	LaCrescent	New Ulm
1990	Glencoe	Lamberton
1991	Benson	Lamberton
1992	New York Mills	Benson
1993	Sebeka	Mt. Lake
1994	La Crescent	Cannon Falls
1995	Pine Island	Plainview
1996	Big Lake	Cannon Falls
1997	LaCrescent	Perham
1998	Milroy	Ely
1999	Nashwauk-Keewatin	Paynesville
2000	Sacred Heart	Montgomery
2001	Parkers Prairie	Morris
2002	LeSueur-Henderson	Blue Earth

The Shelly Hanson Championship Trophy is awarded annually to the Division II State Champion and is named in honor of G. Sheldon Hanson of Austin, for his long time service as State Secretary from 1966-1987.

MINNESOTA'S HALL OF FAME

1962	Frank Momsen, Tracy
1963	W. H. Mulligan, St. Cloud
1964	Robert Marshall, Dilworth
1965	Mark Hayward, St. Paul
1966	Thomas Warner, Marshall
1967	Harry Moldenhauer, St. P.
1966	Frank Fust, Minneapolis
1968	Robert Farrish, Litchfield
1969	Ted Peterson, Minneapolis
1970	Maurice Godsey, Winona
	Mathew Stukel, Ely
1971	Sheldon Hanson, Austin
1972	Gaylrd Zelinske, Brainerd
1973	S.C. Qvale, Austin
1975	M.E. Dekko, Gary
1976	George Medvic, Mpls.
1977	John Koch, Trimont
1978	Dale Van De Walker, St. P
1979	Robert Schabert, St. Paul
	Spike Piper, Blue Earth
	Leonard Grill, Mpls.
1980	Louise Kainz, Ely
	Joe Kastelic, Ely
	Sheldon Hanson, Austin
1983	Dale Timm, Owatonna
	Al Schmidt, Shakopee
	Tony Sipe, Ada
1984	George Marsnik, Ely
	Rueben Nathe, Litchfield
	Rodney Wedin, Wells
	Ken Swartz, Bloomington
1986	Hal Johnson, Moorhead
1989	George Bodlovick, St. P.
	Red Haddox, Blmngton.
1990	Al Schoenthaler, Roseville
1991	Tom Mattson, Albert Lea
1992	Jim Peck, Minnetonka
1993	Tom Elliot, St. Cloud
	Ray DeZurik, Waite Park
2000	Joe Baker, Moorhead
	Al Davis, Princeton
	George Karnas, Richfield

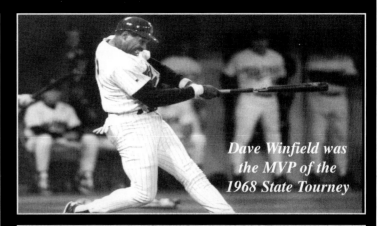

Dave Winfield was the MVP of the 1968 State Tourney

AMERICAN LEGION DIVISION I STATE TOURNAMENT OUTSTANDING PLAYER AWARD
(The Fred Wannamaker Award)

YR	PLAYER	POS.	LEGION POST #
1960	Barry Johnson	P	Fergus Falls #30
1961	Cliff Warnke	P	Winona #9
1962	Bob Williams	P	St. Paul Christie De Parcq #406
1963	Dennis Denning	SS	St. Paul Christie De Parcq #406
1964	Jerry Wickman	P	Mpls. Grain Exchange #403
1965	Dennis Coleman	P	Rosetown Memorial #542
1966	Jim Myers	P	North St. Paul #39
1967	Tim Hadro	C	St. Paul Attucks-Brooks #606
1968	Dave Winfield	P/SS	St. Paul Attucks-Brooks #606
1969	Mike Shea	3B	Little Falls #46
1970	Mike Semling	RF	Winona #9
1971	Terry Johnson	P-1B	Kenyon #78
1972	Mark Stevens	P	Duluth Lakeview #342
1973	Chuck Engle	P/1B	St. Louis Park #282
1974	Peter Maus	P/IF	Bemidji #14
1975	Tim Fagley	P	White Bear Lake #168
1976	Greg Berling	P	St. Cloud #76
1977	Bill Peterson	P	Edina #471
1978	Terry Steinbach	2B	New Ulm #132
1979	Bill Larson	P	St. Paul Arcade Phalen #577
1980	James Burns	3B	Minneapolis Falldin #555
1981	Bill Cutshall	P	Rochester #92
1982	Rob Wassenaar	P/3B	Edina #471
1983	Rob Wassenaar	P/3B	Edina #471
1984	Tim Piechowski	P/SS	Willmar #167
1985	Vince Palyan	P/SS	St. Paul Jacobsen #487
1986	Jeremy Mendal	C/OF	Waite Park #428
1987	Bob Divinski	P/3B	St. Louis Park #282
1988	Todd Hoffman	CF	New Ulm #132
1989	Al Stoye	P	Apple Valley #1776
1990	Wes Denning	CF	St. Paul Hamline #418
1991	Jason Pflaum	2B	Excelsior #259
1992	Ben Griffin	LF	Cold Spring #455
1993	Matt McDonough	C	Osseo #172
1994	Robb Ramacher	CF	Tri-City #513
1995	Brady Ranweiler	1B	New Ulm #132
1996	Joe Siple	2B	Rochester A's #92
1997	Charlie Brookins	P	St. Paul Park #98
1998	Ryan Klocksien	P/IF	Excelsior #259
1999	Billy Schneider	2B	Tri -City #513
2000	Josh Krogman	P/IF	Waite Park #428
2001	Danny Anderson	P/IF	Coon Rapids #334
2002	Dan Brosnan	IF	Apple Valley

VFW BASEBALL

Providing countless opportunities for kids who love to play the game, the V.F.W. (Veterans of Foreign Wars) has become synonymous with summer baseball. From its modest beginnings in 1955, V.F.W. Baseball has emerged as one of the nation's finest youth baseball programs. The first state tournament was held that year — with West St. Paul Post #4462 winning the four-team invitational event. (Because the program was in its infancy and only a handful of teams were participating throughout the state, the numbers were obviously limited.)

From there the program slowly grew thanks to the efforts of so many state V.F.W. officials who saw the need for more youth-oriented programs. Participation quickly grew and it wasn't long before youth baseball champions were being crowned in a number of the state's districts as a prelude to the grand finale — the V.F.W. State Tournament.

The first tournaments were set up with 10 teams, and has since grown to a program that now boasts some 87 Junior Baseball teams (15 & 16 year-olds) and another 34 teams in cub and midget programs throughout the Land of 10,000 Lakes. All 121 teams are sponsored by Minnesota Veterans of Foreign Wars Posts. Focusing on sportsmanship, discipline and having fun, the V.F.W. — which also supports many other sports, has played a huge role in helping to promote the game of baseball in the state of Minnesota.

YEAR	STATE CHAMPION	YEAR	STATE CHAMPION
1955	West St. Paul	1979	St. Paul
1956	St. Paul	1980	St. Paul
1957	Bloomington	1981	New Ulm
1958	St. Paul	1982	Bloomington
1959	St. Paul	1983	Cold Spring
1960	Fergus Falls	1984	St. Paul
1961	Ely	1985	Bemidji
1962	Bloomington	1986	Rochester
1963	Wells	1987	Minneapolis
1964	Winona	1988	St. Paul
1965	Bloomington	1989	Marshall
1966	Morris	1990	Blaine
1967	New Ulm	1991	Lakeville
1968	Keewatin	1992	Cold Spring
1969	Winona	1993	Alexandria
1970	Little Falls	1994	St. Paul
1971	Winona	1995	Rochester
1972	Ely	1996	St. Paul
1973	Austin	1997	Hastings
1974	Bloomington	1998	St. Paul
1975	Bloomington	1999	St. Paul
1976	St. Paul	2000	Crystal
1977	St. Paul	2001	Alexandria
1978	St. James	2002	Duluth East

WOMEN'S BASEBALL

"There's no crying in baseball..." That was just one of the classic lines sputtered from Tom Hanks (A.K.A.) "Jimmy Dugan," in the 1992 movie "A League of their Own." The movie focused on two of the teams from the All-American Girls Professional Baseball League (AAGPBL), the Rockford Peaches and Racine Belles, during the league's inaugural 1943 season. That year the league was started by famed Chicago Cubs Owner Philip Wrigley, who saw girls baseball as a way to keep his ballpark occupied during World War II — while our boys were overseas.

That first year there were just four teams in the AAGPBL: the Racine Belles, Rockford Peaches, Kenosha Comets and South Bend Blue Sox. What many people don't realize, however, is that

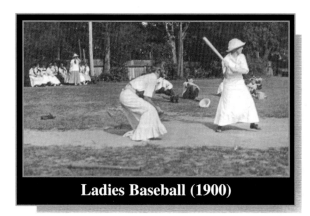

Ladies Baseball (1900)

Minnesota also had a team in the league. That's right, that next year, in 1944, the Minneapolis Millerettes were brought in as an expansion franchise — thus giving the Gopher State its first ever professional women's baseball team. (The Milwaukee Chicks were also added that year as well.)

Women in baseball is nothing new to Minnesota though. In fact, there were records of women's town ball teams playing as far back as the turn of the century. In 1934 Minnesota got its first taste of women's pro baseball when a traveling team called the "House of David" made an appearance here. The team, which was on a barn-storming tour of the Midwest, featured several former major leaguers, including Grover Cleveland Alexander. But it also featured one of the greatest athletes of the 20th century, Babe Didrickson, who would later become famous for being the top female golfer in the world.

What really put women's baseball on the map was the creation of the Millerettes. This, at a time when women were being called upon by the government to take a more active role in the workplace. Rosie the Rivetor was out front-and-center, and America needed them to pick up the slack with the men away. But, while the ladies were being called upon to play the manly game of baseball, Wrigley and other league officials made sure that

they remained as "lady-like" as possible. Etiquette classes, charm school, proper posture and appropriate dress attire were all mandated by the league. A code of conduct was highly enforced for the girls, and their every move was scrutinized. Teams even had chaperones, to ensure their behavior. Mrs. Wrigley herself even designed special

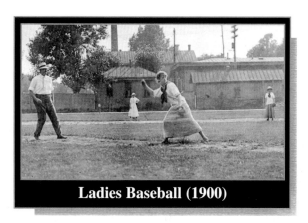

Ladies Baseball (1900)

short-skirted uniforms with satin shorts for the ladies so that they could keep their feminine figures without giving the men any ideas.

The women who wound up making the rosters of these teams were some of the best athletes of their day. Many had been stars in other sports such as basketball, field hockey and even softball, so for them to pick up the new game was no problem at all. It was a fun time for women and for the sport. Seemingly all of the gals had nicknames and the league, as a whole, gave many Americans a sense of normalcy during this troubling time in history.

After that first season of 1943 was deemed as a success, the Millerettes club was brought together under the tutelage of Manager Bubber Jonnard, a former pitcher for the New York Giants. The team, which played its home games at Nicollet Park, opened its schedule

The 1944 Minneapolis Millerettes

Back Row: Bubber Jonnard, Dorothy Wiltse, Vivian Kellogg, Audrey Haine, LaVonne Paire, Kay Blumetta, Lillian Jackson, Ada Ryan (the team chaperone) Middle Row: Faye Dancer, Elizabeth Farrow, Marge Callaghan, Audrey Kissel, Margaret Wigiser Front Row: Ruth Lessing, Annabelle Lee, Helen Callaghan, Betty Trezza

That's right. Way back in 1895, Lewis Robar, a firefighter from Minneapolis' Engine Company No. 11, on Southeast Second Street, invented the game of softball. At the time, Robar was searching for a way to keep his fellow firefighters entertained between calls to action. So he suggested rallying the troops to play baseball in an empty lot next to the fire station. But the lot simply wasn't big enough to handle a standard game of baseball, so Robar got an idea. He then went back to the station, where he proceeded to stitch together a leather ball — about one and a half times large than a baseball. From there he had a local carpenter make him a thinner than-usual bat, and with that, softball was born. The fellas loved the new game, and it allowed them to play ball, while still being able to be close to the old office.

From there the game of softball evolved into several different names, each with its own subtle nuances differing from Robar's first official set of rules. Among them were "pumpkinball," "kittenball" and even "sissyball" — which was how the game was referred to by the die-hard baseball players who thought the game was a joke. Before long the game's popularity grew and grew until it became somewhat of a phenomenon.

For Robar, however, the game's success was a bitter-sweet ride. You see, after inventing the game, he started his own softball production plant. But shortly thereafter, when the game started to take off, he was driven out of business by the larger sporting goods companies who cashed in on the games sudden appeal.

Before long the game had emerged not only as a legitimate sport, but also as a lifestyle, eventually becoming one of the most popular participatory activities around. Today, slow-pitch softball is everywhere, played by an estimated 20 million players worldwide. Eventually, pro leagues emerged for both men and women and it even became an Olympic sport. It still remains all the rage at the high school and college levels, and continues to grow annually. In fact, there are more men's leagues now than can even be counted! (Now, as far as pro softball in Minnesota goes, we had two teams which played at Midway Stadium back in the early '80s called the "Goofys" and the "Norsemen."

there against the Rockford Peaches in front of around 500 fans. The Millerettes jumped out to a 3-0 lead in this one, only to see the Peaches rally for a 5-4 victory.

The star of the team was Helen Callaghan, who would go on to hit .287 that season with three homers, 17 RBI's and 81 runs scored. (It is also interesting to note that Callaghan, who went on to lead the league in hitting that next season, would later have a son named Casey Candaele — who, in turn, would go on to play for more than 10 seasons of major league baseball with Montreal, Houston and Cleveland.)

And, according to renowned baseball author Stew Thornley, Callaghan wasn't the only member of the squad who would have a relative in the major leagues. Annabelle Lee, the team's star pitcher, was also the aunt of Bill "Spaceman" Lee, who would go on to pitch for the Expos and Red Sox in the 1970s and '80s. (The Spaceman would later even credit his Aunt for teaching him how to pitch!)

As the season went on the ladies got better, but the fan support dwindled. In addition, the opposing teams, from as far away as Indiana, were getting tired of taking long bus trips to the Twin Cities, only to have a couple hundred fans show up to watch them. But, the team played on. They knew that they had to make it interesting for the fans to stay involved, so they spiced up their act a bit. One player

The 1909 Spring Valley Ladies Team

The Cokato Ladies Town Team (1918)

in particular did this better than the rest, Center Fielder Faye Dancer, a real crowd-pleaser who oftentimes did somersaults in the outfield between pitches. Other players stepped it up too. Millerettes' hurler Dorothy "Dottie" Wiltse won 20 games that year while LaVonne "Pepper" Paire dazzled the crowd with her amazing range at shortstop.

That 1944 six-team season was divided into halves, with the winners of each half then meeting in a post-season tournament to determine a league champion. The Millerettes played respectably early on in the season, but then slumped big time. From there the club hit the skids and wound up finishing out the first half of the season in the league basement with a dismal record of 23-36. And, while optimism ran high for the second half, it didn't get much better as the club finished with an identical 22-36 tally in part II. The fans were staying away in droves, the media was ignoring them and the players were playing lousy baseball. When you added it all up, it was a recipe for disaster.

With that, in late July the Millerettes' remaining home games were relocated to other cities. The team, which would then become known as the "Orphans," played the rest of its season on the road. That next year the franchise was moved to Fort Wayne, Indiana, where they became the "Daisies." (The Daisies, incidentally, would go on to play for 10 more seasons, winning league titles in 1948, 1952, 1953, and 1954. And, the star of that 1954 club was St. Paul's Jean Havlish, who would go on to become a Hall of Fame bowler.)

While the AAGPBL would go on well into the 1950s, that would be the end of professional women's baseball for some time.

(In 1988, a display of women in baseball opened at the Baseball Hall of Fame in Cooperstown, NY., immortalizing the efforts of the AAGPBL and giving our Millerettes an interesting footnote in Minnesota baseball history.)

However, other prominent Minnesota women would go on to excel individually during this era as well. The most prominent by far, though, was St. Paul's Marcenia Toni Stone Alberga. Toni became the first woman to ever play professional baseball for a men's team, when she signed a contract to play second-base with the Indianapolis Clowns of the old Negro Leagues in 1953. Stone was truly a pioneer. As a kid she grew up playing on the local boys teams in her St. Paul neighborhood. But from there she moved to San Francisco, where, after playing with an American Legion team, she joined the San Francisco Sea Lions, a semi-pro team of African Americans who barnstormed around the area playing exhibition games. Toni then went to New Orleans, where she would play with the Black Pelicans and the Creoles, both minor league Negro League teams. By

1949 she was making $300 a month playing ball.

Then, in 1953 Toni got her big break when she signed a one year contract worth about $12,000 with the Indianapolis Clowns. (It is interesting to note that while the AAGPBL was still going on at this point, Stone couldn't have played in it because it was a "white only" league.) The Clowns were one of the preeminent Negro League

The Phyllis Wheatley's (1925)

teams of this era and Stone would definitely have some pretty big shoes to fill at second base. That was the position recently vacated by future Hall of Famer Hank Aaron, who had just signed with the Boston (soon to be Milwaukee) Braves. And, while the Clowns were previously much like the Harlem Globetrotters, who were known their showmanship as well as for their gamesmanship, by this time they were legit and played it straight. Stone hit .243 that year and even got a hit off of future Hall of Fame Pitcher Satchel Paige. She would later say it was the greatest thrill of her life.

That next year her contract was sold to the Kansas City Monarchs, a traveling all-star team which had won several pennants in the "Colored World Series." Then, after just one season with the Monarchs, Stone retired from professional baseball. The color barrier had finally been broken in baseball and the Negro Leagues were about to be history. When it was all said and

Toni Stone

done, Stone would be inducted into the Women's Sports Hall of Fame, in 1993, and also be honored in two separate sections of the Baseball Hall of Fame in Cooperstown — "Women in Baseball" and "The Negro Leagues."

Minnesota's next great women's ball player was Krissy Wendell, who led Brooklyn Center to the 1994 Little League World Series. At the time, Wendell was just the fifth girl ever to play in the World Series, but she made her mark nonetheless, batting third and

starting as the team's catcher. (Krissy would go on to become, arguably, the world's greatest female hockey player as well, leading the U.S. Women's team to a silver medal in the 2002 Winter Games.)

Finally, in 1997, another great thing happened for women's baseball in Minnesota. That was the year that Pitcher Ila Borders became the first woman ever to pitch in a regular-season professional game when she suited up for the independent minor league St. Paul Saints and Duluth-Superior Dukes of the Northern League.

Ila Borders

Borders would pitch in the league for four seasons before finally retiring in 2000 at the age of 25. (To learn more about Ila's amazing career, please check out the chapter on the Northern League!)

So, despite the fact that women have made huge strides in advancing their role in the game of baseball, it seems that for now that they are destined to be labeled as softball players. Hey, that is all right. Women have gone on to dominate this global sport and turned it into a national obsession. But just wait until the next phenom comes along, just like Toni Stone, Ila Borders or Krissy Wendell before her, who decides that she wants to play hardball with the boys... watch out America!

Good Thunder native Rachel Nelson was an All-American centerfielder on the University of Minnesota's Golden Gopher Softball Team. The Gophers are one of the Big Ten's top programs and recently had a new stadium built.

THE LITTLE LEAGUE WORLD SERIES

Krissy Wendell

Minnesota has had a long affiliation with Little League Baseball and its ever popular World Series, which was first played back in 1947. Played annually in Williamsport, Pa., for 11-12-year-olds, the Series is now a nationally televised prime-time global event. The world's largest organized youth sports program, with approximately 2.8 million children and 1 million volunteers in every U.S. state and 103 other countries, nothing says Americana like Little League Baseball.

Minnesota's first team to advance through the Midwest Regionals and into the World Series was Duluth, back in 1963. Representing the US Central Region, Duluth beat Latin America, 5-2, in the opener, then lost to Stratford, Conn., 5-0, in Game Two, but then rallied back to beat Europe, 3-1, in their finale of the consolation bracket.

It would be 23 years later before another team from Minnesota would make it back to the big dance, and this time it was East Tonka, Minnetonka, in 1985. There, East Tonka lost to Morristown Tennessee, 5-1, in opener, then beat Europe, 4-2, in Game Two, but lost to Latin America, 9-0, in the Consolations.

In 1994 Minnesota made it back to the Show thanks to Brooklyn Center American. Brooklyn Center beat Northridge California in opener 4-2, lost to Springfield, VA, 4-1, in Game Two, and then lost to Middleboro Massachusetts, 11-5, in the consolation finale.

Minnesota made it back-to-back in 1995 when Little Lakes West, Arden Hills, represented the U.S. Central Region at the World Series. This team, however, did not fare quite as well as the others, losing in Game One to Yorba Linda, California, 17-5, and then to Toms River NJ, 11-4, in Game Two, followed by yet another loss to Spring, Texas ,12-1, to finish the tourney.

(It is important to note, however, that the star of that 1994 Brooklyn Center team was Krissy Wendell, who, at the time, was just the fifth girl ever to play in the Little League World Series. Krissy, who became the first girl ever to be named as a starter at the catcher position, was awesome, even batting third in the team's lineup. Brooklyn Center, which beat Duluth to win the Minnesota title, became the media darlings of the World Series because of Wendell, who was such a great player. While nearly every team refused to try and steal second base on her cannon-arm, as a switch-hitter she belted out several home runs from both sides of the plate throughout the year. So amazing was her story, that Sports Illustrated for Kids Magazine even did a big feature story about her at the time. From there, Wendell went on to become, arguably, the greatest women's hockey player in the world. After leading her Park Center High School hockey team to the state title in 2000, Krissy led the U.S. Olympic team to a silver medal in Salt Lake City in the 2002 Winter Games. The 2002 USA Hockey Women's Player of the Year then committed to the University of Minnesota, where she will continue to rewrite the record books.

"That was such an exciting time for me," said Krissy, whose father, Larry, was the team coach. "I was so young and everything was so knew. It was really the first time I ever played in front of a large crowd with so many people rooting for us. It was amazing, I mean people actually flew in to see us play and that really blew me away. The attention they (the press) gave me was, at times, overwhelming though. I just wanted to play, but it was definitely a distraction to be under the microscope like that. Overall it was easy being a girl on the team though, because I basically grew up playing hockey with the same group of guys. They treated me like their sister, it was great!")

MINNESOTA TEAMS IN THE LITTLE LEAGUE WORLD SERIES

1963 Duluth	1985 East Tonka	1994 Brooklyn Center	1995 Little Lakes West
Richard Alstead	Mike Beach	Sean Aasen	Brian Christianson
James Barnsdorf	Jim Brower	Jerry Cogswell	Brian Clark
Gary Berg	John Crist	Chris DeMars	Chris Clifford
Franklin Cicalello	Justin Harder	Dwayne Erickson	Mike Grant
Sherman Erickson	Brad Kearin	Jason Erklouts	Wally Grant
Howard Fitch	Michael Mahady	Dan Erklouts	Joe Jorgenson
Mandel Green	Justin McHugh	Tony Kempf	Steve Jorgenson
John House	Matt Oakley	Steven Kruger	Brad Krebsbach
Jack House	Mark Oster	Luke LaChance	Wes McFarland
Delano Huhta	Don Oster	Mike Langhoff	Mark Mirocha
Terry Johnson	Kip Peterson	Jermar Larkins	Mark Newman
Charles Ness	Jas Pflaum	Glen Linder	Drew Partanen
Richard Pearson	Brent Rowley	Paul Nesheck	Jim Pitt
James Salmi	Pat Seamans	Eric Tauscheck	Luke Stasson
Kevin Scanlon	Brock Waterbury	Krissy Wendell	Dan Stuart
Gregory Swor			
Steven Trachsel			

In memory of Paul Giel — a great athlete, a great person and a great friend.

1932 - 2002

AFTERWORD BY PAUL MOLITOR

Arguably the greatest baseball player ever to hail from the state of Minnesota, Paul Molitor is a real life home-town hero. His baseball career is a seemingly endless series of success-stories, and will come to a pinnacle soon enough with a trip to Cooperstown, and a much deserved spot in the Hall of Fame.

Molly grew up as one of eight children in a middle-class St. Paul neighborhood loving the game of baseball, and worshipping his home-town Twins. He went on to become a star at Cretin High School, where he led his Raiders to a pair of Catholic League High School titles in 1973 and 1974. That same year the baseball and basketball All-Stater led his St. Paul Attucks-Brooks American Legion Team to the state title as well. It was the second Legion title for Paul, who was just an eighth-grader on the 1968 championship team which was led by a kid named Dave Winfield.

Molitor then turned down a pro contract out of high school to sign instead with his hometown Gophers. Legendary Coach Dick Siebert would later say that Paul had the best base-running instincts of any player he ever saw in amateur or professional baseball, and that he was, without a doubt, the best major league prospect he'd ever seen. As a junior Paul led the Gophers to the 1977 College World Series before being selected as the third overall player by the Milwaukee Brewers in the Major League Baseball Draft. During his tenure in Gold Country Paul had become the programs career leader in hits, RBI's, runs-scored, home-runs, triples, total bases and stolen bases. He also set five single-season records and seven college-career records as well. The two-time All-American shortstop would finish his college career with an awesome career batting average of .350.

From there Molly went on to play 15 seasons with the Brewers, making it to the World Series in 1982 before losing to the Cardinals in the "Suds Series." He gave Joe DiMaggio's consecutive hits record a run for the money in 1987 and in 1993 he left Milwaukee to head north of the border. There, he led the Blue Jays to a World Series championship and was named MVP in the process.

On December 5, 1995, Paul Molitor came back to Minnesota, fulfilling a childhood dream of getting to play for his hometown Twins. In 1996, he posted a .341 average and led the league in hits with 225. Then, on September 16th of that same year, in a road game against the Kansas City Royals, Molly made history. With the entire state of Minnesota waiting in anxious anticipation for the big event to finally happen, Paul became the 21st player in major-league history to get 3,000 hits. And, in typical Molly style, he did it his own way, becoming the first player ever to reach the millstone with a triple.

After 21 seasons in the Bigs, Paul finally hung up his cleats in 1998 with a gaudy life-time batting average of .306. He would remain with the Twins as a hitting coach until finally taking a breather in 2002 to contemplate his future. His storybook career has certainly made us all very, very proud. So, who better to talk about the state-of-the state of the next 100 years of Minnesota baseball than a man who has quietly become a legend in the Land of 10,000 Lakes — our very own Paul Molitor.

"I grew up loving baseball and loving the Twins. My mom was a big fan of the game and I can still remember her telling me stories about Willie Mays and Roy Campanella, when they played for the Millers and Saints. I can also remember dragging my dad out to the back yard to play baseball, and staying out there all day long playing with my buddies. I mean I was one of those kids who used to listen to Twins games on the radio while I was doing my homework. I always dreamt of someday wearing a Twins uniform and getting to finally do that was a real dream-come-true. To finish my career back home was like coming full-circle, and getting my 3,000th hit here made the entire experience just that much more special. I was disappointed that I didn't get to play on a winning team and also that I didn't get to play with Kirby Puckett, but being able to wear a Twins uniform meant everything to me. So I guess the love of the game that I first got as a kid has just stayed with me, it is a wonderful thing.

"We have an amazing baseball tradition in Minnesota, but the game is at a real cross-roads right now. I do think, however, that the state of the game looks pretty good, but there is room for improvement. For starters, baseball is not has healthy as it once was, that is for sure. A combination of the emergence of other sports, the cloud that has seemed to hover over Major League Baseball over the past decade or so, along with 10 consecutive losing seasons from the Twins have all contributed to the game's downside here.

"Plus, I think the mindset of young people nowadays is more about quicker, faster and more instant gratifying forms of entertainment — things that have been fueled by the development of computers, video games and even MTV. Everything seems to be geared to a faster pace with today's kids and baseball is something that, for better or for worse, is still a little slower. So, I think the amount of people that are interested in playing the game has simply gone down. The bottom line is that the kids have a lot of other choices out there to entertain them and baseball has not done the best job of capturing their imaginations.

"I think we are at a real crossroads. For whatever the reason, baseball has been more vulnerable than many of the other sports with regards to the number of athletes it has lost over the years. While football and basketball have remained relatively strong, other sports such as soccer and golf have taken a big leap in popularity through the years as well. As a result, baseball has lost not only some of its fan base, but also some of its athlete base.

"I think that a part of the stabilization of the game and the security of

game entertaining to the young people. Somehow baseball needs to make sure that enough parents think it is important enough to expose their kids to the game. Whether that means taking them to a game or signing them up for a youth league, we just need more kids getting into it at all levels. I really think that sustaining the interest of the next generation is going to be the biggest challenge facing baseball in the future.

"As far as Minnesota goes, we still have a lot of great programs in place to promote the game. Some of the Twins efforts to improve little league facilities and things of that nature have been great and their instructional clinics are good too. Overall, the game is pretty strong at all levels here I think, but there is always room for improvement

"I will say though that when you drive by the baseball diamonds in the summertime you just don't see a great number of kids playing the game like you did years ago. I mean it wasn't that long ago that it seemed like kids had a real passion for the game and were just consumed by it during the summertime. That was a big deal, considering the fact that our summers are so short and kids don't have that much free-time.

"I think our high school programs are pretty strong and our youth leagues, which include things like American Legion and VFW, look good too. But I don't know if you have the same number of kids wanting to dedicate themselves to baseball by giving up their summers. It is tough with the cold weather up here, and that makes a difference too. I know that there has been some talk of pushing high school games back into the summer, like they do in Iowa and some other places, and that would probably help out a lot. We'll have to see what happens.

"As far as getting the kids into the college ranks, things are good, but could be better here as well. I do think, however, that the University of Minnesota has a very strong program under Coach John Anderson, and that is leading the way for all of the other division II and III schools in the state. They continue to produce solid teams year in and year out over there and that is great to see.

"As far as the pro game, what can you say about this year's Twins? I guess I picked a bad year to step away from the team! I mean this has been such a great story. I have worked with most of those guys for the last couple of years and seeing them reach the benefits of all their time and commitment is great. Watching guys like Torii Hunter, Jacque Jones, Corey Koskie and Eric Milton go from rookies to where they are now has just been amazing. Seeing their growing pains along the way from wondering if they would ever get over the hump to now, when they are in the post-season, is a lot of fun as well. I am happy for them and really get a lot of personal satisfaction from it too.

"Overall I would have to say that they are a humble group, they are a hungry group and they really don't have any cliques on the team either. They have bridged their cultural differences and come together as a team to play tremendous baseball. It's also a fun group which has good chemistry together, and that breeds a winning attitude. And, they have found their character through all of this adversity. It is just a great story when you think about what they have had to go through to get to this point. From strikes to contraction to stadiums, it has been quite a ride for these guys.

"As far as the strike situation, I was surprised that they worked the strike out to tell you the truth. I mean I had been a part of several work stoppages since I first got into the league back in 1981, and this was a very different situation. There was just so much on the line now with the fear of public repercussions, the economy, September 11th and the fact that the game is losing its fan base. For whatever the reasons, I am just really glad that they were able to work it out. It will really help the Twins too. They are talking about a billion dollars being transferred in revenue sharing to the smaller market clubs over the next four years and that is significant. And I guess if the players were going to compromise with regards to revenue sharing and luxury taxes, then it only made sense that baseball would drop the whole contraction issue in return. Hopefully this agreement will bode well as to how the negotiations are done in the future and that there will be no more work stoppages as a result.

"But, I think the fact that they have announced that there will be no contraction for at least the next four years might potentially hurt this team's chances for a new stadium. Because now the politicians might relax and say it is not an emergency. So, I just hope that whole thing stays on course and they can find a way to get it done sooner than later. And who knows, maybe Carl (Pohlad) will study the deal and decide to keep the team if it is financially lucrative to him after all. Because that is how he is, he understands good business. But then again if someone offers him $150 million he might sell it too. I don't know. He has done a lot of good things for baseball but there were some misjudgments made when his initial stadium deal, which was perceived as a big donation, in reality turned out to be just a loan. So, for the next couple of years he lost some of the public's trust, and that has in turn hurt the teams stadium situation.

"As far as my future goes, I am still contemplating what I want to do. Part of me says I can teach, coach or even manage, but for right now I am considering whether or not I want to return to the game. The game has really changed since I first got into the league 25 years ago, that is for sure. As for right now I am happy being around the Twins and helping them out whatever way I can. I love Gardy (Manager Ron Gardenhire) and wish this team nothing but success. They will certainly be fun to watch in the coming years if they can keep this nucleus of guys together.

"All in all, I miss playing the game but am happy with the way things have turned out. I do have to say though that I really can't thank the fans enough for all of their support they have given to me over the years. We have some great baseball fans here and I feel very fortunate to have been a part of their lives. From my days at the U of M, where being a Gopher was just an awesome experience, to coming home to play for the Twins, it has been great. I mean to wear a uniform with my state's name on it, twice, was a real honor. I wouldn't trade any of it for the world.

"I still believe that baseball is a beautiful game and in some ways it is like a reminder that our lives have become too fast paced. I would still like to think that there are simple things in life that are reminders of just how we should all stop and just take things in. And baseball is like that. While we like the things that are faster in sports today, it is also important to not forget the sometimes slower paced beauty of simplicity. That is what this great game is all about."

HERE'S TO...

THE NEXT...

100 YEARS OF...

MINNESOTA BASEBALL!

INDEX

Bibliography

1. Ross Bernstein: Interviews from over 50 Minnesota sports personalities and celebrities
2. "Fifty Years o Fifty Heroes" A Celebration of Minnesota Sports, by Ross Bernstein, Mpls, MN, 1997.
3. "Hubert H. Humphrey Metrodome Souvenir Book": compiled by Dave Mona. MSP Pubs., Inc.
4. "ESPN Outtakes," by Dan Patrick, Hyperion Books, NY, 2000.
5. "Sid!" by Sid Hartman & Patrick Reusse - Voyager Press, 1997
6. "Minnesota Trivia," by Laurel Winter: Rutledge Hill Press, Nashville, TN, 1990
7. "NCAA Championships": The Official National Collegiate Champs & Records, by the NCAA, 2001.
8. The Star Tribune Minnesota Sports Hall of Fame insert publication
9. "Can You Name That Team?" by David Biesel
10. "Scoreboard," by Dunstan Tucker & Martin Schirber, St. John's Press, Collegeville, MN, 1979.
11. "Awesome Almanac Minnesota," by Jean Blashfield, B&B Publishing, Fontana, WI, 1993.
12. "The Encyclopedia of Sports," by Frank Menke, AC Barnes Pub., Cranbury, NJ, 1975.
13. "My lifetime in sports," by George Barton, Stan Carlson Pub., Minneapolis, 1957.
14. "Professional Sports Teams Histories," by Michael LaBlanc, Gale Pub., Detroit, MI, 1994.
15. "The Encyclopedia of North American Sports History," by Ralph Hickock, 1992.
16. "Minnesota State Fair: The history and heritage of 100 years," Argus Publishing, 1964.
17. "Concordia Sports - The First 100 Years" by Vernon Finn Grinaker, Concordia Website.
18. "Sports Leagues & Teams," by Mark Pollak, McFarland and Co. Pub., Jefferson, NC, 1996.
19. Minnesota Almanacs - (various 1970s)
20. "Season Review": ESPN Sports Almanac by Jerry Trecker, Total Sports Publications, 1983.
21. "Before the Dome," by David Anderson: Nodin Press, 1993.
22. "On to Nicollet," by Stew Thornley, Nodin Press, 1988.
23. MSHSL Media Guides (various 1940-2002)
24. Minnesota Twins Media Guides (various)
25. University of Minnesota Men's Athletics Media Guides (various 1900-2001).
26. Media Guides: Bemidji State, Moorhead State, UM-Duluth, Minnesota State, Mankato, St. Cloud State, Augsburg, Bethel, Carlton, Concordia, Hamline, Macalaster, St. John's, St. Mary's, St. Olaf, St. Thomas
27. "Winfield: A Players Life, by Dave Winfield.
28. "The Living Legend: Ray Christensen," by Brad Ruiter, Fast Break Magazine, March 4, 2001.
29. "Gustavus Athletics: A Century of Building the Gustie Tradition," by Lloyd Hollingsworth, Gustavus Adolphus Press, 1984.
30. NSIC Web-Site & Corresponding Member Web-Pages (Men's & Women's)
31. NCC Web-Site & Corresponding Member Web-Pages (Men's & Women's)
32. MIAC Web-Site & Corresponding Member Web-Pages (Men's & Women's)
33. Minnesota History Center Online Archives
34. Steve Dimitry's Extinct Sports Leagues
35. gophersports.com
36. mshsl.com (baseball section)
37. usoc.org
38. umdbulldogs.com
39. varsityonline.com
40. hickocksports.com
41. Star Tribune archives
42. baseball-almanac.com
43. "Mn. Twins chronology," Star-Trib, Nov. 28 2001.
44. http://www.vfw.state.mn.us/baseballtournament.htm
45. "Split Doubleheader: An unauthorized history of the Minnesota Twins," by Bill Morlock and Rick Little.
46. "How Major League Baseball Came to Minnesota," by Charles O. Johnson.
47. "Calvin Griffith: Not Even My Family Knew We Were Moving to Minnesota," by Dave Mona.
48. "Metropolitan Stadium: The Park Built for Outdoor Baseball," by Joe Soucheray.
49. "Supreme Court rejects Twins appeal; team likely to play in '02," by Randy Furst, Star Trib, Feb 5, 2002.
50. "Bigger twin more coy about stadium," By Judith Yates Borger, Pioneer Press, Jun. 17, 2002.
51. "On to Nicollet: The Glory and Fame of the Minneapolis Millers," by Stew Thornley
52. "The Nights the Lights Went On in the Twin Cities," by Stew Thornley
53. "Pay Days: Millers vs. Saints," By Stew Thornley, 1985.
54. "Minneapolis Millers Protested Games," Excerpted from On to Nicollet, 1982.
55. "Minneapolis Millers: 1959 Junior World Series vs. Havana," By Stew Thornley, 1994.
56. "The Rise Of Minneapolis Baseball" (My Lifetime in Sports Book by Barton)
57. "Williams' greatness was evident even as a Miller,: by Sid Hartman, Star Tribune, Jul 6, 2002.
58. "Minnesota Baseball History," By Stew Thornley, Twins Media Guide, 2002.
59. "Metropolitan Stadium: The Park Built for Outdoor Baseball," by Joe Soucheray
60. "History of the Met," by Charlie Johnson for Midwest Federal Bank, 1971.
61. "Yesterday," by Joe Soucheray. (Before the Dome Book)
62. "Touching Bases with our Memories," by Dean Urdahl, North Star Press, St. Cloud, 2001.
63. "Old Lexington," by Mark Tierney (Before the Dome Book)
64. "Baseball Minnesota - The Northern League," by Rich Arpi and edited by Joe Block
65. "Baseball in St. Paul - From Comiskey to Veeck," by Rich Arpi and edited by Joe Block
66. "Riverfront baseball in St. Paul had short-lived run in 1888," by Jackie Crosby, Star Tribune, Jul 5, 2002.
67. "Great Saints," by Rich Arpi
68. "Popular Saints hope to do more on the field," by John Millea, Star Tribune, May 23, 2002.
69. "When the Saints Came Marching In," by Ken Haag (Before the Dome Book)
70. "Saints get their manager," by Mike Wells, Pioneer Press, Feb. 26, 2002.
71. "Lexington Park: Campy, The Duke, The Babe, and Oh, That Coliseum!," by Patrick Reusse
72. "Midway Stadium: Built to Lure the Big Leagues." by Patrick Reusse
73. "Minnesota Baseball History," by Stew Thornley, Twins Media Guide, 2002.
74. "Riverfront baseball in St. Paul had short-lived run in 1888," by Jackie Crosby, Star Tribune, Jul 5, 2002.
75. "The 100 greatest Minor League Baseball teams," By Bill Weiss & Marshall Wright, www.minorleaguebaseball.com.
76. "Forty-Five Years of Baseball in Minneapolis: From the Unions of 1867 to the, Millers of 1912," By Joe McDermott, Mpls. Journal, March 21, 1912.
77. "Base Ball History," by Mary Jane Schmitt, Rooster Coordinator.
78. "Game of baseball may predate Doubleday," Associated Press, July 09, 2001.
79. "Bud Fowler and the Stillwaters," by Bob Tholkes (Before the Dome Book)
80. "The St. Paul Unions: Minnesota's First Major League Team," By Stew Thornley, 1980.
81. "On to Nicollet: The Glory and Fame of the Minneapolis Millers," By Stew Thornley.
82. "Twin Cities played role in formation of American League," by Brian Murphy, Star Trib, May 20, 2001.
83. "The National Game." by Alfred H. Spink, 1911.
84. "The American League," by Joel Zoss and John S. Bowman, 1986.
85. "Baseball: The Early Years," by H. Seymour, 1960.
86. "Minneapolis' First Downtown Baseball Park," by David Wood, Lake Area News, March, 1984.
87. "An Informal History of The Northern Baseball League,' By Herman D. White & Walter H. Brovald, Gryphon Press, St. Paul, 1982.
88. "The Northern League," By R. Arpi & Joe Block.
89. "An Informal History of The Northern Baseball League,' By Herman D. White & Walter H. Brovald, Gryphon Press, St. Paul, 1982.
90. "My Twenty Years on the St. Paul Sandlots," by Wally Swanson (Before the Dome Book)
91. "Wade Stadium: 60 Years of Baseball in Duluth," by Todd Whitesel, 2001 Dukes Media Guide.
92. Madison Black Wolf 1997 Souvenir Program.
93. "Baseball in St. Paul - From Comiskey to Veeck," by Rich Arpi and edited by Joe Block
94. "Popular Saints hope to do more on the field," by John Millea, Star Tribune, May 23, 2002.
95. "The Northern League: Proud Tradition," by David Kemp, www.northernleague.com.
96. "Concordia Men's Sports - The First One Hundred Years," by Vernon Finn Grinaker,
97. "Saints get their manager," by Mike Wells, Pioneer Press, Feb. 26, 2002.
98. "Duluth Superior Dukes: 2000 Central Division Champs," by Todd Whitesel, Media Guide, 2001.
99. "Who is Ila Borders? By Phil Borders, www.ilaborders.com.
100. "The Rise of Baseball in Minnesota," By Cecil Monroe, MN History, June 1938.
101. "Minnesota Townball Alive and Well," by Rocky Nelson, balldiamondnews.com, 2002.
102. State Amateur Baseball Tournament Program, collectors edition, 2000.
103. "Babe Ruth comes to Sleepy Eye in 1922," From Randy Krzmarzick's column "Weeds" which appeared in the Herald-Dispatch in 1992.
104. "A Glove Affair: Baseball and Brown County"
105. "Town ball remains a grand Minnesota tradition," by Patrick Reusse, Star Tribune, Sept 4, 2001.
106. "My Life in the Great Soo League," by Eugene McCarthy (Before the Dome Book)
107. "My Turn at Bat," by Ted Williams
108. "The Millerettes," By Stew Thornley.
109. "Diamonds in our Backyard," by Jack El-Hai, Mpls.-St. Paul Magazine, June, 1987.
110. "How We Can Have Our Big-League Ballpark and Afford it Too," by Jay Weiner, Minnesota Law & Politics, May 2000.
111. "Stadium Games : Fifty Years of Big League Greed and Bush League Boondoggles," by Jay Weiner, University of Minnesota Press, 2000.
112. "Fulda to have its own Hall of Famer," by Patrick Reusse Star Tribune, August 4, 2001.
113. "Such a one is Willie," by Rolf Felstad Minneapolis Tribune, May 27, 1951.
114. "Minnesota's Greatest Baseball Player," by Gary Clendennen, Minnesota Monthly, August, 1983.
115. "Holy Cow! The Life and Times of Halsey Hall," by Stew Thornley, Nodin Press, Minneapolis, 1991.
116. "St. Paul Unions: Minnesota's First Fling in the Majors," 1980 Baseball Research Journal by the Society for American Baseball Research.
117. "Minneapolis Millers vs. Havana Sugar Kings," The National Pastime by the Society for American Baseball Research, 1992.
118. "Twin Cities Had True Rivalry in Early 1900s," Star-Trib, April 25, 1999.
119. "Minnesota Baseball History," Minnesota Twins 2000 Media Guide.
120. www.SABR.com.
121. "Northern Lights," by Mike Augustin, St. Paul Pioneer Press, July 23, 1991.
122. "A History in St. Paul," by Richard W. Arpi, Saints Souvenir Program, 1993.
123. "A New Beginning," by Dave Wright, Saints Souvenir Program, 1993.
124. "Minnesota Majors," by Glenn Gostick, Saints Souvenir Program, 1993.
125. St. Paul Saints Website
126. Duluth-Superior Dukes Website.
127. Fargo-Moorhead RedHawks Website.
128. www.Northern League.com
129. Bennett, Bruce. Dukes capture the flag. http://www.duluthnews.com/dnt/sports/dukes2.htm, September 2, 1997.
130. Coste, Chris. Hey ... I'm Just the Catcher: An inside look at a Northern League season from behind the plate. Fargo, ND: Jan Plaude Creations, 1997.
131. Baseball America (Allan Simpson, editor), Simon & Schuster, 1996.
132. Johnson, Lloyd and Miles Wolff. The Encyclopedia of Minor League Baseball (First Edition). Durham, NC: Baseball America, Inc., 1993.
133. Obojski, Robert. Bush League: A History of Minor League Baseball. New York: Macmillan, 1975.
134. Perlstein, Steve. Rebel Baseball: The Summer the Game was Returned to Fans. NY: Onion Press, 1994.
135. White, Herman D. An Informal History of the Northern Baseball League. Gryphon Press, 1982.
136. "State of the Game," by Tom Tuttle, Beaver's Pond Press, Edina, 2000.
137. "Twenty Five Seasons: The first quarter century of the Minnesota Twins," by Dave Mona and Dave Jarzyna, Mona Publications, Minneapolis, 1986.
138. "Base Paths," by Ken Lazebnik & Steve Lehman, Brown Publishing, 1987.

ABOUT THE AUTHOR

Ross Bernstein is the author of several regionally best-selling coffee-table sports books, including: **"Hardood Heroes: Celebrating a Century of Minnesota Basketball," "Pigskin Pride: Celebrating a Century of Minnesota Football," "Frozen Memories: Celebrating a Century of Minnesota Hockey"** and **"Fifty Years • Fifty Heroes: A Celebration of Minnesota Sports."**

Bernstein first got into writing through some rather unique circumstances. You see, after a failed attempt to make it as a walk-on to the University of Minnesota's Golden Gopher hockey team, he opted to instead become the team's mascot, "Goldy." His humorous accounts as a mischievous rodent, back at old Mariucci Arena, then inspired the 1992 best-seller: **"Gopher Hockey by the Hockey Gopher."** And the rest, they say... is history!

Bernstein also writes children's and young-reader sports biographies as well. Among these books include bios about such superstars as: Seattle Supersonics All-Star Point Guard **Gary Payton**, Minnesota Vikings All-Pro Wide Receiver **Randy Moss**, Minnesota Timberwolves All-Star Forward **Kevin Garnett**, Minnesota Vikings All-Pro Quarterback **Daunte Culpepper**, and Los Angeles Lakers All-Star Guard Kobe Bryant. (Culpepper and Bryant are due out in 2003.)

In addition, Bernstein also writes an annual book for the U.S. Hockey Hall of Fame, enti-tled: **"The Hall: Celebrating the History and Heritage of the U.S. Hockey Hall of Fame."** Proceeds from the sale of the book, which chronicles and updates the history of the Eveleth, Minn., based museum and its more than 100 world-renowned enshrinees, go directly to the Hall of Fame.

Ross Bernstein

Today the Fairmont native works as a full-time sports author for several Midwest and East Coast publishers. He is also the co-founder and Senior Editor of a start-up life-style based hockey magazine entitled: **"Minnesota Hockey Journal."** A sister pub-lication of USA Hockey's **"American Hockey Magazine"** — the nation's largest hockey publication, the **"Journal"** has a regional circulation of nearly 50,000 Minnesota hockey households.

Ross, his wife Sara, their new daughter Campbell, and their sock-snarfing Jack Russell Terrier, "Herbie" (named in honor of local hockey legend Herbie Brooks), presently reside in Eagan. *(Oh yeah, his new coffee-table book celebrating the history of Minnesota Coaches will be out in the Fall of 2003. Stay Tuned!)*

To order additional signed and personalized copies of any of these books, please send a check to the following address:
(Ross Bernstein • P.O. Box #22151 • Eagan, MN 55122-0151)
*Prices include tax and bubble-packed Fed-Ex Ground shipping. Thank you!

1.) *"Batter-Up!: Celebrating a Century of Minnesota Baseball"* — *$30.00*
2.) *"Hardwood Heroes: Celebrating a Century of Minnesota Basketball"* — *$30.00*
3.) *"Pigskin Pride: Celebrating a Century of Minnesota Football"* — *$30.00*
4.) *"Frozen Memories: Celebrating a Century of Minnesota Hockey"* — *$28.00*
5.) *"Fifty Years • Fifty Heroes: A Celebration of Minnesota Sports"* — *$25.00*
6.) *"Gopher Hockey by the Hockey Gopher"* — *$18.00*
7.) *"The Hall: Celebrating the History and Heritage of the U.S. Hockey Hall of Fame"* (Class of 2000) — *$18.00*
8.) *"The Hall: Celebrating the History and Heritage of the U.S. Hockey Hall of Fame"*(Class of 2001) — *$18.00*
9.) *"The Hall: Celebrating the History and Heritage of the U.S. Hockey Hall of Fame"*(Class of 2002) — *$18.00*
10.) *"Gary Payton: Star Guard"* — *$25.00*
11.) *"Randy Moss: Star Receiver"* — *$25.00*
12.) *"Kevin Garnett: Star Forward"* — *$25.00*
13.) *"Daunte Culpepper: Star Quarterback"* (Due out in 2003) — *$25.00*
14.) *"Kobe Bryant: Star Guard"* (Due out in 2003) — *$25.00*

WWW.BERNSTEINBOOKS.COM